John McGahern and Modernism

Also available from Bloomsbury

Modernism at the Microphone, Melissa Dinsman
Reframing Yeats, Charles I. Armstrong
Samuel Beckett and The Bible, Iain Bailey

John McGahern and Modernism

Richard Robinson

BLOOMSBURY ACADEMIC
LONDON • NEW YORK • OXFORD • NEW DELHI • SYDNEY

BLOOMSBURY ACADEMIC
Bloomsbury Publishing Plc
50 Bedford Square, London, WC1B 3DP, UK
1385 Broadway, New York, NY 10018, USA

BLOOMSBURY, BLOOMSBURY ACADEMIC and the Diana logo are
trademarks of Bloomsbury Publishing Plc

First published in Great Britain 2017
Paperback edition first published 2018

Cover design: Eleanor Rose

A catalogue record for this book is available from the British Library.

A catalog record for this book is available from the Library of Congress.

ISBN: HB: 978-1-4411-2578-1
PB: 978-1-3500-7512-2
ePDF: 978-1-3500-0091-9
ePub: 978-1-6235-6259-5

Typeset by Deanta Global Publishing Services, Chennai, India

In Memory of W.P.R.
(1937–2009)

Contents

Acknowledgements

I would like to thank the Research Institute of the Arts and Humanities at Swansea University for my recent sabbatical. Portions of an earlier essay, 'An Umbrella, a Pair of Boots, and a "Spacious Nothing": McGahern and Beckett', appeared in *Irish University Review* 44, no. 2 (Autumn/Winter 2014) and have been quoted here, with the permission of Edinburgh University Press. Many thanks go to John Kenny for his generosity. Fergus Fahey at NUI Galway helped with the McGahern archive, a little of which has been discussed in Chapter 8, by kind permission of the estate of John McGahern. I am particularly grateful to the following for their invaluable comments on the typescript: Alistair Cormack, Richard Hibbitt, Neil Reeve, Victor Sage and Barry Sheils.

List of Abbreviations

B	John McGahern, *The Barracks* (London: Faber and Faber, 2009 [1963]).
D	John McGahern, *The Dark* (London: Faber and Faber, 2002 [1965]).
N	John McGahern, *Nightlines* (St Albans: Panther, 1973 [1970]).
L	John McGahern, *The Leavetaking*, 2nd edition (London: Faber and Faber, 1989 [1974, 1984]).
GT	John McGahern, *Getting Through* (London: Faber and Faber, 1988 [1978]).
P	John McGahern, *The Pornographer* (London: Faber and Faber, 1990 [1979]).
AW	John McGahern, *Amongst Women* (London: Faber and Faber, 1991 [1990]).
CE	John McGahern, *Creatures of the Earth* (London: Faber and Faber, 2007 [1992]).
RS	John McGahern, *That They May Face the Rising Sun* (London: Faber and Faber, 2002).
M	John McGahern, *Memoir* (London: Faber and Faber, 2005).
LW	John McGahern, *Love of the World*, ed. Stanley van der Ziel (London: Faber and Faber, 2009).

Introduction

A Giotto postcard

There is a moment in John McGahern's final novel, *That They May Face the Rising Sun* (2002), when Joe Ruttledge is absorbed in a postcard of Giotto's *Flight into Egypt*. He finds the blue of Mary's robe paler than the sky, and the brown of Joseph's robe like that of the earth. 'The whole world had an extraordinary and deeply affecting serenity: it was as if they had complete trust in the blessed light as they travelled to a place or state where nothing cast a shadow' (*RS* 108). The early fourteenth-century frescoes at the Scrovegni chapel are stylized, iconographic, their friezes lit with an as yet crude perspectival awareness. It goes too far to say of the 'blessed light' of Giotto's painting that *nothing* casts a shadow, but the fully fleshed, three-dimensional Renaissance humanism of Michelangelo, or the chiaroscuro of Caravaggio, is still a long way off. In the short story 'The Wine Breath', the priest, recognizing the future company of his own ghost, uses a similar phrase: 'Absence does not cast a shadow' (*CE* 120). For the priest, the shadow-less place is the afterlife of eternity; for the artist, it is, after Yeats, the artifice of eternity.

A contemporary novel in the age of mechanical reproduction is less like an early Renaissance fresco and more like a postcard. It is a form of art which is both miniaturized and secularized. Denis Sampson has drawn attention to the importance in the same novel of the unfinished, four-pillared structure on which Patrick Ryan is working next to the Ruttledges' cottage: what is significantly called 'that whole cathedral of a shed' (*RS* 297).[1] The implication is, perhaps, that the medieval faith which actuated Giotto's art and, say, Chartres cathedral cannot be recovered. Neither can the aura of the artwork. Towards the end of his writing career, McGahern expresses his reverence for the vocation of art and the viewer's contemplation of it, but also knowingly encodes in the *mise-en-abîme* of the shed and the postcard that his own aesthetic ambition, and our expectations of art, have been scaled-down.

In a recent polemic, *Whatever Happened to Modernism?*, Gabriel Josipovici argues that the radical energies of modernism have been marginalized in much contemporary middlebrow culture.[2] Modernism is not to be thought as finished, a super-structural cultural manifestation of an early twentieth-century bourgeois crisis, but should remain a pressing aesthetic imperative, a perpetual questioning of representation which any work of art should pose. Perhaps Josipovici's boldest intellectual leap is to argue that modernism still best represents the 'disenchantment of the world' that occurred in the sixteenth century (there is no talk here of 'December 1910, or thereabouts'). The legacy of verisimilitude is bequeathed by Renaissance humanism, and the Reformation's dispelling of medieval superstition lays the foundation for realism. But there is a 'hidden madness in every realist novel' (34), as those anti-realist progenitors of the genre, *Don Quixote* or *Tristram Shandy*, happily expose. I refer to Josipovici's book because it incorporates modernist literature (and art) in an argument about art and the loss of faith, our emergence from a pre-modern world into one in which, after Hegel, the 'oracles are silent'. The book models modernist disenchantment not as haughtily dismissive of primitive culture, nor as a triumphantly demythologizing force which proclaims the false god of the new. It shows how modernism is continuous with the erosion of 'our confidence in the sacramental', a remark which must chime with any reader of McGahern's work.[3]

The moment in which Ruttledge is engrossed in the postcard is emblematic of McGahern's sense of his own art. It is conceded that this art is a reproduction, an imitation without aspiration to originality. However, this is not conflated with an unquestioning acceptance of secular realism. The world cannot be re-enchanted, and contemporary art cannot hide from its endless reproducibility and diminishment. Yet the 'whole world' of the artwork still bears the sign, albeit in a characteristically oblique and coded way, of a continued yearning for metaphysical meaningfulness: to be freed from the particularizing solidity of a place where everything casts a shadow. If this is to be regarded as regressively nostalgic or anti-modern, it is a charge of disenchantment also to be levelled at much modernist work.

Word and image

It should be acknowledged from the outset that McGahern's fiction cannot easily be thought of as late modernist, neo-modernist or belatedly modernist in form. His work does not radically 'dislocate' language into meaning, as Eliot put it.[4] There is no crisis of representation, no shock of defamiliarization or distantiation; no avant-garde poetics; little processual sense of a world unfolding in language and perhaps withheld by it. Although the interior life is explored, most memorably perhaps in *The Barracks*, it is not with that aspiration to imitate the grammar of consciousness – to turn the mind inside out and make the external world remote. Aesthetic ambition is not foregrounded in the fiction: the artist in the text may be an implied, surrogate or emblematized figure, like Ruttledge looking at the postcard, but is never fully exposed, let alone flaunted. McGahern is not writing evidently self-begetting, decentred, indeterminate or self-deconstructing narratives which play with the provisionality of its authored worlds or open epistemological cracks in the surface of the text. There is a good deal of individual solitude and existential expressiveness in his writing, but finally this does not seem to serve the broader ideological privileging, in the view of theorists like Georg Lukács, of the fractured psychopathological consciousness of the modern bourgeois subject. The quasi-allegorical or apocalyptic modernist mode is alien to the privacy or constriction of McGahern's work. It is not the future-directed art of the new nor is its representation of history charged by Benjamin's *Jetztzeit*, 'the time of the now'.[5] If anything, its constant recourse to past time suggests a deliberate turning away from technological modernity, an attempt to 'make it old': McGahern used the epithet earned from John Updike, 'oldfashioned', as a title for a short story in the *High Ground* collection.[6] Taken as a whole, McGahern's work appears to be an unheroic, belated art of stasis and remembrance, and there is little to suggest that this body of rooted writing – still centripetally attached, for good or ill, to the home – should represent a continuation of the exilic art of expatriate, 'unhoused' modernism.[7]

Nevertheless, McGahern's fiction should not be viewed as being solely reactive against modernism. McGahern is typical of a generation of Irish writers after Yeats and Joyce who, in Neil Corcoran's words, ran a gamut of responses: 'imitation, admiration, dependency, modification, hesitation, anxiety, separation, subversion, rejection, reaction'.[8] Reaction is one in a series of terms. If McGahern does not pick up the baton of modernism with the serio-comic panache of, say, Flann O'Brien – and it is hard to think of more different writers, despite the shared bicycles and police barracks – this does not mean it is less worthwhile to read his work through the prior inscriptions of modernism. Such an impression is confirmed in McGahern's interviews, critical essays and journalistic articles, many of them now collected in *Love of the World*. It is worth briefly turning to these sources to underline how McGahern was constantly evaluating – extrapolating and contesting – modernist aesthetics.

McGahern is never more modernist than when discussing the materiality and autonomy of language itself. He continually refers to words in a kind of mystical way: words are 'things' or have 'presences' (*LW* 9). Like the modernist, he is alive to the generative rather than reflective properties of the word – the word which makes rather than mirrors the world: 'By concentrating on words, all kinds of revelations appear in language rather than the other way round'[9]; 'Through words I could experience my own life' (*LW* 9); 'It was through words that I came to understand the little I do know about the world, and it was through words that I came to see the world.'[10] It is appropriate, then, that McGahern should quote Yeats's happy shepherd, for whom 'words alone [are] certain good' (*LW* 185). McGahern's statements follow this apotheosizing of the world-begetting word: as for Joyce's Stephen Dedalus, it is *through* words that 'he had glimpses of the real world about him'.[11]

This reverence for the word is balanced by an awareness of the alienating politics of language. In the essay 'What is my Language?' McGahern, like many, lights upon the word 'tundish' in *Portrait* as paradigmatic of the fretful, foreign-familiar politics of colonized language, and also alludes to Beckett's Maddy, who says in *All that Fall* that it is 'unspeakably excruciating' to speak a language which contains the ghosts of our 'own poor dear Gaelic' (*LW* 260–1). McGahern is aware that Irish writing is, in Deleuze and Guattari's terms, a deterritorialized and thus potentially innovative 'minor' literature. Nevertheless, in the same essay McGahern also quotes Pirandello: 'But don't you see the whole trouble lies here in words, words. … We think we understand each other, but we never really do' (*LW* 261). The Irish 'trouble' with English words is not separated from a more general modernist scepticism towards language as an instrument of mimesis. This helps us to understand that the isolation of McGahern's early protagonists may not be exclusively associated with a mid-century existential sensibility, but may after all have some sort of genealogical connection to the *anomie* of the modernist subject.

McGahern's assertion that 'the art of fiction should be supremely difficult', seems to confirm a modernist view that form – or in McGahern's Flaubertian word, style – should be hard-won. Again, he approvingly refers to Yeats: 'When your technique is sloppy, your matter grows second-hand; there is no difficulty to force you down under the surface. Difficulty is our plough.'[12] Though he read modernist texts at different stages – he knew Yeats's work before Joyce's, for example – McGahern registered that modernism, at least as it is conceived as a literary period, had retrospectively been named and had 'happened', and that subsequent writers, including himself, were conscious of its legacy. Equally, though, he identifies himself as a traditional writer with 'no interest in experiment for experiment's sake': for him 'the way of seeing is the real experiment'.[13] Such statements speak of his remoteness from the ludic aspects of contemporary postmodernist poetics, but also bring into question his relationship to modernism, if that is primarily conceived as 'experimentally' avant-garde. It is not surprising, then, that it is likely that McGahern expressed his admiration for early chapters of *Ulysses*, such as 'Hades', because they continued the scrupulous method of *Dubliners*. His silence about later parts of the novel is eloquent. Acknowledging 'the incredible energy of that comic genius' in *Finnegans Wake*, 'always expanding, expounding, playing', McGahern writes that 'we have left the world of letters and reached impure sound': though the *Wake* may be a work of genius, 'one such is enough' (*LW* 185). McGahern's belief that words themselves have presences may be aligned with what Beckett said of later Joyce ('His writing is not *about* something; *it is that something itself*'), but such comments nevertheless reveal in McGahern a discomfort with the difficulty of high or late modernist prose forms.[14] Beckett is acknowledged as coming 'at the end of the great modernist movement', but the 'elemental sparseness' of his style (*LW* 264), purged of erudition, is not related to contemporaneous forms of *écriture blanche*, or to the supposed exhaustion of literature at mid-century. Rather, McGahern sees Beckett's language as similar to that of Thomas Ó Criomhthain's *An tOilenách* (1929), an Irish language work set in the Blasket Isles and translated into English as *The Islandman*.

McGahern's short essay on *Dubliners* is as much about Flaubert, whose correspondence with George Sand is quoted liberally, as it is about Joyce. McGahern is drawn to Flaubert's defence of depersonalization, a method which is not coldly unfeeling but proceeds from the necessity that the writer remains glued to the earth because 'everything moves [him], everything lacerates and ravages [him]' and that he makes 'every effort to soar' (*LW* 203). Met with Sand's accusation that the 'supreme impartiality' of his writing is 'antihuman', Flaubert uncompromisingly emphasizes linguistic autonomy: '*To write well* is everything'; the 'word is never lacking when one possesses the idea' (*LW* 204). Flaubert's proto-modernist poetics of impersonality lie behind McGahern's repeated objection to what he calls 'self-expression', which is regarded as 'always bad writing', 'the opposite of creativity'.[15] Elsewhere McGahern discusses the necessary artifice of language: 'All that matters … is style'; writing should be a 'clear mirror … the reflection of personality that we call style'.[16] If the supposedly inexpressive objectivity of McGahern's narratives is taken to be realist, then it has its origins in that realism Flaubert said he execrated, though he was 'regarded as one of its high priests' (*LW* 204). McGahern's acknowledgement that *Dubliners* continues Flaubertian aesthetics is tempered by his hostility to the Romantic notion of the artist as hero that, at least initially, he saw Joyce as cultivating: 'a sort of … Victorian sentimentality'.[17] However, it seems that McGahern reconciles this mistrust of the artist-cult, for in another essay he approvingly quotes Joyce's more humble reference to Hardy as a fellow clerk. The neo-Romantic Joyce is thus implicitly accepted as one of Hugh Kenner's stoic comedians – a Bouvard or Pécuchet, a 'great clerk' (*LW* 186).

McGahern's sensitivity to what, faintly echoing Dylan Thomas, he called the 'colour' of words, and the premium he places on objective style, must be read in connection with his emphasis on the image as the foundational source of his writing.[18] The supreme difficulty to which McGahern refers is not that of the reader's encounter with the rebarbative text, but rather that of the authorial quest for the image. In an essay that McGahern regarded as the summation of his aesthetic credo, 'The Image', he writes of 'the rhythm and the vision' (*LW* 7) of the artist's struggle towards the single image. As James Whyte has pointed out, parts of this essay resemble Yeats's account of the Great Memory: 'But now image called up image in an endless procession, and I could not always choose among them with any confidence; and when I did choose, the image lost its intensity or changed to some other image.'[19] Similarly, for McGahern, although memory-images may flow, the writer seeks 'the one image that will never come' (*LW* 7). McGahern's aesthetic may be psycho-biographically regarded as governed by a transcendent Mnemosyne, but it should also be recognized that the limits of memory are also registered. Art is figured as a world of imagination over which the author may reign, viewing the intolerable pain of life as if in Perseus's shield, transforming the immovable solidity of the world. A note of bathos, or at least disappointment, is struck. Language is presented as 'the absurd crown of Style', and the vocation of art in the age of modernist disenchantment is figured as a struggle towards 'something which may be no more than a yard of lead piping we saw in terror or in laughter once' (*LW* 8). On the one hand, McGahern's work may gravitate towards a transcendent romantic image, such as that in the short story 'Parachutes', where the thistledown of Grafton Street and the waltzing couple are symbolically fused in the eponymous turning shape (*CE* 165). Equally, though, the image recovered by the author may be lost to the reader, as is the case in *Amongst Women*, whose image of a London flat used by long-distance lorry drivers originally engendered the novel's centripetal, reverse-diasporic narrative, but which is eventually omitted from the completed text.[20]

In what may be broadly thought of as broadly Proustian terms, McGahern referred to the 'art that abolishes time and establishes memory'.[21] McGahern's work emerges from a Proustian descent into the depths of oneself – what

Dermot McCarthy, foregrounding McGahern's early loss of his mother, has symbolized as an Orphic journey to the underworld.[22] However, the importance of Proust to McGahern's work, first brought out by Sampson, must also take account of the ways in which a poetics of profundity risks becoming reductively synonymous with the wholesale recuperation of original experience. What is equally Proustian in McGahern is an objection to the crude transferring of personal memories into autobiographical narrative. McGahern was drawn to a distinction in Proust's *Contre Sainte-Beuve* (*Against Sainte-Beuve*) between two selves: the personality of the author explored by biographical critics, and the *moi profond* which, in McGahern's words, was an 'inner spirit that creates [and] operates according to its own laws'. Thus, McGahern summarizes the Proustian description of the biographical method as 'essentially idle, since the recognizable, everyday personality of the artist bears, at best, an uncertain relationship to the inner spirit that creates' (*LW* 352–3). Something more than 'me' – for Proust, laws and analogies – must be brought up from the depths of the self. Seamus Heaney describes McGahern as a writer of 'ruminant' imagination, of 'compulsive return to certain themes and landscapes': in repeatedly 'retrieving himself', Heaney goes on to say, McGahern is 'achieving a new self'.[23] McGahern's suspicion of self-expression should warn us against the privileging of confessional truth telling, and remind us that a lifetime of reading mediates expressive fidelity to personal experience. Successive fictional articulations of the self must be 'achieved'.

For those less familiar with McGahern's work, it is worth rehearsing how the overall trajectory of his six novels may be configured in relation to this compulsive self-refashioning. In the broadest terms, it might be observed that McGahern moves from concentrating on the suffering, victimized, remembering or self-abasing individual to a more impersonal, formally memorializing mode. Although his first novel, *The Barracks* (1963), is a third-person narrative not completely confined to Elizabeth's consciousness, it is nevertheless intimately focalized through her. The philosophical problem of others and the present suffering and memories of a dying subject are explored within the claustrophobic provincial confinement of a police barracks. *The Dark* (1965), a novel which was banned in Ireland, is an episodic representation of a boy's growing up under the tyrannical law of the father. The narrative of Mahoney's formation is variously narrated by *I*, *you* and *he*, suggesting the grammatical splintering of selfhood. An existential rawness characterizes these early novels, both of which are set in the countryside of County Roscommon. *The Leavetaking* (1974) is narrated by a soon-to-be-dismissed teacher on his final day in a Dublin school: this departure re-enacts and recalls the childhood day on which his mother died. The narrator's descent into traumatic memory is shown to be eventually emancipating, healing the rupture between the lost day of his past and the last day of his present. In the next first-person novel of the 1970s, *The Pornographer* (1979), the contingencies of the perpetual present force the eponymous narrator into a tragicomic form of abjection which, in contrast to the previous novel, leaves very little room for irruptions from the past. The chronological gap between these novels and McGahern's next, *Amongst Women* (1990), marks what appears to be a formal shift, though it is difficult to articulate this accurately. The daughters of an embittered veteran of the War of Independence continue to be drawn back to the patriarchal domain of Great Meadow. If one emphasizes a new kind of impersonality in *Amongst Women* – a performed and faintly archaic remoteness – then this risks misrepresenting McGahern's continued attentiveness towards the pulsions of cruelty and love within the republic of the family. *That They May Face the Rising Sun* (2000) extends the movement away from the subjective towards the interpersonal, but is no less intimate. The formal austerity of this representation of a Leitrim community by the lakeside, taken together with an emphasis on seasonal rhythms and a strategic evasion of 'deep' selfhood, should not be held as synonymous with an exercise in framed naturalist objectivity, nor with a culturally incurious retreat into benign pastoralism. If an anthropological or elegiac value is to be conferred upon this last novel, it must take account of its covert aesthetic and philosophical questioning.

McGahern's essay on *Dubliners* expresses a certain anxiety about what he refers to as that 'dubious enterprise, the Irish Short Story' (*LW* 200). Nevertheless, he wrote three volumes of acclaimed short stories, *Nightlines* (1970), *Getting Through* (1978) and *High Ground* (1985), which were collected, with a number of omissions and new additions, in *Creatures of the Earth* (1992). It is this uncertainty – dubiety in a benign sense – which makes McGahern's short stories distinctive. A tension emerges between the fluency of the storytelling or expository voice, on the one hand, and the modernist drive to contain or ironize expressive lyricism, on the other. What appears to be an updated type of tale may be transfigured into a compressed, crypto-symbolic artefact: a piece of writing after modernism. The implicitly interconnected stories often have a familiar topography: the narrator's often-repeated dialectical movement between city and country – the compulsion both to take leave and to go back – carries him between generations and between two inimical but mutually constitutive 'Irelands'. These stories test the idea of vernacular tradition as a cultural and formal legacy.

For many, McGahern's autobiographical fiction *Memoir* (2005), published the year before his death, represents a final restoration of the lost image. Towards the beginning of the book, McGahern has returned to walking the lanes of his childhood, where he experiences a deep peace: 'I suspect it is no more than the actual lane and the lost lane becoming one for a moment in an intensity of feeling, but without the usual attendants of pain and loss' (*M* 24). This prepares the ground for the very last page of the book, in which the narrator and mother are brought together in those same lanes around the lake, fringed by wild orchid and windflower. Narrated in the conditional mood, a lost memory is also a future resting place: 'I would take her by the beaten path'; 'I would show her the green lawns'; 'I would want no shadow to fall on her joy' (*M* 272). The extraordinarily moving transcendence of this reunion with his mother is imagined in that same extra-temporal realm – of art and the afterlife – where nothing casts a shadow.

This is Proust writing in similar terms on the countryside of *his* childhood, in *Against Sainte-Beuve*: 'Was it on those walks around the town where I was happy as a small boy, was it only in that imaginary country where later I was to dream that Mother was so ill, beside a lake, in a forest where it remained light all night, a country dreamt of only but almost as real as the country of my childhood which was already no more than a dream?'[24] McGahern's own 'imaginary country' is made up of remembered images from his early life – but also of remembered texts which are interposed into this experience. An insistence upon intertextual readings of autobiographical writing seems to run the risk of being intrusive and bloodlessly analytical. For this reason, as well as that of space – there are ten chapters in this monograph, six on the published novels, four on selected short stories – I have decided not to write on *Memoir*, though I acknowledge that it is a major work, already held in great affection, and of much importance to scholars of life writing or autofiction. *Memoir* could indeed be read intertextually, but this monograph concentrates on McGahern's fiction.

After modernism

McGahern's absorption in modernist writing is evident from interviews and critical essays, and yet the trace of modernism in his fiction is often peculiarly obfuscated. Denis Sampson's ground-breaking work of the early 1990s, *Outstaring Nature's Eye*, to which this book is in debt, makes it abundantly clear what a profoundly literary writer McGahern is, despite what may be conceived of as his lack of flamboyance – a tendency, perhaps, towards tactical concealment. Although McGahern's allusiveness is not confined to modernism, the writings of Joyce, Proust, Yeats and Beckett, as well as Flaubert and Chekhov, among others, are shown to have acted upon McGahern's imagination and to be sometimes unexpectedly present in his work. Taking their lead from Sampson, a new generation of scholars, among them Stanley van der Ziel and Frank Shovlin, have continued to unearth the quietly connotative richness of McGahern's fiction.

The very coyness and latency of McGahern's literary practice encourages what Shovlin described as a form of critical detective work.[25] We see how the 'content' of modernist writing can be unearthed from McGahern's work, but also that a new interpretative problem arises from this. Rather than being an anchor which secures the canonical status of the text, the allusion may become the place of dissonance or abrasion. The canonical validation of the Proustian or Joycean McGahern may bring with it the feeling that modernism is absent: the return of the repressed modernist text creates a conspicuous differential – what is conspicuously *not* Proustian or Joycean. Alternatively, the crowding of literary forbears, often conspicuously those of Irish modernism, may unmask an intertextual contest: the text becomes a site of over determination. Allusive plurality suggests the polarization of interpretative undecidability – Proust versus Joyce, as it were – but also makes the limits of emulation more obvious. The urge to confer canonical respectability on McGahern risks effacing the differential. As Beckett wrote, 'the danger is in the neatness of identifications'.[26]

The reader cannot pretend to an objective evaluation of modernist 'content'. Harold Bloom is withering about the 'kind of critic who spends his time dissecting what he reads for echoes, imitations, influences, as if no-one was ever simply himself but is always compounded of a lot of other people', and refers to 'the wearisome industry of source-hunting, of allusion-counting'.[27] The critic, this one included, may always be thought complicit in his or her anxiety not to miss the echo. Such source-hunting has been a necessary defence against the classifying of McGahern as a respectable but formally unambitious writer – as one who, more interested in 'matching' than 'making', to use J. P. Stern's distinction, wields language with instrumental purpose.[28] The task remains as to how to discuss McGahern's allusiveness while not being overawed by those intimidating canonical adjectives, Proustian, Joycean, Yeatsian, Beckettian.

To continue with modernism is to be condemned to depart from it. Derek Attridge has written that 'modernism after modernism necessarily involves a reworking of modernism's methods, since nothing could be less modernist than a repetition of previous modes, however disruptive they were in their time'.[29] Modernism is identified by its own processes of bricolage and of cannibalizing the canon, but then becomes petrified as an object-text of unique particularity, of an imitative 'voice'. Is to repeat the parodic art to be naively mimetic or to continue the mode of the parodic-modernist? Margot Norris has written that the narrator of Joyce's 'An Encounter', primed by his precocious consumption of literature and now retrospectively fashioning his story, presents the reader with 'the construction of an encounter'. For McGahern, then, 'Lavin', a quite conspicuous rewriting of the *Dubliners* story, may be thought of as the construction of a construction of an encounter – but one which lacks any postmodernist relish for parody. If 'trying to be a modernist' (in Tom McCarthy's phrase) is fraught and futile, condemned to the fate Attridge spells out, then McGahern's often reticent intertextual practice begins to look more strategic than reactive.[30]

Covert but insistent, McGahern often digs subterranean channels to modernist texts under the cover of the benighted provincial realist. As McGahern scholars know, thanks to Sampson's service, the eponymous 'dark' of his second novel is not only the representation of childhood experience, of psychological darkness, but is a quotation from Yeats's 'The Choice', a poem which contrasts the 'heavenly mansion' of a perfected life to the fate of the artist-worker who rages 'in the dark'. But we should not brush over the interpretative problem that 'the dark' is a very private allusion which is nowhere else underwritten by the text. We cannot say that such a title may not equally point, say, to the 'proper dark' of the Irish – 'we Irish' – in 'The Statues'. Such coded quoting of Yeats is not of the same extrovert order as, for example, John Montague's mock-heroic tribute to 1960s' Ireland: 'Puritan Ireland's dead and gone/A myth of O'Connor and O'Faoláin'.[31] In McGahern, there is a deliberate diminution, a voluntary type of debasement, in the refusal to make aesthetics a more conspicuous and self-reflexive matter of content. Learning is more often concealed than incorporated, and McGahern's language is largely shorn of the specialized vocabularies of philosophy and academicism. Pronouncements on aesthetics – be they in critical essays or in the mouths of characters – can sometimes have a deliberately homespun quality, particularly as they touch on deeply considered epistemological or metaphysical questions. I take this to be a pre-emptive reluctance to thrust art forward as an overly intellectualized, self-reflexive, 'public' content of the work. This is an important difference from modernism and explains the patterns of downplayed surrogacy which can be detected in much of the fiction, and to which this book pays particular attention.

It is also true to say that McGahern's work cannot be comfortably pigeon-holed as realist. When claims are made for McGahern's realism, they often point straight back not to the classical realism of the nineteenth century but to a nascent or gestational modernism. Terence Brown argues that a Joycean 'inexorable realism' is evident in McGahern's early fiction, and that when the more 'self-regarding' poetic passages creep in, expressing imponderable metaphysical questions, they merely obtrude on a 'controlling import' which for Brown is 'resolutely realistic'.[32] The implication is that the world of implacable objects in the early *Nightlines* may in part derive from a modernist solidity of specification, one which for Joyce brings weight to Bloom's kettle, 'dull and squat, its spout stuck out'.[33] Other critics, including Neil Corcoran, Maria DiBattista, and John Wilson Foster, all attribute to McGahern a strain of Joycean realism.[34]

McGahern's belated realism, if that is what it is, is thus haunted by a prior body of writing whose own verisimilar or self-fashioning status is contested. One of the first surveys of literary modernism which did not yet name that phenomenon, Edmund Wilson's *Axel's Castle*, argued that the 'imaginative literature of 1870-1930' – of Yeats, Valéry, T. S. Eliot, Proust, Joyce and Gertrude Stein – emerged from the 'fusion or conflict' of Symbolism with Naturalism. Joyce is termed by Wilson as 'a master of Naturalism'.[35] If the high modernist is simultaneously an extreme realist, having been a naturalist, then the holding apart of mimetic and self-reflexive modes becomes problematic. *Ulysses* could not be a more materially solid representation of Dublin; *Ulysses* could not be more linguistically self-conscious. It is not a matter of a later literary 'movement' superseding another, but rather of its thriving 'in the teeth' of what has preceded it, as Wilson conceives it.[36] If McGahern's work continues to be classified as realist – be it psychological, symbolic, poetic, expressive or provincial realism – it must be acknowledged that this too has survived, if not thrived, 'in the teeth of' modernism. In some ways, his earlier writing may be consistent with a recent characterization of 'anti-heroic, post-imperial' British fictions which, after modernism, 'could almost be said to radicalize the diffidence for which they are perhaps better known'.[37] Such diffidence, common in the mid-century period, is symptomatic of the self-conscious reconfiguring of realism into a mode which may quietly inscribe rather than discard modernism.

'No one comes out of nowhere'

After the foundational work of Seamus Deane and Declan Kiberd, it is now axiomatic in Irish studies to associate the historical rupture of Ireland's revolution with the aesthetic rupture of modernism. The idea that 'Irish modernism' could ever have been regarded as oxymoronic has been overturned: rather, both nationalism and modernism are to be seen as outgrowths of modernity: manifestations of the 'shock of the new'.[38] Deane has written that to 'be colonial is to be modern' and that it 'is possible to be modern without being colonial; but not to be colonial without being modern'.[39] The act of rebellion and the act of writing become inseparable, as the fictive and the political merge in the act of 'completing' uncreated Ireland. Not having known the idea of totality, a so-called minority culture is primed to produce the 'imperial' art of modernism.[40] The Irish Revival, for example, has been re-conceptualized by critics such as John Wilson Foster and Terence Brown as coterminous with, rather than oppositional to, international modernism: both are forms of resistance to bourgeois individualism and realism; both make expressive form out of supererogation and pluralism; both accommodate symbolism; both relish the autotelic structures of storytelling and celebrate its textuality. The Revival has been termed 'a figure of a recurring European cultural pattern' whose versatile arts could 'invade' and be accommodated by modernism, and whose construction of a national consciousness could cut across time, creating an 'endless present'.[41] The tendency to associate the Revival with post-Romantic originality and with reactionary realism can thus be overturned. The question more often asked, then, is not what is modernist about early twentieth-century Irish literature but what is Irish about modernism.

McGahern was aware of how critical debates about Irish modernism were changing. His review of Declan Kiberd's *Irish Classics* acknowledges Kiberd's generosity to his late teacher, Richard Ellmann, but nevertheless refers to Kiberd's 'direct reversal' of Ellmann's accounts of Yeats, Joyce, Wilde and Beckett, which 'had the strange effect of convincing a whole generation of readers that the great Irish modernists were not, in any meaningful sense of the word, "Irish"' (*LW* 411). In this admiring review, McGahern retains a woolly agnosticism about the ramifications of Kiberd's statement, similar to that quoted above, that 'to be Irish was to be modern anyway' (*LW* 411). There is a certain defiant self-projection in McGahern's sense that he could not be anything other than an Irish writer, and that he did not wish to be regarded solely as one. Elsewhere he writes sceptically about the tag 'Latin American literature', which subsumes writers who not only 'have little or nothing in common' but who 'passionately conflict with each other' (*LW* 183). The analogy is faulty, of course, but it does suggest ways in which McGahern may be thought alive both to the exceptionalism *and* typicality of Irish modernism – how it may be different from itself, or comparable to other modernisms.

McGahern's often-acknowledged debt to Joyce, Yeats and Beckett equates to a literary inheritance which assumes the very inextricability of nationalist and modernist narrative modes, as well as the plurality and capaciousness of Irish modernism. The legacy of formal modernism is equivalent to the legacy of political modernity, and the difficulty of rejecting or resuming one project mirrors the difficulty of rejecting or resuming the other. More specifically, the post-war context of that Irish cultural phase after modernism must be taken into account. On the one hand, McGahern initially follows the pattern of the withdrawn, understatedly literary writer whose accent on privacy and solitude is not wilfully subjective but symptomatic of languishing in the shadow of monumental modernism. But when McGahern first started writing in Ireland, modernism was the censored, oppositional and defeated art. Declan Kiberd depicts the emergence of the stage-artist, the artist-as-drinker, in 1950s and early 1960s' Ireland, performing a self-conscious and 'newly visible' macho Bohemianism in resistance to bourgeois conformism.[42] A guilty delight of McGahern's stories is the satire of just such types: of the dyspeptic, Kavanagh-like poet who may indeed have been banned, but from a pub ('My Love, My Umbrella'); or of those who strike the pose of aesthetic disaffection ('Parachutes'). In both cases, McGahern's narrator is the artist as failed lover, neither committed to the smallholder's idyll nor to the fatigued barfly Bohemianism of the aspirational neo-modernist. Nevertheless, the banning of *The Dark* briefly consigns McGahern to the same reception as the dissident modernists, something with which he later makes implicit play in *The Pornographer*. This book explores the oblique ways in which McGahern's work registers this metamorphosis from subversive to canonical Irish modernism.

If the now unfashionable notion of Bloomian 'misprision' were to be applied to McGahern's work, perhaps the most meaningful categories would be either *kenosis*, characterized by a movement away from the precursor, a humble process of ebbing or 'emptying out', a discontinuity; or of *askesis*, a movement of self-purgation, a willed curtailment which defines the aspiration towards solitary achievement.[43] But McGahern does not really fit Bloom's taxonomy of 'anxiety' at all. Sampson's recent biography of the young McGahern revealed the excitement, reverence and sense of artistic vocation which the discovery of literature inculcated in him in the 1950s. There is little evidence that his work really aspires to enter the fray, to express itself wilfully as *agon* to the canonical parent. We cannot imagine, as Bloom does for Wallace Stevens and Yeats, and as Borges does in his 'Kafka and his Precursors', that the canonical forefather could, by reversing literary chronology, be thought of as 'imitating' his ephebe. In this sense, McGahern is simply not Joycean, Yeatsian, Beckettian 'enough'. This marks a clear limit to McGahern's un-Olympian re-staging of modernism which this book bears in mind, even as it draws out comparative cross-readings with modernist intertexts.

How may we conceive of McGahern's relationship to the idea that Ireland has an oblique relationship to the middle-class form of the novel – that the Irish writer does not directly inherit the monumental tradition of the Anglo-French realist novel but rather Ireland's adjacency to it? J. P. Stern conceives of the realist novel as providing a 'middle distance' which 'places individual people and their institutions in one working perspective': it 'gets them all into the picture'.[44] The middle distance does not seem to be compatible with the subjectivism of McGahern's earlier work, and even the interconnectedness of a late novel like *Rising Sun*, which though it seems to get all the members of the community 'into the picture', is intimately particularized rather than purposively metonymic. In response to Stern, Stephen Heath has written that 'middle and completeness look less likely if you are marginal to the centre, the consensus of the established realism'.[45] A Lukácsian version of comprehensive and typical realism does not easily fit the Irish writer, who has accelerated into Irish modernity, in a recently decolonized society whose frictional movements between residual, dominant and emergent cultures, in Raymond Williams's terms, destabilize fixed notions of representative community. Confidently panoptic realist totalism is not assumed to be the indigenous narrative form to re-adapt after the wreckage of modernism.

In a recent revisionist account of the Irish novel, Derek Hand challenges the normative assumption that the novel has an exclusive affinity to so-called developed nations with dominant bourgeoisies, and that it was therefore incompatible with pre-modern Irish culture. Hand justifies a selective study of Irish novels from the late seventeenth century onwards, rebutting the notion that if 'Irish writers bothered at all it was only to write great novels'.[46] It is true that in some statements McGahern subscribes to the orthodoxy that Hand is challenging: he refers to their having been no 'structured society' in which the novel could flourish, and suggests that Irish novelists have had to invent new forms.[47] But Hand is generally concerned to treat the novel as a capacious form, and this is in sympathy with McGahern's sense of 'the most social of all forms', as he called it – the genre which most satisfactorily presents 'a completed world'.[48] McGahern indeed feels at home in the novel, and the eclecticism of his reading, which includes an unapologetic affection for writers like Austen and Hardy, signals a lack of postcolonial mistrust about such an inheritance. At any rate McGahern's work fits Hand's universalist modelling of Irish novel writing as answering 'the demand to recognise Ireland as a space where it is also possible to be simply human'.[49] If this suggests McGahern's humanist lack of sympathy for the anti-novel, or what he termed the 'art' novel, it should not be taken to mean that the difficulty of Irish anti-realism is simply ignored.[50] What remains of interest is the way in which McGahern attempts to accommodate, and in some ways contain, a body of writing which constantly threatens to breach generic limits.

McGahern's credo of complex localism has a distant antecedence with Yeats's project for modern Irish fiction: in his 1893 *Representative Irish Tales* Yeats wrote that 'A man need not go further than his own hillside or his own village to find every kind of passion and virtue,' and quoted Paracelsus: 'If thou tastest a crust of bread, thou tastest all the stars and the heavens.'[51] McGahern's attachment to the local is also similar in some ways to Kavanagh's claim for the meaningfulness of the parochial. For the artist, the pressing claims of the world, such as the 'Munich bother' of 1938, need not override those of the locality: 'I still made the *Iliad* from such/ A local row' ('Epic').[52] In McGahern's case, at least, this emphasis on the self-identity of the particular may be seen as one way of responding to the potentially monologic legacy of independence and partition. In a late lecture, McGahern wrote: 'No one comes out of nowhere; one room or town or locality can be made an everywhere. The universal is the local, but with the walls taken away' (*LW* 11). McGahern described Ireland as 'an island containing thirty-two independent republics'.[53] This conjoining of the local 'republic' to the universal everywhere – the idea of the walls being taken away is from the Portuguese writer Miguel Torga – has appealed to many scholars, including Eamon Maher, as it offers a way of establishing McGahern's appeal as a writer of the Irish west midlands and of the world.

This should not be mistaken for a naively borderless utopianism, however. McGahern lived near a militarized border which has not been 'taken away'. The supposedly pastoral *Rising Sun* includes a scene at the checkpoint: sandbagged compound and camouflaged steel hut form part of the nearby scenery: as for Seamus Heaney, McGahern is aware of his proximity to the 'frontier of writing': a political space of 'tightness and nilness' which is yet the site of continual return for the poet, a place 'where it happens again'.[54] A political unconscious is apprehensible in stories like 'Korea', as Joseph Cleary has pointed out, and also in 'Sierra Leone', in which the narrator's envy of his lover's symbolic irredentism in a new African state – 'it must be wonderful to have your mind full of a *whole country*' (*CE* 226, my italics) – can be read doubly.[55] McGahern's continual reconstruction of his 'one world' encodes a defence of the local which speaks of scepticism towards technological globalization, of state centrism and of cultural modernity in its late capitalist or postmodernist phase. 'No one comes out of nowhere': such a declaration arises from the same expression of the need for discrete communal identities to articulate a resistance to the bland but acquisitive monocultures of globalism. To Michael Cronin, for example, autonomous localism is hardly in opposition to a benign cosmopolitanism – because it is, *in toto*, constitutive of it: 'Mixtures are mixtures of something.' The conventional terms of the lofty dismissal of provincialism may be inverted, so that we may understand how 'diversity universalises' whereas 'uniformity provincialises'.[56] McGahern is reaching out for the truth of the universal but always through the empirical fragment. This is a localism – a rich and subtle parochialism – which is nevertheless unillusioned and demythologizing, and in which is encoded a recognition that Yeats's stonily emergent independent nation remains off-stage, 'in the midst of all', even as one of its symbolic fathers weakens and dies.

Just as there are clear limits to whatever modernist properties we may wish to claim for McGahern, so the idea that his body of work is consistently smoothed out into unquestioning mimetic realism is wide of the mark. The opening chapter's analysis of McGahern's first novel, *The Barracks*, explores how those discourses of naturalism and existentialism which have been discerned in the novel unexpectedly overlap and interpenetrate. The recent return to considering Beckett in some sort of relationship to Sartrean existentialism – long held to be problematic – opens up ways of placing the novel's claustrophobic representation of the thinking subject in its mid-century intellectual context. Chapter 2 turns to McGahern's next novel, *The Dark*. Though not radically defamiliarizing, it is nevertheless a fragmented, multipersonal narrative which exploits the fluidity of second-person narrative. The unstable positioning of the subject is traceable, I argue, to the burden of genre – what has been bequeathed by traditional narratives of maturing selfhood, inevitably including Joyce's belated refracting of the *Bildungsroman*. Unlike Joyce, McGahern is uneasy with placing the artist in the text. The third chapter turns to four stories, three of them in McGahern's first volume of short stories, *Nightlines*, which quote proto-modernist or modernist texts (by Joyce, Yeats, Chekhov and Beckett) with a greater or lesser degree of conspicuousness. The perhaps surprising emergence of a palimpsest-like McGahern suggests the importance of discriminating between different theoretical models of intertextuality. This prepares the ground for my commentary in Chapter 4 on *The Leavetaking*, a novel which 'presents' as a psychological casebook but whose sheer allusiveness faces the text towards the schoolroom of literature in which the lost mother taught. The traumatic experience is recuperated through prior reading, and its narration may be fruitfully compared to Proust's rendering of memory, loss and solitude. Both the psychonanalytic and interpretative untying of this text requires the reader to follow the path of the signifier, in Lacanian terms. *The Pornographer* makes cunning play with the abjection of writing, and with the separateness of art from life, implying a self-awareness about following the rarefied but censored aesthetics of modernism. Close cross-readings with Wilde, Joyce, Yeats and Lawrence in Chapter 5 bring out the strange juxtaposition of low and high sex-writing in this novel, and its encrypted allegorical significance for McGahern's poetics.

The intertextual presence of Yeats in *Amongst Women* has long been noted. In Chapter 6, I consider the novel's representation of will through Nietzsche and what is sometimes Nietzschean about Yeats. In an increasingly gynocentric narrative, will (*Wille*) is shown not to be synonymous with power (*Macht*). Rose and the daughters' willingness to keep the patriarch propped up reveals that they are no less agents of volition. Moran is a theatrical historical protagonist, but his will turns upon an undoing rather than overcoming of the self, in Nietzschean terms. Unlike one of Yeats's two speakers in 'A Dialogue of Self and Soul', who is 'content to live it all again', Moran shockingly claims that it would have been better if the War of Independence had never happened.[57] The next section of the book turns to groupings of short stories. In Chapter 7, I consider the positioning of the typically reticent first-person narrator in a number of short stories. An individual moral evolution can be traced between these fictions of education: the narrator's consciousness is divided by a crisis of mobility, in Raymond Williams's terms, so that he is brought to an ethical brink – whereupon he falls silent. The confessional voice is finally censored. The third-person objectivity of the almost novella-like 'The Country Funeral' can be framed not as an aestheticized type of formal impersonality but more as a vehicle for ideological contestation. Chapter 8 brings out the ways in which this story encircles the dialectic of country and city, and of myth and reason, by relating it to debates about the fraught inheritance of European Enlightenment thought and to definitions of Irish modernity. The story is briefly contrasted to two country funeral stories by Frank O'Connor.

The overarching autobiographical sense of McGahern as a writer whose memory, pursuing the elusive image, recuperates the lost experience of childhood, should not disguise that his fictions are also drawn to the philosophical abysses of time. In Chapter 9, short stories are read through Proust, Beckett, Bergson and Kavanagh in order to explore the complicated relationship between habit and memory, and also to show how time is embodied and emblematized in narrative. McGahern's work is not unquestioningly dependent on wheel-like figures of circularity and cyclicity, in which beginnings are embedded in endings, and vice versa, but also tries to make sense of the telic experience of an ending, as the irresistibly self-referential last word of 'Gold Watch', 'conclusion', makes clear. To Josipovici, the disenchanted art of modernism follows Kierkegaard's dialectical movement: 'To find the conclusion it is necessary first of all to observe that it is lacking, and then in turn to feel quite vividly the lack of it.'[58] This keenly felt experience of lack is manifest in the many figures of emptied absence in McGahern's work, and in the way an ending may be conferred in his fiction, to quote the last words of his last short-story collection, 'as if it was at last a fact' (*CE* 408). This book makes its own ending with McGahern's last novel, *That They May Face the Rising Sun*, an ostensible novel of place which is no less a complex 'time-book'. Even though it is for the most part austerely resistant to what Ricœur has termed the 'implied immensity' of the modernist time of the mind, *Rising Sun* represents the reticular lakeside space as a chronotope, or site of time. Its characters are shown to be 'standing put while going past' (*RS* 293): they are 'living in Time', like Proust's narrator. Lingering over aporias of Augustinian time, the novel 'keeps' its moments but conveys duration, revealing the gapped temporality of national history and the recurrent arrival of modernity.

Since this book reads McGahern after modernism, evaluating allusion and difference, often comparing what Gérard Genette calls the hypotext to the hypertext in a two-way process, it cannot offer conventionally comprehensive interpretations of all of McGahern's work. Avoiding too great a dependence on those ambiguity-erasing adjectives (Joycean, Proustian, Yeatsian, Beckettian) requires a frequent mobilizing of modernist intertexts, and thus a reduction of exegesis on McGahern's fiction. Not only are certain texts regrettably omitted (most notably *Memoir*, a number of major short stories, and the play *The Power of Darkness*), but the readings of the included texts may themselves be somewhat selective, and are not designed to exhaustively 'cover' elements of plot and character. Neither is there space for a volume-by-volume treatment of the short-story collections. The comparative methodology of this book, contained in the titular word 'and', demands that McGahern's fiction is thoroughly juxtaposed to the body of modernist writing, which also must be explicated rather than stowed away in a series of footnotes.

Notes

1 See Denis Sampson, '"Open to the World": A Reading of John McGahern's *That They May Face the Rising Sun*', *Irish University Review* 35, no. 1 (Spring/Summer 2005): 136–46, 143.

2 Gabriel Josipovici, *What Ever Happened to Modernism?* (New Haven and London: Yale University Press, 2011).

3 Josipovici, *What Ever Happened to Modernism?*, p. 36.

4 T. S. Eliot, 'The Metaphysical Poets', in *Selected Prose* (London: Penguin, 1953), pp. 111–20: 'The poet must become more and more comprehensive, more allusive, more indirect, in order to force, to dislocate if necessary, language into his meaning', p.119.

5 Walter Benjamin, 'Theses on the Philosophy of History', in *Illuminations*, trans. Harry Zorn (London: Pimlico, 1999), pp. 252–3.

6 John Updike, quoted in Denis Sampson, *Outstaring Nature's Eye* (Washington: Catholic University of America Press, 1993), pp. 191–2.

7 See George Steiner, 'Extraterritorial', in *Extraterritorial: Papers on Literature and the Language Revolution*' (Harmondsworth: Penguin, 1972), pp. 14–21.

8 Neil Corcoran, *After Yeats and Joyce* (Oxford: Oxford University Press, 1997), p. viii.

9 Quoted in James Whyte, *History, Myth, and Ritual in the Fiction of John McGahern: Strategies of Transcendence* (Lewiston, NY: Edwin Mellen, 2002), p. 233.

10 Quoted in Denis Sampson and John McGahern, 'A Conversation with John McGahern', *Canadian Journal of Irish Studies* 17, no. 1 (1991): 13–18, 13.

11 James Joyce, *A Portrait of the Artist as a Young Man*, ed. Jeri Johnson (Oxford: Oxford University Press, 2000), p. 52.

12 John McGahern, 'Entretien de John McGahern avec Nicole Ollier: Step-by-Step through *The Barracks* with John McGahern ', *La Licorne* 32 (UFR Langues Littératures Poitiers, 1995): 55–86, p. 75; McGahern, 'Entretien de John McGahern avec Liliane Louvel, Gilles Ménégaldo and Claudine Verley', in *La Licorne* 32, pp. 9, 19–31, in which McGahern alludes to W. B. Yeats's letter to Margot Collis of early April 1936.

13 Sampson and McGahern, 'A Conversation', p. 16.

14 Samuel Beckett, 'Dante ... Bruno. Vico. Joyce', in *Our Exagmination Round His Factification for Incamination of Work in Progress* (London: Faber, 1972), pp. 1–22.

15 See Whyte, *History, Myth, and Ritual in the Fiction of John McGahern*, p. 235 and McGahern, *La Licorne* 32, p. 9.

16 Sampson and McGahern, 'A Conversation', p. 14; McGahern, *La Licorne* 32, p. 9.

17 McGahern, *La Licorne* 32, p. 26.

18 Sampson and McGahern, 'A Conversation', p. 13.

19 W. B. Yeats, 'The Trembling of the Veil', quoted in Whyte, *History, Myth, and Ritual in the Fiction of John McGahern*, p. 127.
20 See McGahern, *La Licorne* 32, p. 28.
21 Whyte, *History, Myth, and Ritual in the Fiction of John McGahern*, p. 231.
22 Dermot McCarthy, *John McGahern and the Art of Memory* (Oxford and Bern: Peter Lang, 2010).
23 Seamus Heaney, quoted in *Young John McGahern*, p. xi.
24 Marcel Proust, *Against Sainte-Beuve and Other Essays*, trans. John Sturrock (Harmondsworth: Penguin, 1988), p. 6.
25 Frank Shovlin, 'Four Ducks', in *The John McGahern Yearbook*, ed. John Kenny, vol. 4 (Galway: NUI Galway, 2011), pp. 48–53.
26 Beckett, 'Dante ... Bruno. Vico.. Joyce', p. 3.
27 Harold Bloom, *The Anxiety of Influence* (Oxford: Oxford University Press, 1973), pp. 31, 70.
28 J. P. Stern, *On Realism* (London: Routledge & Kegan Paul, 1970), p. 75.
29 Quoted in David James (ed.), *The Legacies of Modernism* (Cambridge: Cambridge University Press, 2012), p. 6.
30 Quoted in James (ed.), *Legacies*, p. 6.
31 See W. B. Yeats, 'The Choice' and 'The Statues', in *Collected Poems* (London: Macmillan, 1985), pp. 278, 376; Montague quoted in Corcoran, *After Yeats and Joyce*, p. 81.
32 Terence Brown, 'Redeeming the Time: The Novels of John McGahern and John Banville', in *The British and Irish Novel Since 1960*, ed. James Acheson (New York: St Martin's Press, 1991), pp. 159–73.
33 James Joyce, *Ulysses*, ed. Jeri Johnson (Oxford: Oxford World's Classics, 2008), p. 53.
34 Neil Corcoran argues that McGahern's prose 'is a limpid development of the "scrupulous meanness" of Joyce's *Dubliners* ... whose realism is capable of sudden vivid fractures into depths of both lyrical plangency and stomach-turning disgust', p. 87. Maria DiBattista explores Joycean realism in her discussion of *Amongst Women*: 'Joyce's Ghost: The Bogey of Realism in John McGahern's *Amongst Women*', in *Transcultural Joyce*, ed. Karen Lawrence (Cambridge: Cambridge University Press, 1998). See also John Wilson Foster, *Colonial Consequences: Essays in Irish Literature and Culture* (Dublin: Lilliput, 1991) for comments on Joycean realism.
35 Edmund Wilson, *Axel's Castle: A Study in the Imaginative Literature of 1870-1930* (Harmondsworth: Penguin, 1993), pp. 24–5.
36 Wilson, *Axel's Castle*, p. 11.
37 Marina MacKay and Lyndsey Stonebridge (eds), *British Fiction After Modernism* (Basingstoke: Macmillan, 2007), p. 8.
38 For a recent and lucid summary, see Carol Taaffe, 'Irish Modernism', in *The Oxford Handbook of Modernisms*, ed. Peter Brooker, Andrzej Gasiorek, Deborah Longworth and Andrew Thacker (Oxford: Oxford University Press, 2010), pp. 782–96.

39 Seamus Deane, 'Dead Ends: Joyce's Finest Moments', in *Semicolonial Joyce*, ed. Derek Attridge and Marjorie Howes (Cambridge: Cambridge University Press, 2000), p. 26.
40 Seamus Deane, 'Joyce and Nationalism', in *Celtic Revivals: Essays in Modern Irish Literature 1880-1980* (Winston-Salem, NC: Wake Forest University Press, 1987), p. 97. See also Emer Nolan, *James Joyce and Nationalism* (London: Routledge, 1995).
41 See Wilson Foster, *Colonial Consequences*, pp. 55, 51; and Terence Brown, *The Literature of Ireland: Culture and Criticism* (Cambridge: Cambridge University Press, 2010), pp. 96, 101–2.
42 Declan Kiberd, *Inventing Ireland* (London: Vintage, 1995), pp. 582–3.
43 Bloom, *The Anxiety of Influence*, pp. 87–8, 121.
44 Stern, *On Realism*, p. 121.
45 Stephen Heath, 'Realism, Modernism, and "Language-Consciousness"', in *Realism in European Literature: Essays in Honour of J.P. Stern*, ed. Nicholas Boyle and Martin Swales (Cambridge: Cambridge University Press, 1986), p. 119.
46 Derek Hand, *A History of the Irish Novel* (Cambridge: Cambridge University Press, 2011), p. 5.
47 Whyte, *History, Myth, and Ritual in the Fiction of John McGahern*, pp. 227–8.
48 Eamon Maher, *John McGahern: From the Local to the Universal* (Dublin: Liffey, 2003), pp. 159, 144.
49 Hand, *A History of the Irish Novel*, p. 13.
50 Quoted in Maher, *John McGahern*, p. 144.
51 W. B. Yeats, *Representative Irish Tales* (Gerrards Cross: Colin Smythe, 1979), p. 32.
52 Patrick Kavanagh, 'Epic', in *Collected Poems*, ed. Antoinette Quinn (Harmondsworth: Penguin, 2005), p. 184. See Sampson, *Outstaring Nature's Eye*, for intertextual readings of McGahern with Kavanagh's poetry.
53 See Kiberd, *Inventing Ireland*, p. 496.
54 Seamus Heaney, 'From the Frontier of Writing', in *Opened Ground* (London: Faber, 1998), p. 297.
55 Joe Cleary, *Outrageous Fortune* (Dublin: Field Day, 2007), p. 206. Cleary's comments are addressed to Cathal Black's film 'Korea' rather than McGahern's story.
56 Michael Cronin, *Translation and Globalization* (London and New York, 2003), pp. 73, 91.
57 Yeats, 'A Dialogue of Self and Soul', in *Collected Poems*, p. 267.
58 Josipovici, *What Ever Happened to Modernism?*, p. 108.

1

'Useless Passion': Naturalism, Existentialism and Christianity in *The Barracks*

The Barracks and naturalism

Joe Cleary places McGahern's fiction squarely within a canon of what he terms 'Irish naturalism' in the mid-to-late twentieth century. Cleary argues that the continuation of this naturalist mode is symptomatic, rather than diagnostic, of an aesthetic retreat from the radical potentiality of modernism, and represents a passivity or loss of nerve in exploring Irish modernity in a future-oriented way. The impetus of McGahern's fiction, Cleary contends, is

> to evict history altogether and to discover a narrative form adequate to an essentially existentialist philosophy premised on the futility of worldly struggle and on the need to discover some inner authority and calm in the face of life's evanescence. In short, McGahern the socially engaged investigator of the secrets and lies of Irish rural life and McGahern the detached philosophical existentialist do not cohere in any satisfying way, and yet McGahern's admirers have never fully attempted to resolve this dilemma or even acknowledge it.[1]

Although this informs Cleary's critical assessment of *The Dark*, it also helps us to confirm two approaches to reading *The Barracks*, as an existentialist and naturalist novel, and thus to begin that process of acknowledgement which Cleary feels is lacking. The question which persists is the extent to which these modes are in fact oppositional or in need of an act of authorial cohering which never arrives. If a book like *The Barracks* is to be considered naturalist, it is a naturalism that has been resumed immediately after the intervention of French existentialism.

First, in what ways does *The Barracks* fit the model of the foundational French naturalist novel? David Baguley, also cited by Cleary, has conceived of the entropy of later naturalist literature. In a Flaubertian kind of naturalism, a Schopenhauerian world view predominates, in which a single life, ensnared in static daily routines, is 'frittered away on the path of extinction', so that it steadily goes downhill while going nowhere.[2] *L'Éducation Sentimentale*, for example, may be taken as part of this naturalist grouping of texts, with its description of repetitive, homogeneous, habitual days which pass away ('les jours s'écoulaient dans la répétition des mêmes ennuis et des habitudes contractées').[3] In novels such as Henry Céard's, argues Baguley, everything is shown to merge ('tout se confondait'); discriminations and distinctions are dissolved; and the 'representation of the nullity of hopes and illusion' gives way to a sense of fatalism. The naturalist vision is thus typically dysphoric and entropic, representing a world in which the destructive processes of time predominate, and what is recorded is the slow ebbing away of a life in which 'the human being [is] hopelessly and irretrievably subjected to his or her *natural* condition'.[4] The trajectory is towards deterioration, disintegration and even decomposition.

McGahern convinced his publisher that although he wanted 'to write a book about boredom' it would not fall in the trap of being boring itself.[5] The time scheme of *The Barracks* conveys something of the viscosity of Flaubertian time, as Bakhtin puts it: that ancillary time of pre-industrial or provincial existence.[6] The unit of the day, which McGahern related to both Greek and Gaelic temporality, is enclosed by the ringing of the alarm and the raking of the coals, and is compared to the fluctuation of the tides (*B* 21). Sylvie Mikowski refers to the novel's 'chronique naturaliste', though she also mentions that this is importantly interrupted by Proustian passages of memory which suggest an alternative, interior temporality.[7] Nevertheless, the emphasis on the habitual and routine in Elizabeth's life confirms the naturalist chronicity: what Baguley calls 'the traumatism of the Same'.[8] Mid-century sociopolitical stagnation is associable to Seán Ó Faoláin's satirical likening of de Valera's idyllic vision of cosy homesteads to a 'dreary Eden'.[9] The barracks can be seen as replicating a paradigmatic naturalist enclosure in which diurnal work is carried out, an environment in which people undergo 'the drag and burden of their lives together' (*B* 202), and which encourages trapped female characters, like Zola's Thérèse Raquin for example, to break out. Elizabeth sometimes thinks of her plight in terms of entrapment and escape, and of being 'shut in a world of mere functional bodies' (*B* 76). The novel rarely leaves the barracks: what is more, when it does, it is to other typical naturalist settings, like the hospital and indeed the cemetery.[10] This increases the sense of what Liliane Louvel conceives of as a series of '*emboîtements*' or encasements – a concentric boring down to Elizabeth's imprisonment in her own faulty cells.[11] Reegan also feels 'tethered' to family life and dreams of clearing out 'to blazes' so that 'he'd go free yet out into some life of his own' (*B* 109–10). Elizabeth's death finally precipitates the routing of his superior, Quirke, thus enabling Reegan to leave the barracks, even though the notion of 'clearing out' remains idealized.

The language of *The Barracks* carries echoes of the nineteenth-century naturalist inheritance, in particular the post-Darwinian discourse of biological determinism. To some extent, we can view the barracks as a cage in which physiological forces are working themselves out. Critics have noticed the conspicuousness of animal imagery. Reegan is agonized by his interview with the doctor: 'It was too horrifying, a man or woman no more than a caged rat being given over to scientific experiment' (*B* 110). But he is just that animal when in the barracks: after Elizabeth's burial, the guards avoid returning to the wake where they imagine Reegan 'standing silently like a caged animal' (*B* 223). Elizabeth too sits in the barracks kitchen 'with the abjection of beaten animal' (*B* 21); she is 'a thieving animal held at last in this one field' (*B* 51); she hears the mating foxes, their 'raw cry of animal heat' (*B* 90), with terror. In the doctor's waiting room, Elizabeth finds 'the most deserted corner of the table like a half-dazed animal' (*B* 78). Later, she thinks of her working life as that of 'a performing animal' (*B* 188). These analogies suggest the problem which Elizabeth is facing: on the one hand, her own human uniqueness, that 'being was her ridiculous glory as well as her pain' (*B* 94), and the sense of purpose that can be derived from this; on the other, the relentless and inescapable causality which dictates the downward trajectory of human life. The erasure of humanist 'glory' brings man down to the level of just another zoological form: not the Aristotelian *zoon politikon*. In the hospital, Elizabeth observes her fellow patients undermining a vain woman: 'They had her by the heels. They'd drag her down' (*B* 137). The correlation between human and animal cruelty within the species is made explicit: she remembers a pack of greyhounds turning on a brindled dog in their midst, threatening to tear it to pieces.

The conspicuousness of the scene in which Mullins's pig is slaughtered thus hints at the idea that Elizabeth may herself be a type of *bête humaine*. Elizabeth vividly imagines rather than sees the 'the long knife driven into the heart', 'the screaming choke into silence' and then the carcass 'scalded with boiling water and the white hairs shaved away' (*B* 170–1). This disturbingly brings her thoughts into alignment with an earlier description of her own body in the operating theatre, shaved, washed, 'painted with iodine': the shame of a body once 'excreted by her mother' (*B* 119), as it is put with Beckettian brutality, but now anaesthetized and knifed. Mullins's pig has been fed up in order to be killed: it is unconscious of its rude good health and its imminent death. We might say that Elizabeth thinks of the pig's slaughter 'without emotion' not only because of her familiarity in childhood with stuck pigs but also because she feels a kind of companionship with the pig; she conceives of her body as other, just as the animal is supposed to be other. The reader is discomfited by the proleptic analogy between the mortality of Elizabeth and the death of the pig, perhaps questioning that distinction which Heidegger draws between human dying (*sterben*) and animal dying (*verenden*).[12]

Another way of tracing the remote archetypal structure of naturalist narrative in *The Barracks* is to consider the much debated relationship between realism and naturalism. One strand of the discussion concerns how, in the naturalist novel, there is an ebbing away – indeed a satirical scrutiny – of bourgeois confidence. Of course, satire may often have a prominent role in bourgeois realism, but what we find is that the naturalist is, as Flaubert said, ever more motivated to paint 'the topside and the underside' – to expose what is underneath the dominant stratum of society.[13] In this sense a dramatist like Ibsen may be understood as a naturalist. It is the relevant lack of such a dominant bourgeois culture in nineteenth-century Ireland which is conventionally seen as foreclosing the possibility of an Anglo-French classical realist tradition. If we compare the narrator's final consideration of Dorothea at the end of *Middlemarch* with the representation of Elizabeth, continuities and distinctions can be appreciated. Eliot writes,

> A new Theresa will hardly have the opportunity of reforming a conventual life. … But we insignificant people with our daily words and acts are preparing the lives of many Dorotheas, some of which may present a far sadder sacrifice than that of Dorothea whose story we know. But the effect of her being on those around her was incalculably diffusive: for the growing good of the world is partly dependent on unhistoric acts; and that things are not so ill with you and me as they might have been, is half owing to the number who lived faithfully a hidden life, and rest in unvisited tombs.[14]

St Teresa of Avila's motto was 'Lord, either let me suffer or let me die': her early experience of ecstatic, self-mortifying pain is behind the 'ardent deeds' of a 'conventual life' – the founding of Carmelite nunneries in Europe. Elizabeth owns a valuable relic of St Teresa of Avila enclosed in the carved crucifix attached to Elizabeth's antique rosary beads (*B* 74). Teresa, who McGahern referred to as an intellectual, is to be distinguished from another St Thérèse (de Lisieux), whose statue stands on the mantelpiece next to the clock (*B* 24, 49).[15] Like

Middlemarch, *The Barracks* also implies the value of the ordinary lives that it has recorded, despite the fact that such lives lack the heroic 'significance' of acts such as Teresa's or Antigone's. Elizabeth's chores are 'so colourless and small that only on a reel of film projected slowly could they be separated and named; and as no one noticed them they were never praised' (*B* 21). They too are unnoticed, hidden or 'unhistoric' acts, intimately known only to the sympathetic and private fellowship of novel readers. In both cases, it is the solicitude of both writers to attend to what is latent but extraordinary in the ordinary, to what lies outside of the idealized forms of romantic or heroic historical narratives.

And yet we see the difference between the two 'new Theresas' in relation to the social confidence of one, the existential isolation of the other: crudely, the classic realist and the neo-naturalist. Dorothea's idealistic good works – for instance, her interest in improving local cottages – may be overlooked at the macro-historical level, but they have contributed in their 'incalculably diffusive' way to the progress of middling English society. No such improvement is available for Elizabeth: 'Her woman's days had no need of change. They were full and too busy, wanting nothing but to be loved' (*B* 21). This work is part of the repetitive continuum of habitual labour – one chore is 'always unfinished and two more eternally waiting' (*B* 21). There is no question of the 'diffusion' of such individual deeds, despite the constancy and implied goodness of the life. This is partly an index of the different social positions of the two characters, in which the idea of Dorothea's 'sacrifice' (she marries the penniless Ladislaw and foregoes Casaubon's inheritance) is of a different order from Elizabeth's. Juxtaposing the texts emphasizes the extent to which *The Barracks* occupies a more pessimistic, static naturalist mode which represents a break from classic realism.

A case has been made for the ways in which *The Barracks* may indeed manifest certain distant generic similarities to late nineteenth-century French naturalist narrative. However, the differences from such a model of naturalism are quite clear. This is not an adultery narrative. Elizabeth is not a fallen woman, whose malady is supposedly caused by her libidinous behaviour. The cancer is not caused by the 'nature' of human behaviour but visited upon Elizabeth, and thus marks cruel existential randomness rather than moral determinism. This is not a degraded or sordid enclosure telling of, say, alcoholism and prostitution. Elizabeth is not an object of social investigation to be documented but a subject whose consciousness is plumbed. *The Barracks* is not a narrative of dissipation or degeneration in Baguley's fully entropic sense.

Like the laundress Gervaise in Zola's *L'Assommoir* (1872), often taken to be a *locus classicus* of European naturalism, Elizabeth dies early, but it is worth looking at how the former's death is described:

> And it was there, on some straw, empty and frozen to the bone that she starved to death. Apparently the earth was in no hurry to have her. … Death meant to take her little by little, bit by bit, dragging her along the wretched path she had made for herself. It wasn't even clear what she did die of. People mentioned the cold and the heat, but the truth was that she died of poverty, from the filth and exhaustion of her wasted life. As the Lorilleux put it, she died of slatternliness. One morning, as there was a nasty smell in the passage, people recollected that she hadn't been seen for two days, and she was discovered in her hole, turning gently green already.[16]

The naturalist body is objectified to this extreme: 'C'était là dedans' ('… it was in there'). At the end of *Madame Bovary*, Charles's corpse is also an 'it'.[17] For all Elizabeth's shame at her trussed, shaved and mutilated body in the operating theatre, her sense of its otherness ('a few stone of agonized flesh' (*B* 122)), and her acknowledgement that people 'rotted apart' (*B* 90), we are not allowed to follow her own disintegration into something green and foul-smelling. Dehumanization is not carried to this extreme. Elizabeth's subjectivity – her life of the mind – has been so dominant that a literary effect such as Zola's, insisting ultimately upon an objectification of the individual as putrid matter, would be out of keeping. Treating Elizabeth as a 'human beast' does not imply any sort of post-evolutionary, atavistic regression. In naturalist novels, nature may often appear to be 'ontologically evil', in Baguley's phrase, something which threatens the human order.[18] *The Barracks* is far from a celebratory pastoral: the 'singing' from the sawmills and the digging of the turf remind us that this landscape is worked upon. Yet the ways in which the narrator observes the red light of dusk at the top of the trees, or the Wordsworthian 'wonder of yellowness' (*B* 49) of daffodils, argue against any such naturalist demonization of nature.

If we return to the analogy with the pig's body, we may note the merest hint of the crucifixion: Elizabeth visualizes the tangled-up pig as it 'rise[s] to its highest when it was caught on the snout-hook' (*B* 170), and Casey comments that the pig 'got more publicity than a Christian' (*B* 171). The boiling of the pig may be associated to the 'quick death' of the lobster, boiled *alive* in 'Dante and The Lobster', admitting in both cases a certain Christian symbolism. Belacqua motions towards fellow-feeling with the lobster – 'it's a quick death, God help us all' – but the concluding voice which comes out of nowhere, 'It is not', points to the unknowability of the animal and thus to the limits of zoomorphism.[19] The lobster has a slow, lingering death and its sentience is unknown to us. Likewise for McGahern, that such symbolism touches on the 'quickness' of Christ's, Elizabeth's and the pig's death – all of which prematurely end within the middle of healthy lives – works against the notion of her body being functionally analogous to the animal other as 'it', a material object. The implied symbolic association cuts more deeply.

Elizabeth, far from indulging solely consolatory memories, is of the opinion that she has used Reegan just as she was used by Halliday: 'They all lived on each other and devoured each other as they themselves were devoured' (*B* 210). Such devouring may be a socio-biological naturalist trope: the hierarchy of society will always produce such relationships of cruelty and dependency: 'a system of arselickin' which is in 'the natural order of things' (*B* 69), as Reegan explains it. But it is more than the naturalist determinism of 'dog eat dog' which defines Reegan's masculinist world view. The idea of a cannibalistic devouring, what McGahern elsewhere describes as selves drawing 'closer to a meal of each other's flesh' (*N* 79), may equally be framed in existentialist terms and Beckettian terms. We devour and are repelled by others: desire is a hunger whose obverse is what Dermot McCarthy refers to as the 'nausea that results from feeling the surfeit of identity'.[20]

Finally, a strain in studies of American naturalism, in particular, suggests the Marxian economic determinism of the late nineteenth century: the tyranny of capital, the individual's relationship to labour and the consequent loss of individual agency. Although Reegan's life of work could be usefully investigated under such a rubric – his entrepreneurial turf-providing on a rented conacre coexisting with his violent relationship to the work he does for the state, some of it imaginary – *The Barracks* cannot be placed in a broader context of urban naturalism, for obvious geographical reasons. Reegan epitomizes professional stasis in the civilian era: the novel is not fully disengaged from mid-twentieth-century Irish history, but attuned to the disjunctive relationships within the structure of the polity. The attention intermittently paid to his 'sour reflection of a disappointment ... both personal and Irish' represents for John Cronin a 'saving context' which speaks to a post-independence narrative of the nation.[21] The sense of the provincial locality as cut off and insularized, and the numerous references to emigration, emphasize socio-economic marginalization, rural stagnation and disconnection from the state centre. By dwelling not only on Elizabeth's plight but on Reegan's resentful relationship to 'the institution of Eire'

(*B* 118), with its 'floral screens' and 'anthems of faith-and-fatherland' (*B* 28), McGahern demonstrates that although he resists fully objectifying the human he does not simply take apolitical refuge in the fetishizing of Elizabeth's interior life.

The Barracks and existentialism: Habit and work

Habit is a recurrent word in *The Barracks*. The emphasis on habit as a salve for boredom fits the naturalist paradigm: Flaubert's 'répétition des mêmes ennuis et des habitudes contractées'. However, the fact that *work* is Elizabeth's habit also points to unexpected continuities between naturalism and existentialism. Camus wrote of Sisyphus's fate as a 'series of unrelated actions' (*B* 110): Elizabeth too faces an eternal present of unnoticed identical chores, interrupted by nocturnal periods of renewal, and experiences time as tidal rather than teleological. A life's changeless domestic work atomizes into separable instants which make up an overlooked existence. Drudgery is a condition of existence. When Elizabeth rides home from the doctor's surgery she has to dismount on the steeper hills. The note is one of stoic perseverance: '"All answers are stupid and questions too, … I am pushing the bike because I am pushing because I am pushing. I am going home because I am going home because I am going home"' (*B* 96). The struggle of life is conceived as an endless repeated loop of Sisyphean 'pushing', free of causal explanation – what Liliane Louvel describes as the 'cercle tautologique et absurd de la vie'.[22]

To take another intertextual example from Camus, we see that *La Peste* (*The Plague*) is about both the habit of work and of living with death, as Elizabeth does. Soon after the word 'plague' has first been uttered, Rieux, the doctor, draws courage in the certitude of work and the daily round: 'The thing was to do your job as it should be done'.[23] *The Plague* argues against the exceptionalism of pestilential visitation: rather, death is within life, inescapably part of our experience of life. This is what the old asthma patient implies when he says: 'But what does that mean – "plague"? Just life, no more than that'.[24] Oran's citizens become habituated to death, for them a statistical part of daily life. Elizabeth's last year, in which she lives and she dies, is utterly ordinary too. Rieux does his repetitive doctor's job on earth as one of the less deceived, without resort to any romantic illusions of overweening human agency; nor does he assume that the plague will behave in a rational way. We are warned to be on our guard against the roused, dying rats of a death-dealing future: we work and fight and do not submit, but we cannot sanitize life of death. Elizabeth's former job as a nurse in war-torn London is significant, then. Like Rieux, she too has toiled in a struggle with death-in-life: there will always be another dying body to treat, and hers will not be exempt.

As a young woman, Elizabeth, under the tutelage of Halliday, has defined a potential life of freedom through literature as a shedding of the unthinking repetition of custom: habit, in this meaning, is blind emulation, the safety of the 'ensured imitation of other people's lives' (*B* 87). Instead, in a classically existentialist articulation of joyful freedom, she realizes the singularity of her own life, 'when a single human being discovers his or her uniqueness ... when after having slept for ever in the habits of other lives, suddenly, one morning, the first morning of the world, she had woken up to herself' (*B* 87). Elizabeth's blazing youthful realization that, in Hegelian-Sartrean terms, she can be-for-herself (*für-sich-sein*, *être-pour-soi*), that she can fashion her life in her own image, does not last and cannot sustain her. The habits of 'other people's lives' take over again. Not only her later skivvying, but also her work as a nurse in London, becomes 'repetitive and menial and boring', and in her account it is because she grows 'simply sick of living' there that she marries Reegan (*B* 49). Although Elizabeth cannot find meaning in her work, as Camus has Rieux do, neither is she rendered wholly un-free: she will not be fully 'broken into the deadness of habit like most of the rest...' (*B* 188).

Prayer is significantly represented as a conspicuous cultural habit, a collective guarantor handed down through generations, an 'ensured imitation'. McGahern often acknowledges the cultural importance of ceremony in communal life, and thinks of ritual structures as aesthetically meaningful, indeed analogous to art itself: he said that 'all art approaches prayers'.[25] The value of religious habit is recognized in *The Barracks*. The fourteen stations are a pattern which gives dignity to Elizabeth's life. She says of the rosary that 'she'd come to love its words, its rhythm, its repetitions, its confident chanting, its eternal mysteries; what it meant didn't matter. ... It gave the last need of her heart release, the need to praise and celebrate, in which everything rejoiced' (*B* 220). However, the novel does not shy away from registering that semantic emptiness which seems to accord with Alain's saying, quoted by Camus, that 'prayer is when night descends over thought'.[26] Christian ritual is another learnt and empty habit. Reegan's prayers are answered in chorus, 'murmurs and patterns and repetitions that had never assumed light of meaning, as dark as the earth they walked, as habitual as their days' (*B* 73). Prayer is an inculcated habit to '*help ... unbelief*' (*B* 123), and may itself carry an interdiction against loss of faith in terms of hellish enclosure: '*I must necessarily live within the gates of my hell for ever*' (*B* 73). The odd-looking syntax of one sentence, just before it is specified that Elizabeth has cysts in her breasts, describes Reegan's relentless and monotonous prayers being repeated 'without urge or passion, no call of love or answer, the voices simply murmuring away in a habit or death' (*B* 33). Unbeknownst to the others, Elizabeth is now living 'in death' as well as in habit, though not defended by it. Elizabeth says eleven Hail Marys, the new sense of her mortality leading her to exceed the decade. Existence is a surplus which the eschatological narrative cannot contain.

The phrase 'deadness of habit' (*B* 188) reminds us of a modernist lineage to McGahern's emphasis on habit in *The Barracks*: the Proustian-Beckettian. In an interview, McGahern said of the novel that 'we work in the same material, Beckett and I'.[27] Beckett's early book on Proust includes memorable epithets about habit: 'the generic term for the countless treaties between the subjects … and their correlative countless objects'; or more brutally, 'the ballast that chains the dog to his vomit'.[28] A young Beckett is sifting out from Proust what will, as it were, become Beckettian, leading to the gestural language of *Godot* as well as lines such as Vladimir's 'habit is a great *deadener*' (my italics).[29] If we are to regard Elizabeth's chores as Sisyphean, this does not tally with the Beckettian conception of habit: although he accorded importance to *L'Étranger*, he was characteristically caustic about Camus's apotheosis of this particular myth, presumably because it still ennobles the idea of work. Elizabeth holds herself aloft from 'the rest' who are fully broken into dead habit, signifying that she does not find much glory in her continual pushing, even though it may insulate her from the nakedness of her existence.

'Habit' gathers together multiple meanings or connotations: devotion as repetition, the domestic space as *habitus* or dwelling, inherited custom, the cultural 'mantle' of clerical vestments, and in a biological sense, habit as *mode of growth* (an archaic meaning of habit as bodily condition). Elizabeth's body is constituted by deathly growth so that death has now become her habit. She suffers from a Flaubertian-naturalist 'traumatism of the Same' but this may also be read through existentialism, hinting at the daily work of suffering and struggling. It also derives from a less affirmative view of work which Beckett extricates from Proust: that habit is an analgesic to daily suffering. The preoccupations of post-war existentialism, which were at their height in the years before the publication of McGahern's first novel, can be seen to overlap, in these perhaps unexpected ways, with those of late nineteenth-century naturalism, suggesting a shared erosion of confidence in religion and in humanism.

Existentialism and Beckett: Thought

The Barracks extrapolates existential questions from its naturalist confinement. As we have seen, though, it is not the determining forces of social turmoil or deprivation which bring about the death of the protagonist, as in many naturalist novels, but the fickle visitation of cancer. Like Camus's plague, cancer acts randomly but remorselessly, unconnected to human will, and even though it leads to an inevitable end, it nevertheless problematizes our sense of causality and intelligibility. In *The Barracks*, illness is not 'produced' by society but opens out upon universal questions of existence, as with Kierkegaard's biblical metaphor of the 'sickness unto death'. Thinking of a miser saving for a rainy day, which represents the cheapening of our 'passion to live for ever', Elizabeth dismisses 'the lunacy of building an outer wall against something that's impregnably entrenched in every nerve and cell' (*B* 156). Although Elizabeth acknowledges that death, in the form of impregnable cancer, cannot be bricked out of life, in another sense she does want to keep death distinct from life, in order to preserve the sense of an individual, full and finished life, and to confirm that final determination that she has 'lived in health, not in sickness in death' (*B* 220). Although the sheer fatigue of dying also prompts a sense of futility, she does not fear death because only through it can the uniqueness of her own healthy life be completed and appreciated. The way in which the fluctuations of Elizabeth's last moments are recorded suggests that, as Heidegger says, 'Dying is something that every *Dasein* must take upon itself' (*Sein und Zeit/Being and Time*) – that it is not 'delegatable'.[30]

Elizabeth's existential courage is bound up with the representation of her as, above all, a thinking subject – as one who is burdened by the curse and freedom of being a thinking reed. To Louvel, this relates to an affirmation of the individual: the text celebrates the victory of the subject over death.[31] Nevertheless, thought itself is regularly convicted for the suffering that it causes and for its futility: 'It was no use trying to think anything, it was too painful, it all got on the same claustrophobic road back to yourself' (*B* 56); her 'thinking only made bad worse' (*B* 150); 'human understanding' is deemed not to matter 'because it understood nothing' (*B* 118); a quick death is desirable as it would be 'without time for terror or thought' (*B* 160). As Ciaran Ross has argued, these thoughts are reified as part of a painful process which cannot defend Elizabeth from the void: her thoughts 'unthink' or 'unfix' her.[32] Elizabeth distinguishes between the act of thinking as a continuous Cartesian process (the 'road back to yourself'), and the produced object of that thinking, thought: 'There was no end of thinking and she could even think away the need to think. An age of thought can pass before the mind and be lost in the same flash' (*B* 154). This is more than homely wisdom. If philosophy is the history of thought, then it too – an 'age of thought' – must be borne in evanescent thoughts. Thought, conceived of as a massive body of passed-on understanding, seems to be the parent of our thoughts, but its only vehicle is our own consciousness, on which it depends to be perpetuated.

At one point, Elizabeth wishes to get rid of her mind because her 'thought could begin on anything for object and still it travelled always the same road to the nowhere of herself' (*B* 176). This idea of thought 'working on' the object world, of objects being continually changed by the perceiving consciousness, is explored by Beckett, and particularly relates to his interest in Proust and in Husserlian phenomenology, which is concerned with how objects are explored as phenomena in the consciousness of subjects. This eventually leads to the subjectivity of *The Unnamable*, in which the object world is eventually reduced to the 'nowhere' of oneself and one's thoughts – to a consciousness which cannot be given objective identity but which nevertheless goes on expressing itself. It is not necessarily a question of arguing for direct analogies with such difficult late modernist texts, but rather in identifying in *The Barracks* an anti-humanist scepticism towards thought which spreads throughout Beckett. One of the key debates in *Waiting for Godot* relates to the cursed inheritance of the *cogito*. Vladimir asserts that 'what is terrible is to *have* thought' but also that 'thinking is not the worst': the compromise position seems to be that though it is 'not the worst to have thought', we could have done without it.[33] Oddly, then, Elizabeth the naturalist *bête humaine* and existentialist thinker has a kind of kinship with that other tethered thinking subject, Lucky. Lucky's speech, recited on the command 'Think, pig!', is the ruin of Enlightenment thought, now as useful as gobbledegook. Despite the incomplete philosophical labours of Puncher, Wattmann, Belcher and Fartov, and their attempts to prove the existence of a white-bearded God, man is still destined to 'waste and pine', to 'shrink and waste', to 'the skull the skull the skull in Connemara'.[34] Here is Beckett's rendering, in accelerated monologue, of that 'flash' of thoughts which, to Elizabeth, comprises an 'age of thought' whose authority has waned as she shrinks and wastes.

The problem of thought is also related in *The Barracks* to the Sartrean problem of others. While visiting town, Elizabeth considers her withdrawal from the pleasantries of small talk: social interaction is viewed as if through a closed window: a kind of screened-off, grotesque dumb show which emphasizes that '*they* did not exist any more, but *she* did' (*B* 95). The idea that the narrative 'shares round' its centres of consciousness through the fluid use of free indirect discourse should not disguise the centripetal movement towards the solitude of its principal subjectivity. Although others have minds, the subject can never think like them, and thus imagines them as alienated from her thinking and from thought in general. The other is inert, in Sartrean terms, and comes to represent something that is unthinking. At one point, and despite the fact that at times we are given access to his thoughts, Reegan's mind is described (by Elizabeth, we intuit) 'as a painless blank', of containing a 'total blankness' which is disturbed by the thought of his wife (*B* 45). While he complains about Quirke, a debate is carried out in her mind between his adversarial approach to the Darwinian struggle, and how such 'ceaseless activity' (*B* 193) defines life, and her own fatalistic acceptance of universal mortality, something which to Reegan would represent a death-driven pacifism. A distinction is set up in Elizabeth's mind between those for whom 'fullness of life … was not thought' and the solitary subject whose thinking is 'to be free and lonely and to die' (*B* 193). It is significant that although Elizabeth rehearses this debate and imagines her husband's response, these thoughts remain unspoken, as if the private life ousts the coded exchanges of married life. As has already been established, she does not assert the superiority of her thoughts: they may not be worth the penny which Reegan offers for them (*B* 154), and can be figured as poisonous (*B* 128). What emerges from the provincial social milieu is the isolation of a subjectivity for whom 'praying and thinking and reading' are 'just pale little sideshows' (*B* 188). The legacy of thought is now reduced to the same level as prayer, 'when night descends over thought'. Autonomous and unitary selfhood is not taken for granted but shown to be vulnerably constituted by scattered thoughts and memories: it would 'need years to gather the strewn bits of her life into the one Elizabeth' (*B* 72).

The idea Sartre expresses in *L'Être et le Néant* (*Being and Nothingness*) that 'my being-for-others is a fall towards objectivity' – that such a fall is 'an alienation' – aptly describes Elizabeth's feelings about the priest on her deathbed.[35] Elizabeth refuses to engage with the priest's potential *objectification* of her as yet another soul: he does not become her secret sharer. It is not only that the man at the bedside is a priest, though it is clearly important to note, as Eamon Maher does, the problematic history of a relationship that has earned Elizabeth 'the reputation of being a renegade, an eccentric'.[36] Her refusal certainly does not proceed from atheistic antagonism or from what David Coad regards as a mocking, deriding, meanly cynical portrait of Catholicism in this novel.[37] The priest is, simply, an other: he 'would have to examine and try to understand what she'd say in the light of *his own life*' (*B* 218). In the end, she reaffirms her subjectivity, her being-for-itself, against the social role of being-for-the-other: 'The whole of her vital life was in herself' (*B* 218). After the priest's administering of Extreme Unction which she has only ever imagined 'other people' receiving (*B* 216), she is protective of her own thoughts which 'had been with her too long', and of 'her own truth … within herself' (*B* 217). The priest is just another interpreter of mysterious reality and Elizabeth will not cling to anything other than the reefs of her own consciousness. But, as for Beckett, the continuing role of her failing body, which was once 'excreted', and then 'strutted in the rouge of its youth' (*B* 119), is not disowned by talk of the soul. The priest's anointment of her 'organs of sense, through which sin had entered the soul', a supposedly purifying ritual, prompts the refractory Elizabeth to think that 'all things else had entered that way too' (*B* 216). What the sexual body has known and what the decrepit body now knows cannot be disowned or overridden by transcendent words spoken directly to the soul.

The singularity of *The Barracks* is in part effected by the way free indirect discourse does not translate and manage thoughts into conventional novelistic parcels. Terence Brown refers to how the prose of the novel is 'reflective, open syntactically and rhythmically to accumulation of event, deed, detail of milieu and to narrative comment'.[38] That open syntax of Hiberno-English prose, with its roots in the art of the storyteller, is similar to what the Russian formalists, identifying the diegetic staple of fiction often camouflaged in realism, referred to as *skaz*. In *The Barracks*, the paratactic piling up of clauses and semantic repetition suggests a resistance to the sophistry of grammatical subordination, and to the scripted 'finish' of literary prose: 'They were all the same, they would not change, the same day would follow the same day and day and day, nothing more would happen' (*B* 160). However, this is a form of 'open' writing which comes after the syntax of Irish modernism, whose deliberate resistance to elegant variation calls to mind Beckett's comments on the iniquities of literary style and his aspiration to write in French 'without style' (*sans style*). McGahern's disabused allusion to the 'absurd crown of Style' in his essay 'The Image' recognizes this Flaubertian–Beckettian inheritance – a style which may 'work on' the object of nothing. Immediacy and spontaneity are manifest in the disruption of syntactic order: 'She could make no statement other than that here, she had no right, she was only waiting and she could not say or know more' (*B* 211). McGahern does not get near to processual writing at 'degree zero', that '*écriture blanche*' Barthes argued was characteristic of Camus and Blanchot, but by avoiding the mediating or elegant ordering of thoughts, he still gestures towards the potential of imitative form.[39] The terror and freedom of thoughts certainly come ceaselessly to Elizabeth, and are represented without an overseeing authorial presence to 'correct' the prose.

Christianity and existentialism

Despite his demurral that he 'wouldn't read Camus for his ideas', McGahern conceded that *The Barracks* could be called 'an existential novel'.[40] Roger Garfitt claimed that McGahern's work is that of 'the most truly Existentialist writer working in English today'.[41] Commentaries on the novel such as Denis Sampson's, rich in the existentialist vocabulary of authenticity, personal freedom, anguish, choice, revolt and commitment, suggest that this is an appropriate way to discuss Elizabeth's 'ridiculous being' (*B* 94). The sense that her ordinary life must be borne with heroic responsibility is stamped with existentialist conviction, articulating struggle in the world rather than evasive quietism. Elizabeth's being, however, was her 'glory as well as her pain' (*B* 94): the liturgical overtones tell us that the ridiculous struggle takes place in a conspicuous Christian context. Elizabeth's attachment to the 'beautiful, beautiful ceremonies of Holy Week' is not only an aesthetic appreciation (of candlelight, the scarlet of the altar-boys, shuffling on flagstones (*B* 194)) but an expression of a dying woman's fellow-feeling with the suffering of Christ. *The Barracks* integrates the vocabulary of existentialism with that of ingrained rituals which, though metaphysically hollow, remain culturally meaningful. These apparently mutually exclusive worlds are held in suspension, their claims unresolved, as if McGahern is reaching out to an 'existentialist theology' or a 'religious existentialism' – categories which though for Sartre were self-contradictory, suggest both the inheritance of Kierkegaard and the attempts of Catholic philosophers like Gabriel Marcel, who probably first coined the term existentialism, to reconcile the two.

Elizabeth is not presented as one who would easily accept Pascal's wager: 'Her life was either under the unimaginable God or the equally unimaginable nothing' (*B* 59). Though her straitened existence within the barracks 'with these others' (*B* 152) limits the scope of experience, she instinctively objects to moderation, to life taken in 'small doses': 'how that mean of measurement degraded and cheapened all passion for life and for truth' (*B* 152). Both Christianity and existentialism exclude the middle, philosophically speaking. Father Paneloux, in *The Plague*, preaches a fundamentalist credo of 'All or Nothing': his congregation must 'believe everything' – including the active willing of apparently meaningless cruelty, such as a child's death – or they must 'deny everything'.[42] Existential *néant* is the enemy here: an undifferentiated *everything* must be accepted under God. But the moderated middle ground is inimical to existentialism as well: Sartre opposes a 'secular moralism which seeks to suppress God at the *least* possible expense'.[43] Such an attitude allows the idea of intelligibility to remain without God, whereas, to the existentialist, it is embarrassing that God does not exist, because it forces individuals to design their own intelligible patterns and construct their own morality. Sartre concludes *Being and Nothingness* by writing that man is 'a useless passion'.[44] Elizabeth may be seen as equally suffering Christ's and Sartre's passion, and cannot be imagined solely 'under' one or the other.

It is for this reason that the role of Halliday finally remains undecidable. He is not unrelated to a stock figure in naturalist fiction, the disaffected intellectual, or Flaubertian *fruit sec*, who may briefly offer a way out for the doomed heroine but who always disappoints. Mainly, though, Halliday recurs in the text as a ghostly agent of degraded existentialism. Under his tuition, Elizabeth discovered her own 'uniqueness', when she had first 'woken up to herself' (*B* 87): these are represented as 'a few impassioned months of her life' (*B* 188). Later, she recasts the very same period as 'some months of bitterness' (*B* 194) – the single time she had 'fallen away' from attending mass, we infer. Sampson refers to Halliday as 'the spokesman, though not the representative, in the novel for the supreme authenticity of calm and lucid observation in the face of mutability'.[45] For all that, he succumbs to cynicism and suicide, lacking existentialist affirmativeness. It is rather Elizabeth, able to avoid the nihilism abhorrent to Sartre, who may be the more representative figure. Importantly though, the memory of Halliday is not exorcized from the narrative but returns to Elizabeth as she lies dying. He had taught her to name the terror of living rather than to cower behind superstition, but this has been a questionable legacy: can huddling together as a crowd 'in the dark' of superstition or belief be any worse than 'this lonely terror of broad daylight' (*B* 210)? As with 'The Country Funeral', no decision is reached. Elizabeth finally chooses to identify herself with the dignity and meaning which Christ gives her, life to individual life; she submits to Extreme Unction. Equally, though, she chooses *not* to say what the priest wants her to say, not to submit to institutional expectation; the possibility of an 'unimaginable nothingness' is by no means discarded. The existentialist damage has been done for Elizabeth: just as she cannot unlearn Christian habit, she cannot unlearn the new terror.

This interpenetration of Christian and existentialist vocabularies defines the particular form of its modern disenchantment. Elizabeth refers to the lives of others which 'had to overflow or cripple and die', and wonders whether it matters 'where the overflow ran' (*B* 218). This overlaps with the Sartrean notion of things being superfluous (*de trop*). Sartre conceives of beings not conscious of themselves (*en-soi*) as viscous and defiant substances whose quiddity ('thingness' or 'itness') escape anthropomorphized pattern. But the being-for-oneself (*pour-soi*), the thinking subject, is not exempt: in *La Nausée* (*Nausea*) Roquentin says, 'And *I* – weak, languid, obscene, digesting, tossing about my dismal thoughts – *I too was superfluous*.'[46] Although Elizabeth's expression of inter-subjective relations and of contingent 'overflow' can be profitably viewed in this Sartrean light, it must also be acknowledged that it does not sit easily with her spiritual appreciation of the natural world as part of something which may indeed imply theistic design, and which seems more akin to what Gabriel Marcel thinks of as a creative fidelity to the sacred gift of existence.

This indeterminacy is a manifestation of what Eamonn Grennan has called the 'implicit (post-Catholic) religious accommodations' of McGahern's fiction.[47] For all of her metaphysical speculations, there is an element of empirical materialism to Elizabeth's response to Extreme Unction. She thinks twice of the '*65 per cent wax* candles', and of the *olive* oil (my italics) in the priest's bottle (*B* 216–17), which triggers memories of childhood through the senses. Matter persists: the numinous is not victorious. In another illustration of this 'post-Catholic' or 'post-Christian' accommodation, Elizabeth looks up from her sickbed:

> With the flickering night light she could follow the boards across the ceiling, then the knots in the boards, dark circles in the waxen varnish, but soon they were lost, the ceiling in as much confusion and emptiness over her eyes as she didn't know what'. (*B* 200–1)

These inscriptions, which tease us with the magic of potential intelligibility, could be compared to the scene in Beckett's *Molloy* in which Jacques Moran takes personal confession in his room with a priest who carries a portable pyx that he calls his 'kit'. The priest sees something on the ceiling: 'Heavens … what is that stain?'.[48] Ceilings are now heavens: the vaulted firmament has been replaced by a travestied set of arbitrary patterns – stains, or wooden knots and circles. Lest this seem far-fetched, we may remember a late scene in *The Barracks* when Mullins and Casey are in the Protestant cemetery. Before heading off to the pub, they decode the inscription of the local gentry, *spes tutissima coelis* (or, 'the surest hope is heaven'), by musing upon Ascension from a rotating, orbiting world. They wonder which 'way up' (*B* 224) heaven is, and conversely whether hell might be in Australia. This comically points to the impossibility of such 'renegades' rejecting Christianity *tout court*, and how existential 'confusion and emptiness' may be rendered in terms which are materialist, absurd *and* culturally Christian.

Conclusion

Elizabeth insists on excluding the middle: her Christian faith and her existential freedom are 'all or nothing'. She thinks of an unspecified 'mystery', out of which she has come and to which she will return, 'surrounding' her life (*B* 211) – a mystery defined by liturgical culture but also standing for the existential unknown. Her passion for life, either Christian or Sartrean, resists the middling 'mean of measurement'. The text must allow its metaphysical indeterminacy, the aporia of either/or, to persist, and thus to represent both the unknowingness of the human condition and the autonomy of the thinking subject. This relates to the claim which this chapter began by considering – that the naturalist and existentialist modes do not satisfactorily 'cohere' in McGahern's fiction.

It is difficult to see how such coherence could be achieved and how these modes could be reconciled without detracting from the singularity and resistant undecidability of this novel, at least. In a work which aspired to be about boredom but not itself be boring, the naturalist and existentialist modes are revealed to be distinct but mutually constitutive. Elizabeth is hedged in by a constrictive provincial environment, tethered to domestic life, un-free and doomed to die, described variously as an abject, half-dazed or performing animal. She is objectified by work, which 'had to go on, grinding, incessant, remorseless; breaking her down to its own dead impersonality' (*B* 188). Yet she is also thinking subject, a consciousness 'for herself' who, sensitive to the otherness of the world, knows that it is 'terrible to have thought' but also that this is what constitutes her uniqueness and authenticity as an individual. Naturalist and existentialist elements are interdependent. Elizabeth *thinks about* her entrapment, her life of habit which determines her daily behaviour, and thus escapes the life of naturalist abjection not only through remembering but also by intellectually tussling with a torturous 'age of thought'. Beckett's dramaturgy has been described as a 'caged dynamic'.[49] With its cognate ideas of imprisonment, internment, or encasement, or what French scholars of the novel perhaps punningly call *enfermement* (hellish enclosure, the Sartrean *huis clos*), the figure of encasement resurrects a naturalist trope. The effect of experiential impoverishment and decrepitude, played out through the Flaubertian 'traumatism of the Same', is produced, as for the solitaries of Beckett's fiction, within the plethoric richness of a self-interrogating consciousness.

There is no need to make over-stretched claims that *The Barracks* continues the defamiliarizing and dissident project of modernism – it does not – to assert that, equally, it is hardly exemplary of a retrenchment into unambitious, plot-driven or mimetic realism. The realism that has been attributed to the novel is peculiarly fissile or implosive. Sampson argues that it is 'restrictive to think of [it] as a realistic novel' although he also refers to its 'poetic realism'.[50] Garfitt calls McGahern's writing realist too, but with the caveat, as we have seen, that he is the 'most existentialist' of Anglophone writers.[51] The often cited influence of Tolstoy's 'The Death of Ivan Ilyich' in turn suggests a debt to the psychological realism of canonical Russian fiction. The hoary question of the relationship between realism and naturalism, briefly touched on in this chapter, confirms the inappropriateness of aligning the novel with a confident bourgeois tradition, and we might remember that even Ivan Ilyich has a book by Zola on his shelves. Even if Elizabeth's centrality as a subject may seem to perpetuate the idea that this is 'expressive realism', in Catherine Belsey's term, this is difficult to reconcile with McGahern's often stated beliefs that art must not be expressive.[52] It cannot be proposed that *The Barracks*, dominated as it is by Elizabeth's centre of consciousness, communicates an essentialist sense of the unitary subject of mimetic humanism. Rather, the reader is aware of Elizabeth's fragmented, self-questioning subjectivity, tied to a body she wishes to 'get shut of' (*B* 122), disabused of anthropocentric assumptions. She is indeed not granted the years she would need 'to gather the strewn bits of her life into the one Elizabeth' (*B* 72). If *The Barracks* is realist, it eludes all but the broadest definitions of realism.

Notes

1 Joe Cleary, *Outrageous Fortune: Capital and Culture in Modern Ireland* (Dublin: Field Day, 2007), p. 165.

2 David Baguley, 'The Nature of Naturalism', in *Naturalism in the European Novel*, ed. Brian Nelson (New York and Oxford: Berg, 1992), p. 22.

3 David Baguley, *Naturalist Fiction: The Entropic Vision* (Cambridge: Cambridge University Press, 1990), p. 93.

4 Baguley, 'The Nature of Naturalism', pp. 25–6.

5 McGahern quoted in 'Entretien de John McGahern avec Nicole Ollier: Step-by-Step through *The Barracks* with John McGahern', in *La Licorne* 32 (UFR Langues Littératures Poitiers, 1995), p. 60.

6 M. M. Bakhtin, *The Dialogic Imagination*, ed. Michael Holquist (Austin, TX: University of Texas Press, 1981), pp. 247–8.

7 Sylvie Mikowski, 'L'Expérience Fictive du Temps dans *The Barracks*', *Études Irlandaises: Études sur* The Barracks *de John McGahern* (October 1994): 27–44, 42.

8 Baguley, *Naturalist Fiction*, p. 221.

9 Seán Ó Faoláin quoted in Michael Mays, *Nation States: The Cultures of Irish Nationalism* (Lanham, MD: Lexington, 2007), p. 99.

10 This is pointed out by David Malcolm, *Understanding John McGahern* (Columbia: University of South Carolina Press, 2007), p. 11.

11 Liliane Louvel, 'John McGahern: *The Barracks*: Requiem un Jour Ordinaire', in *La Licorne* 32 (UFR Langues Littératures Poitiers, 1995): 87–105, 89.

12 See Derek Attridge on Derrida's *Aporias* and animals in J. M. Coetzee's *Disgrace*, in *J. M Coetzee and the Ethics of Reading: Literature in the Event* (Chicago: Chicago University Press, 2004), p. 185.

13 Quoted in Philippe Hamon, 'The Naturalist Text and the Problem of Reference', in *Naturalism in the European Novel*, ed. Brian Nelson (New York and Oxford: Berg, 1992), p. 31.

14 George Eliot, *Middlemarch* (Harmondsworth: Penguin, 1988), p. 896.

15 McGahern refers to Thérèse de Lisieux as 'a sentimental saint, a sentimental kind of make-believe' and Teresa of Avila as 'an intellectual … a very interesting saint'. See 'Entretien de John McGahern avec Nicole Ollier', in *La Licorne*, 55–86, 73.

16 See Sarah C. Alexander, 'The Residuum, Victorian Naturalism and the Entropic Narrative', *Nineteenth-Century Contexts: An Interdisciplinary Journal* 35, no. 2 (2013): 99–120, 109.

17 Gustave Flaubert, *Madame Bovary*, trans. Gerard Hopkins (Oxford: Oxford University Press, 1991), p. 339: 'He fell to the ground. He was dead. … Thirty-six hours later, Monsieur Canivet, summoned by the apothecary, arrived. He opened the body, but found nothing.' In the French: 'Il l'ouvrit et ne trouva rien', *Madame Bovary* (Genève: Droz, 2011), p. 490.

18 Baguley, *Naturalist Fiction*, p. 216.

19 Samuel Beckett, 'Dante and the Lobster', in *More Pricks than Kicks* (London: Faber and Faber, 2010), p. 14.

20 Steven Connor has coined the wonderful term 'emetic aesthetic' in thinking of a shared Sartrean-Beckettian interest in alimentation and nausea. To Connor, existence is figured as indigestion: most pertinently to a line that McGahern cut from 'My Love, My Umbrella', and which connects to this idea of mutually devouring selves, human interaction means that the self can get 'a taste of the

Other's taste of himself'. See Steven Connor, 'Beckett and Sartre: The Nauseous Character of all Flesh', in *Beckett and Phenomenology*, ed. Ulrike Maude and Matthew Feldman (London: Continuum, 2011), pp. 61–4. McCarthy, *John McGahern and the Art of Memory*, p. 55.

21 John I. Cronin, '"The Frightful Mill of Love": John McGahern's *The Barracks*', *Études Irlandaises: Études sur* The Barracks *de John McGahern* (October 1994): 107–18, 109.

22 Liliane Louvel also relates these lines to the Sisyphean: 'John McGahern: *The Barracks*: Requiem un Jour Ordinaire', in *La Licorne*, 87–105, 92.

23 Albert Camus, *The Plague*, trans. Stuart Gilbert (Harmondsworth: Penguin, 1948), p. 37.

24 Camus, *The Plague*, p. 250.

25 Denis Sampson, *Young John McGahern: Becoming a Novelist* (Oxford: Oxford University Press, 2012), p. 154.

26 Albert Camus, *The Myth of Sisyphus*, trans. Justin O'Brien (Harmondsworth: Penguin, 1975), p. 63.

27 John McGahern, 'Entretien de John McGahern avec Nicole Ollier: Step-by-Step through the *The Barracks* with John McGahern', *La Licorne* 32 (UFR Langues Littératures Poitiers, 1995): 55–86, 77.

28 Samuel Beckett, *Proust and Three Dialogues with Georges Duthuit* (London: John Calder, 1999), p. 19. See Sampson, *Young John McGahern* for further comparisons between Beckett and *The Barracks*.

29 Samuel Beckett, *Waiting for Godot* (London: Faber and Faber, 2010), p. 87.

30 Quoted in David E. Cooper, *Existentialism: A Reconstruction* (Oxford: Blackwell, 1999), p. 136.

31 Louvel, *La Licorne*, p. 104: 'Le texte alors célèbre la victoire du sujet sur la mort'.

32 Ciaran Ross, 'Some Painful Thoughts about *The Barracks*', *Études Irlandaises: Études sur* The Barracks *de John McGahern* (October 1994): 119–30, 129.

33 Beckett, *Godot*, p. 55.

34 Ibid., pp. 35–8.

35 See Cooper, *Existentialism*, p. 101.

36 Eamon Maher, *The Church and Its Spire: John McGahern and the Catholic Question* (Dublin: Columba, 2011), p. 39.

37 David Coad, 'Religious References in the Barracks', *Études Irlandaises: Études sur* The Barracks *de John McGahern* (October 1994): 131–8.

38 Terence Brown, 'John McGahern's *Nightlines*: Tone, Technique and Symbolism', in *The Irish Short Story*, ed. Patrick Rafroidi and Terence Brown (Gerrards Cross: Colin Smythe, 1979), pp. 289–301, 291.

39 Roland Barthes, *Writing Degree Zero*, trans. Annette Lavers and Colin Smith (London: Jonathan Cape, 1967).

40 Sampson, *Outstaring Nature's Eye*, p. 34. McGahern quoted in *La Licorne*, p. 81.

41 Roger Garfitt, 'Constants in Contemporary Irish Fiction', in *Two Decades of Irish Writing: A Critical Survey*, ed. Douglas Dunn (Cheadle: Carcanet Press, 1975), pp. 207–43, 208.
42 Camus, *The Plague*, p. 183.
43 Jean-Paul Sartre, *Existentialism and Humanism*, trans. Philip Mairet (London: Methuen, 1973), p. 33.
44 Jean-Paul Sartre, *Being and Nothingness*, trans. Hazel E. Barnes (London: Routledge, 1996), p. 615: 'Thus the passion of man is the reverse of that of Christ, for man loses himself as man in order that God may be born. But the idea of God is contradictory and we lose ourselves in vain. Man is a useless passion.'
45 Sampson, *Outstaring Nature's Eye*, p. 55.
46 Jean-Paul Sartre, *Nausea*, trans. Robert Baldick (Harmondsworth: Penguin, 1965), p. 184.
47 Eamon Grennan, '"Only What Happens": Mulling Over McGahern', *Irish University Review* 35, no. 1 (Spring/Summer 2005): 13–27, 19.
48 Samuel Beckett, *Molloy* in *Trilogy* (London: John Calder, 1994), p. 101.
49 Lawrence Graver, *Waiting for Godot: A Student Guide* (Cambridge: Cambridge University Press, 2004), p. 22.
50 Sampson, *Outstaring Nature's Eye*, p. 36.
51 Garfitt, 'Constants', pp. 208, 224.
52 Catherine Belsey, *Critical Practice* (London and New York: Methuen, 1980), p. 7.

2

Mining the Self: *The Dark*

Multipersonal narrative

A pronoun may seem a small matter, but she matters, he matters, it matters, they matter.[1]

John Berryman

If at least he would dignify me with the third person, like his other figments, not he, he'll be satisfied with nothing less than me, for his me.[2]

Samuel Beckett

That beautiful English word for the Other is Thou.[3]

John McGahern

The Dark is what narratologists call a multipersonal novel: the short chapters are mainly narrated through the third or second person, and in fewer instances, the first. Some reviews of the novel downplayed or reacted against the formal strategy of the novel. John Cronin was generally critical of the novel's 'confessional form', a kind of bleak narrative entrapment from which we are given no remit, and did not refer at all to the portions of second-person narrative that take up approximately half of the narrative.[4] F. C. Molloy endorsed the view that, though the variation in narrative person is designed to deepen our intimacy, what is absent from *The Dark* is the sort of retrospective understanding of the subject that is provided in *The Barracks*.[5] In contrast, however, others have claimed a self-conscious objective scrupulosity for the novel, one which implicitly derives from the aesthetics of modernist impersonality. In an early review, Vivian Mercier argued that by the last chapter, which is mainly rendered in dialogue and whose person is indeterminate, 'complete objectivity has been achieved' and that it is 'this objectivity-in-the-subjective, constantly growing throughout the book, that sets this novel of adolescence somewhat on a par with Joyce'.[6] Paul Devine addressed the unexpected switches in what he (rather misleadingly) called point of view: such narrative fluctuation eliminates authorial 'didacticism' and compels readers to evaluate on their own terms. Although remarking that the distribution of narrative persons is not easily schematized into a pattern, Devine argued for the gradually increasing objectivity of the novel, and like Mercier, for the significant 'absence of narrative presence' in the last chapter.[7] This critical model of an aesthetically achieved objectivity, not to be confused with naturalist objectivity, suggests that the eventual withdrawing of the self is somehow akin to the Flaubertian–Joycean method of 'refining' the authorial voice out of existence.

More recently, Stanley van der Ziel's analysis of *The Dark*'s multiform narrative, particularly in relation to Beckett's narrating 'I', has convincingly proposed another way to conceive of the movement from the multipersonal to the concluding impersonality of the last chapter.[8] Van der Ziel argues against the idea of an implicitly retrospective narrator looking back with irony from the vantage point of the future, emphasizing instead the unstable and continual fragmentation of grammatical person-in-process. Despite being 'cursed' and fissile, Beckett's 'I' stoically 'goes on', whereas the eventual disappearance of McGahern's pronouns is, for van der Ziel, a marker of how the narrator not only stops being narrated but stops narrating.[9] This confirms that *The Dark* is an existentialist novel which recognizes the limits of the Joycean *Bildung* as well as the Beckettian need to keep saying 'I'. The novel thus acknowledges both its lack of aesthetic triumphalism and its stoic compulsion to express: that failure is its success, in van der Ziel's view. What is particularly suggestive about this conception of the novel is that it views impersonality not in the classically Flaubertian-Joycean, proto-modernist sense but from the other end of the telescope, at or beyond mid-century generic exhaustion, emerging from the post-Trilogy, *nouveau roman* period in which selfhood has been evacuated and subjectivity erased.

This in turn allows us to evaluate the way in which the oscillation of pronouns has attracted the equivocal epithet 'experimental', particularly in relation to the novel's surprising use of the second-person voice. The narratologist Monika Fludernik suspects that texts such as *The Dark*, which alternate between first-, second- and third-person mode, 'provide a very strong impression of "mere" experimenting with the pronominal choices … although the foregrounding of different perspectives that are inherently contradictory and repetitive might constitute just such a motivation for the "experimental" use of pronominal alternation'.[10] David Malcolm is more laudatory of the 'intriguing narrative experiment', noting that the complex narrative organization inevitably draws attention to itself and makes the novel 'an artistic artefact' and an example of how McGahern's fiction 'inhabits a border land between the relatively invisible conventions of realism and the foregrounded art of other kinds of fiction'.[11] Rather than a modernist or late modernist model of impersonality, we might infer an outward-facing, foregrounded or experimental narrative which may, at least to some degree, be associable with the self-referential poetics of *post*modernist narrative.

This mid-1960s novel may be surprisingly placed in the unexpected company of international postmodernist works which make complete or extensive use of the second person: Michel Butor's *La Modification* (1957), Günter Grass's *Katz und Maus* (1961), Carlos Fuentes' *La Muerta de Artemio Cruz* (1962), Thomas Pynchon's *Gravity's Rainbow* (1973), Clarice Lispector's *Agua Viva* (1978), Italo Calvino's *Se una Notte d'Inverno un Viaggiatore* (1979), Gabriel Josipovici's *Contre-jour: A Triptych after Pierre Bonnard* (1986), Nuruddin Farah's *Maps* (1986), Nathalie Sarraute's *Tu ne t'aimes pas* (1989).[12] This reads like an orthodox university postmodernist fiction course and one to which, so the academic taxonomizing of post-war literature dictates, *The Dark* ought not belong. Certainly, *The Dark* is not a ludic, frame-breaking meta-narrative. McGahern himself would of course dissociate himself from accusations of metafictional flamboyance: 'I would think that while I am a traditional writer – I have no interest in experiment for experiment's sake – I actually think that the real experiment is a constant experiment, and that's the experiment of the voice, of the way of seeing… .'[13] Yet, on a technical or formalist level, the novel can be smuggled into that category of so-called 'experimental' post-war world fiction which seeks alternatives to the confessional but unreliable first person or to the stony substantiality of third-person narrative. The general multipersonal structure of *The Dark* may not be a radical instrument of defamiliarization, but it does disrupt the univocality and discursive hierarchies of classic realism.[14]

McGahern's gesture towards a splintering of selfhood is actuated by something more than the ludic desire to experiment. The protagonist must remain nameless, attached to a grammatical substitute rather than a proper name, his as yet unformed identity a site of conflictual process. The early third-person sections show how the anonymous 'small-he' is bound to the patriarchal-He, Mahoney, whose surname is the only one we have for the first son, and thus acts as a kind of unwanted patronymic. Grammatical sharing imitates bed sharing. In a rare first-person chapter, this sharing is oddly reinforced by the refusal to name him 'Daddy' in his thoughts: 'And all I did for her [his mother] now was listen to Mahoney's nagging…' (*D* 33). Early resistance – the children shutting out the father after a fishing trip – takes the form of an unindividuated sibling 'they' which subsumes the small-he but keeps the tyrannical-He shut out: 'Let him play alone' (*D* 16). In *Le Degré Zéro de l'Écriture* (*Writing Degree Zero*), Barthes tells us that, for Paul Valéry, the conventions of the novel were epitomized by the third-person statement 'The Marchioness went out at five o'clock'. Such sentences are part of a fabricated narrative code which allies the novel to history, naturalizing and giving solidity to social relations. Thus, to Barthes, the massiveness of the bourgeois realist novel banishes our sense of existence.[15] His antipathy for the third-person pronoun which such naming necessitates is clear. Elsewhere he writes that '"he" is wicked: the nastiest word in the language: pronoun of the non-person, it annuls and mortifies its referent', and that to say 'he' about someone is to envisage 'a kind of murder by language'.[16] The violence of *The Dark* is not just in its represented scenes of beating or psychological bullying, but also connected to this annulment and mortification of individuated selfhood in narrative. The symbolic Law of the Father structures narrating language, and that language must be destabilized. The boy is never given a forename, a Christian name. Although local place names are 'bedded for ever in [his] life, as eternal' (*D* 139), his own name is a lack: staring at it printed in the newspaper, he wonders to himself, 'Was that his name, was that him?' (*D* 162). 'Young Mahoney' must evade the inheritance of the patrilineal pronoun, but neither is his confidently confessional, defiantly individualistic 'I' allowed to fully emerge. His personhood is cleft, and this is manifest in the novel's extended use of *second-person* narrative.

The interstitial subject

Narratologists have accommodated some second-person narratives within a relatively simple schema – that of the displaced, disguised, dissimulated or even counterfeit 'I'.[17] In such texts, there is a so-called 'deictic transfer' – in essence, a change in the way we understood the context of utterance and address – from the 'I' to a substitute 'you'. An apparently uncomplicated translation is pulled off. The implication is that such texts are perhaps toying with a device which, to a more radical writer, would more convincingly implicate the reader. It turns out that 'you' may not be much of a base-level guarantor of anti-realist poetics at all. Such is the strict focalization and governing consciousness of young Mahoney, it is not surprising that Fludernik places *The Dark* in this category and regards the second person as having 'little inherent appropriateness to the topic of the story'.[18] For the 'you' to function solely as a 'disguised-I' seems to duck the challenge of dialogism, and to fall back on the hidden circumscription of the first person. However, 'you' is not necessarily condemned to being a counterfeit 'I'. Brian McHale has argued, in relation to *Gravity's Rainbow*, that 'you' can simultaneously entertain more than one signified and thus preserve the very strangeness, equivocality and irreducibility of fiction.[19] McHale has written that '*you* is a sign of dialogue, conveying some vocative appeal, some sense of address, even in its most "innocent", impersonal instances'.[20] This pronoun is more apt to 'slide' between its possible uses, encouraging readerly hesitancy. Though *The Dark* has been categorized as a 'displaced-I' text, I would argue that, as well as hinting at the potential indeterminacies within the self, it does indeed draw on the 'vocative appeal' of the second person, creating an interpersonal 'aura of intimacy' between the narrator and the addressee.[21]

In the following example, a dialogue with the father on the subject of university gives way to a voice no longer watchful, non-committal or pessimistic. Education is conceived of as an initiation into mystery:

> All day you could pore over the marvel and delight of the books of the world if you chose the arts. You could walk under trees and talk with men and women who were initiates with you too, men your own age, and walk with a girl of your own who was studying the same as you. (*D* 124)

As we enter the mistily naïve realm of the hypothetical future – 'the long golden evenings in the boats on the Corrib' (*D* 124) – the 'you' shifts slightly and necessarily to the impersonal, the colloquial 'one'. Rewriting the passage with an undisguised-I would limit this sense of hope and opportunity, by enclosing the experience within the first person:

> All day I could pore over the marvel and delight of the books of the world if I chose the arts. I could walk under trees and talk with men and women who were initiates with me too, men my own age, and walk with a girl of my own who was studying the same as me.

There is too much first person here. But there is not too much 'you' in the first passage because it implicitly shares, gathering the other students and a girl who may become a wife into a gilded future which does not take place. The solipsism of the narrator on the farm, projecting himself into a fantasy, is rendered more acute by the cadence of the second person: this 'you' could be 'me'.

The second-person form enables the representation of young Mahoney's consciousness to be dialogically structured. We gain intimate access to an interior life in which the catechistic form has been absorbed. As Dermot McCarthy has argued, young Mahoney is both penitent and his own confessorial superego, the would-be priest trying to control the sexual guilt of the adolescent.[22] The 'you' marks a form of self-address, self-enquiry and self-interrogation:

> Why are you here? the questioning started.
> To sit and read a book.
> But no, beyond that, why did you come, why are you alone here?
> To think about being a priest. (*D* 82)

This is interior monologue without speech marks, but it is not rendered as stream of consciousness. The reader is *not* addressed by the narrator: young Mahoney only has himself these questions to ask, something which deepens our sense of his isolation and encourages potentially empathic proximity. Swapping the 'I' for the 'you' would win a type of flat coherence but lose richly interrogative confusions. Rather than being thought claustrophobic, the second-person voice of the narrator-protagonist may be thought as fissile and dialogic, as McCarthy has argued.[23]

Discussing his choice of the second person, one writer has said that it is like 'standing (raging) outside yourself … of not wanting to be that person'.[24] The displacement of the first person may be seen as a protection from oneself, and the suppleness of the second-person form shows how 'you' may act as 'I''s shadow-self or anti-self. In *The Dark*, for example, a curious aggressiveness breaks out while the boy is in the priest's quasi-Marvellian garden, a 'green prison': 'Suddenly you jumped and trampled bee and flower into the earth of the grave' (*D* 85). This is an oddly shocking moment, and part of the shock is that the second person has lulled the reader with the flow of paratactic clauses, inducing the 'heat and nothingness' of high summer. Everything is being focalized through young Mahoney's eyes, but his control of the narrative has been modified not only by his idling but by the 'vocative appeal' of the 'you'. He has taken a book into the garden and is thinking: that is all. Action, when it comes, irrupts this inertia in a literal and unexplained 'annihilation' of the world's living matter, but without Marvell's conception of the transcending, creative imagination. Later in the day, young Mahoney hurls a big history book on the floor and stamps on it: this is designated as 'rage' or a 'fit' (*D* 87). The reader eavesdrops on these thoughts, and understands that a fierce battle is being waged within the 'you', but the sting of the action still comes as a surprise. The more inter-subjective 'you' leads the reader to expect confessional complicity, and not the potentially mendacious suppressions or unreliable justifications of the first person.

Barthes thinks of the wicked 'he' as belittling and conquering the 'I', a person which stands for existential density and darkness, yet to be objectified in material history. 'I' is anonymous and can thus conceal. Barthes refers to how in *The Murder of Roger Ackroyd*, Agatha Christie hides the murderer under the 'I', taking advantage of the novel's conventional implication that the observed third person will be the main actor.[25] This is a useful context in which to interpret Mahoney's bee-trampling, book-throwing rage, suggesting the potential for violence admitted in an earlier confrontation with the father. In Beckett's *Molloy*, Moran conceals his murder of a man between sentences, but is still apologetic, like the petit bourgeois 'smallholder' he is: 'I do not know what happened then. But a little later, perhaps a long time later, I found him stretched on the ground, his head in a pulp. I am sorry I cannot indicate more clearly how this result was obtained, it would have been worth reading'.[26] The subject is split open, unable to account for actions governed by his unconscious, by the 'mollose' Molloys inside him. Young Mahoney's bee trampling is not of this order. Beckett's Moran is locked into what linguists call an 'illocutionary', self-justifying contract (writing a report for his boss), whereas young Mahoney indulges in reproachful forms of self-address. Nevertheless, the boy's bee trampling remains an action of unexplained motive which suggests self-estrangement. McGahern does not surrender the existential darkness of 'I' and the promised confidentiality of the second person does not always materialize.

Finally, another aspect of second-person narratives, evident in texts like Butor's *La Modification*, is the importance of tense. The past tense creates the effect, according to one narratologist, of 'deixis am Phantasma'. In it, 'the speaker conjures up a past version of himself and talks to and about it as if it were present in his immediate deictic field, while distinguishing it from his present identity through the difference in tense and person'.[27] The curious transpositions of tense in the following spectral passage from *The Dark* may thus be suggestively linked to the 'you'-form. Young Mahoney is sleepless in the priest's house, which is situated next to a graveyard. He imagines the souls who, like the purgatorial, Yeatsian spirits abroad (see 'The Wine Breath') have 'left their graves to walk in search of forgiveness':

> The presence of the dead seemed all about, every stir of mouse or bird in the moonlit night, the crowded graves, the dead priest who'd collected the grandfather clocks. You grew frightened though you told yourself there was no reason for fear and still your fear increased, same in this bed as on the road in the country dark after people and cards, nothing about, till haunted by your own footsteps your feet go faster. You tell yourself that there's nothing to be afraid of,

you stand and listen and silence mocks you, but you cannot walk calm any more. The darkness brushes about your face and throat. You stand breathing, but you can stand for ever for all the darkness cares. Openness is everywhere about you, and you at last take to your heels and run shamelessly, driven by the one urge to get where there are walls and lamps. (*D* 69)

The event-in-memory, walking in the country after dark, is rendered more present than the consciousness of the narrating 'you'-voice, lying in bed in the priest's house, and attached to the conventional preterite. His and our impression that the dead are present is emphasized through a switch in tense. The 'you' can range about, drawing the reader into a similar position: we are led away from the particularity of a circumstantial episode, the single night of 'people and cards', into a universally available human condition, fear of the dark. The ubiquity of the second person, together with the deliberate vagueness about the memory, opens up the possibility that the reader may thrillingly tiptoe into the text to be abandoned in the present: 'You can stand for ever for all the darkness cares.' The internal dialogue, the self-addressing default of I-to-you, briefly shifts, as though this atavistic communicative act is somehow addressed to our fears.[28] Although this is not the ontologically destabilizing 'you' of an apostrophized reader-as-character, as in some works of high postmodernism, the transgressive capaciousness of the second person nevertheless spreads an almost gothic disorientation.

As we trace the multipersonal positions of each chapter in *The Dark*, we see that the second person is an intermediary vehicle to show how the coerced self, on whom prohibition acts, threatens to stunt the process of individuation. It is significant that McGahern was not alone in evading the circumscriptions of the first- and third-person voice in post-war Irish fiction. Edna O'Brien's *A Pagan Place* is a second-person novel of rural childhood, too. O'Brien explains why she chose this form: 'As a child you are both your secret self and the "you" that your parents think you are. So the use of the second person was a way of combining the two identities.'[29] The 'you' may be intimate but it is also the prescriptive voice of the superego which commands 'Thou shalt not'. At the end of *A Pagan Place*, the protagonist is about to leave Ireland to enter a convent:

I will go now, was what you said, hoping that she would emerge from the house and say good-bye and have done with you, but since no such thing happened you went anyhow and the last thing you heard was a howl starting up, more ravenous than a dog's, more piercing than a person's, a howl that would go on for as long as her life did, and his, and yours.[30]

The narrating 'you' will assume a new saint's name as a nun in Brussels. This leavetaking is narrated in the interstices of the fragmenting family, and any Joycean confidence in voluntary self-exiling, 'I will go now', is immediately dissolved by the necessary infelicity, 'was what you said', which still binds the parental 'you' to the secret 'you'.

While discussing the unbridgeable separateness of self and other in *The Leavetaking*, and the way in which 'the person cannot emerge from the Self', McGahern remarked that the 'beautiful English word for the Other is Thou'. The archaic, intimate, religious, blasphemous second person seems in this conception to capture both what is most loved and most other – what, in the preface to *The Leavetaking*, McGahern calls the 'otherest' (*L* 5). But there is no completed leavetaking in *The Dark*. The novel can be retrospectively constructed as having represented the internalization of this schism between self and other within the formative subject. 'Thou art' abjectly what you are told to be, although 'thou art' potentially beautiful: indeed 'hallowed be thy name'. As for O'Brien, McGahern's choice of grammatical person, which builds into the narrative the interdiction placed upon identity-formation and self-determination, relates to the genre of these narratives. The distinctive narrative form of *The Dark* is symptomatic of the generic inheritance of *Bildungsroman*, albeit that this legacy is refracted and contested in its European, Anglophone and Irish disseminations.

The modernist *Bildungsroman* and genre memory in *The Dark*

Critical approaches to *The Dark* have both invited and disavowed the relevance of the *Bildungsroman*. Eamon Maher categorizes the novel in this way but observes that 'this may have unconsciously led McGahern into territory that didn't quite suit his artistic temperament'.[31] Sampson writes that '*The Dark* is less a *Bildungsroman* or a portrait of the artist as a young man (although it has elements of both) than an existential study of a consciousness in an indeterminate state'.[32] Although David Malcolm concedes that '*The Dark* shows affinities to the class of novel called the bildungsroman', he wonders more broadly about the applicability of the term outside of German-language contexts to any novel of maturation.[33] The taxonomic diffuseness of the term is indeed unhelpful, but *The Dark* nevertheless 'invites readings both autobiographical and generic', as Neil Corcoran puts it.[34]

For this reason, it is worth pursuing how to read *The Dark* as generically exemplary or exceptional of the *Bildungsroman*. The morphological fragmentation of the developing individual, an uncertainty about the authority of voice, is traceable to a generic legacy, whether that is knowingly inscribed in the text or not. Writing on Bakhtin, David Duff has coined the term 'genre memory' to express how literary works may evoke a genre which 'is reborn and renewed at every stage in the development of literature' and 'lives in the present, but always remembers its past, its beginning'.[35] The multipersonal and briefly episodic structure of *The Dark*, with its almost exaggerated fragmentation (thirty-one chapters in under two hundred pages), is in some form of understated alignment with the more radical distantiation of Brechtian epic form, which insists that 'nobody can be identically the same at two unidentical moments'.[36]

Franco Moretti has argued that, after the Enlightenment, the narrative trajectory of the *Bildungsroman* gave symbolic shape and meaning to modernity itself.[37] The newly mobile protagonist, with his or her great expectations, was a self-cultivating subject whose youthful experiences – no matter how testing – represented an induction into the bourgeois order. We see the *Bildungsheld*, deliberately anti-heroic and ordinary, in the process of eventually becoming a full socialized member of a normative community. The *Bildung* is the youthful individual's apprenticeship into selfhood and autonomy, directed towards an endpoint of eventual integration, paradigmatically represented by the Society of the Tower in Goethe's *Wilhelm Meister*. However, questions of self-determination and integration within society cannot be extricated from how personhood is enunciated in narrative. This is immediately apparent from exemplary nineteenth-century *Bildungsromane* in English. The first chapter of *David Copperfield* is entitled 'I am born'. The narrative of development immediately and comically points to the impossibility of its own enunciation: the 'I' who narrates is not the same as the 'I' who is narrated. The wholeness and continuity of the first person itself is seductive and chimerical. Philip Pirrip mispronounces a name founded on unknown origins, and engenders himself in language. The orphan Jane Eyre, who often refers to herself in second or third person, is finally reconciled with herself as well as Mr Rochester: 'I am Jane Eyre … I am come back to you'.[38] For all that such first persons may eventually overcome obstacles to enter the bourgeois order, their selfhood is narrated through an unstable, aporetic subject position. The overarching *telos* which retrospectively charts how *I was* became *I am*, and which demands smooth teleological development, is betrayed by the instability of subject positions in language.

Generally speaking, there is a change in the personhood of early twentieth-century *Bildungsromane*: Mann's *Tonio Kröger*, Musil's *Die Verwirrungen des Zöglings Törleß*, Lawrence's *Sons and Lovers* and Joyce's *Portrait* are written in the third person. At the beginning of *Portrait*, the emergent subject is being narrated to the extent that it cannot speak as 'I': 'His father told him that story'; 'you wet the bed'; 'Stephen will apologize'; 'He hid under the table'; '*Pull out his eyes*'. John Paul Riquelme has referred to the way in which the reader is increasingly required to 'translate' the third person into the first-person voice during Stephen's narrated monologues.[39] The increasing resemblance in *A Portrait* of teller and character, their mutual self-engendering presence, allows the narrative to stand as both process and product: the 'writing of the story becomes the story of a writing'.[40]

Moretti argues that these late *Bildungsromane* are often more novella-like – certainly the case for *Tonio Kröger* – and that they incorporate the poetics of the emergent short story and lack the novel's sense of totalization. They are also characterized by a new moral climate in which the alienating power of the institution threatens to punish and do violence. What were opportunities for the expectant hero have now turned into accidents (233). Moretti conceives of *Portrait* as a 'dead branch' of the nineteenth-century mode: Stephen Hero 'cannot survive' in the twentieth century. The *Bildungsroman* is a residual form whose utility has been exhausted, and to Moretti no novel shows this better than *Portrait*. To Weldon Thornton, too, it is an 'antimodernist' narrative which does not endorse the 'atomic individualism' of the modernist self, and whose oscillating movement between self-assertion and self-abnegation can be attributed to a valid psychological wholeness and determination: a reconstituted psyche which has 'an entelechy'.[41]

This is one way of briefly sketching the generic history which precedes McGahern's own development or anti-development novel. In James Calahan's view, McGahern may have sought to undo rather than outdo Joyce: *The Dark* 'could not more deliberately invert, subvert, and deflate the dénouement of *Portrait*'.[42] This is hardly a unique anxiety of influence, however. Many, if not most, coming-of-age Irish novels with literary aspirations in the last eighty years have borne such scrutiny.[43] However, the inevitability of comparing late twentieth-century Irish development novels to *Portrait* – an obeisance to a once new but now canonical modernism – is perhaps more justifiable if Joyce's own work is placed in *its* generic context, as a self-conscious outgrowth of the nineteenth-century European tradition. *The Dark* succeeds an earlier belatedness or exhaustion of form, signalling its own generically residual identity. If it deliberately deflates *Portrait*, as Calahan has claimed, it may be deflating a clapped-out genre.

The opening of *The Dark* is a deliberate provocation, an early retaliation against the censor, so to speak: after twenty-three words, to be precise. *The Dark* spells out but does not write 'F.U.C.K': in a sly communication with the censor, the word is there and not there – a fragmented signifier. In the light of later fiction like *The Pornographer*, we cannot but reread the first lines of *The Dark* as part of a continuous narrative of authorial self-awareness, concerning the reception and cultural status of the work in Ireland. *The Dark* replays a Joycean matrix of linguistic evasion, obscenity, prohibition and taboo. The opening scene, in which the boy is beaten by the Father for uttering the obscenity, is a familiar narrative structure of which *Portrait*'s pandybat episode is the best known. Before administering the beating, Mahoney refers to that 'profane and ugly word' (*D* 7). At the very beginning of *Portrait*, the interdiction relates not to the boy's obscenity but to his blasphemy: expressing a desire to marry a Protestant. Nevertheless, the fear instilled into Stephen, who hides coweringly under the table, obliquely suggests a sexual anxiety. Dante has called up the Prometheus myth, but voices the threat that the eagles will pluck out Stephen's *eyes* rather than his liver – in Freudian terms, she invokes the displaced terror of castration. The crouching young Mahoney's fear of sexual violation, as well as of physical violence, returns to such oedipal symbolism.

The sexual and the lavatorial are connected in the early pages of *Portrait*. Stephen muses, 'Suck was a queer word … the sound was ugly'.[44] According to Derek Attridge, for Stephen the word has subliminal associations with adult male sexuality, centring on his memory of being in the lavatory of the Wicklow hotel with his father: it possesses 'an aura of the forbidden, the sinful, the unclean' and 'echoes the primary taboo word "fuck"'.[45] Stephen remembers the sound of 'suck' when his father 'pulled the stopper up by the chain and the dirty water went down through the hole in the basin'. (In such circumstances, the basin 'cocks' or taps are implicated.)[46] 'Suck' also suggests homosexuality at Clongowes, and is linked to the 'smugging' (masturbation or mutual masturbation) which Stephen puzzles over in the 'square', or latrine, as Attridge has observed. The bedroom is also lavatorial in *The Dark*. As he lies in the chair completely naked, and waiting to feel his father's obviously phallic leather on his flesh, the boy's own 'dirty water' escapes him. The boy is not beaten: rather the father strikes the arm-rest. Incestuous homosexual violence is narrowly averted, suggesting the terrifyingly close displacement of desire. The belt, which had 'twitched against his trousers, an animal's tail' (D 8), is now described as 'hanging dead' (*D* 10). For young Mahoney and his siblings, it is the lavatory, with its 'reek of Jeyes Fluid' (*D* 10), that is a dark refuge from sexual threat. The father nearly hits the boy. The early impact of 'the profane and ugly word' (*D* 7) in *The Dark* recalls those queer Joycean words which are also near misses, such as 'suck' for 'fuck'.

However, *The Dark*'s narrative of self-determination does not exclusively evoke Joyce. As many commentaries point out, McGahern's intention was to refer to Yeats's poem 'The Choice' in the title of the novel. The narrator of the novel must choose between the 'perfection of the life, or of the work', and by refusing 'the heavenly mansion' guaranteed by either leading a good spiritual life (heaven) or by material comforts (mansion), the artist devoted to the work has chosen the path of 'raging in *the dark*' (my italics).[47] Though uncovered authorial intention may centre on the Yeatsian 'old perplexity', life or art, it is important to recognize that this choice is not made at all explicit in the text itself. The choice elaborated in the novel is rather between 'heaven' and 'mansion'. Mahoney thinks of a priest saying that he had '*chosen* God before life' (my italics, *D* 83). The father's fear of the 'poor house', a frequent refrain which touches on his so-called 'race-memory' and is emphasized by the prominence of the potato in the novel, is juxtaposed to the rising bourgeoisie, a term defined by Father Gerald (*D* 99). The Church is now being supplanted by what he calls Society, and 'Society influences the Word far more than the Word influences Society' (*D* 100). The secular aspiration for bourgeois materialism has, in the priest's account, ousted the people's dependence on religion. To young Mahoney, education is playing the game, cramming information which will be forgotten after the exam, and paving the way for 'roses and vegetable gardens and semi-detached house' and for 'Sunday outings from the Dublin suburbs' (*D* 129). Education is a route to the 'rathole of security', the umbrella in the office (*D* 136), and the way to escape emigration to England, that doom-laden refrain of the 1950s. The protagonist's dream of academia, to become a 'gowned professor under the chestnuts' (*D* 167), is threatened by a fellow student's talk of dentists' salaries, but there is no bourgeois triumphalism in his choice to take a civil service job. Mahoney's consciousness is still underwritten by a louring existential awareness that 'death was all that mattered' (*D* 123) or that everything was 'riveted' into death (*D* 83). What is absent from his choice is the articulation of an affirmative, life-combating perfection offered by art. This refusal marks a resistance to that type of *Bildungsroman* which self-reflexively brings to the foreground questions of aesthetics.

Against the *Künstlerroman*

McGahern expressed a sceptical attitude to the Romantic egoism of the artist which is consistent with the critical idea that *The Dark* deflates *Portrait*: 'I did object very much to the Romantic notion of the artist, you know, that was cultivated by Joyce, when I was very young. I actually resented the notion of the artist as hero … a sort of nineteenth-century sentimentality, Victorian sentimentality'.[48] The end of the novel can be best understood in relation to this reluctance to follow a generic pattern and finally cry out as a heroically self-achieving artist.

The last paragraphs of *The Dark*'s penultimate chapter, which aim at a culminating expressiveness, have attracted particular critical attention. Cronin and Molloy cavilled at the changes of unexplained mood, the supposed 'triteness of thought' and inconsistency of characterization. Cronin levelled the charge that the reader is left stranded and that 'the novelist fails utterly to justify this particular *epiphany*'.[49] This has rather set the trend for implying an enactment of post-Joycean failure, be it involuntary or deliberate: what has later been called a 'false' or 'weak' epiphany.[50] There is, according to these critics, an inherent confusion over what might be meant by the concluding 'real authority':

> One day, one day, you'd come perhaps to more real authority than all this, an authority that had need of neither vast buildings nor professorial chairs nor robes nor solemn organ tones, an authority that was simply a state of mind, a calmness even in the face of the turmoil of your own passing. …
>
> You were walking through the rain of Galway with your father and you could laugh purely, without bitterness, for the first time, and it was a kind of happiness, at its heart the terror of an unclear recognition of the reality that set you free, touching you with as much foreboding as the sodden leaves falling in this day, or any cliché. (*D* 188)

Joe Cleary reads 'authority' as an essentially existential acceptance of mortality which allows father and son to reach a form of *rapprochement*. Social achievement and human struggle are rendered in their properly comic or absurd perspective.[51] Sampson too underlines the narrator's stoic equanimity.

The critical view that the epiphany has failed is mainly prompted because Mahoney's final rejection of university education, in particular the interview with the Dean of Residence, and the episode in the rowdy science lecture theatre, bring to mind the university scenes in *Portrait*. Young Mahoney feels that he is being perceived by the scornful Dean as a menial 'to the race he'd come from' (*D* 188) who should be grateful for the pickings of a desk job, although McCarthy has argued he is acting in bad faith and has deliberately manoeuvred the Dean into assuming such superiority. In Joyce, it is the English Dean's obsequiousness which points up the colonial and linguistic asymmetry ('How different are the words *home, Christ, ale, master,* on his lips and on mine!'), but the interpersonal dynamic with the Dean of Residence in Galway now has a social, class-based significance.[52] Entering bourgeois society is the default option of the non-artist, and one that the Dean sneers at. If we are to imagine the protagonist as a would-be artist, it is under these unpromising conditions: still accompanied by his father, he is not yet ready to strike out as an artist. It is true that young Maloney rehearses the same rejection of traps or Joycean 'nets' (turning his back both on church and academy), but he does so without now embracing the Word of Art. He is not given Stephen's intellectual agency. It is no coincidence that rather than voluntarily sauntering out of the lecture theatre, he is thrown out of it for being a hooligan (*D* 180). A deliberately parodic, post-Joycean self-abasement is at work.

Mahoney is not granted the eventual power of self-cultivation, nor the confidence of eventual socialization as a classical *Bildungsheld*. If we are to imagine his acceptance of the Electricity Supply Board clerkship as integration, it is as a form of coercive bourgeois expediency, and the fact that he is back in bed with his father at the end of the novel points claustrophobically – even atavistically – to the stunting of development. Neither does Mahoney give full voice to the defiant individualism formed in resistance to alienating institutions in late *Bildungsromane*. According to Gregory Castle, who takes issue with Moretti's view of genre-failure, Joyce's specifically Irish *Bildungsroman* indeed does not follow a path to harmonious socialization, or the realizing of the self through valuable pedagogical processes. Nevertheless, to Castle the genre remains fertile, as it expresses a willed resistance to an alien, colonial system, and an individualist defiance of being instrumentalized as a subject.[53] That Joyce's narrative does not 'complete' itself as might a traditional *Bildung* is appropriate to these new 'modes of inharmonious but achieved development'.[54]

In contrast, we might say that *The Dark* achieves a regressive type of familial harmony through its unachieved development. The young man's apparently throwaway remark that 'the sodden leaves [are] falling in this day, *or any cliché*' (my italics) hints, in the most understated way, that he may be inspecting the conceit of his own conclusion. The merest shoot of self-referentiality can be glimpsed in his hope for the calmness of 'real authority' – which may be read as signifying the calmness required to transform turbulent experience into authorship. Maloney has previously read the catalogue of concrete objects in Galway – 'wild grass and sea and fish boxes' – as a 'confusion of all these scattered images' (*D* 168). Perhaps the experiential 'reality that set you free' (*D* 188) will now set him free to capture these images in art? Although McGahern's frequently cited comments make this inference that he is an artist-*manqué* easy enough to supply, the self-inspecting quality of this novel remains almost completely covert – or, as Sampson has put it, a way of seeing like an artist that is 'oblique'.[55] McCarthy convincingly frames the ending as a negative freedom *from* the hold of the spiritual, erotic and academic, and thinks of the mystery the protagonist is advancing towards as 'implicitly' that of the 'writer's craft'.[56] The key word, though, is 'implicitly': in other proto-modernist *Bildungsromane*, in which the narrator is also beset by traumatic experience, a state of greater aesthetic confidence is often reached.

Such novels finish with a gap where, it is implied, transformative agency of art must be imagined by the reader: the self-begetting art of the protagonist who will come to write the work we have just read. Whether or not that rather uncommonly applied name should be used, the sub-genre of the *Künstlerroman* is intimated. It is implied that such a lived life is now worthy of telling, and that the teller is a writer, even if not yet a *writer*. The trajectory is circular, so that the end of experience, the end of represented time, is succeeded by the beginning of narrative. Put like this, Proust's *À la Recherche du Temps Perdu* – hardly novella-like – is an extended set of *Künstlerromane*. There is a splitting of the 'I': between, on the one hand, Marcel as character, recessively set back but participative in a quietly catalytic way; and on the other, the narrator of the books. As Roger Shattuck has written, Marcel 'metamorphoses into the Narrator of his own life', so that his experience of life as failure is transformed into the success of narrative composition.[57] A second reading replaces our attentiveness to Marcel's life with a new way of seeing the events as part of the *narrator*'s past in the process of being written.

The final aesthetic intent of Thomas Mann's *Tonio Kröger* points up the obliquity of *The Dark*. *Kröger* ends with a final letter which is within the main narrative but also paratextual, suggesting a new form of writing, one which contains the 'I'. It is comparable to Stephen's concluding journal, interpreted as two documents, one 'kept by a character', the other 'a portion of a narrative reported by the teller'.[58] Kröger characterizes himself not as the Nietzschean man apart but as 'a bourgeois who strayed off into art' and 'a bohemian who feels nostalgic yearnings for respectability'. Such is the pain of not belonging, but it is necessary for the art he wishes to achieve in the future:

> The work I have so far done is nothing or not much – as good as nothing ... I am looking into a world unborn and formless, that needs to be ordered and shaped; I see into a whirl of shadows of human figures who beckon to me to weave spells to redeem them: tragic and laughable figures and some that are both together – and to these I am drawn.[59]

Unsurprisingly for the author of *Buddenbrooks*, Mann does not impute to his artist a chilly contempt for the bourgeois, but a tragicomic sense of the equilibrium of art and life. The mood is lacking in bitterness and accepting of bourgeois caricatures. Proud Luciferian defiance is not a prerequisite of the proto-modernist hero. But the order and shape of 'the work' must be incorporated, and the weaving of the artist's spells included in the end. Similarly, the Joycean artist of *Portrait* – whose villanelle remind us how far he still has to go – must specify that the forging and forgery of art will issue from his 'encounter' with the 'reality of experience'.

In the last chapter of *The Dark*, a governing consciousness barely extrudes. An important impersonality is aimed for which may be said to imitate the Flaubertian mode of *Dubliners*, rather than *Portrait*, or a post-Beckettian model of stasis and arrest, not development. The young man is pushed back down into his social role as 'the son', as one objective term in the universal paradigm of the consubstantial Christian family, here rendered idiomatically as 'the father and the son and the whole shoot' (*D* 191). The idea that the son is 'going out into the world' on his own (*D* 190) does not ring out with the son's aspiration: it is spoken by the father. It may be that the reader is affected by the son's longing for the world to give him some proof of life's suffering, that paradoxically he might be privy to some sign of the existential indifference which will confirm his own isolation. Such pathos is qualified by the boy's residual acceptance of the 'whole shoot': the father and the Holy Ghost; thus, the symbolic Father. In the end, all young Mahoney hears are the contingent noises of footsteps and a shunting train. The indeterminacy of the ending is bound up with the lack of person and retreat of consciousness: he is no longer the 'little-he', nor the occasionally telling 'I', and his invisibility is also made more acute by the relinquishing of the predominant role of the 'you' as shadow-self and secret sharer. The subject is evacuated from the text.

If it continues to be read in its generic context as a belated modernist *Bildungsroman*, *The Dark* concludes with more of a regressive falling back than an Icarian falling down. The lack of aesthetic 'development' is built into the end of the narrative. The son may be separated from the father in the country but is still in the thrall of his father's narrative for him, and is unable to complete the path of self-determination which the artist's *Bildung* requires. Compare *Portrait*'s 'Old father, old artificer, stand me now and ever in good stead'. For all that we may infer the disappointed future of the filial artificer, Stephen as Icarus has cast off the real father, Simon Dedalus, that 'praiser of his own past', supplanted by the Daedalean father who has become the symbolic artist as craftsman.[60] In addressing the so-called 'failure' of *The Dark*'s protagonist to match Joycean aspiration, van der Ziel has argued that McGahern redefines the object of aspiration and achievement: the need to face 'life-in-mediocrity' is an existential rather than artistic triumph.[61] This in turn reminds us that Stephen must indeed fall and be joined by the 'mixed-middling' Bloom for the high modernist work to avoid egoistic triumphalism.

The young Mahoney's expression of love for his father, and the backward-looking structure of the chapter itself, which reprises the undressing and 'obscenity' of the first, nevertheless suggests a kind of recidivism. The epiphanic form of *Portrait* requires an artistic self-undercutting: 'Disapprove of this last phrase'; 'Read what I wrote last night'.[62] In McGahern's case, the egoist-artist hesitantly acknowledges a supposedly clichéd image, but is still dominated by the experiential: existential indifference occludes aesthetic agency. The formal impersonality of the last chapter is not synonymous with the dark object-world of a brutally deterministic naturalism, but the gap between life and art remains much greater than in modernist *Bildungsromane*. The implication that *The Dark* self-reflexively aspires after Yeats to choose 'perfection of the work' is indeed very deeply buried. Aesthetic self-encryption is particularly difficult to decode, because there are no overt reflections about 'the work', even in its formative imperfections. Perhaps the final voiceless chapter, formally distinct from the multipersonal refractions of the preceding episodes, can itself be regarded as kind of adjunct of impersonal, belatedly modernist narrative. If so, it remains an aesthetically diffident coda.

Notes

1 Quoted in Brian McHale, *Constructing Postmodernism* (Abingdon and New York: Routledge, 1992), p. 89.
2 Samuel Beckett, *Texts for Nothing IV* (London: John Calder, 1999), p. 23.

3 Sampson and McGahern, 'A Conversation', p. 16.
4 John Cronin, '*The Dark* is Not Light Enough: The Fiction of John McGahern', *Studies: An Irish Quarterly Review* 58, no. 232 (Winter 1969): 427–32, 427.
5 F. C. Molloy, 'The Novels of John McGahern', *Critique* 19, no. 1 (1977): 5–27, 16.
6 Quoted in Sampson, *Outstaring Nature's Eye*, p. 70.
7 Paul Devine, 'Style and Structure in John McGahern's *The Dark*', *Critique* 21, no. 1 (1979): 49–58, 53.
8 Stanley van der Ziel, '"All this Talk and Struggle": John McGahern's *The Dark*', *Irish University Review* 35, no. 1 (Spring/Summer 2005): 104–20.
9 Van der Ziel, '"All This Talk and Struggle": John McGahern's *The Dark*', p. 115.
10 Monika Fludernik, 'Second-person Narrative as a Test Case for Narratology: The Limits of Realism', *Style* 28, no. 3 (Fall 1994): 445–79, 469.
11 Malcolm, *Understanding John McGahern*, pp. 32, 43.
12 Even a modernist forbear which includes second-person narration, Faulkner's *Absalom! Absalom!*, is notable for being what Brian McHale calls a 'limit-text' which tips over from the epistemological dominant of modernism into the ontological displacements of postmodernism.
13 Sampson and McGahern, 'A Conversation', p. 16.
14 The second person is not the exclusive property of 'extraterritorial' postmodernists. Nathaniel Hawthorne used it in a short story called 'The Haunted Mind'; Tolstoy in a Sevastopol story.
15 Barthes, *Writing Degree Zero*, p. 37.
16 Roland Barthes, *Roland Barthes by Roland Barthes*, trans. Richard Howard (New York: Farrar, Straus and Giroux, 1977), p. 169.
17 See John Capecci, 'Performing the Second Person', *Text and Performance Quarterly* 1 (1989): 42–52.
18 Fludernik, 'Second-person Narrative', *Style*, p. 469.
19 Brian McHale, '"You Used to Know What These Words Mean": Misreading *Gravity's Rainbow*', *Language and Style* 18, no. 1 (Winter 1985): 93–118.
20 McHale, '"You Used to Know What These Words Mean": Misreading *Gravity's Rainbow*', p. 112.
21 Fludernik, 'Second-person Narrative', *Style*, p. 469.
22 McCarthy, *John McGahern and the Art of Memory*, pp. 89, 100, 102.
23 Ibid., p. 103.
24 Peter Bibby, 'Taking the Road Out', *Imprint: The Short Story Magazine* 8, no. 3 (1986): 62–7, 64–5.
25 Barthes, *Writing Degree Zero*, p. 40.
26 Samuel Beckett, Molloy, in *Trilogy: Molloy, Malone Dies, The Unnamable* (London: John Calder, 1994), p. 152.

27 Karl Bühler quoted in David Herman, 'Textual "You" and Double Deixis in Edna O'Brien's *A Pagan Place*', *Style* 28, no. 3 (Fall 1994): 378–410, 396.
28 See Herman, 'Textual "You" and Double Deixis', *Style*, for an elaboration of 'covert apostrophes', pp. 395–6.
29 Edna O'Brien, 'The Art of Fiction', *Paris Review*, no. 82 (Summer 1984): 92.
30 Edna O'Brien, *A Pagan Place* (Harmondsworth: Penguin, 1970), pp. 202–3.
31 Maher, *John McGahern: From the Local to the Universal*, p. 30.
32 Sampson, *Outstaring Nature's Eye*, p. 63.
33 Malcolm, *Understanding John McGahern*, p. 35, 141.
34 Corcoran, *After Yeats and Joyce*, p. 89.
35 David Duff, 'Intertextuality versus Genre Theory: Bakhtin, Kristeva and the Question of Genre', *Paragraph* 25, no. 1 (March 2002): 54–73.
36 Quoted in Belsey, *Critical Practice*, p. 89.
37 Franco Moretti, *The Way of the World: The Bildungsroman in European Culture*, 2nd edn (London and New York: Verso, 2000).
38 Charlotte Brontë, *Jane Eyre*, ed. Stevie Davies (Harmondsworth: Penguin, 2006), p. 500. See Davies's introduction, p. xx.
39 John Paul Riquelme, *Teller and Tale in Joyce's Fiction: Oscillating Perspectives* (Baltimore and London: John Hopkins Press, 1983), p. 54.
40 Riquelme, *Teller and Tale in Joyce's Fiction*, p. 59.
41 Weldon Thornton, *The Antimodernism of Joyce's* 'A Portrait of the Artist as a Young Man' (Syracuse, NY: Syracuse University Press, 1994), p. 81.
42 See Malcolm, *Understanding John McGahern*, p. 36.
43 Flann O'Brien's *At Swim-Two-Birds* may be notably *Ulyssean* in its stylistic high jinks, but the presence of a cerebral student and would-be author from University College Dublin reminds us that it is a deliberate de-sacralizing of the belated Romanticism which *Portrait* contains, albeit ironically. Even a book such as J. P. Donleavy's *The Ginger Man* was thought of as Joycean, simply by dint of presenting in its knockabout way a young man in the down-at-heel Bohemia of 1950s Dublin. To take a more recent example, Bernard MacLaverty's *The Anatomy School*, with its scenes of seminary retreat and later episodes in university science halls, self-consciously harks back to *Portrait*. That the protagonist's erotic adventure is brought to halt when his girlfriend looks upon glass jars which contain foetuses curiously literalizes the 'sudden legend' which startles Stephen's blood in the Cork physics theatre.
44 James Joyce, *A Portrait of the Artist as a Young Man* (Oxford: Oxford University Press, 2008), p. 8.
45 Derek Attridge, *Joyce Effects: On Language, Theory, and History* (Cambridge: Cambridge University Press, 2000), p. 61.
46 Joyce, *Portrait*, pp. 8–9.

47 Yeats, 'The Choice', p. 278.

48 Quoted in 'Entretien avec Liliane Louvel', in *La Licorne*, p. 26.

49 Cronin, '*The Dark* is Not Light Enough: The Fiction of John McGahern', p. 429.

50 For the term '"false" epiphany', see Maher, *The Church and its Spire*, p. 63. McCarthy uses the term 'weak epiphany', but argues that it is befitting of the character, 'convincing in its conjunction of "terror" and "unclear recognition" and as yet appropriately lacking the "authority" of the individuated self', p. 112.

51 Cleary, *Outrageous Fortune*, pp. 161–2.

52 Joyce, *Portrait*, p. 159.

53 Gregory Castle, 'Coming of Age in the Age of Empire: Joyce's Modernist *Bildungsroman*', *James Joyce Quarterly* 40, no. 4 (Summer 2003): 665–90.

54 Castle, 'Coming of Age in the Age of Empire: Joyce's Modernist *Bildungsroman*', p. 674.

55 Sampson, *Outstaring Nature's Eye*, p. 75.

56 McCarthy, *John McGahern and the Art of Memory*, pp. 116–17.

57 Roger Shattuck, *Proust* (Glasgow: Fontana, 1974), p. 131.

58 Riquelme, *Teller and Tale in Joyce's Fiction*, p. 60.

59 Thomas Mann, *Tonio Kröger*, trans. H. T. Lowe-Porter (Harmondsworth: Penguin, 1955), p. 191.

60 Joyce, *Portrait*, p. 203.

61 Van der Ziel, '"All This Talk and Struggle"', p. 116.

62 Joyce, *Portrait*, pp. 211–12.

3

Quoting Modernism in the Short Stories: Joyce, Yeats, Chekhov and Beckett

Introduction

'Any text is constructed as a mosaic of quotations; any text is the absorption of another.'[1] Thus Julia Kristeva introduced Bakhtinian theories of the novel into French literary studies and beyond, along with the term intertextuality. 'Any text' has assumed some importance. Kristeva suggests that the polyphonic, radical or 'unreadable' modernist text (she mentions Proust, Joyce and Kafka) represents a break in literary history where the problem of intertextuality becomes conspicuous. There is a sense that modernist textuality can be said to illustrate the insights or even have done much of the work of post-structuralist theory. What better 'mosaic of quotations' is there than *The Waste Land*? Roland Barthes acknowledges that 'the labour of semiosis', the 'intensity of the *significance*' of so-called 'texts of modernity', seems to privilege them as text rather than work. However, to Barthes, the text is not a determinate object but a critical practice, and Barthes himself is at great pains, in his analysis of Balzac, to reveal 'the sumptuous rank of the signifier' in the concealments of realist narrative.[2] Any text is intertextual.

Many intriguing points of intertextual contact with specifically proto-modernist or modernist writing are to be found in McGahern's short stories. The prior text – what Genette calls the hypotext to which the later hypertext is grafted – may be named, as is the case with Chekhov's 'Oysters' and 'The Beginning of an Idea', or it is so directly signalled that a consideration of the earlier hypotext is assumed, as in 'Lavin' and Joyce's 'An Encounter'.[3] In the first instance, this still appears as a type of authorial edict rather than the assertion of the (some would feel presumptuous) reader's production of meaning: the earlier text makes itself known, almost forces itself upon the reader. This correlates to what Genette describes as manifest 'writing in the second degree', in which the palimpsest-like text advertises that it is not a singular entity but has rewritten and stands in a coexistent relationship to a previous text, something which suggests a determinate relationship of intentional intertextuality.[4]

For these two McGahern stories, the intertextual signposting suggests the emulation of genre: the form of the short story for which McGahern is often admired. The mandatory 'content' of Chekhov and Joyce poses an implicitly self-reflexive question about McGahern's own practice of the short story, revealing that Bakhtinian sense of 'genre memory' discussed in the previous chapter. Manifest allusiveness in these stories remains a model of intertextuality under the authorial signature. However, for post-structuralism such a volitional uncovering of the will-to-quote must be held separate from the more general rendering of the text as a complex of borrowed discourses which cannot merely be controlled by a fixation upon canonical literary influence. Even by narrowly pursuing the literary relationship, it becomes clear that the limits of 'allusion' are undecidable, although it is only the interpretative process itself which can bring the reader close to appreciating whether a particular intertextual analysis is, in Michel Riffaterre's terms, more aleatory than obligatory.[5] The presence of Yeats in 'Christmas' rests on a minor detail, perhaps, but this may be thought of as a wormhole which opens out on to an unexpectedly subversive miniaturization of the Gregory poems. If the reader ventures further forward, as maker of the *lisible* text, more expansive intertextual possibilities present themselves. Another story in McGahern's first collection, *Nightlines* (1970), regarded as a particularly Joycean volume, prompts the reader to wonder what sort of iconographic inheritance an umbrella, that overdetermined psychological symbol, may trail in its wake. The choice here to read 'My Love, My Umbrella' through Beckett is not directed at proving influence or imitation, but as with all the other intertextual cross-readings, to evaluate difference as well as similarity.

A quare pair: 'Lavin' and 'An Encounter'

'Lavin' manifestly rewrites Joyce's 'An Encounter' and expects the reader to have foreknowledge of the prior text. Any crudely conceived thematizing of 'Lavin' – that it is a story about the transition from childhood to adulthood, about the sexuality of experience, forbidden knowledge, and so forth – implicates the reader quite directly. A most piercingly painful, exciting and traumatic experience is recalled as the 'shiver' of the pubertal body, and yet the reader cannot forget that the interposing *textual* relationship must awkwardly mediate this felt experience. The near repetition – 'in my heart I hated him' ('Lavin', *N* 74), 'in my heart I had always despised him a little' ('An Encounter') – is just a part of a coded communication.[6] The gap- and yellow-toothed old man of Joyce's story is transformed into the stump-toothed Lavin, and the sexual dynamic is reproduced in the same triangular structure: two boys (one bookish, one sporty), and an old pervert. Margot Norris has written that the narrator of 'An Encounter', primed by his precocious consumption of literature and now retrospectively fashioning his story, presents the reader with 'the construction of an encounter': for McGahern, then, 'Lavin' may be thought of as the construction of a construction of an encounter. If the hypotext is open to the post-structuralist exposure of its duplicitous concealments, its Derridean 'graft', 'Lavin', for all that it plugs some (self-) censored Joycean gaps, may be equally susceptible to its own gaps or new indeterminacies.

The 'queering' of Joyce returns to textual occlusions and indeterminate subject positions, offering explicatory narratives which, within the heteronormative contract between author and reader, could not previously speak their names. It is said of Father Flynn in 'The Sisters', that 'there was something queer about him…' (1) and 'something gone wrong with him…' (10). One way of interpreting the 'crossing' of Flynn's life, marked in language by elliptical tailing off, is to construe his putative sexuality in relation to the 'missing' sexuality of the priesthood to which he is bound: an unspeakable queerness may fill the textual gap, articulating the sexual discontents of society. 'An Encounter' announces its queerness, too. When his companion, Mahony, exclaims, 'I say! Look what he is doing', the narrator neither answers nor raises his eyes, so that Mahony has to continue, 'I say … he's a queer old josser'. We are not told what the old man is doing in the corner of the field, but that his action represents queerness for Mahony. The obscene behaviour does not quite take place in front of the boys, but in the ambiguous region of the 'near end' (16), as if hiding in plain sight. It was Joyce who alerted his publisher to what he might have missed in blithely overlooking the content of this story, if not others, in *Dubliners*: 'The more subtle inquisitor will denounce "An Encounter", the enormity of which the printer cannot see because he is, as I said, a plain blunt man.'[7] The sexual act missed by the 'plain blunt' printer, most commentators seem to agree, is the unnamed act of masturbation. Such was the 'enormity' of the obscenity, that the possibility was raised, and accepted by Joyce, that 'An Encounter' would be entirely omitted from *Dubliners*, as long as a note was supplied testifying to 'the incompleteness of the book'.[8] Queer textual silence is not only a matter of gapped aposiopeses, of gnomonic missing parts, but of the incrimination of the whole.

The degree of sexual explicitness in 'Lavin' may be taken to be a rebellious assertion of authorial autonomy as the power of the censor waned in Ireland and the *Chatterley* ban was lifted in Britain. 'Lavin' seems to make good the necessary exclusions of 'An Encounter' with some deliberateness, bringing centre stage the genitals (pubic hair, 'John Charles' – the phallus combines the forenames of the boy and man but is also a post-Lawrentian joke, perhaps); and in the frank admission of a pubertal form of gay love. The narrator admits that he was in love with Charley Casey, and later that he was 'stiff with excitement' when he imagines them 'doing it together' (*N* 75). There is no concealing of the homosexual 'shiver' here: while in 'An Encounter' the narrator wonders 'why he shivered sometimes' (16), in 'Lavin' the 'image of the monstrous penis … made me shiver with excitement' (*N* 74). The whipping fantasy indulged by Joyce's old man is transferred to McGahern's boy. In general, the sado-masochistic combination of the 'pleasant and vicious' (4) imagined but euphemistically unexplained by the boy in 'The Sisters' is lingered over more explicitly in 'Lavin'.

To what extent does 'Lavin' replicate the formal pattern of the short first-person narratives of early *Dubliners*? The story starts off with the idea that the behaviour of Lavin, once handsome and fastidious, causes 'puzzlement' (*N* 70), lack of comprehension, just as the boy in 'The Sisters' 'puzzled [his] head to extract meaning' (4). No final explanation is given for what made Lavin, like Flynn, 'go wrong', and this seems to advertise where the typical frustration of the modernist epistemological quest may be located. However, reading 'An Encounter' as a queer text shows how this puzzlement may be deflected away from the narrator himself. Despite the signposting towards sexual perversion, it is the narrator's patchy account, with its curious insistence on silence ('…we remained silent', 'After a silence of a few minutes'; 'We said nothing further to each other' (18)) which begins to look queer. Margot Norris conceives of 'An Encounter' as 'a doubled text that conceals a noncanonical homosocial fantasy whose desirous homosexual undercurrents affright it and oblige it to mask itself as a canonical cautionary tale of imperilled innocence'.[9] Whether we conceive of the narrator as either a preternaturally eloquent boy or backward-looking adult, there is a strategic withholding of knowledge, with the sexual implications of that word, from the narrative. The possibility is raised that he will not look at what the old man is doing because he already knows, and already knows he would enjoy watching, what he is doing. The story ends by insisting on the exclusion of the 'despised' Mahoney, and with it the frightening or exciting prospect of teaming up with the pervert, whose viciousness may be dangerously pleasant. Textual silence begins to look complicit.

The ending of 'Lavin' imitates the structural re-triangulation of 'An Encounter': in similar ways, the fellow child is disturbingly excluded in the face of paedophiliac sexual violence. The reader is asked to grant a privileged narrative status to a 'picture' – imagined, not remembered – of Lavin, who had inherited a wealthy farm and could have had the pick of the girls, as a young man in the 'clean wheatfield' (*N* 76). That this figure of yet-to-be perverted innocence is insistently troubling to the narrator shadowily hints at the untold disappointments of his own life. The ageing narrator's indifference to his first love, Casey, and his banal conformity – married with children, running a pub – reveals the narrator's belated affiliation to the child molester, and his own implied feelings of exclusion from heteronormative adulthood. His identification may be with the handsome, affluent Lavin, but the signs of Lavin's sexual delinquency are already apparent in his supposedly innocent state: his pernickety gathering of tools and urge to close gaps (*N* 70) suggests a Flynn-like excess of scrupulosity, and his avoidance of dance halls a suspect prurience. We may take the narrator's inability to let Lavin go as an attachment to the irretrievability of his childhood: orthodox enough in one sense, but also dangerously hinting at an alignment with the initiatory moment of sexual trauma when he too 'went wrong', and led a different sort of life from that of Casey: disquietingly, perhaps, a queer sort of life.

The conspicuous Joycean trace in 'Lavin' should alert the reader to textual desire. Literature – in the form of Joe Dillon's little library of magazines – is anterior to, and in some ways shapes the expectations of the boys' experience in 'An Encounter'. As R. B. Kershner has revealed, these 'chronicles of disorder' (12) were far from wholesome but purveyed sado-masochistic discourses.[10] The old man exploits the authority of the canon to seduce the bookish narrator into what Norris calls 'displacements and cathexes' which meld 'bibliophilic and libidinal desires'.[11] The boy condemns himself by pretending to have read everything, including those portions of Lord Lytton's works mentioned by the old man as not suitable for children. Perversity does not just lie ahead of the venturing truants but is formed from the disorder of their secretive reading.

In 'Lavin' the narrator chastizes the boy he is in love with for not sharing his love of a 'beloved book' (*N* 72), *David Copperfield*. The implication is that for him literature is pre-sexual, and that he wishes to keep the experience of the body at arm's length, delaying the moment when forbidden knowledge will initiate his fall. The boy's chaste love is an imagined, eternal homosocial confection which transposes David Copperfield's Yarmouth to the west of Ireland. It is noteworthy that it is Charley's betrayal of the literary brotherhood which motivates the narrator to take him to Lavin in order to punish him with adult perversion.

The narrator can be read double: his attachment to literature and childhood is self-aware and willed, a resistance to what is, in fact, broadly known about fallen adulthood. But Charley, who has previously been 'measured' by Lavin, already knows, too – and knows more. The episode between Charley and Lavin brings out a new, unchaste passion, first exhibiting itself as 'smouldering anger and outrage' and then as 'puritanical bitterness' (*N* 73–4), the latter phrase hinting at retrospective self-diagnosis. The correction to adolescent bibliophilia is implied, hinting at the fall of beloved literature. There is an acknowledgement that beloved words are not the pristine bearers of personal experience but are tainted by prior use.

For a story seemingly centred on homosexuality, it is worth noting the fluidity of erotic desire, even in its pederastic form. Lavin is aroused by the thought of the sexual maturation of girls, as well as boys; the narrator is in love with Charley partly because of 'the glamour of a house of ripe women' (*N* 71) in his family. It is consistent, then, that the gay fantasy of 'doing it' with each other, possibly hurting each other, emerges from the proto-patriarchal inheritance of violent heterosexual subjugation – doing to a number of women 'the way the bull does' (*N* 75). The sexual positions are not fixed or evaluated. Charley has visited Lavin before and seems enthusiastic about repeating the same-sex encounter, but it is the narrator who admits to taking the lead later. Generally, the story's speaking of the sexual name allows the 'shameful truth' (*N* 75) of polymorphous desire, unacknowledged in the discourse of conventional fiction, to be brought out into the open.

The reader cannot look upon such exposure with detachment, because our own knowledge, literary and sexual, is liable to supply meanings which incriminate our own desires: we too emerge, in Norris's words, as an equally doubled, 'devious and self-disguising figure'.[12] The reader is expected to lovingly 'know' *Dubliners*, but is also aware of putting the canonical library to devious uses, as is the case with this chapter, indulging a bibliophiliac play which implicates its own intertextual *jouissance*. The exposure of 'An Encounter' inside 'Lavin' forces an interpretative question about whether the reader's knowledge will block a pathetic response to this representation of youthful experience (the long-term effects of childhood sexual abuse), and that by evasively retreating into intertextual comparisons – by reaching for a book, like the child reached for *David Copperfield* – the reader is merely playing with her or himself.

Finally, if 'Lavin' unmasks or 'outs' the queerness of 'An Encounter', plugs the Joycean gap, does it follow that an attempt to subject it to Norris's unmasking, 'doubled' reading must be less subversive? If more is exposed, less can be concealed. Nevertheless, the recurring Joycean structure of re-triangulation, now with the narrator and Lavin as the pair, and Casey as the conformist 'other', leads us back to the disturbing similarities between the book-loving innocent, who describes himself as once having been 'puritanical', and the fastidiously asexual Lavin, who 'clos[es] gaps' (*N* 70) while others carouse. What remains deliberately hidden is the narrator's disappointed adult life, and why the 'pre-sexual' Lavin of the '*clean* wheatfield' (my italics, *N* 76) should be so meaningful to him. It surely speaks of the continuing of sexual shame. The boys avoided each other as if they 'vaguely glimpsed some shameful truth we were afraid to come to know together' (*N* 75). We may decode this is a general post-Edenic shame – they are lying naked on a riverbank, inflicting cruelty on a frog – or we can interpret it as a 'queer' fear that they might 'remain' gay, never passing out that so-called phase. The narrator's 'outing' of his own sexual puritanism, sado-masochistic desires and gay pubertal 'shiver' is not enough to prevent readerly suspicion about the stunting of his *Copperfield*-like maturation, and about the way the backward glance upon childhood is trained upon the image of the paedophile.

Lady Gregory and Mrs Grey: 'Christmas' and Yeats

'Christmas' is another of the *Nightlines* stories marked by the prior texts of Irish modernism. As Frank Shovlin has noticed, that a Mrs Grey should have lost her son in aerial combat over Italy is for some likely to recall Lady Augusta Gregory and her son Robert, a pilot who was killed over Italy the First World War, and who is the subject of a number of Yeats's poems in *The Wild Swans at Coole* collection (1919).[13] Bearing in mind the shared opening letters of the surnames, we cannot easily dismiss this as coincidence, though Lady Gregory is 'transformed' into a widow who had come from America and built the 'huge house' (*N* 31) after the son's death in the Second World War.

That the Anglo-Irish lifestyle of the Gregorys could not seem more remote from the hard-bitten provincial environment depicted in the story may initially suggest the apparent disposability of the allusion. That indeed seems to be the very point of embedding Yeats – that the homeboy-narrator, maligned by the men in the shop as a 'little fucker', a 'bad piece of work' (*N* 32), eventually sent back to where he came from, is the inverted, anti-heroic image of Yeats's Gregory, the Sidney-like aristocrat of the elegy, the 'Soldier, scholar, horseman'; 'our perfect man'.[14] The boy is responsible in the story for an action – the trampling to pieces of a model aeroplane given to him as a Christmas present by the mourning Mrs Grey – which also restages Gregory's heroic moment in miniaturized or 'model' form, suggesting that we may compare the liberating and self-destructive actions of Gregory and the homeboy. Gregory's flight into the clouds has been interpreted variously. To Balachandra Rajan, 'the lonely impulse of delight' of 'An Irish Airman Foresees his Death' is embodied in a Sartrean *acte gratuit*, a moment 'freed from all motivation and therefore totally self-expressive'.[15] Edward Larrissy is more sceptical: although it sounds finer than 'adolescent images of heroism', Gregory's action is presented equivocally: he is 'more truly the hero because of the tragic imperfection of his choice'.[16] Frank Kermode argues that the complexities of Gregory's self-realization are only fully understood in relation to 'In Memory of Major Robert Gregory', which emphasizes that Gregory is, above all, a painter. His escape is not that of Lionel Johnson, from art into action, but rather a fusing of the two. Gregory becomes a poetic image of life-in-death, a 'radiant symbol' of escape which allows the choice between art and life to be held in momentary equilibrium.[17] The perfect act, the culmination of a life in which all has been 'done perfectly' (151), is the act of art.

How, then, can the boy's enraged but apparently unmotivated trampling of the aeroplane, his own lonely act of destruction, be construed? It is not made clear in what 'the horrible hurt of the toy' (*N* 34) consists. It is not the disappointment of not having been given Christmas money, because he recognizes that money would have been drunk away by his guardian. We might speculate that the boy, an orphan, may have wished for some symbol of maternal recuperation, one which corresponded to Mrs Grey's futile attempt to replace her son, the dead pilot. The model aeroplane is not a proper aeroplane but a simulacrum which points to the failure of filial or maternal surrogacy and thus to an irremediable isolation. A less psychoanalytic interpretation may connect the boy's destruction of the model plane as springing from the class-based *ressentiment* of the subaltern within. The narrator has internalized subjection at the hands of the state: in answering Mrs Grey, he says, Bartleby-like, that he 'thought *prefer* was well put for a Homeboy' (*N* 33). His upbringing has left him disenfranchised from the movements of Irish history above, decided upon by the arbiters of cultural nationalism. It is consistent with the rejection of the displaced aristocrat (Lady Gregory as Mrs Grey) and of petty bourgeois provincialism, that he eventually feels kinship with the disgraced drunk Mullin, and that he eventually feels pride in being a 'ward of state' (*N* 30). The boy could be said to be kicking to pieces the gift from the Anglo-Irish 'huge house' in an act of defiance. The heroic act is not available to the outcast for whom the state must now grudgingly provide.

'In Memory of Major Robert Gregory' also lingers in the boy's kinship with the jennet, a beast of burden in the story, and thus another debased iteration of Gregory's noble and daring equestrianism. As the jennet delights in the smell of smoke, the boy burns dry straw while kicking the aeroplane. The act of destruction and self-realization coincides with an expression of affinity not, as it were, with the horseman but with the horse, imagined in Yeats's poem as 'outrun' by Gregory's mind. Gregory's 'blaze of total accomplishment' is contrasted to the pedestrian condition of growing old[18]:

> Some burn damp faggots, others may consume
> The entire combustible world in one small room
> As though dried straw, and if we turn about
> The bare chimney is gone black out
> Because the work had finished in that flare. (151)

The self-reflexive emphasis is on 'the work' – what is finished in the artwork, and implicitly what all artists will leave unfinished or undone. As Larrissy has written of this poem, the 'death of the potential artist is proleptic of the death of all artists'.[19]

The boy in 'Christmas', though, is far from being an artist drawn to the cleansing fire of Byzantine art, and the pile of straw hardly produces for him a 'hard, gem-like' Paterian flame. At the end of the story, he does find a way forward: 'A new life … had already started to grow out of the ashes' (*N* 36). Lest this phoenix-like regeneration appear too affirmative, a vantage point of retrospection has already been supplied: the brutalized boy has already underlined that this is a story about a 'stupid wish' (*N* 30), both his own and Mrs Grey's: the stupidity is seeking happiness or trying to confer it upon others. The boy and the mourning mother both briefly let down their guard, forgetting the inhospitability or tragedy of life. They are both punished for it. The lesson, since thoroughly absorbed by the adult narrator ('what happened has struck me ever since' (*N* 36)), may also be read in the earliest Gregory poem, the schematic pastoral duologue 'Shepherd and Goatherd', in which the old goatherd despondently says that 'Nor bird nor beast/ Could make me wish for anything this day … Let the young wish' (159).

The narrator's self-determination and rejection of petty hypocrisies may point to a shaking off of *ressentiment*. Trampling the aeroplane and burning dried straw injects 'new sweetness' (*N* 36) into the homeboy's blood: Yeats had written that Gregory's paintings 'had majesty and austerity, and at the same time *sweetness*' (my italics).[20] The 'new life' has been initiated by a sweetly heroic act, then, but the resolve to 'not wish' is a bleak form of emancipation, and remains a code of behaviour derived from the unkindness of his upbringing. His guardian contemptuously wishes the boy 'a good flight' in the plane (*N* 36) this Christmas: the implication is that the boy's 'flight' will take him back to the incarceration of the brutal home, in contrast to an escape beyond the clouds. In such ways, the story encrypts the difference in scale and aspiration between the heroism of the homeboy and the aristocrat.

The coded allusions to the Gregory poems prompt a set of perhaps surprisingly subversive speculations about the circumscribed legacy of Irish modernism in the social context of de Valera's Ireland. The animus of the story can be linked with the idea that there can be no indulgent symbolizing of an aristocratic artist choosing to make an image of his action. The flying of the plane is both Art and Life, but McGahern is writing from the point of view, as it were, of one of the tenants deserted by Gregory's heroism.[21] The homeboy smashes the artwork to free himself, but the writer of supposedly naturalist provincial fragments is not in the modernist business of smashing. A cunning interlacing is at play, and it would be mistaken to dismiss such an apparently slight short story as too formally conservative. McGahern is 'citing' and miniaturizing Yeats to point to the unassimilable remainder of literary modernism and to a new phase of postcolonial modernity in the Irish state. Such combustible intertextual moments ask the reader to decode this uneasy misalliance with heroic tradition.

'Oysters' and 'The Beginning of an Idea': Chekhov

This is Chekhov, in excerpts from a letter of 1892:

> Do you need my biography? Here it is. In 1860 I was born in Taganrog. … In 1891 I toured Europe, where I drank splendid wine and ate oysters. … I have been translated into all languages with the exception of foreign ones. … Among writers I prefer Tolstoy, among physicians – Zakharin. However, this is all rubbish. Write what you want. If there are no facts, substitute something lyrical.[22]

In a letter of 1960, McGahern referred with an equal degree of scepticism to what he called 'the autobiographical stunt': that 'the common notion you can make art out of your life' was 'pure moonshine'.[23] In 'The Beginning of an Idea', McGahern boldly opens *Getting Through* with a lengthy paraphrase of a brief Chekhov short story, 'Oysters'. Like other short-story writers who have incorporated Chekhov as subject-content, such as Raymond Carver and Bernard MacLaverty, McGahern implies his indebtedness of form to the so-called progenitor of the modern short story.[24] The protagonist of 'The Beginning of an Idea', Eva Lindberg, is a theatre director and also a translator of the plays she directs. McGahern's story asks us to question the metaphorical translation of life into art, following that Chekhovian scepticism about biography. However, in quoting the Chekhovian story so extensively, the story emphasizes its own sense of self-reflexive 'genre memory'. It implicitly positions itself as emulating Chekhovian form as well as marking its intertextual 'content'. Does it avoid that sub-Chekhovian mode in which, as one critic put it, stories 'expire into ellipses, or seem to end in the middle of a thought'?[25]

Eva leaves behind her career as a successful theatre director, and a prolonged though doomed love affair, in order to '*try* to write' (*GT* 19) – rather than the more complacent 'to write'. She is poised between composing an imagined life of Chekhov, a hybrid of biography and fiction, as either a play or a novel. She does neither, defeated by 'the solitary white page' (*GT* 24), unable 'to pluck the life of Chekhov out of the unimaginable air' (*GT* 25), finding it easier to translate Mayakovsky. She is, then, a surrogate but failed author-figure. Denis Sampson writes of the 'warning to the reader' sounded by Eva's failure to write.[26] The reader must indeed read with care in order to realize that the manifest intertextuality of the story implies a form of self-reflexive commentary. McGahern's second collection also 'begins with an idea' and begins with borrowed marks which fill the white page. A metafictional question is posed: to evaluate Chekhov-in-McGahern in relation to Chekhov-in-Eva.

It is suggestive that McGahern substantially paraphrases an early, not much anthologized story, 'Oysters' (*Ustritsy*). The story was one of hundreds that Chekhov produced during his Grub Street existence in St Petersburg in the early 1880s. It was published for the periodical *Oskolki* ('Fragments' or 'Splinters'), for which Chekhov would write twice a week. It has been described as part of a 'literature of commiseration' popular at the time, in which a 'wringing of social conscience' is expressed. For Donald Rayfield, this context points to an aesthetic defect akin to the death of Little Nell: 'The child's mingled revulsion and hunger are well described, but the story has the same touch of the spurious that vitiates many of Chekhov's stories of children and animals. … The author has sensed the fashion of shedding tears and is assiduously pandering to it.'[27] To other readers of 'Oysters', the rendering of the callousness of the upper-class Muscovites – which would have been pleasing to the St Petersburg readers – implies an urgent demand for social reform which is rather too gestural and undeveloped.

The reader more interested in the evolving genre of the modernist short story is drawn to the symbolic potentiality of the oysters themselves. The child sees 'oysters' on a placard and thinks it 'a strange word'. It is a signifier without a signified, a piece of language which he can fill with his imagination. Conditioned by the father's definitions (respectively delicious and disgusting), 'oysters' becomes a split sign. The boy's eating of the oyster shell, taking the signified (something to eat) for the referent (the indigestible thing itself), is not only a marker of desperate privation but also an act of confused literalization, in which the child's growing appreciation of language is surreally distorted.[28] Not writing about oysters, Janet Malcolm refers to Chekhov's art as 'a kind of bark of the prosaic in which Chekhov consistently encases a story's vital poetic core, as if such protection were necessary for its survival'.[29] The symbol must be delicate but also tough – naturalistically blended in but resonant with meaning. The oysters of 1884 are rather too obtrusive, but a foretaste of symbols to come in Chekhov's work: a prototype of the symbol as symbol. Sampson mentions the seagull in relation to the drama – Eva is working on a translation of that play – and this can be extrapolated to include the symbolism of the later stories. In Chekhov's 'Gooseberries', for example, the gooseberries sustain an illusion of happiness though they taste sour in reality, standing for just that gap between the idea and reality which Eva cannot capture in her artistic vision.

Confusing the art with the life, Eva asserts without substantiation that Chekhov *was* that boy outside the restaurant, although as a boy he actually remained behind in Crimea while his father roamed Moscow. This points to what is not Chekhovian in her putative approach: she has not respected the separateness of art. Her whole urge to write was predicated on the 'moonshine' of a symbolic neatness, a fetishizing of 'order and calm' in her life which does not 'translate' to 'calm and order' in art (note the chiasmic reversal: *GT* 24). Rather it leads to the blank page. Janet Malcolm disputes the lazy idea that Chekhov would have been amused at the idea that his body was carried to Moscow in a carriage marked 'oysters', and that some mourners then followed the wrong coffin. In a notebook, Chekhov had mentally addressed a corpse being taken to the cemetery thus: 'You are dead, you are being carried to the cemetery, and I will go and have my breakfast.' Chekhov would not have been 'amused at being dead'. Malcolm argues that 'incidents without consequences had no interest for Chekhov' and that although he 'sometimes creates an illusion of lifelike pointlessness', every action has a point, which indeed is endowed with significance.[30]

In contrast, Eva, exemplary of authorial naivety, wishes to follow just this afterlife in order to impose a specious narrative circularity – to 'begin with oysters and end with oysters' (*GT* 14) – on to the messy though meaningful contingency of life. Eva is initially confident because she 'had an end … and a beginning'; 'what she had to do was imagine the life in between' (*GT* 24). She will fail to emulate Chekhov's method of deleting beginnings and ends – of writing stories which are 'all middle, like a tortoise', in Galsworthy's often-quoted comment.[31] Chekhov wanted to jettison the ready-made mould, the well-wrought tale, to make an arbitrary-seeming cut in the fabric of reality but not one which apotheosized randomness or lack of causation. This decentring or obliquity is what made an impression on modernist writers like Mansfield and Woolf. The latter said of the ending of Chekhov's 'The Post' that it 'produces at first a queer feeling that the solid ground upon which we expected to make a safe landing has been twitched from under us, and there we hang asking questions in mid air. It is giddy, uncomfortable, inconclusive.'[32] Victor Shklovsky wrote of 'Misery', a story in which an old man tells his grief to his horse and from which Mansfield borrowed, that the 'denouement here is the lack of denouement, the endless grief, the lack of an answer, the absence of an end … suspended in the concluding conversation as if in tragic parody'.[33]

How then do we assess the ending of 'The Beginning of an Idea' in relation to what was regarded as the apparent suspension of Chekhov's endings? Waking up on the train, Eva thinks she can taste bitter oysters in her mouth. The life and the art have contaminated one another to the extent that she experiences a somatic intrusion. Sampson suggests that Eva has now grasped the meaning of Chekhov's story – that is, a full apprehension of her mortality and suffering – and that 'a new beginning' is possible for her.[34] It is shocking that a double rape is the index of punishment for her artistic failure. The idea of an embedded beginning-in-ending, despite the idea of deletion, is thoroughly Chekhovian, as evidenced in the obvious example of 'The Lady with the Little Dog': 'And it seemed – given a little more time – a solution would be found and then a new and beautiful life would begin. And both of them clearly realized that *the end* was far, far away and that the most complicated and difficult part was only just *beginning*' (my italics).[35]

Antoinette Quinn is less affirmative about the end to McGahern's story, arguing that Eva's 'inarticulate re-enactment' of Chekhov's death indicates that Eva is still inserting herself into a Chekhov-shaped autobiographical narrative.[36] Eva remains the object of a discovered reality which she cannot quite apprehend; she has not yet reached a fully undeluded sense of life's suffering. The final sentence includes the phrase 'but then she saw that…' (*GT* 28): the typical threshold moment of the short story's ending. A post-epiphanic structure is suggested, but it is indistinct – indeed inarticulate – about the ironic revelation of self-understanding, and how this may be translated into a newly fashioned Chekhovian art. However, such inarticulacy is far from rendering the story un-modernist, as may be suggested by the notion of the 'non-epiphany' suggested by Dominic Head.[37]

Eva's writerly aspiration had already seemed to carry with it an appropriate humility about human mortality: the sea 'would not grow old' but its 'tides would ebb and flow' and 'it would still yield up its oyster shells long after all the living had become the dead' (23). This Joycean inflection may legitimize Eva's literary enterprise, although again it underlines that lyrical language, as well as symbolic 'idea', is inevitably borrowed. The metafictional implication for McGahern is that of a fruitfully belated and compromised poetics: that after Chekhov, after Joyce, he too is '*trying* to write' a short story which symbolizes its own form. This anxiety of modernist influence is not quite fully suppressed by the unusual prominence of the intertextual allusion, perhaps explaining the story's exclusion from *Creatures of the Earth*.

'My Love, My Umbrella': Beckett

So far in this chapter, the discussed stories have brought prior texts or hypotexts to the surface, with the consequence that the process of reading across or between texts is encouraged. What appears to be an authorial guarantee points to an obvious interpretative principle: texts cannot be read as single, self-bounded sites of meaning. The more or less conspicuous quoting of Joyce, Chekhov and Yeats may be a strategic shot across the bows to the reader who would concentrate too readily on the object of representation at the expense of the medium of representation, language itself, including all the traces it bears of other texts. However, intertextual interpretation must explore what is beyond the 'intention of the text', or *intentio operis*, as Umberto Eco has put it, so that the critic is free to render the text as writable (*scriptible*) – in conventional terms, to practise a riskier type of reading.[38]

In 'My Love, My Umbrella', another story in the early *Nightlines* collection, the 'constant weather' (*N* 77) of Dublin rain requires the constant protection of the umbrella for two lovers who must make love outdoors. They stand under trees in an unlit 'dead end' (*N* 79) behind a church while she holds the umbrella; he always ejaculates on the mud and decomposing leaves. These are the habits of love and of each other. Sex is merely another aspect of repeated human behaviour, not a romantic fulfilment: according to the narrator, its renewable singularity is only made possible by the penis having no memory (*N* 81). The relationship is threatened when the narrator tells a story about two London 'city gents' being tried for assault (on each other) by umbrella, and then extinguished when he asks her to hold the umbrella while making love on a clear moonlit night.

The consensus that *Nightlines* is a response to what has been termed Joycean realism includes commentary on 'My Love, My Umbrella'. Pascal Bataillard, for example, relates the story to 'A Painful Case', arguing that the narrator persists in his obtuse symptoms in the manner of James Duffy, who is taught a lesson about the desiring and symptomatic body – that it is not 'just a carnal envelope but the message itself'. Bataillard argues rather contentiously that whereas McGahern's poetics are disabused of ironic constriction or alienation, the irony Joyce targets against Duffy is itself aloof – and that it is only 'The Dead' which finally concedes that the artist must go beyond being the 'high priest of the imagination'.[39] Denis Sampson has also pointed to the bathetic Dublin settings and to the mock-heroic tone of 'My Love, My Umbrella', which may bring to mind the romantic 'gallantry' of Corley, for example. However, he also refers to a 'hint of existential urgency' in the story, which works against the comic or mock-heroic tone.[40] This touches on a certain shortfall in the Joycean properties of the story, and I would like to suggest that the tonal difference – the way in which the story balances the grim manifestations of sexual cruelty against its more ludic or clownish absurdity – can be further understood by comparing it to Beckettian humour. It is unclear whether it is possible to laugh at this absurd story: perhaps if we do, it is like that laughter defined at its typological extreme in *Watt* as 'the laugh of laughs, the *risus purus*, the laugh laughing at the laugh, the beholding, the saluting of the highest joke, in a word the laugh that laughs – silence please – at that which is unhappy'.[41]

McGahern's story clearly symbolizes the body in the umbrella itself. The umbrella is very much a borrowed, intertextual object, laden down with comic, quasi-philosophical possibilities, and full account must be taken of its over-determined iconographic meanings.[42] The story borrows its situational humour from the fetishizing of the umbrella as an object of desire, and this in turn may lead us to consider the vaudevillean, tragicomic aspects of Beckett. Umbrellas are part of the paraphernalia of *Mercier and Camier* and *Endgame*. The umbrella is an appendage for the rickety post-Cartesian Beckettian carapace, an intermediary piece of equipment or surrogate limb. The umbrella in *Malone Dies* is yet another version of the liminal elongated instrument – a kind of prosthetic used by the self to negotiate what is outside of it. The pen, prehensile stick, punt pole, umbrella or murderous hatchet are thrust out to scratch, poke, probe, grasp, intrude into or strike at the void. Winnie has a parasol rather than umbrella, but she too is trying to keep out 'the constant weather' – in this case, pitiless sun rather than endless Dublin rain. The parasol spontaneously combusts and is replaced for the second act, the object of Marxian utility flouted as mere theatrical prop.

The narrator's story about assault-by-umbrella suggests the sexual cruelty and potential violence of his own 'lovemaking': he too has been wielding a sexual 'weapon' (the word used to describe Lavin's phallus). The Beckettian umbrella can be a weapon, too. Malone is worried that a man dressed like an undertaker may use his tightly rolled umbrella, bent and with a shaper point, to plunge into his heart. Later, one of his characters, a thin man, breaks his umbrella against a rock.[43] Beckett's sexual comedy can be clinical – Malone looks at his sex, 'the tube itself, and in particular the nozzle [which] he does not expect to see again' – not to say gruesome, if we remember the coupling of Molloy and his captor, sometimes called Lousse.[44] As he feels the cold metal of the umbrella shaft, the narrator of 'My Love, My Umbrella' relates sex to veterinary insemination (also a feature of 'A Ballad'), and is similarly detached from his own un-sentient 'glass plunger'. The prominence of the umbrella complements the emphasis in *Nightlines* on objects or things, many of which Terence Brown has enumerated, including chainsaws, mallets, whips with metal tips, steel hoppers, as well as the insemination plunger, in order to illustrate the ubiquitous tyranny of the machine, its 'iron physical law', artificiality and lack of creativity.[45] Interestingly, the umbrella is missing from Brown's list. In the case of the city gents, the judge found only for common assault because a more punitive judgement would have conceded that the umbrella is indeed a dangerous weapon – in Bataillard's view, a piece of normative and normalizing casuistry.[46] The narrator's interest in the gents' case suggests how this story is poised between grimly asserting the instrumentalism of human 'objects' – the 'desire to hurt' – and a more leavened sense of 'growing absurdity' (*N* 86). As a supposed weapon the umbrella cannot rid itself of a certain Heath Robinson-like comedic quality. This reminds us of the umbrella's role at the inception of surrealism, known from Lautréamont's remark that a boy's beauty is like the chance meeting on a dissection table of a sewing machine and an umbrella. The umbrella is like the bowler hat, an exotically normal object in a Magritte painting. An umbrella cannot only be an umbrella, even if it sometimes is. It is this playful frustration of self-identity which alerts the reader to the tonal difference of this story from others in *Nightlines*.

On the one hand, the umbrella is synonymous with the woman's body: the narrator says it reminds him of her body; he hides it when trying to forget her, loses it when he loses her and retrieves it when trying to retrieve her. He has, precisely, objectified the woman, who is the 'body I'd tried to escape from' (*N* 86). On the other hand, the umbrella is inevitably phallic and thus symbolic of the narrator's own body. Of course, it appears in Freud's dream list: all 'elongated objects, such as sticks, tree-trunks and umbrellas (the opening of the last being comparable to an erection) may stand for the male organ'.[47] But there is a splitting of the sexual signified: Freud's deterministic code may undo itself. In a dream, the block-hat can be uterine as well as phallic, and the jutting umbrella can be inverted into a vaginal receptacle. The umbrella 'stands for' and 'opens out as' *both* bodies, but it is also as something which comes between and protects the bodies it represents. In short, the umbrella is hopelessly overdetermined. Bataillard enumerates wonderfully: it is 'the mockery of a phallic symbol, a regressive womb, a fetish, a dangerous supplement, a prosthetic sex toy'.[48] It is unsurprising that Derrida should have leapt at Nietzsche's marginal comment in an unpublished manuscript, 'I have forgotten my umbrella', as a curiosity which would encourage a hermeneutical will to explain and master the symbol.[49]

What is more, the umbrella also emblematizes the split sign of prophylaxis and procreation, rather like the eponymous parachutes of a later story, those similarly shaped 'machines of prevention' which are transformed into drifting thistledown, 'organisms of propagation', in Nicola Bradbury's words.[50] Beckett described Proust's desired object, enveloped in time and space, as being 'endowed with what might be described as an abstract, ideal and absolute *impermeability*' (my italics).[51] Watt speculates about 'that presence without, that presence within, that *presence between*' (my italics).[52] In McGahern's story, the umbrella – or *parapluie* – represents a protective epidermis but also the interpenetration of bodies: the all too permeable, stitched-up self in its contact with otherness, a screen which is neither within nor without but a 'presence between'.

The narrator's lover only accepts the umbrella in its improperly proper function, during sex in the rain, as a sensible object of utility. She tells a story about driving a farmer mad with lust for her: a testament to the dangerous enchantment of the sexualized human body. It cannot be admitted that the body is ridiculous. Eventually, she does not want to marry the narrator because there is nothing more for them to 'discover': the body has been uncovered and is no longer *terra incognita*. The narrator longs for the habits of cosy domesticity but also fears suburban family life in a Clontarf housing estate, or a rainy day on the coast with the children in a hired Volkswagen. For him, the umbrella may be initially tainted by the sort of bourgeois connotations memorably captured by Nabokov, who dismissed Freud as 'an Austrian crank with a shabby umbrella' at the centre of deadly middle-class Viennese life.[53] This represents an existential vacillation: should the narrator cling to the rock of others or the rock of self? Solipsism expresses itself with the reprobate desire to defamiliarize the everyday object by wrenching it out of its habit-forming context. Holding the umbrella to the moon during lovemaking is a lunatic, relationship-killing act, a cocked snook at the lover's conventionality.

The narrator is finally routed by his lover's ruthless disengagement from him, disguised perhaps by her conformist desire for the covered 'magic' of the body, rather than its discovered mechanics. The earlier unimpassioned routine is supplanted by a belated and caricatured heartsickness: he returns to the scene of the lovemaking standing under the umbrella, but now suffers from rather than celebrates 'growing absurdity' (*N* 86). The narrator finally determines to return to his state of 'unknowing happiness' under the trees, with the gripped umbrella as consolatory support, but the scene of the absurd ends as a kind of lost paradise, suggesting a somewhat reductive nostalgia. Such silly behaviour hints, in a possibly didactic way, that the narrator has been put in his place. It is indeed shocking that sex has been such a grimly depersonalized, potentially sadistic affair, but its need for the rejuvenating powers of the imagination should not solemnly exclude some sort of laughter at the surrealist tableau or the umbrella-wielding gents. The narrator's yearning for the primal scene is not really convincing, as the earlier habits of the body hardly represented innocence or happiness. It does not admit of the idea that there may have been something admissible in seeing the funny side in the ungovernably polymorphous or perverse forms of erotic desire. Having found a 'relief in movement' (*N* 86) by riding on buses to the terminus, the narrator does not in the end 'go on' with the resolve of Beckett's stoic comedians.[54] By the end of the story he has been unable to develop a conception of 'better failure': no bitter or pure laugh is recorded to accompany the narrator's plangent desire 'to be as [he] was before' (*N* 87).

Nevertheless, the surrealist centrality of the umbrella points to a certain tragicomic, Beckettian scepticism in the story. The umbrella is, in yet another of its manifestations, a mnemonic trope in reverse: it is what is forgotten, and to the psychoanalyst a staple parapraxis with determinate cause. Leonard Bast forgets his umbrella in *Howards End* – in order to get to know the Schlegels. Stephen's disquisition about Shakespearean brothers in the 'Scylla and Charybdis' episode of *Ulysses* includes the comment, which Stanislaus must have read with interest, that 'a brother is as easily forgotten as an umbrella'.[55] By emphasizing the evidence of *forgetting* rather than remembering, it may be said that in this story McGahern makes comic capital out of suffering and also, obliquely, of his own dependence on what Dermot McCarthy terms his 'art of memory'. The lovers' remembered stories destroy the eternal present of their lovemaking. Forgetting is not apotheosized here as a necessary process in advance of the involuntary recapturing of time but is mockingly represented by the conjunction of that forgetful instrument of habit, the penis, and the thing most forgotten, the umbrella.

Conclusion

This chapter has gathered a rather strange set of stories together, one of which was cut from the *Creatures of the Earth* collection. An apparently unflinching realism, which brings to light what has previously been censored or occluded, is here characterized by actual or imagined acts of violence – the fantasy of whipping the gypsy girls, the trampling of the model aeroplane, the rape of Eva by two Spanish policemen and common assault-by-umbrella. Such short fiction neatly fits the construction of early McGahern as a writer whose gaze is fixed upon brutality in the parish or disaffection in the city. Two of the short stories are backward-looking: the boy imagining the 'clean' Lavin in the wheatfield; the lovelorn narrator yearning for a state of 'unknowing happiness' under the umbrella. In the other two, the end also marks a transitional beginning of something, poised between then and now: the homeboy's blaze of accomplishment releasing a 'new life ... out of the ashes'; the failed writer at last seeing, albeit in an as yet inchoate way, how the meaningful contingency of existence frustrates the telic patterning of art.

Bearing in mind the weight of traumatic personal experience, it is all the more surprising that these stories are so conspicuously mediated by the presence of extrinsic texts. The transmutation of suffering into art is not direct but catalysed by literature. The retrospective structure is not only the training of the memory on childhood, but the memory of the library. McGahern's allusiveness stretches throughout the canon, as Sampson and more recently van der Ziel's work has demonstrated, but in these selected stories we see the work of modernist writers obtruding – even if such writing is, significantly, not representative of fully fledged or high modernism but is adjacent to it in various ways. The intertexts which are signposted or intimated in these stories have a disruptive effect on their apparently mimetic imperative, and this itself can be thought of as a formal legacy of modernism.

There is a certain curiosity and atypicality about this selection of short stories, and it can be argued that McGahern's later masterpieces of the form – say, 'Gold Watch' and 'The Country Funeral' (see Chapters 8 and 9) – achieve a more successfully ruthless suppression of intertextual obtrusion. The quotation of prior texts becomes less assertive, though this does not exempt such self-contained artefacts from also being interpreted as *lisible* palimpsests, silently dialogic with and rewritable through prior texts. It is not quite right to say that the ever more canonical modernists are conclusively cast off, but rather that their writing becomes more deeply embedded in the 'genre memory' of the short story or that their aesthetic preoccupations are increasingly overlaid by the naturalized idiom of the narrating voice. Though the later short stories are all the more shorn of overt self-reflexivity, this does not equate to a wilfully naïve or homespun poetics, but rather one which has passed through modernism, bearing its traces.

Notes

1 Julia Kristeva, *Desire in Language* (Oxford: Blackwell, 1980), p. 66.
2 Roland Barthes, *The Pleasure of the Text*, trans. Richard Howard (New York: Hill and Wang, 1980), p. 65.
3 See Gérard Genette, *Palimpsests: Literature in the Second Degree*, trans. Channa Newman and Claude Doubinsky (Lincoln: University of Nebraska Press, 1997), pp. 1–6.
4 Genette, *Palimpsests*, p. 5.
5 Michael Riffaterre, 'Syllepsis', *Critical Inquiry* 6 (Summer 1980): 625–38, 627–8.
6 James Joyce, *Dubliners*, ed. Jeri Johnson (Oxford: Oxford University Press, 2008), p. 18. All subsequent references to this edition of *Dubliners* will be made in the text.
7 James Joyce, *Selected Letters*, ed. Richard Ellmann (London: Faber and Faber, 1966), p. 83.
8 See Margot Norris, 'A Walk on the Wild(e) Side: The Doubled Reading of "An Encounter"', in *Quare Joyce*, ed. Joseph Valente (Ann Arbor: University of Michigan Press, 1998), p. 21.
9 Norris, 'A Walk', p. 21.
10 R. B. Kershner, *Joyce, Bakhtin, and Popular Literature: Chronicles of Disorder* (Chapel Hill: University of North Carolina Press, 1989), pp. 31–46.
11 Norris, 'A Walk', p. 10.
12 Ibid., p. 26.
13 Frank Shovlin, 'The Ghosts of W.B. Yeats', in *John McGahern Yearbook*, vol. 2, ed. John Kenny (NUI Galway, 2009), pp. 42–51.
14 W. B. Yeats, 'In Memory of Major Robert Gregory', in *Collected Poems* (Basingstoke: Macmillan, 1985). All subsequent references to Yeats will be made in the text.

15 Balachandra Rajan, *W.B. Yeats: A Critical Introduction* (London: Hutchinson, 1969), p. 110.
16 Edward Larrissy, *Yeats the Poet: The Measures of Difference* (Hemel Hempstead: Harvester Wheatsheaf, 1994), p. 131.
17 Frank Kermode, *Romantic Image* (London and New York, 2002), pp. 37–51.
18 Rajan, *W.B. Yeats*, p. 108.
19 Larrissy, *Yeats the Poet*, p. 130.
20 Cited in Kermode, *Romantic Image*, p. 39.
21 See Larrissy on Yeats's 'Reprisals', unpublished in his lifetime, which accuses Gregory of irresponsibility to his aristocratic responsibilities, p. 131.
22 Quoted in Robert Louis Jackson (ed.), *Reading Chekhov's Text* (Evanston, IL: Northwestern University Press, 1993), p. 19.
23 Quoted in Sampson, *Young John McGahern*, p. 131.
24 Raymond Carver crosses the boundary of fact and fiction in 'Errand', a rendering of Chekhov's famous dying moments, during which a German doctor ordered up champagne. In Bernard MacLaverty's 'The Clinic', a man reads 'Beauties' in a doctor's waiting room, prompting him to remember how 'the wind blow across his soul' when he first saw his wife.
25 James Wood quoted in Adrian Hunter, *The Cambridge Introduction to the Short Story in English* (Cambridge: Cambridge University Press, 2007), pp. 125–6.
26 Sampson, *Outstaring Nature's Eye*, p. 170.
27 Donald Rayfield, *Chekhov: The Evolution of his Art* (London: Paul Elek, 1975), p. 30.
28 Anton Chekhov, 'Oysters', in *Short Stories*, ed. Ralph E. Matlaw (New York and London: Norton, 1979), pp. 2–6.
29 Janet Malcolm, *Reading Chekhov* (London: Granta, 2001), p. 21.
30 Ibid., p. 92.
31 John Galsworthy, *Selected Essays and Addresses* (London: Heinemann, 1932).
32 Virginia Woolf, 'Tchehov's Questions', in *Virginia Woolf: Essays 1912-18*, vol. II, ed. Andrew McNeillie (London: Hogarth, 1987), p. 245.
33 Viktor Šklovskij, 'A.P. Čexov', in *Anton Čexov as a Master of Story-Writing: Essays in Modern Soviet Literary Criticism*, trans. and ed. Leo Hulanicki and David Savignac (The Hague and Paris: Mouton, 1976), p. 62.
34 Sampson, *Outstaring Nature's Eye*, p. 168.
35 Anton Chekhov, 'The Lady with the Little Dog', in *The Lady with the Little Dog and Other Stories*, trans. Ronald Wilks (Harmondsworth: Penguin, 2002), p. 238.
36 Antoinette Quinn, 'Varieties of Disenchantment: Narrative Technique in John McGahern's Short Stories', *Journal of the Short Story in English* 13 (1989): 77–89, 81.
37 See Dominic Head, *The Modernist Short Story* (Cambridge: Cambridge University Press, 1992), pp. 37–78.
38 See Umberto Eco, *Interpretation and Overinterpretation*, ed. Stefan Collini (Cambridge: Cambridge University Press, 1992), p. 64.

39 Pascal Bataillard, 'Love and Solitary Enjoyment in "My Love, My Umbrella": Some of John McGahern's Uses of *Dubliners*', *Journal of the Short Story in English* 53 (Autumn 2009): 79–90, 86.

40 Sampson, *Outstaring Nature's Eye*, p. 100.

41 Samuel Beckett, *Watt* (London: John Calder, 1976), p. 47.

42 Stanley van der Ziel has brought out the Beckettian qualities of that other *Nightlines* story 'Wheels', suggesting that the emphasis on purgatorial waiting in the train station, and the story about the failed suicide (hanging-by-tree) hint at *Godot*. See '*Nightlines*', in *The British and Irish Short Story*, ed. David and Cheryl Malcolm (Oxford: Wiley-Blackwell, 2009), pp. 489–90.

43 Samuel Beckett, *Malone Dies*, in *Trilogy: Molloy, Malone Dies, The Unnamable* (London: John Calder, 1994), p. 288.

44 Beckett, *Malone Dies*, p. 235.

45 Brown, 'John McGahern's *Nightlines*', p. 296.

46 Bataillard, 'Love and Solitary Enjoyment', p. 83.

47 Sigmund Freud, *The Interpretation of Dreams*, trans. James Strachey (Harmondsworth: Penguin, 1985), p. 470.

48 Bataillard, 'Love and Solitary Enjoyment', p. 80.

49 Jacques Derrida, *Spurs: Nietzsche's Styles/Éperons: Les Styles de Nietzsche* (Chicago and London: University of Chicago Press, 1978). Derrida speculates that Nietzsche's marginal note may have meant nothing or only pretended to mean something, whereas psychoanalytical symbol-hunters must confer significance. They would say of the umbrella-phallus that one 'doesn't just happen onto an unwonted object of this sort in a sewing-up machine (*machine à recoudre*) on a castration table' (p. 129). Derrida undermines such highly determined readability by gruesomely extrapolating this surrealist dismemberment: sewing becomes sewing-up; dissection, castration.

50 Nicola Bradbury, 'High Ground', in *Re-reading the Short Story*, ed. Clare Hanson (Basingstoke: Macmillan, 1989), p. 86.

51 Beckett, *Proust*, pp. 57–8.

52 Beckett, *Watt*, p. 43.

53 Vladimir Nabokov, *Strong Opinions* (New York: McGraw-Hill, 1973), p. 116.

54 Cf. Murphy in his rocking chair, or in the rocking and stopping of *Rockaby*. It is 'time she stopped': female time coming to a stop, the woman trying to stop time, the woman stopping trying to stop time. The narrator of McGahern's story is unable to stop trying to recover lost time.

55 Joyce, *Ulysses*, p. 203.

4

Psychoanalytical Signification and the Remnants of Literature: *The Leavetaking*

The remnants of literature

Although this chapter contains sections in which canonical modernist texts are considered, this is not at the service of proving influence but as part of a broader assessment of intertextual practice – that of writing and reading. The more or less conspicuous words of, among others, Arnold, Wordsworth, Hopkins, Yeats, T. S. Eliot, Dylan Thomas and Patrick Kavanagh have been acknowledged or unearthed by commentators, and sometimes assimilated into critical discussion. *The Leavetaking* seems to make a point of inviting intertextual interpretation, and this extends to the unusual rewriting of the novel: in 1984 the second edition re-emerged, after translation into French, from the ashes of the original text of 1974. From the outset, the reader's awareness of the novel's compositional history prompts a particular attentiveness to the palimpsest-like processes of writing and the recirculation of language.

The Leavetaking equally invites psychoanalytical interpretation. The temptation of viewing Patrick, the first-person narrator, as a victim of early trauma – a type of self-confessing patient whose behaviour in the present is wedded to and determined by the death of his mother in childhood – was certainly apparent to the author. In the 1984 edition of the novel, McGahern cut a reference to Freud from the first edition, and significantly reduced the story of Isobel's own family romance, which has a certain caricatural quality. Crudely psychoanalytical decipherments of *The Leavetaking* were apparently to be discouraged. The revision itself suggests that the narrative of the Freudian casebook can be 'doctored', and that our response to the representation of foundational trauma, and to repression and recurrence, must attend to what is concealed and revealed in language itself.

Dermot McCarthy argues that the whole of McGahern's writing, synthesizing conscious or unconscious processes, can be figured as a 'poiēsis of mourning' in which autobiographical fact, the shadow of the loss of the beloved, is shaped into 'personal mytheme'.[1] The very act of narration is related to a psychoanalytical working-over, -out or -through of trauma. *The Leavetaking* is evidence of a particular phase in the therapeutic movement down to the underworld, an Orphic revisiting of the primal scene, in which the psychic wound is reopened so that it can eventually be sutured. This is not only because the second edition, according to McCarthy, emerges as 'a conscious effort to excise that ghostly presence' of the former, but also because the late publication of the autobiographical *Memoir* recycles the text of *The Leavetaking* so conspicuously – a point that may take the reader aback but which does seem symptomatic of the author's having returned to the site of trauma in order to close with 'the climactic re-union' (144) of mother and son on the last pages of the last work, *Memoir*.[2] The uncanny recirclings of McGahern's imagination are thus given a curative determinism.

Notwithstanding the potency of such a psycho-biographical approach, the critic is still faced with granting *The Leavetaking* its own self-sufficient signifying power, freed from affiliation to the author, and not necessarily forming part of an end-directed narrative of long-deferred psychotherapeutic cure. Representing the text in terms of psychological healing risks critical complicity, for it places the reader as an explicatory master of the textual analysand, putting Humpty Dumpty back together again. An interpretative model ought also to accommodate the autonomous signifying potential of literature beyond the idea of the casebook. Denis Sampson observes that there are strands of narrative that 'do not "explain" according to analytical principles', and that the 'flow of Patrick Moran's consciousness is governed by laws that are not, finally, psychological or wholly available to logical scrutiny'.[3] Richard Kearney has written of how in *The Leavetaking* the 'notion of a psychoanalytical transformation of memory into imagination serves … as a metaphor and model of the activity of writing: a creative retelling of one's past by communicating it to others i.e. the readers'.[4] This usefully shifts the emphasis from the experience of trauma to its belated representation in Patrick's 'creative' act of writing.

The question remains, though, about the creative act of *reading*. To Jacques Derrida, psychoanalysis is only ever capable of finding itself. As Barbara Johnson puts it, 'what has been left out' from a psychoanalytical reading 'is precisely literature itself'; the 'remnant is still literature'.[5] The aim of this chapter is to show how recognition of the novel's psychological depths – in which the rupture of self and other, the obvious behavioural pattern of repetition compulsion and the final promise of psychic healing all figure strongly – must still account for the plentiful remains of literature. The intertextuality of the novel may be thought symptomatic, particularly given that literature binds mother and son together, but the process involves the symptoms of the reader, too. Patterns of substitution, surrogacy and transference are clearly evident in the novel as structural and intertextual processes, and the reader comes to see that what chains the subject to the loss of the other also chains the signifier to the transmission of 'the dead letter' of writing, as Derrida called it.[6] Although *The Leavetaking* 'presents' pathology, it also points to psychological overdetermination. In the end, the novel's pathology (novel as casebook narrative) and its intertextuality (text as mosaic of quotations) cannot be held apart: in both cases, as Lacan would put it, the path of the signifier must be followed.

Freud 'under erasure'

Most commentaries on *The Leavetaking* grapple with the short preface to the second edition, which seems to offer a *clou* to the reworked narrative to come:

> It [the first edition of the novel] was an attempt to reflect the purity of feeling with which all the remembered 'I' comes to us, the banal and the precious alike; and yet how that more than 'I' – the beloved, the 'otherest', the most trusted moments of that life – stumbles continually away from us as poor reportage, and to see if these disparates could in any way be made true to one another. (*L* 5)

Remembered experience is at its most richly transcendent, 'most trusted', when it is of moments shared with the beloved; it is also when the subject feels most strongly his lack of unity with the other, in the Platonic sense. The wish-fulfilment of perfect unity is always deferred: the otherest 'continually stumbles away'.

This proclaimed structural principle of self and other(est) suggests why Freud was prominent in the first edition of the novel. In *Civilization and Its Discontents*, Freud writes: 'At the height of being in love the boundary between ego and object threatens to melt away. Against all the evidence of his senses, a man who is in love declares that "I" and "you" are one, and is prepared to behave as if it were a fact'.[7] Love is the desire to become one with the beloved, whose otherness makes this impossible. Similarly, a melancholic such as Patrick seeks to introject the lost object – a recuperation of absence which impoverishes the ego. Just as Freud refers to how the 'shadow of the object fell upon the ego', so Patrick writes that a 'shadow was to fall forever on the self of my life' (*L* 64), and later that the 'shadow had fallen on the life' (*L* 82).[8] The novel is dramatized as Patrick's eventual breaking-free from the long shadow of childhood trauma, from a coercive shaping process akin to the sea-wind bending trees to its will (*L* 71). The pathologies of love and melancholia are brought together as the fantasy of absorbing and uniting the 'disparate' of other to the self. Unlike in *The Barracks*, otherness here has little to do with Sartrean *l'autrui* but is rather a psychological index of the love-object: the superlative of love is the superlative of otherness.

However, the novel inscribes the process by which the shadowed ego inscribes a necessary distance from the object as (m)other, suggesting the patient's self-knowledge. The novel retains the fracture in form, the gap between the two sections, but eventually offers itself as a new fictional whole which heals that fracture. Patrick's account of three relationships at the beginning of the second section is framed as a quest for a mother-surrogate, both as the One and the Many: 'the dream of another woman' and 'the dream of woman' (*L* 85). It records a sacrifice or betrayal of the mother, who had encouraged him to become a priest – what would be a posthumous guarantee of his lifelong virginity and fidelity to the Marian woman. Patrick rejects the sexual self-denial of this 'living death' (*L* 85), but his dream of other women cannot be dissociated from the presence of the originary bond with 'woman', the woman. The pickup artist, dreaming of woman in other women, is still pursuing the mother.

At the same time, though, that pursuit is retrospectively condensed to emphasize its futility. Markers of structural substitution are deliberately made conspicuous in all three relationships with the unnamed women, but most obviously with the first of them, who comes from the same area of Leitrim's iron mountains as his mother, went to the same convent and training college, and who, like Kate, becomes a schoolteacher, taking 'the same beaten path a generation apart' (*L* 87). In admitting to seeing past the dance-hall scene to his mother, 'the girl with the emery stone' (*L* 87), Patrick knowingly signals that his experience is being narrated as if in an exemplary case study. The closeness of this identification of lover and mother is presented to the reader as fatally unhealthy, confirming a too schematic return of the repressed, a regressive filling of the mother-shaped void. The final leavetaking from the first woman is deliberately symbolized as her return to *her* own mother: daughter is merged with the indistinct dark shape of her mother in a restitution of the primary family scene from which Patrick is excluded.

The truncated erotic sequence with the three women inevitably points to repetition compulsion, in particular the Freudian observation that in retaining a still-infantile fixation of tender feelings for the mother, a man may supply himself with an endless series of mother-surrogates.[9] However, Patrick is diagnostician as well as analysand. Thinking of this third lover, he writes: 'I had transferred the dream of my own life to another ... she was the one irreplaceable world everybody is, but which we feel only ourselves to be' (*L* 99). He is implicitly writing about his 'irreplaceable' mother as well as the brief love affair, and this will also define his need to respect the beloved otherness of Isobel, the American woman he falls in love with in the second part of the novel. Being completely subsumed in the other is equated with a return to an originary 'state of self' (*L* 99), but such a reconciliation of self and other in a Platonic whole is recognized as impossible. Isobel too must enact her own leavetaking of the parent – in her case, the quasi-incestuous protectiveness of the Father. Patrick and Isobel are mirror images of each other who have come 'towards one another from opposite directions' (*L* 143). The structural symmetries of substitution and repetition are thoroughly schematized. The narrator's representation of his and Isobel's sloughing off of psychological bondage is akin to the patient's working-through (*Durcharbeitung*).

Patrick banishes his own ghosts, explains his own symptomatic dependencies, and prepares the reader to understand how the formal fracture of the narrative is analogous to psychic wounds and their suturing. His subjectivity is shown to be self-diagnosing and potentially curative. Obvious shaping patterns of surrogacy and repetition are allowed to remain in place so that they may be scrutinized: the Freudian casebook, with its excavations into the strata of 'deep' selfhood, is not removed but placed *sous rature*, under erasure, in Derridean terms. In the end, the conspicuously constitutive narrative elements of the casebook emphasize the making of fiction.

Post-memory and the path of the signifier

Transference and substitution are everywhere we look in *The Leavetaking*. Take, for example, the interlocking symbolism of stones: the mother's breaking of the black emery stone; Isobel's white oblong stone, 'cold and soothing' (*L* 169); the lapis lazuli she hands to Patrick (*L* 110); the emerald her father steals (*L* 114). The stone is not so much to be decoded as a psychoanalytical symbol but rather in Lacanian terms as a relayed signifying function which the reader must follow. Language effects the repetitions, substitutions and structure of surrogacy and attempts to make true the shortfall between 'pure feeling' and 'poor reportage'.

Denis Sampson remarks upon the novel's impersonally 'symbolic order of art', shaped 'by means of this ritual of return': 'Only a poetic fiction woven of symbols and refrains, of repetitions and variations, can enact that appropriate sense of mystery and objectify the efforts of the self to grow into its own authority'.[10] This can be specifically related to a Lacanian sense of Patrick's consciousness as determined by language. One episode in particular, in which Patrick is told a story by his father about a shopping bag, reveals how the psychological phenomenon of traumatic recurrence is structured in the symbolic order of the signifier.

In a story of emigration and paternal desertion which is historically familiar, Patrick's paternal grandfather promised to send money from New York to his wife and son on the 'island'. He never returned from America. The grandmother is under the delusion that money will be sent, but letters stop arriving. No speech marks are used to signal that the first-person narrator has shifted between father and son. The pronoun silently and disturbingly slips, suggesting that the narrative will not only anneal the division between Patrick and the lost mother, but also allow the empathic workings of the imagination to recover the relationship with the less beloved. The son remembers the father's remembering. By repeating his father's story, Patrick can possess it as his own.

The delimiting of the pronoun draws attention to the structural function of the narrative. In particular, the unseen joining together of remembering and remembered 'I's signifies the transferring of memory – of memory becoming 'post-memory', as Marianne Hirsch called it.[11] This term, now used widely in Holocaust studies, refers to how the second generation indirectly experiences traumatic events which preceded their births. Their memories of such events cannot be literal but they have been transmitted so forcefully, both within the family and more broadly between generations, that they become second-order memories in their own right. As Hirsch argues, post-memory distinguishes itself from the direct experience of memory in that it is an 'imaginative investment, projection, and creation' within the closed space of the family, and that in crossing over the generations it becomes a 'performative index, shaped more and more by affect, need, and desire as time and distance attenuate the links to authenticity and "truth"'.[12] Patrick *performs* the remembering of his father, takes it upon himself, allowing the other into the 'I'.

The father remembers walking 'in the shelter of that hardness as I have seen foals move in the mare's shadow' (*L* 54), but the reader is likely to attribute it to Patrick's symbolizing sensibility, always emphasizing the maternal shadow. The consistency of the telling voice is surrendered, and grammatical 'migration' surprisingly makes father like son. The anecdote is not a singular oddment from the past but rather a mnemonic inheritance in which a persistent familial trauma is transmitted. The memory is a displacement of Patrick's own experience: the grandmother's vomiting through bus-sickness stands in for his mother's illness, and the grandfather's absence in America is repeated through the father's abandonment of his dying wife. The child is bound to a recurring psychodrama of leavetaking.

The slipping of the narrating signifier is a mechanism and manifestation of repetition. The boy listens to the story of the shopping bag while inside an ash tree; he will also hide inside a (laurel) tree during his mother's funeral, displaced from a funeral scene he may only imagine, not memorize. His father's story is one he is overhearing as if for the first time, but also one which has been repeated in childhood, with variations. Patrick 'trace[s] it out one last time' (*L* 52), a story as either first told or last remembered, one chained to its other iterations and to its intergenerational repetitions, and never a single site of irreducible meaning. As a principle of narrative recuperation, the key and often-quoted notion of 'memory becoming imagination' (*L* 45) must also include this transferring of enunciated subject positions. What is suggested is not only a kind of inherited boundedness between generations but also the constitutive role of narrating language. Parts of the main narrative of Part One turn out to be a kind of repetition of an earlier scene, in which the protagonists have replaced their counterparts from the previous generations. Patrick is a subject who 'must pass through the channels of the symbolic', as Lacan puts it, one who is not just bound to and unbound from the mother (and father), but who articulates and is articulated by them as a subject-position in the narrative.[13] Patrick 'lends his voice' to the familial other, just as his voice has been lent to him.

If we think of the narrative of the grandparents as a Lacanian triangulation of desire whose pattern will be repeated in the main traumatic memory (of the mother's death), we might note the following. The father and the son occupy the same apex position as teller and young sufferer of parental abandonment, with their parents at either vertice. It is only that the role of the abandoner has changed from father to mother. Structurally, then, it is appropriate for Patrick to 'become' his father in the telling, in order to repeat similar feelings. '"When I grow up we'll never be poor, mother," I said to her, and though she is gone I'm not going to be poor now either' (*L* 56). We could imagine such a similar sort of promise being made by Patrick to *his* mother – perhaps about avoiding spiritual poverty – but instead it is uttered as a boy by his father to his paternal grandmother. For Patrick, parental abandonment is not only the death of the mother but also resentment that his father abandoned his mother in the death room. In the tale of the previous generation, the abandoned grandmother occupies the maternal position in the household and is therefore a substitute of Patrick's mother. The remembered/remembering father is proleptically, unknowingly, as it were, telling the story at his own expense. The supposed generosity of Patrick's narrative transference seems to offer a brief period of filiative self-effacement, but only in the end, to underline how the father's guilt is structured.

It is not to exculpate the father to emphasize how structure determines identity. With Lacan in mind, it cannot be seen as coincidental that the shopping bag story centres on a letter which does not arrive. The grandmother imagines receiving the money from America and filling the shopping bag with foison: instead she vomits into it when the letter does not arrive. She turns it inside out to clean it: the shopping bag is a reversible sign of plenitude and emptiness, a receptacle of material absence. In this, it is like the registered letter itself, which supposedly contains money, and which she and her son go all the way to Derry to collect. In Lacan's seminar, he draws attention to Dupin's avidness in securing from the Prefect a great reward for the stolen letter: 'the signifier most destructive of all signification' is money.[14] The sign of the letter is, for the grandmother, the promissory note of another sign (the banknote) which can eventually be redeemed into material presence. 'Will the letter ever come now?' asks the father (*L* 55). No: the signifier is perpetually deferred and displaced. It is not that the letter arrives empty, without content; it is that the letter is imaginary. To Lacan, the text is a lack, an allegory of the signifier, and has meaning only in the effects it produces.

Lacan's seminar enigmatically concludes that 'a letter always arrives at its destination'.[15] The grandparental non-letter is in its turn a substitute for the letter that Kate sent to Patrick's father, enclosing the engagement ring in order to break off from him. This letter did exist and did arrive, thereby bringing life to Patrick but perhaps also a premature death to his mother. The repeatedly transmitted story of the letter would seem to suggest that a letter needs to be written to arrive. This intergenerational episode confirms Lacan's reassessment of Freud: 'Everything that might be considered the stuff of psychology, kit and caboodle, will follow the path of the signifier'.[16] The very lack of the letter is, to the grandmother, vomit-inducing signification itself: it still has its effect in – structures – her world. This episode suggests ways in which *The Leavetaking* points beyond the orthodoxy of a Freudian family romance, and shifts the emphasis on to the repeating structures of language and narrative. Patrick's casebook may be the 'stuff of psychology', but the truth of its stories and memories follows the path of the signifier.

'I' and other: Proust

The self/other structure mentioned in the preface to *The Leavetaking* encourages the interpretative discourse of psychoanalysis. This preface is reworded in the novel itself: 'The whole dear world of the beloved comes to us with the banality of news reports, while our own banalities come to us with the interest of poetry' (*L* 143). The 'interest of poetry': narrating the self and its discontents is also a question of language, be it banal or poetic. A fashioned, literary subjectivity wishes to give way to inadequately objective, 'secondhand' (*L* 143) reporting of the other, whose subjectivity is beyond reach and unrepresentable. The reader turns to the casebook of literature itself, in which the same breach of self and other is dramatized. As Denis Sampson was the first to insist, the relationship of the Proustian 'I', the *moi profond*, to *its* 'dear world of the beloved', was of great importance to McGahern. Superficially, the Proustian narrative may be thought of as incorporating the plenitude of the past life, centring on its lost images of greatest affect, and thus promising a kind of subjective wholeness within the circumscription of the first-person voice. But the Proustian problem which McGahern is trying to work out in *The Leavetaking* is that of reconciling 'the subjective reality of the individual self and the other reality of what is not part of the self', as Sampson puts it, and of revealing the limitations of the restorative consciousness: 'the egocentricity of remembering to the point of solipsism'.[17]

The psychoanalytical critic Hanna Segal said that for Proust, 'writing a book is like the work of mourning in that gradually the external objects are given up, they are reinstated in the ego, and re-created in the book … all creation is really a re-creation of a once loved and once whole, but now lost and ruined object, a ruined internal world and self'. Art is supposedly akin to mourning. But in a postscript, Segal, citing Adrian Stokes, places the emphasis differently: the artist's wish is to 'maintain simultaneously an ideal object merged with the self and an object perceived as separate and independent, as in the depressive position'.[18] Although we might think of Patrick in Freudian terms as melancholic rather than mournful, this gives Patrick and the reader of *The Leavetaking* a way of reconciling what seem to be competing aspects: on the one hand, the evocation of the mother as the 'irreplaceable' other, whose presence as 'ideal object' is retained (or 'reinstated in the ego') and with it the hope of merging or subsuming of the self and 'otherest'; on the other, a mature acknowledgement that love, be it of the mother or of Isobel, can only flourish if the otherness of the love-object is accepted as other, outside of the ego – in this sense, as 'lost'. Marcel writes of his delayed realization, after his grandmother's death, that 'we had not been created solely for one another; she was a stranger to me'.[19] As with Deleuze's reading of Proust, the accent is less on recreation and more on the ideal essence of the artistic sign – what is both in past and present, 'real without being actual, ideal without being abstract'.[20] Art may wish to represent the healing process, the unifying of 'I' and 'other', in which fiction is used as 'a balm or therapy', in Eamon Maher's words, but it also asserts itself as distinct from, supplementary to, coherent or cured psychic self-identity.[21]

The 'I'/Other structure is related to the Proustian question of friendship, too. Patrick's friend Lightfoot believes, after Proust in *Le Côté de Guermantes* (*The Guermantes Way*), that friendship 'is the halfway house between physical exhaustion and mental boredom' (*L* 30).[22] Lightfoot is the solitary who would feel, as Marcel does when thinking about St Loup, that friendship tends to make us sacrifice 'the only part of ourselves that is real and incommunicable ... to a superficial self which unlike the other, finds no joy in its own being, but rather a vague, sentimental glow at feeling itself supported by external props, hospitalised in extraneous individuality'.[23] In an essay on Ruskin which McGahern would have read in *Against Sainte-Beuve*, Proust had traced back such a 'sentimental glow' about friendship to a passage in Goethe:

> The world is so waste and empty, when we figure only towns and hills and rivers in it; but to know of someone here and there whom we accord with, who is living on with us, even in silence – this makes our globe of earth into a peopled garden.[24]

Ruskin opposes the affinity expressed in *Wilhelm Meister*, saying instead that '*my* times of happiness had always been when *nobody* was thinking of me'.[25] And Proust is of Ruskin's party:

> In comparison with the all too human eighteenth century, which de-poeticizes the world by filling it with people and deprives it of mystery by anthropomorphizing it, it seems to us that Ruskin is right. And, by not having everywhere a friend 'whom we accord with', he has discovered the inspiration afforded only by solitude.[26]

The quoting of Proust-on-friendship in *The Leavetaking* seems, then, to reinforce our sense of creative solitude. Elsewhere McGahern's alludes to bourgeois socializing as that 'eternal business that Proust describes as "Moral Idleness"' (*LW* 87).[27] However, Lightfoot is a minor character and not a mouthpiece for McGahern. Rather, Patrick's temperamental difference from Lightfoot points to a small resistance to Proust. In saying that 'the simple feeling that such as he [Lightfoot] is alive is enough to make my own life more bearable…' (*L* 31), and by heading for what the priest calls the 'vastly overcrowded place' (*L* 167) of the metropolis, we glimpse something in the narrator of an *anti-solipsistic* impulse which has an affinity with 'the all too human eighteenth century' uncongenial to Proust. Stanley van der Ziel has shown the extent of McGahern's appreciation for 'manners' in Jane Austen, and how it provides a model for the novelist's own need to read and indeed write the minds of others, to efface selfhood in the exercise of sympathetic imagination. Although Proust is of course a brilliant 'mind-reader', like one of his heroes, George Eliot, this does not detract from a clinging to the solitary, a cultivation of acquaintances rather than friends. For McGahern, the allusion to Proust makes the point that it is indeed the homosocial code of manners, rather than the apotheosizing of solitude, which lies behind the narrator's comment that he respects Lightfoot 'too much to claim him for a friend against his will' (*L* 30–1). Thus, there is a small early sign in *The Leavetaking* that the 'immaculate imaginative tact' of the characters in the final novel *Rising Sun*, as van der Ziel puts it, will act as compensation for – perhaps a reproach of – the imprisoned subjectivities of the earlier career.[28] More broadly, we intuit a tension between competing literary inheritances, a testing of the limits of modernist egoism and of Augustan sociability.

The overall structure of *The Leavetaking* seems to derive from an apparently Proustian structure of temporal recuperation. In his aesthetic credo 'The Image', McGahern includes the idea that 'dead passions and their days' can be called up in memory, just as Patrick calls up his own 'dead and dead days' (*L* 64), joining the 'last day' of the present to the past day in the 'deathroom' (*L* 31). The 'loss and joy' (*L* 65) of the restoration of the dead day is a Proustian structure. Sampson notes the similarity of the Overture in *Du Côté de Chez Swann* (*Swann's Way*) to 'The Image': 'Will [the image] ultimately reach the clear surface of my consciousness … this old, dead moment which the magnetism of an identical moment has travelled so far to importune, to disturb, to raise up out of the very depths of my being?'[29] McGahern invokes Proustian involuntary memories elsewhere in his work (see Chapter 9), describing them as 'more true because they surprise us, evading will and habit'.[30]

It must be admitted, however, that in *The Leavetaking* there is no sensory 'trigger' into the past. Rather, memories of 'old, dead moments' are called up with a greater or lesser degree of consciousness. It is the mechanical routine of teaching and 'its arid discipline' (*L* 25) which allow the narrator to place himself elsewhere: 'Her dead world comes to life in my mind as I drift away from the classroom and out of this last day in it on a tide of memory' (*L* 25); 'I turn to memory and images out of my own life' (65). Of a family memory, Patrick 'trace[s] it out a last time' (*L* 52). There is a degree of self-doctoring volition about the recollection of memory which suggests that it is a *voluntary* part of Patrick's self-healing, which will soon be completed: 'By evening the life would have made its last break with the shadow, and would be free to grow without warp in its own light' (*L* 82). This botanical analogy – the tropism of the human plant – may be a Proustian figure, but points to how the triumph of art in *Le Temps Retrouvé* (*Time Regained*) may come at the cost of the life. It is unlikely that Marcel will be similarly free to grow 'without warp' in his own light.

The central idea in McGahern of 'memory becoming imagination' (*L* 45) is similar to but distinct from Proust. Patrick has given himself licence, as it were, to accrete experiences from the past beyond the strict bounds of selfhood. In *Du Côté de Chez Swann*, Marcel also accommodates a narrative of frustrated love (with Odette) that happened before he was born, in what is a structured foreshadowing of his own struggle with the beloved other. But there is a slight difference. Proust effaces the first-person voice but does not pass the baton of self to another teller, allowing the signifier 'I' to slip, as McGahern does. The Proustian 'I' is multiple and successive but it is also the case that Marcel muses over being imprisoned to his perpetual selfhood, wondering how after a deep sleep a person resumes being who he or she was the night before. The subject is often present though silently catalytic, as in the Guermantes dinner party. In *The Leavetaking*, for all the acknowledgement of the superlative otherness of the beloved, the 'I' still seems more willing to surrender itself into the familial other. Patrick turns 'to memory and images out of [his] own life to imagine the night that [his mother] conceived' (*L* 65). It is difficult to conceive of Proust transgressing the borders of his imagining subjectivity, or allowing a narrative transition in which Marcel 'becomes' his mother or grandmother.

For memory to 'become' imagination is a consolatory narrative act in *The Leavetaking*. In Proust, the relationship between memory and imagination turns on the frustrated desires of the remembering subject. Malcolm Bowie has written of Proust as an example of a human type that Jane Austen called 'the imaginist' – a person who spends too much time fantasizing and who always seems to be in flight from real events and binding obligations. This again confirms how McGahern's Augustan sympathy may be held distinct from a delimited modernist egoism. The 'nomadism' of the Proustian imaginist can always be centripetally traced back to the isolated rock of selfhood which is 'lost, and found, and lost again'.[31] Albertine is a series of figments of the narrator's imagination, products of jealous desire. The narrator comes to realize 'an ineluctable law which ordains that we can only *imagine* what is absent' (my italics); as Shattuck has put it, it is an imagination which 'seeks its object forever elsewhere'.[32] Edmund Wilson had recognized in Proust a similar process in 'the tragic subjectivity of love', that 'what we love in [a woman] is merely the creation of our own imagination: we have supplied her with it ourselves'.[33] Imagination in this Proustian sense generates lengthy, super-sensitive examinations of the self's multiple constructions of the beloved most other to the narrator: thus, we are aware of the significance of Albertine having a personality diametrically opposed to Marcel.

This does seem close to McGahern's sense of the self continually missing or falling short of the precious and disparate other, and in both writers the apparent paradox is explored that the closer the approach to personal memory, the greater the role of the imagination. However, for Patrick, memory can 'become' imagination with a degree of restorative power, notwithstanding the Lacanian structuration discussed earlier, whereas for Proust's narrator, the repeated recreations of his life contain a succession of inventions which undermine the status of absolute memory. Memory is replete not only with (lost) visual images but also with all the things Marcel *imagined* to be the case at the time: it is replete with a succession of fabricated signs, in Deleuze's sense. Memory has a signalled provisionality and exfoliating multiplicity in Proust which aligns it with imagination. No single border of memory becoming imagination is pointedly drawn and crossed, as in *The Leavetaking*, because Marcel is constantly imagining things as he remembers them.

This is not to claim that the willed replenishment of memory is taken for granted as automatically successful in McGahern. For example, after the end of the relationship with the first woman, the clearly indicated mother-double, Patrick finds a photographer's ticket in a suit pocket and has the photograph developed:

> The more I looked the further she went away. I was looking at celluloid that merely looked back. There was not even the sense of persons missing from empty spaces that will never be filled that way again. (*L* 91)

Patrick 'should' feel what Barthes calls the *punctum* of the photograph, but the greater the attempt to reconstitute the person (the closer he peers), the more that time distends. The lover is a different type of other or false 'disparate' –

someone never fully loved and therefore never lost, whose doomed integration into a symbolic structure may not even be attempted. Marcel measures being bored by attending an exhibition of photographs, and describes the failure of his memory when it tries to recall Venice *as if in snapshots*.[34] As Barthes puts it, there is 'nothing Proustian in a photograph'.[35] In this episode, McGahern is replaying a Proustian frustration that time cannot be abolished at will.

Nevertheless, while Proust's narrator remains alone in time, accompanied only by his art, Patrick finally merges with Isobel into a continuous or continuing 'we' at the end of *The Leavetaking*. Reading the novel after Proust reminds us that the relationship of the 'I' to the 'other' is not a privately pathological set of co-ordinates belonging to an individual case study. It is rather a persistent literary problem of how the subject's desire for and memory of the object may be structured in narrative. What McGahern apprehends as 'disparate' is not only the object of the lost mother. The question of discrepancy, of what remains or 'stumbles away', cannot be separated from the 'other' of literature itself. Patrick calls up his dead days, and in doing so enlists the 'dead letter' of literature, beloved of 'I' and other: 'Our own banalities come to us *with the interest of poetry*' (my italics, *L* 143). A set of intertextual relationships are suggested, some of them directly indicated, others covert. Whether they are conscious or unconscious is not a matter for the critic, but their marked or unmarked allusiveness signals that the act of reading may be creative, increasingly testing how the intersubjective may be reconfigured as the intertextual.

Psychological symbolism and intertextuality

The Derridean idea that literature is what is omitted from the narrative of the casebook prompts a new way of approaching the distinctive literariness of *The Leavetaking*, particularly as literature is enlisted in the novel as succour by mother and son, and is intrinsic to the aspiration to heal and make whole. If 'poor reportage' is purged, the preface claims, we are left with the supposedly 'pure' subjectivity of the remembered 'I'. That subjectivity is, however, communicated in an allusive style which critics have thought of as lyrical or poetic. We come to realize that the memory of the beloved is inextricable from the shared love of reading, but the interpretative implications stretch further. What is at stake for the reader when reading this poetic language is an encounter with the remains of discrepant literature itself, with what Derrida calls 'the very open letter which fiction is'.[36]

The reader's approach to the allusiveness of *The Leavetaking* seems to imitate that of the psychoanalyst. There is a play on intertextual surface and depth: on what is manifest, quoted and attributed; or on what is latent, unmarked, writing in need of disinterment. In a brilliant piece of detective work, Frank Shovlin has shown how unattributed lines of poetry, such as Yeats's 'trivial event/ That changed some childish day to tragedy' ('Among School Children'), echo in an account of Patrick's mother, the young Kate, 'playing at the edges that turn a child's day to tragedy' (*L* 68).[37] Kate reflects on how the poems she learnt pass through her mind, 'not unlike old friends or stray strands of music' (*L* 37), and how she encourages her pupils to learn poems by heart. We are alerted to the signifying practice of the text itself: both Patrick and his mother are 'among schoolchildren' and among literature. Yeats's intertext is unmoored from a single consciousness. The son may have used the line to describe the mother's experience because she had passed it on to him, as if he were her pupil.

In one way, the precious line of poetry is indeed possessed by the characters in the secret sharing of mother and son, and its embedding in Patrick's consciousness may be seen as an authorial index of the privacy of their love. But the unhitching of the line from its source, its blending into the texture of supposedly pure subjectivity, remains a marker of the 'open letter' of literature. Much has been made of the condensed poetic symbolism in *The Leavetaking*, in relation to gulls, shadows, trees, water and so forth. A case can be made that, in at least one instance, the 'symbol' itself is less a nucleus of psycho-symbolic meanings by which realist prose is lifted from its mimetic function, and more an agglomeration of canonical literary signifiers.

To illustrate this, let us take the dominant imagery of sea and water – the neatly circular joining of the 'first constant' (or supposed element) of water at the beginning of the novel (originating with the ancient philosophy of Thales of Miletus) to the signposted quoting of Arnold's 'Dover Beach' at the end. The Howth harbour tide reminds Patrick of Arnold's 'ebb and flow/ Of human misery' at Dover, and the explicit thematic connection is made that, like Arnold's speaker, Patrick feels himself to be living in a world from which faith has withdrawn.[38] Arnold has been smuggled in earlier to describe the very start of Patrick's loss of faith in childhood – in this case, being told that Santa Claus does not exist: 'It was the first break in the *sea of faith* that had encircled me, for what if God was but the same deception' (my italics, *L* 62). The last day in the schoolroom, including his sacking by the priest, represents the cutting of the final link to religious affiliation. This time Arnold is quoted *and* named: '"Begin and cease, and then again begin". It was Matthew Arnold. The bright girdle he spoke of had been long broke for me before this last night' (*L* 169).

The mid-Victorian tension in Arnold's poetry between evolution, faith and existence informs *The Leavetaking*. 'Dover Beach', whose speaker appears to be on honeymoon, can still allow Patrick to imagine the lovers being united on the shared 'boat of our sleep' – thus his apparently romantic repetition of Arnold's 'Ah, love, let us be true/ To one another!' But Patrick also thinks of the lovers slipping their moorings and trusting to 'the open sea: and no boat needs so much trust to put to sea as it does for one body to go human and naked and vulnerable into the arms of another' (*L* 170). That this open sea is in contrast to the withdrawn 'sea of faith' may extend rather than limit the Arnoldian associations. In 'To Marguerite', for example, human beings, each 'in the sea of life enisl'd', have been sundered from one other: 'We mortal millions live *alone*'.[39] The severed islands will not be reunited into a continent. The Arnoldian sea suggests a kind of proto-existentialist modernity.

With its insistence on the physical and Darwinian – 'The odour of our lovemaking rises, redolent of slime and fish' (*L* 170) – the end of *The Leavetaking* asserts a return to the primordial soup, or the returning of human love to 'the prime element', in Roger Garfitt's words.[40] Isobel's musing on the potential conception of her child adds to the sense that the lovers are like mammals crawling back to their origins in the sea, biologically engaged in continuing human life. Garfitt emphasizes how this sense of organic cyclicity, which encircles eschatological narrative, lies behind the forming of existentialist 'belief'. The symbolic association of the sea with sexual fertility is a breaking-free from non-procreative celibacy, as another encrypted poem, Hopkins's 'Heaven-haven', intimates. Patrick imagines his mother copying the poem, subtitled 'A nun takes the veil', on to the blackboard (*L* 36–7). The implication is clear: Hopkins's nun opts out of the stormy 'swing of the sea' or 'the green swell', unlike the mother, who agrees to marry, and unlike Patrick, who does not enter the priesthood and resolves to leave the haven of Howth harbour. The 'sea of faith' is symbolically supplanted by the sea as fecund, swelling, stormy.

The open letter of literature continues to be exfoliated. In writing of the boy's foreknowledge that 'the journey would be dark and inland through sex and death, the sea continually withdrawing' (*L* 63), the narrator continues his manifest engagement with Arnold. The 'dark … inland' is like 'the darkling plain' of historical struggle. 'Going inland', associated with the child's isolation on uncovered land, is inscribed as psychic topography: Patrick looks between a woman's thighs on the day of his mother's death, suggesting the dark interiority where the erotic life of the young adult will be shadowed by the dead mother. But the image refuses to be pinned down to the psycho-symbolic. Denis Sampson has recently pointed to the possibility of a lurking, covert allusion to a line in Patrick Kavanagh's 'Prelude': 'And you must go inland and be/ Lost in compassion's ecstasy'.[41] 'Prelude' voices an anxiety about expressing sincerity in literature – how vulnerable it is either to ape or to be the target of satire's 'unfruitful prayer'.[42] The commitment to be made in the end is to the 'mundane problems of the lover', not to the 'schismatic sect' of the literary establishment. Kavanagh's final line, 'Lovers alone lovers protect', speaks in sympathy with Arnold's apostrophe to his lover.[43]

Whether such texts have been purposefully buried together is not the question. If we are to call up an image of the lovers reborn in water, this is mediated by prior texts. The last words of *The Leavetaking*, 'the first death', are used in Dylan Thomas's 'A Refusal to Mourn the Death, by Fire, of a Child in London', as Victor Sage points out.[44] With its proximate image of burning, the earlier use of the phrase – 'the first death and its suffering *burned away*, welded into one desire for this new love, for a life with her, a life with her forever' (my italics, *L* 88) – deepens a potential connection to Thomas's poem. The first death in turn implies the second death of the *Book of Revelation*, a text which leaves traces in *The Pornographer*, as the next chapter considers. It is clear from McGahern's texts that a literary allusion does not represent the 'haven' of origin: the signifier does not stop once a source is supposedly mined.

Like his mother, Patrick copies poetry on to the blackboard. When a boy speaks out a line from Wordsworth's 'My heart leaps up when I behold', we are implicitly invited to complete the poem:

> The Child is Father of the Man;
> And I could wish my days to be
> Bound each to each by natural piety.

The concatenation of days 'each to each' implies Patrick's traversing of his last day as a teacher and the last day of his mother's death. The man wishes to inherit the boy's sense of natural wonder, such as when he chased and tried to hold 'the flaming ball of heaven' (*L* 48). Retaining the identity of the child keeps the mother, rather than the father, alive; the reader silently adjusts the intertext. However, the parental chain may also be tyrannically causal, a force of bad determinism which beats the present 'into its shape' (*L* 48) with the same hammering, percussive rhythm with which the beds were uncoupled in the empty rooms as Patrick's mother was dying. Days are traumatically bound 'each to each', but the psychological explanation is caught within a signalled movement between texts.

Generally, it can be seen that the symbolic images within Patrick's creative consciousness are formed by means of interlinked literary signifiers. What is 'inland' in the text is to be found outside it, enmeshed in other texts. What explains deep selfhood, the 'journey' into the narrator's unconscious, is a borrowing from literature. We are invited to psycho-analyse and analyse the text simultaneously – to 'untie the text' – as we disentangle what passes through the mind of Patrick and his mother.[45] The analyst must seek out latencies, paying attention to what has been exposed and concealed. If the text recuperates 'lost images', and if it finally achieves a sort of transcendent unification of evolution and psychology, it does so through the mediation of writing. It is as if *The Leavetaking* has a textual memory, in which allusions are conspicuous, and an intertextual unconscious, in which literature floats free of narrative agency.

Peter Brooks has written about the kinship between Freudian repetition compulsion and the experience of reading a text: 'All the mnemonic elements of literature and indeed most of its tropes are in some manner repetitions which take us back into the text'; repetition 'creates a *return* in the text, a doubling back. ... We cannot say whether this return is a return *to* or a return *of*: for instance, a return to origins or a return of the repressed.' We may move backward and forward, so that 'the end is a time before the beginning'.[46] This describes quite accurately why the couple are said to be 'continuing' rather than 'departing' at the end of *The Leavetaking* (*L* 170). Patrick has thought of 'the beginning only in the end' (*L* 85), echoing Eliot. The novel establishes an intra- and intertextual pattern of 'mnemonic elements' which, once the spectre of traumatic repression has been exorcized, performs just such a 'return to origins'. Remembering is co-extensive with the remembering of literature. Patrick may be 'driven' towards a fusing of Thanatos and Eros, to a fertile, amniotic pre-Symbolic unity which, in the words of Juliet Mitchell, 'is death and has to be death'.[47] But the text is equally driven towards its extra-literary signifiers, 'first death'. The novel concludes by intimating the regressive, evolutionary journey into the psyche at the very time it is most highly intertextual. The enactment of a return to the primal takes place under the sign of literary allusion, so that the dead letter of the lost text is itself eroticized. Writing returns to its 'origins' in writing.

'Nestor' and *The Leavetaking*: History and poetry

A debate about the extent of certain literary influences on McGahern should not be too constrictive, remembering Michael Riffaterre's emancipating, some would say irresponsible, claim that the only requirement for reading may be a 'presupposition of intertext'.[48] This final section indulges such a presupposition, remembering that, in the words of John Frow, texts 'are not structures of presence but traces and tracings of otherness … shaped by repetition and the tracings of other textual structures'.[49] The unattributed quotation of Yeats's 'Among School Children' may allow Patrick to be placed, as it were, in the same classroom as Yeats's 'sixty-year-old smiling public man'. As we have seen, though, the allusion does not 'stop' at an origin, but suggests other chains of meaning – in this case, the trace of another absent classroom in canonical Irish modernism. The 'Nestor' chapter of *Ulysses* also allows Patrick to be associated with an unsmiling twenty-two-year old private man in Dalkey. The pursuit of such presupposed relations is not to fetishize impersonal structural processes at the expense of the dethroned author, but rather to bring out how, in Kristeva's terms, intertextuality is a passionate affair, signifying those conscious and unconscious desires implicated in language. In what appears to be a privately psychological novel like *The Leavetaking*, this latent intertextual passion importantly bears on how the competing narrating languages of Irish history are bequeathed in the language of Irish *literary* history.

In an early review of *The Leavetaking*, Jonathan Raban emphasized McGahern's fruitful 'collusion' with Joyce, celebrating the shared tradition of history and language as their 'family affair', and neatly side-stepping Harold Bloom's Oedipal agon. Raban seems to have 'Nestor' in mind when describing, though discriminating between, Patrick and Stephen: the former 'does not have to go through the anguish of rejecting history; his history gives him the sack'.[50] It is as if the controversial circumstances of McGahern's dismissal from his job as a schoolteacher, here transmuted into the fictional sacking of Patrick, had neatly made good a *Ulyssean* promise: Deasy 'foresees' that Stephen 'will not remain … very long at this work', and that he was 'not born to be a teacher'.[51] What the comparison of McGahern's and Joyce's schoolrooms initially reveals is that conversations about Irish history replay and recast earlier ones, projecting and sometimes inverting historical images. History has moved on but its roles are repeated, with a difference.

Patrick, like Stephen, is a schoolteacher in a suburban Dublin school trying to resist the historical articulations imposed upon him by the educational authorities. Maloney, described as an 'ardent nationalist', is a mirror-image of the Protestant Unionist Deasy, who champions Anglo-Saxon values to a sceptical Stephen. Maloney reminds Patrick of England's past imperial brutality – 'They tramped us into the dirt' – and refers to England's 'great civilization' with a 'gleeful sarcasm' (*L* 153) that has a faint resemblance to the citizen's scorn about English 'syphilisation' in 'Cyclops'. Like his counterpart Deasy, the Headmaster is positioned in the narrative as a mouthpiece of the educational Law of the Father, though it is another master-father, the priest, who will sack Patrick later in the day. In both texts, the reader is attuned to how colonial history may describe contested postcolonial futures. The contemporaneity of *Ulysses*'s publication with partition retrospectively informs our reading of Deasy's Unionism ('*For Ulster will fight/ And Ulster will be right*', 35). When Patrick says that the English have left Ireland, he is told by the Headmaster that 'they're not out of all of it yet. But they will be one day, *buichas le Dia*' (*L* 153). The novel takes place well before its publication in 1974 and 1984, but such comments seem to hint at the violence of its historical future.

Patrick's political self-positioning is double-voiced and performative. He remembers his servility as a very young teacher, and is embarrassed by 'the slavish caution of [his] whole forever overmastered race' in his voice (*L* 150). He sees his current unwillingness to bend to the school authorities as 'shaking off some of the slavishness' (*L* 151), though he still plays the role of Anglophobe for Maloney's benefit, 'echoing the master': 'They are on their way down. … The whole thing is riddled with class distinction' (*L* 153). But this immediately makes him feel disloyal to the friends he has made in the London pub, to the extent that the words of a working-class Englishman, describing his wartime days as a desert rat, are remembered and quoted. Patrick has the courage to parry the Headmaster, criticizing how the Irish 'run one another down'. An internalized dialogical struggle is going on. The question of partition is likened to dangerous waters to be avoided. The typical guardedness of the McGahern narrator should not be equated with the disengaged pose of the egoist-artist, however: Patrick also remarks that his own havering may be unfavourably compared with the Headmaster's conviction: 'I loved his narrow passion, faithful to the person he was, so alien to my uncertainty' (*L* 153). As David Malcolm has written, Patrick is quite affectionate to the 'old fanatical peasant' (*L* 12), who is much more affable than Deasy or the citizen.[52] The conversation may be 'quite hopeless', to the extent that Patrick grows ashamed of his own 'forever overmastered' voice (*L* 150), but his attitude is more rueful than combative.

The narrator's disturbance can be interpreted as a figure of historical and literary recurrence. The masters are different, but the relationship of power into which the teachers are interpellated, in Althusserian terms, is repeated. Stephen, who styles himself as a dogsbody, a type of Caliban, the 'servant of two masters'

(20), an odd job man, another perennial jester at court, can be seen as a 'slavish' forbear of Patrick. History is all too easily performed, adhering to familiar patterns of promise and betrayal. It is so deprived of meaning and agency that it resembles fiction: 'History was a tale like any other too often heard' (25). It is only Stephen's acutely historical consciousness which allows him to figure history as a 'nightmare': he wishes to awake from history only because he is able to conceive of himself as acted upon by its unbearable weight. Stephen muses that the events of history are branded and fettered and not to be 'thought away' or 'ousted' (25), and muses upon Aristotle's contrasting of the actual (what happened, equated with history) with the possible (what might have happened, associated with poetry). He is trying to grasp the meaning of entelechy, to integrate visionary idealism and materialist history, and to see how potentiality might be actualized. In *The Leavetaking*, Patrick's friend Lightfoot, though he quotes Proust, now reads only history because history 'stays still: '*It* at least is settled' (*L* 163). Lightfoot has simply become an apostate from literature: having exhausted the richly disappointing potentialities of poetry, he has reached this masochistic comfort in the pyrrhic victory of material history, recorded in 'gorescarred' textbooks (24).

What has been ousted for Stephen, according to Emer Nolan, is national self-determination, and to awake from history is to awake from the colonial history written by the victors. A distinction ought to be made between 'a purely idealist conception of history and that attempt at a materialist history which, given that it must proceed in the absence of material evidence and in the interstices of a canonical history, can easily be mistaken for such an idealist mode'.[53] When contrasted to the relentlessly teleological sense of historical progress which the Unionist Deasy narrates – towards 'the manifestation of one great goal' – Stephen's fragmented thoughts may be mistaken for a retreat into a universalizing idealist mode. But these constellated responses have an anti-colonial historical materialism of their own, a resistance to the violence of teleological master-narratives which, as Nolan writes, have been occluded by Deasy's account of history.

We may thus interpret Patrick's suspicion of totalizing, end-directed historical narratives as other than an egoistic disengagement from obdurate, 'settled' history. He remarks of the *Notes for Teachers* that

> the cultivation of patriotism is more important than the truth. So when we teach history Britain is always the big black beast, Ireland is the poor daughter struggling while being raped, when most of us know it is a lot more complicated than that. (*L* 162)

As well as Yeatsian echoes of Leda and the foundational violence of historical becoming, we may think too of the gun-carrying Haines's nightmares of a black panther in 'Telemachus', suggestive of the prowling colonial unconscious of self-proclaiming civilization. Patrick's distrust of official history updates the Joycean notion of 'forged' history, and the cautiousness of Patrick's conversation with the Headmaster reveals that history is far from 'settled'. History is not to be thought away, but neither must it be beholden to the sovereignty of state-sanctioned facts. We hear no admiration from Stephen, as we do from Patrick, about his Headmaster's 'narrow passion'. Rather the reader of *Ulysses* may project a sense that Stephen's resistance to colonial history will eventually allow him to gain *aesthetic* confidence and play a new part, not that of the jester, in creatively forging Ireland.

The artistic ambitions of McGahern's subject, covert and deeply embedded, are never brought centre stage, as in modernism. In the schoolroom of *The Leavetaking*, Patrick objects to the complicity involved in the monologic dissemination of the nation, and also implies that literature can be potentially emancipatory in more private ways. The transformative 'possibility' of literature turns inwards upon his relationship with his dead mother – on personal loss, rather than historical dispossession. Such is the pathos of the death of the devout mother that we may forget that it, too, is passionately intertextual. In 'Nestor' Stephen is of course preoccupied by his mother's death – 'She was no more' – and by the notion of mother-love in both its meanings: '*Amor matris*: objective and subjective genitive' (28). He wonders whether the 'only true thing in life' is the love of a mother for her son, and he is haunted by his failure to pray at his mother's bedside (28). Patrick shares an associated guilt with Stephen, for he broke his promise to his mother to enter the priesthood. Mother-love becomes a kind of prohibitive superego from beyond the grave. The young son's own remorseful conscience, in scholarly Stephen's remembered scrap of Middle English, is his 'agenbite of inwit' (16).

In both 'Nestor' and *The Leavetaking*, the remembrance of death in the classroom is counterbalanced by thoughts about conception and heredity. Patrick speculates in boredom-relieving vein about the 'couplings', ably assisted by cut-price Powers wine, which may have created these schoolboys: 'certificates of conception' would be more interesting than birth certificates (*L* 45). Such certificates would, though, be a cruel record of back-street fumblings or banal domestic convenience, and so he is led to consider how he too was engendered from his 'dead parents' (*L* 45). Conception is linked to death in Patrick's mind, particularly through the 'cancer-child' which kills Patrick's mother, but all the way to the potential conception of Patrick and Isobel's child, which would initiate the 'first death'.

The evolutionary discourse of *The Leavetaking* is also *Ulyssean*. Stephen thinks of the infant being born helplessly premature, liable to be 'a squashed boneless snail' without the mother's protection. *Amor matris* is not a sentimental fiction but a species-truth for the likes of the weak-blooded, slope-shouldered schoolboy Sargent. The mother is rendered disposable: 'She had saved him from being trampled under foot and had gone, scarcely having been' (28). Patrick's childhood 'bends beside' him like Stephen's, though his musings on his own conception as a 'casual accident' which stops him from remaining in 'Nothingness' (*L* 35) are not co-opted into a sweeping intellectual argument about the heretical theories of consubstantiality or the legal fiction of paternity. In both cases, though, the 'conceit' of conception and traumatic loss is transferred into recurrent symbolic imagery: in *Ulysses*, the odour of wax, rosewood and wetted ashes becomes a motif, and the mother a revenant who must be exorcized in the 'Circe' chapter. Patrick is shadowed by seagulls and by his 'ghostwoman', to the extent that shadowing becomes a literary as much as psychological symbolic function.

The Hopkins poem Patrick imagines his Yeats-quoting mother writing down, a kind of ironically celibate counterpart to Wordsworth's paean to parental affiliation, eventually suggests that their shared 'heaven-haven' is the schoolroom of literature itself. Patrick is not yet born when he 'remembers' his mother discussing literature with Mother Mary, but compels a possible event to become lodged in the schoolroom of his memory. However, he not only imagines a memory but also makes the poem present on the page: part of this empathic 'bending' towards his mother is to give absent literature its material trace. Thinking of historical potentiality in his classroom, Stephen alludes to Aristotelian entelechy: 'an actuality of the possible as possible' (26). It is poetry, not history, which gives weight to the condition of what might have happened. For Patrick, it was 'possible' that his mother would teach such a poem, and so he gives it 'actuality' in his imagined memories which return, without banality, with 'the interest of poetry' (*L* 143).

Conclusion: 'Let the commentary itself be a text'

Roland Barthes argues that reading and writing should not be held apart as oppositional but regarded as equivalently productive of textual meaning. The *scriptible* may, in the end, be an unachievable ideal, but nevertheless a free and 'full' reading is one 'in which the reader is nothing less than the one who desires to write'.[54] In McGahern's other novel of the 1970s, *The Pornographer*, we will see how the desire to write is profanely inverted in the surrogate outpourings of a pornographer. In *The Leavetaking*, however, literary desire is manifest at the very instance of trauma: Patrick remembers his 'childish day [changed] to tragedy' through the poetry loved by his beloved other. The son and mother are readers, teachers and copyists of literature, who either consciously or unconsciously remember and (re)write 'strands' of poetry.

In this way, the novel discloses the proximity between creative acts of reading and writing, but it also marks the limits of consolation in literature. Following the path of the signifier leads the narrator eventually to the dead or empty letter of literature, to its intertextual 'first death'. The reader of the novel is also complicit in this process. The critical quest for the intertext is encouraged and frustrated. Embedded allusiveness is generally being shown to be characteristic of McGahern's work, but in *The Leavetaking* the more prominent quoting of literature, be it attributed or intonational, folds into an overt thematic design which challenges the reader. Placing the narrator in the modernist schoolroom with too much insistence may imply a critical meta-language which imposes what Barthes calls the jurisdiction of canonical literary history. In the pursuit of critical authority, of proving influence, the critic cannot deliver on the promise of the letter, rather like Patrick's grandfather. A final way of responding to the intertextual remainder of *The Leavetaking* may be to demur from expectations of such authority and, after Barthes, accept that the commentary itself is a text.[55]

Notes

1 McCarthy, *John McGahern and the Art of Memory*, pp. 144, 135.

2 Ibid., p. 144.

3 Sampson, *Outstaring Nature's Eye*, p. 120.

4 Kearney quoted in Whyte, *History, Myth, and Ritual in the Fiction of John McGahern*, p. 130.

5 See Barbara Johnson, 'The Frame of Reference: Poe, Lacan, Derrida', in *Psychoanalytic Criticism: A Reader*, ed. Sue Vice (Cambridge: Polity, 1996), pp. 92, 94.

6 Jacques Derrida, *Of Grammatology* (Baltimore and London: Johns Hopkins, 1976), p. 29.

7 See Mary Jacobus, *Psychoanalysis and the Scene of Reading* (Oxford: Oxford University Press, 1999), p. 20.

8 Sigmund Freud, 'Mourning and Melancholia', in *The Freud Reader*, ed. Peter Gay (London: Vintage, 1995), p. 586.
9 Freud, 'A Special Type of Choice of Object Made by Men (Contributions to the Psychology of Love I)', in *The Freud Reader*, p. 391.
10 Sampson, *Outstaring Nature's Eye*, pp. 116, 136.
11 Marianne Hirsch, 'The Generation of Postmemory', *Poetics Today* 29, no. 1 (2008): 103–28.
12 Hirsch, 'The Generation of Postmemory', pp. 107, 124.
13 Lacan quoted in John P. Muller and William J. Richardson, eds, *The Purloined Poe: Lacan, Derrida and Psychoanalytic Reading* (Baltimore: Johns Hopkins, 1988), p. 178.
14 Lacan, in Muller and Richardson, *The Purloined Poe*, p. 49.
15 Ibid., p. 53.
16 Ibid., p. 44.
17 Denis Sampson, 'The Lost Image: Some Notes on McGahern and Proust', *Canadian Journal of Irish Studies* 17, no. 1 (July, 1991): 57–68, 65.
18 Segal quoted in Jacobus, *Psychoanalysis and the Scene of Reading*, p. 56.
19 Marcel Proust, *Sodom and Gomorrah*, trans. C. K. Scott Moncrieff and Terence Kilmartin (London: Chatto & Windus, 1992), p. 202.
20 Marcel Proust, *Time Regained*, trans. C. K. Scott Moncrieff and Terence Kilmartin (London: Chatto & Windus, 1992), p. 224.
21 Maher, *The Church and Its Spire*, p. 75.
22 See Marcel Proust, *The Guermantes Way*, trans. C. K. Scott Moncrieff and Terence Kilmartin (London: Chatto & Windus, 1992), p. 456.
23 Proust, *The Guermantes Way*, pp. 455–6.
24 Quoted in Roger Shattuck, *Proust's Way: A Field Guide to In Search of Lost Time* (London and New York: Norton, 2000), p. 92.
25 Shattuck, *Proust's Way*, pp. 93–4.
26 Ibid., p. 95.
27 See also Whyte, *History, Myth, and Ritual in the Fiction of John McGahern*, p. 81.
28 Stanley van der Ziel, 'McGahern, Austen, and the Aesthetics of Good Manners', *Essays in Criticism* 63, no. 2 (2013): 203–22, 218.
29 Sampson, 'The Lost Image', p. 16.
30 Whyte, *History, Myth, and Ritual in the Fiction of John McGahern*, p. 230.
31 Malcolm Bowie, *Proust Among the Stars* (London: HarperCollins, 1998), p. 1.
32 Proust, *Time Regained*, p. 223; Shattuck, *Proust's Way*, p. 86.
33 Wilson, *Axel's Castle*, p. 54.
34 See Proust, *Time Regained*, p. 215: 'I tried next to draw from my memory other "snapshots", those in particular which it had taken in Venice, but the mere word "snapshot" made Venice seem to me as boring as an exhibition of photographs.' See also Gilles Deleuze, *Proust and Signs*, trans. Richard Howard (London: Penguin, 1973), p. 56.

35 Roland Barthes, *Camera Lucida: Reflections on Photography*, trans. Richard Howard (London: Vintage, 2000), p. 82.
36 Derrida quoted in Johnson, 'The Frame of Reference: Poe, Lacan, Derrida', p. 93.
37 Frank Shovlin, 'Four Ducks', in *The John McGahern Yearbook*, vol. 4, ed. John Kenny (NUI Galway), 48–53.
38 Matthew Arnold, 'Dover Beach', in *Poems*, ed. Kenneth Allott and Miriam Allott (London and New York: Longman, 1979), p. 255.
39 Arnold, 'To Marguerite', in *Poems*, p. 130.
40 Roger Garfitt, 'Silent Traveller', *The New Review* 1, no. 11 (February 1975): 63–5, 64.
41 See Sampson, *Young John McGahern*, p. 50.
42 Patrick Kavanagh, 'Prelude', in *Collected Poems*, ed. Antoinette Quinn (London: Penguin, 2005), p. 208.
43 Kavanagh, 'Prelude', p. 209.
44 Victor Sage, 'McGahern's Inverted Uncanny', in *Territoires de L'Étrange Dans La Littérature Irlandaise Au XXe Siècle*, ed. Gaid Girard (Rennes: Presses Universitaires de Rennes, 2009), pp. 195–206, 199.
45 See Robert Young, *Untying the Text* (London: Routledge & Kegan Paul, 1981).
46 Peter Brooks, 'Freud's Masterplot', in *Psychoanalytic Criticism: A Reader*, ed. Sue Vice (Cambridge: Polity, 1996), pp. 30–40, 32–5.
47 Juliet Mitchell, 'Femininity, Narrative and Psychoanalysis', in *Modern Criticism and Theory: A Reader*, ed. David Lodge (Harlow: Longman, 1988), pp. 425–30, 429.
48 Michael Riffaterre quoted in Graham Allen, *Intertextuality* (London and New York: Routledge, 2000), p. 121.
49 John Frow, 'Intertextuality and Orality', in *Intertextuality: Theories and Practices*, ed. Michael Worton and Judith Still (Manchester: Manchester University Press, 1990), pp. 45–55, 45.
50 Jonathan Raban, 'Exiles: New Fiction', *Encounter* XLV, no. 6 (June 1975): 77–9.
51 James Joyce, *Ulysses*, ed. Jeri Johnson (Oxford: Oxford World's Classics, 2008), p. 35. Subsequent references to this edition will be made within the text.
52 Bowie, *Proust Among the Stars*, p. 66.
53 Emer Nolan, *James Joyce and Nationalism* (London: Routledge, 1995), p. 71.
54 Roland Barthes, 'Theory of the Text', in *Untying the Text: A Post-Structuralist Reader*, ed. Robert Young (London and Boston: Routledge and Kegan Paul, 1981), pp. 31–47, 44.
55 Barthes, 'Theory of the Text', p. 44.

5

'Low' Modernism: *The Pornographer*

Pornography and modernism

> *I say deliberately that it is the most infamously obscene book in ancient or modern literature. The obscenity of Rabelais is innocent compared with its leprous and scabrous horrors. All the secret sewers of vice are canalized in its flood of unimaginable thoughts, images and pornographic words. And its unclean lunacies are larded with appalling and revolting blasphemies directed against the Christian religion and against the name of Christ.*[1]
>
> James Douglas on *Ulysses* (*Sunday Express*)

Why, in his fourth novel, did McGahern write pornography? The most obvious reason relates to the prior banning of *The Dark* by the Irish Censorship of Publications and Film Board. Society had deemed him to be an obscene writer. In *The Pornographer*, he willingly took that classification to its logical extreme. By opening *The Dark* with the spelling out of a 'profane and ugly word' (*D* 7), McGahern had already shown that he was answering a censorship mentality. But having a teenager masturbate into a sock in *The Dark* was rather too hole-in-the-corner. In *The Pornographer*, vice is given its bold unapologetic play on the canvas, and degenerate proclivities indulged to the full. As Eamon Maher has written, the title itself was a provocation to the Censorship Board: this is what a real 'dirty book' would look like.[2] To write as a pornographer can thus be viewed as a parodic act of self-abjection, in which the artist performs to excess the proscribed role of outcast, pervert and criminal.

It may be argued, from a retrospective and psycho-biographical point of view, that the personal retaliation of the egoist-artist is also cathartic: this last of the first-person novels seemingly clears the way for the more impersonal, less existentially fraught style of McGahern's later work. However, viewing

The Pornographer as a stage in this authorial trajectory should not disguise or confine the broader meanings of the author's decision to write dirty. McGahern was following in a line of venerable proto-modernist and modernist pornographers. Works such as *Madame Bovary* (1857), *Salomé* (1891), *The Rainbow* (1915), *The Well of Loneliness* (1928), *Ulysses* (1933) and *Lady Chatterley's Lover* (1960), among others, were all put on trial for corrupting morality or for obscenity.[3] This chapter assesses how *The Pornographer* encodes within it this shadow-history of modernist 'lowness'.

In 'The Solitary Reader' McGahern records discussions he had with friends which centred on the idea that 'even an obscene book ... could not be immoral if truly written'. This is very close to what Flaubert said to Sand: 'for the moment a thing is True, it is good. Even obscene books are immoral only if they lack truth' (*LW* 91, 204).[4] *Madame Bovary* had been put on trial for posing an offence to morals and religion. McGahern had a Flaubertian sense of the 'truth' of obscenity, but also a prior model of cunningly strategic engagement with the censor: *Madame Bovary* was found not guilty. The famous scene in which Emma rides around Rouen in a locked carriage with Léon had been censored by the editors of the *La Revue de Paris*, but at the trial the defence lawyer was happy to read it out in its entirety precisely because the sex, though unarguably present, was not explicit.[5]

By necessarily keeping art and morality separate, the artist may risk incrimination. Wilde's pronouncements, such as those from the Preface to *The Picture of Dorian Gray*, follow Flaubert: 'There is no such thing as a moral or immoral book. Books are well written or badly written. That is all'; 'Vice and virtue are to the artist materials for an art'.[6] Modern literature could be 'about' anything at all: an ideal nothing, in Flaubert's case, or art itself (but not life), in Wilde's. The interdependence of truth and obscenity lies behind the proximity of canonical modernism and the accusation of pornography. The modernist text, often regarded as too linguistically rebarbative or aesthetically rarefied, found itself on trial for being too materialist, too 'cloacal', too pornographic.[7]

The trial and appeal trial of *Ulysses* centred on whether it had aphrodisiac qualities. Judge Woolsey's statement included a number of 'well-intentioned lies' about *Ulysses* (in Leslie Fiedler's phrase), stemming from the mistaken belief that literature and pornography are mutually exclusive categories. Immersed in the scholarly work of Joycean critics, like that of Stuart Gilbert, which were founded on the principle that Joyce was a 'real artist', Woolsey argued that the author's non-pornographical intention could be established. Here Woolsey was following a self-proving, tautological argument: literary criticism helped him discover the artistic intention which would automatically discount lascivious intent, or 'the leer of the sensualist'. Although he had steeped himself in the text and its critical satellites, Woolsey considered the book's impact on the *homme moyen sensuel* decisive. He was on thinnest ice when declaring that *Ulysses* was '*nowhere* aphrodisiac'. The close-run repeal trial of 1934 would reformulate the grounds for the lifting of the ban by conceding that parts of the book were indeed obscene and libidinous. Joyce himself had described 'Penelope' as more 'obscene' than previous chapters, and had said that 'there is less than 10 per cent of *that* in my book', according to Sylvia Beach.[8] The repeal trial judges decided, *pace* Woolsey, that *Ulysses* was *somewhere* aphrodisiac, but that the book as a whole was not pornographic: while in 'not a few spots' it was 'coarse, blasphemous and obscene', it did not 'tend to promote lust'.[9]

In the foreword to *Women in Love* (1920), Lawrence wrote that he had been 'accused, in England, of uncleanness and pornography'.[10] In the late essay, 'Pornography and Obscenity', he defended this charge by declaring that 'pornography is the attempt to insult sex, to do dirt on it'.[11] He draws a comparison between masturbation and what he thought of as much sentimental and over-analytical contemporary literature, in which 'there is no real object, there is only subject'. In what seems to be a not-so-veiled attack on the fetishistically private and monumental elaborations of selfhood which, to some critics, defined modernism, Lawrence alluded to a type of authorship that was 'productive' but null: 'The author never escapes from himself, he pads along within the vicious circle of himself. … Hence the lack of creation, and the stupendous amount of production. It is a masturbation result, within the vicious circle of the self. It is self-absorption made public'.[12] 'Pornography and Obscenity' was intended to stake out the ground for the writing of sex as spiritual, to write it as a separate field of experience. Thus, in the words of one critic, *Lady Chatterley's Lover* 'is indubitably about sex but is also indubitably moral'.[13] This underlines the difference from the Flaubertian-Wildean separation of art and morality, and also explains why Lawrence distinguished himself from the sexually materialist Joyce, describing Molly's monologue as 'the dirtiest, most indecent, obscene thing ever written'.[14]

It can be seen, then, that McGahern's decision to narrate as a pornographer came laden with a prominent literary history that neither he nor his readers could ignore. In constructing this parodic, second-order model role of pornography, McGahern both literalizes the charge against himself as a dirty writer, and engages in a much broader debate about the relationship between what is true and what is obscene in art. This is filtered through an implicit dialogue with much of the modernist writing in which he had immersed himself. In interviews, McGahern explained that, in writing as a pornographer, he was using an old theory or literary trick – that of writing about something by directly addressing its opposite. To try and approach the mystery of human sexuality, which he compared to looking at the sun, he must trace its patterns in the dust. Pornography was the mechanical backdrop, the lifeless counterpart to unrepresentable human vulnerability.[15]

Critics have disagreed about the importance of the narrator's trade. It is true, as David Malcolm says, that there is not a great deal of pornographic writing in the novel – even less, we might say, than Joyce's ten per cent of *that*. Though conceding that pornography is a motif which develops the novel's broader concerns with love and sex, Malcolm is quite dismissive about the 'straightforward' or 'crude' analogy between art and pornography, and claims that almost 'any dull, repetitive, unsatisfying urban employment would have a similar function'.[16] To Michael Toolan, who had admired *The Leavetaking*, McGahern's decision to assume the role of pornographer was an unjustified and degrading strategy which echoed the narrator's own 'deadness of heart', and represented a 'wilful perversion of [McGahern's] fictional gifts'.[17]

These sorts of readings are at odds with Denis Sampson's view of the self-generating, implicitly metafictive role of the pornographer's transformation from the '*artist manqué* … into the narrator of the novel'.[18] Dermot McCarthy notices the easily overlooked confirmation that the narrator, who had been an English teacher and has 'a priest's face' (*P* 214), lets slip that he is a would-be writer: of Maloney, he says that 'he, *too*, had ambitions of being a poet once' (*P* 25, my italics).[19] To McCarthy, pornography is a quasi-allegorical metaphor for 'bad writing' which enables McGahern to ask questions about the relationship of his life to his art, but by using 'a masking device to temper the serious self-referential dimension of the novel'.[20] Pornography violates the sacred creative process by which memory becomes imagination: it distorts, makes unreal and commodifies the truth of memory.[21] This view lends particular importance to the narrator's transformation of his experiences with Josephine on the Shannon into commercial, pornographic 'art', emphasizing the extremity of the poet's fall. The aesthetic aspirations of the novel are obversely related to the narrator's grubby hack-work, and we see that, characteristically for McGahern, and despite the reactive provocation of the title, those aspirations have been embedded rather than flaunted. The 'lowness' of the writing is a mark of its own secretively allusive, subterranean practices. In order to fathom the metafictional potential of the novel, the reader is required to translate its lowness into highness. This is profitably achieved by tracing how in *The Pornographer* McGahern cunningly invites intertextual comparisons with modernist writing, often a site of contestation between the high and low.

Art and nature: Wilde and Yeats

McGahern's vaguely expressed 'old theory' of writing about something by using its opposite has a good deal in common with late nineteenth-century decadent aesthetics. Matthew Arnold had argued that the aim of criticism was to see the object as it was. Following Walter Pater's modification, Oscar Wilde declared that rather the aim was 'to see the object as in itself it really is *not*'.[22] What predominantly characterized such resistance to mimetic naturalism was a resistance to nature itself, and an insistence upon cleaving art and life apart. In J-K Huysmans's *A Rebours* (literally 'Backwards', but sometimes translated as *Against Nature*) the aesthete des Esseintes claims that 'nature has had her day'.[23] Wilde's defence of telling beautiful untruths forms part of his attack upon 'that dreadful universal thing called human nature', and upon the burdensome facts of life: 'All bad art comes from returning to Life and Nature'.[24] For Wilde, art must be sterile – a 'trick played on nature, an *illicit* creation by man'.[25] This informs Yeats's notion that only in an eternal Byzantium, only when 'out of nature', can experience be safely sealed off from tyrannical teeming of the organic.

The Pornographer explores this idea of being 'against nature'. The novel most obviously alternates between sex and death – the sex of the narrator and the death of the aunt – but lurking under this schema is a more oblique tension between art and nature. Pornography, standing in for art, is the negative image, what life is *not*: it is the object which flouts the mimetically representational principle. The pornographic excerpts may themselves be limited, but McGahern assigns an important role to the dandified Maloney, a failed poet who lost in love and now commissions pornographic work from the narrator. The novel has plenty of room for the aesthetic theories of the Pornographer-in-Chief, who utters quotable or quoted epigrams on the inviolable boundaries between art and life: in a phrase of Goethe's taken up by Wilde, Yeats and Picasso, Maloney states that 'art was art because it was not nature' (*P* 27), that the 'imagination requires distance' (*P* 21), that one 'of the reasons for art's supremacy is just because of the very limitations of life' (*P* 25).[26]

Maloney is first presented adopting a tweedy 'English-country' look, with bow tie and oxblood boots, 'old-boy-ing' the narrator in an unsuccessful English accent: like Wilde, the Irishman playing at being the Englishman. He berates the narrator not for the immorality of his conduct but for behaving stupidly (244), recalling Wilde's 'There is no sin except stupidity'.[27] He advises the narrator on the art of lying – every good lie must be flavoured with a little truth, he says, as whiskey with water (*P* 71) – recalling Wilde's lament for the stigmatization of the beautiful lie in 'The Decay of Lying'. Wilde's aphoristic eloquence and his spirit of *épater les bourgeois* are arrogated to Maloney. Pornography is the art of hyperbole: the avoidance of the prosaically mimetic dimensions of verisimilitude can also be traced to Wilde, who wrote that 'art itself is really a form of exaggeration; and selection, which is the very spirit of art, is nothing more than an intensified mode of over-emphasis'.[28] It has been observed that Wilde's art is often parentless, as if it needs to establish its freedom from the human laws of biological determinism. Viewed like this, the pornographer's creation of an artificial but familiar world with its own laws seems connected to his own parentless state. He says that their death or 'vamoosing' was not 'playing the game' (*P* 68) – so he plays his own. Finally, Wilde the artificer is neighbour to the figure of the incriminated artist, in Richard Ellmann's term: the Wilde of *Salomé*, the incarcerated *poète maudit*, or the Wilde fascinated, for instance, by the poisoner Wainewright. To take vice and virtue as the soiled materials for art is, for McGahern, a Wildean manoeuvre.

Frank Shovlin persuasively argues that Maloney, a failed poet, is an avatar of Yeats. Like Wilde, art for Yeats 'brings us near to the archetypal ideas themselves, and away from nature, which is but the looking-glass'.[29] As Shovlin points out, Maloney's comment that his readers escape into the world of pornographic artifice so that they can get 'someone else to do their living and their dying for them' originates from the French symbolist Villiers de L'Isle-Adam, who wrote 'As for living, our servants will do for that'. Yeats used this as an epigraph for *The Secret Rose*.[30] Maloney tried to make good the emotional failure of his life's experience through art, which he terms 'a vision of the law' (*P* 27), but that art was risible poetry. He insists that life, with its accidents and infirmities, must not be let into the pornographic work. Art dwells in the realm of beautiful, untrue things; pornography the realm of mechanical, untrue things. To Maloney, the boat of life is all too likely to spring a leak (*P* 124), but that of pornographic art must be well caulked; elsewhere, the pornographic protagonist is likened to a deep sea diver, moving in a world which is elementally other. Maloney's desire to create a world free of bodily decrepitude has a particular Yeatsian resonance. That the aesthetics of Wilde and Yeats are voiced by a pornographer prompts a disquieting – or what Shovlin calls puzzling – inference in the reader: that the writing of pornography, which the Leavisite instinct would regard as against literature because against life, is in some ways analogous to the creation of the artwork, rather than oppositional to it. What is true for art often seems true for pornography: the charmed circle of art and the bad magic of pornography are both forms of unreality which stand against dreary old life. Why, after all, are art and pornography both so popular?

There may be a tendency, given the later phase of his career, to associate McGahern with the perhaps uncritical presentation of transcendent nature. It is not surprising that weighty significance has been given in *The Pornographer* to how the lovemaking with Nurse Brady, during which the 'sweet fragrance of the new hay' (*P* 175) suffuses the hospital gardens, offers the potential redemption of countryside and nature. Fintan O'Toole has remarked upon the transition in Irish literature from mythologized natural sexuality (in O'Flaherty and Austin Clarke) through the 'nightmarish and surreal miscegenation' of Patrick Kavanagh's *The Great Hunger*, to works like *The Pornographer*, in which 'nature is, like the sex of the narrator's books, distanced, formalized and packaged for consumption'. Pornography is a metonym of the Anglo-American consumerism which has insinuated itself into traditional Irish culture.[31] Elsewhere, O'Toole also comments on how the Shannon houseboat, with all its mod-cons, presents a mediated view of Irish nature as package-holiday destination. Though this argument acknowledges a subtly mediated conception of Irish pastoral, McGahern's novel is figured as relying on the old mistrust of urban *anomie*, so that the country remains 'the real psychic battleground' where 'the great themes of sex and death' are explored.[32]

Such an account still accommodates those accounts of the novel which seem confident that the narrator will return to his native home and make a healthy new life in the countryside, with or without the nurturing nurse. The citified pariah is ready for moral regeneration, or in Whyte's words, 'a return to, and renewed appreciation for, the rural community, its manners and rituals'.[33] In this view, the country is eventually accepted by the narrator as a place where the pretence of social ceremony, which represents man's attempt to 'master the darkness', is framed as a type of necessary 'kindness' (*P* 239), a riposte to the existential isolation of the individual in the city. The violently cathartic 'cleansing' of the narrator in London allows the bourgeois fantasist Josephine, symbolic of modernized Ireland, to be replaced by the 'natural' nurse.

This would seem to privilege the victory of nature over art-as-artifice. Josephine, with her occasionally transatlantic twang, does indeed seem to import the values of an Americanized or consumerist Ireland. Like pornography, she is fake or ersatz and must be left behind. However, Josephine is also equated with nature at its most tyrannical. Pornography is 'horrible stuff ... twisted and *unnatural*': 'There's so many other decent *natural* things you could do' (*P* 96, my italics). 'Nature' is never more culturally authoritarian than when being wielded as a blunt ideological instrument. She is not a sexual consumer – she detests unnatural pornography – but rather a thirty-eight-year who was recently a virgin: she thus stands for the naïve privileging of the same nature she is packaging. The younger, non-virginal Nurse Brady is a good deal more worldly and accepting of the mechanics of bodily acts, we may imagine. Josephine's abuse or strategic use of the idea of nature confirms the narrator's knowledge that there is nothing innately 'decent' about fecund nature. Her aversion to prophylactics suggests that she is against what is against nature. Josephine is aligned with an old-fashioned, conventional, state-sponsored natural life, and her necessary disappearance from the novel clears the way for the abandonment of 'bad' nature.

The idea of victorious neo-pastoral benevolence should thus be treated cautiously. Josephine's role helps us understand why the narrator, brought up in the country, is estranged from nature in the first place, and how his practice of pornography is, like the decadents or the modernists, explicably 'against nature'. The pornographic writing itself is co-opted to make the point. We read the episode on the Shannon houseboat, where the conception took place in reality, both as 'straight' and pornographic narrative. The repetition of the natural scene as pornographic artifice mockingly justifies the prophylactic sealing-off of art from the rank fecundity of life. The narrator describes the real scene in terms of the unreal: on the river, he comments that there 'had been so many interpretations of beauty as such an evening and scene that it had grown abstract and unreal' (*P* 89).[34] Again, this reflects a Wildean insistence on life imitating art: his idea, for example, that we appreciate a natural phenomenon like a sunset because its beauty has been created in art.

There is no guarantee that the narrator's return to the country will lead to revitalization or renewal, only that there will be another turn of the wheel. The return to nature – nature-as-habitual-work, landscape as worked-over by man, what Maloney terms that 'caper' (*P* 250) – is far from unquestioning. It is quite possible to imagine a future in which the pornographer runs back to Dublin, unable to face milking another cow, or that the healthy nurse tires of the narrator's intellectualized introspection. This helps explain McGahern's risky decision to align Wildean and Yeatsian views of exalted artifice with basest pornography, ranging both against nature. There is no clear-cut Damascene moment when the pornographer decisively throws up his trade. We can only assume that this bad art is abandoned like the bad nature of Josephine. There remains a kind of fatalism, or at least lack of epiphanic transcendence, in the narrator's claim that it won't matter if he is turned down by the nurse, that 'life has to be lived afterwards' (*P* 251), though admittedly this may be an expression of bravado in front of Maloney. Sampson regards the Maloney influence to have waned in the second half of the novel: the implication is that he will be excised from the narrator's future life.[35] In contrast, Malcolm refers to the persistence of his 'dark raillery', and his 'astringent and derisory laughter'; McCarthy argues that though Maloney is initially presented as an inauthentic 'hollow man', he remains heroically ironic – a choric presence.[36] The Pornographer-in-Chief is still going strong at the end.

The novel ends with ourobouros-like figure of the road, conforming to the earlier contention that 'the road away became the road back' (*P* 203). The road is taking both pornographer-artists back to the city but the narrator plans to go back to the country. The road is narrative itself, both line and circle, taking us back to the very beginning of the novel. 'Going back' functions as part of a structural pattern. Urban *anomie* may have been disposed of but it is conceded that 'going back' also means 'going on'. The road 'doesn't answer', and the narrator acknowledges that the 'world won't stop' (*P* 251–2). The existential indifference of the world, rather than of the cynical subject, persists as a remainder which cannot be assimilated into a 'natural' narrative.

'How is that for low, laities and gentlenuns?': Joycean lowness

The pornographer is positioned as an avatar of the fallen Irish artist in the Joycean mould. Maloney imagines the narrator pushing a pram-shaped coffin around a Parisian park – a kind of parody of metropolitan avant-gardism between the wars – but wonders whether it is necessary for him 'to go into exile since [his] whole life and work is an embodiment of the idea of exile' (*P* 125). Maloney claims the altar boy-turned-pornographer has 'a priest's face' (*P* 214), just to remind us of the career he did not pursue, and recalling how, to Buck at least, Stephen the artist is the erstwhile seminarian: the 'fearful Jesuit', 'jejune jesuit' who has 'the cursed jesuit strain … injected the wrong way'.[37] The abjection of the narrator seems designed to place him in a distinctive but problematic relationship to his censored forbears, refusing to emulate their modernist 'highness', but nevertheless extrapolating their 'lowness'.[38]

Stephen's pronouncements on aesthetics, informed by Aristotle and Aquinas, claim a vocational highness for art which must of course exclude pornography. Stephen defines pornography as a type of 'improper' art which excites the 'kinetic' feeling of desire, the reflex nervous urge to possess. He contrasts this aesthetic impropriety with the stasis of Aristotelian tragic art: pity, for example, is a feeling which 'arrests the mind in the presence of whatsoever is grave and constant in human sufferings and unites it with the human sufferer'.[39] Art must be arresting but not excite a compromisingly dynamic interaction with society. This view accords with that of Wilde, that 'all art is quite useless' and that 'the moment an artist takes notice of what other people want, and tries to supply the demand, he ceases to be an artist'.[40] Art should not be put to uses. In contrast, the artist of *The Pornographer* is tasked with inflaming the Irish public, whetting and satisfying their appetites. This extreme pandering to public taste is like a grotesque version of an art hopelessly defined by its commercial and popular uses. The old slogan about an ideal temperance in Ireland – 'Ireland sober is Ireland free', a line which appears in *Ulysses* – is jokingly reworked by Maloney as 'Ireland wanking is Ireland free' (*P* 25).[41] Even if the new permissiveness of the 1960s is so absurdly exalted as servicing a social good, the very usefulness of pornography would condemn it as non-art.

This may seem to weaken the provocative analogy of pornography and literature. However, we must remember that Stephen, the hydrophobe who has not washed for a month, is also a dirty writer. Maud Ellmann has constructed a model of *Portrait* as a book of oozing, trickling and secretion, indifferent to the formal boundaries between writing, excrement and sexuality. One of the problems of literature is that its instrument is the dirtiness of language itself. Stephen's aesthetic 'difficulty' is 'to know whether words are being used according to literary tradition or according to the tradition of the marketplace'.[42] The example he chooses is the word *detain*, which the Dean of Studies misinterprets. As Ellmann has argued, literature must 'hold back' or detain language from common currency, as 'the miser hoards his money and the petulant infant withholds what Lacan calls his "gift of shit"'.[43] *Detain* was an antiquated term for constipation.[44] Language mired in the marketplace is sniffed at, whereas precious language is held within the authorial body. Eventually, though, even the anal author must expel writing: in Ellmann's words, the 'worst stench of all is that of writing'.[45] In addition, Stephen's early encounter with more broadly 'queer' language, like 'suck', 'smugging', 'foetus', is an encounter with obscenity.

The 'Shem the Penman' episode of *Finnegans Wake* revels in the pungency of textual 'issue'. Shem, the persona of the disgraced Irish writer, is above all 'low'. Shem is 'our low hero'; 'Shem was a sham and a low sham'; 'O! the lowness of him was beneath all up to that sunk to!'; 'Talk about lowness! Any dog's quantity of it visibly oozed out thickly from this dirty little blacking beetle…'; 'this disinterestingly low human type, this calumnious column of cloaxity'; 'such porterblack loweness, too base for printink'.[46] This gives us a way of imagining the pornographer holed up in a dark room, whose long velvet curtains shut the world out: a garret for the solipsistic writer, complete with Chianti bottle table lamp, fire in the grate, typewriter and ream of fresh paper. The narrator is content to hunker down in a self-made, claustral space: 'Always the room was still'; 'I reflected as I always did with some satisfaction after an absence that the poor light of day hardly ever got into this room' (*P* 20). It is a masculine space, something which Josephine accepts weakly, but which the nurse, the agent of emotional balance, practically resists by calling for cleanness and light (*P* 214). Shem's supposedly high art and the narrator's pornography are not easily distinguishable: Shem writes in the 'Haunted Inkbottle', 'amid the inspissated grime this glaucous den making believe to read his *usylessly unreadable Blue Book of Eccles, édition de ténèbres* … every splurge on the vellum he blundered over was an aisling vision more gorgeous than the one before t.i.t.s…' (my italics).[47] *Ulysses* (or, the unreadable book of Eccles Street with the blue Greek flag on its dust-jacket) is a low book where the gorgeous dream-vision has 't.i.t.s'.

Whereas McGahern's narrator mixes his blood on the pornographic vellum, Joyce's spilt ink is more cloacal. Although the colonel makes a reference to 'liking the dirt' (*P* 159), McGahern does not on the whole point up the Swiftian misanthropy, the idea of Ireland as Ould Sod, though the phrase occurs in the novel: 'auld sod' (*P* 102). This is a pun relished by Joyce and Beckett, whose relationship of faeces and history, of postcolonial 'writing in the shit', was brought out by David Lloyd.[48] McGahern's pornographer does, however, inherit the general lowness of the Irish modernist tradition, comically associating writing as a tenebrous, self-enclosing and debased art, like Shem's filthy squirtings of the 'squidself', as the blasphemous products of 'lowdown blackguardism'.[49]

The blasphemous ritual of Joycean writing informs the way in which pornography is enunciated in McGahern's novel. The narrator tells us that he goes over to the typewriter and starts 'to leaf through what [he] had written' (*P* 21). We read an account of an altar boy waiting in the sacristy before assisting in the mass. The narrator is, for this rare instant, an eloquent remembering subject, like that of *The Leavetaking*, and we momentarily entertain the idea that this beautifully textured memory – of the scarlet robe, the sacristy window, the covered chalice, the coughing congregation – *is* the prose the narrator has just typed out. And then, after the mediating comment 'Among what rank weeds are ceremonies remembered, are continued' (*P* 21), we read pornography. The main point is that for McGahern's narrator, writing remains ceremonial, even as it is pornographic. The serving up of the daily bread of pornography for an expectant congregation is a *continuation* of church ritual. The writer's lair, with its candles and drawn blinds, is a kind of murkily mystical place for the priest-like pornographer, and the 'mixing' of the author's blood with his writing (*P* 24) – to Maloney, 'blackpudding, pig's blood' (*P* 50) – suggests a type of Black Mass. McCarthy imaginatively extends the paralleling of sacred and profane communion: the typewriter is like a tabernacle, the untouched pages like 'unsanctified hosts'.[50] It may be added, however, that after modernism such parodic practice is itself second-hand, the parody of Buck's parody, in which 'blood and ouns' are demystified as 'corpuscles'. An inverted, pseudo-Joycean transubstantiation is effected, in which the narrator's sinful body (the 'dogsbody', the servant of the Pornographer-in-Chief and of the demanding market place) is mixed with, and artistically transformed into, that paradigm of sexual athleticism, the 'Godsbody' of that Platonic ideal: Colonel Grimshaw.

When Shem asks, 'How is that for low, laities and gentlenuns?' (177), he seems to be addressing the clericalist censorship mentality, rather like McGahern in writing *The Pornographer*. Joyce said of 'Oxen of the Sun', that gestating parody of English prose styles, 'How's that for high?' McGahern does not even allow his pornographer, book-crammed though his haunted inkbottle is, happy though he is to quote Pirandello and de Quincey, to confess to his completely hidden vocation as a poet. That is the dirty secret which dares not speak its name. The abjection is that of a banned writer without the creatively Bohemian subversiveness to go with such a status. Pornography is the production of writing for a marketplace which cannot be 'usylessly unreadable' but is read to be used, kinetically. The pornographer, more existentially alienated than cunningly self-exiled, lacks manifest modernist dissidence and his work lacks textual *différance*. It is interesting to connect two observations: first, how little commentators on the novel – including this one – discuss the pornographic writing itself; second, how dated the pornography is. A randy bald-headed old colonel and a woman named Mavis Carmichael are meant to inflame us. This neatly demonstrates that language which has not been detained, but serves the current needs of the ever-changeable consumer, loses interest to the literary critic.

In mixing his blood with his text, narcissistically turning himself on, the narrator may be commenting on the unachievability of impersonality in the artwork. Textual self-reflexivity is that kind of authorial onanism disapproved of by Lawrence. The narrator asks, 'Is my flush the flesh of others, are my words to be their worlds?' (*P* 24). In reference to the Johannine incarnation, McCarthy notes that though this question is serious, it is 'merely a parody of the kindling of the imagination'. The narrator misses the opportunity to fathom his writerly degeneration – a 'fall from the grace of words'.[51] Again, this re-enacts a prior fall from linguistic grace familiar from Joyce: Stephen walks in a lane among 'heaps of dead language'; Martha's 'I do not like that other world' in *Ulysses* suggests that the author may create the world of the text, but that it is made up of fugitive signifiers: Martha means to write 'word'.[52] The use of words makes literature into a series of dirty letters, like *Ulysses* itself (or, as *Finnegans Wake* puts it, a 'litter'). In the case of Bloom's 'other word', obscenity remains off the page. For all its dirtiness, language is not embodied or 'made flesh' but caught in a process of autonomous signification which the author cannot control.

In *The Pornographer*, the manifestation of excess is limited to the pornographic economy of functional hyperbole. By contrast, text in *Ulysses* is intrinsically and excessively sexy. Rachel Potter has developed the argument that Joycean language makes obscenity inseparable from art.[53] It is not that obscenity would be transformed into art by controlling and making it mythic, nor even that in commingling élite and mass culture, obscenity would be let in, given its textual space, as a sign of the book's inclusive democracy. Rather, as Potter argues, obscenity in *Ulysses* becomes increasingly inextricable from the surplus signification of language. One of Molly's favourite writers, Paul de Kock, is not in fact a pornographer, but he is made into a husbandly porn-sign: 'Poldy cock'.[54] The proliferation of language is its own object, so that the 'artifice' of language and style generates more obscenity.[55] McGahern refuses to write high, instead entering a mechanically artificial world in which excess is the predictably inflated. Rather than the polymorphous superabundance of Molly, *The Pornographer* peddles a denuded, disembodied excess which is unrelated to textuality. Memories of the narrator's occluded prior life remain off the page, as if it is 'that other world' and cannot be brought to life. On the whole, the 'cauterised' existential subject (the adjective is Malcolm's) writes text in the present to avoid giving lyrical expression to the traumatic memory of lost love, so that the crossed out years on his dead mother's calendar can be stopped from 'working on' him (*P* 201). The self-generating property of Joycean language – the dirty hoard of literature which must be detained – is replaced by a sense of obliteration, erasure, crossing-out, or of dealing with language as a currency in the market place.

After the modernist struggle with the censor, the artwork asserts that it must contain 'low' material, just as the artist must contain his anti-self. The opposite or other would not be puritanically excluded but rather brought within the text, indeed flamboyantly and riskily displayed. Although *The Pornographer* follows this Joycean paradigm, it also intimates an un-Joycean reverence for sex, attempting the impossible in *The Pornographer*: to write sex 'straight', indeed 'high'. Although this points to a dissociation from obscene Joycean textuality, it leads to another engagement with the language of modernist sex writing – that of Lawrence.

'A crown of life': Lawrence and 'high' sex

McGahern occasionally writes of sex gravely and mystically in *The Pornographer*. Sexuality may have to be comically traced in the dust, too blinding to be represented, but McGahern nevertheless compels himself to stare riskily at the sun. The sacramental sex is set beside the pornography in a version of Barthes's 'reality effect': the end-of-the-pier silliness of the confected sex implies the authenticity of 'real' sex. McGahern is trying to capture what makes up human sexuality, and his sex writing establishes that, for all the 'doing of the dirt' in its pornographic passages, the novel is concerned with the mystery and transcendence of sex. A lineage can be discerned not only with the supposed obscenity of censored low modernism but also with that ideological strand of modernism which, in its aversion to the consumerizing of sex, sacralizes it.

This is all the more surprising when the narrator's increasing contempt for the vexing Josephine is taken into account. The cynical outlook of the pornographer is carried over to his evaluation of the cattle market of the Metropole dance hall where he pursues 'the ideal greasy warm wetness of the human fork' (30). When Josephine insists on unprotected sex, he crudely thinks to himself 'if it's raw meat you want, raw meat you'll get' (*P* 57), and curiously compares the encounter to 'nights of old, bollock to bollock naked' (*P* 56). He uses what McCarthy calls 'moistly zoological' similes, such as comparing entering the woman as akin to 'any fish feeling the triumph of breasting the hard slimy top of the weir' (*P* 57).[56] Nevertheless, loveless sex is not always depicted in brutal, quasi-evolutionary terms, nor with the increasing 'fear and shame and dismay and revulsion' (*P* 102) he later feels. The fact that it is represented earlier as an uncheapened ideal, that there is an 'apparent shift in rhetorical register toward a pseudo-Lawrentian sexual mystique', is seen by McCarthy as symptomatic of the narrator's psycho-pathology: such writing is 'simply an excrescence of the morbid, predatory "excitement" aroused in the dancehall'.[57] As a psychological explanation of the narrator's behaviour, this is convincing, but it also prompts the reader to compare linguistic difference, and to wonder how the supposedly authentic and 'pseudo' may be distinguished.

The prose of the 'high' sex-writing has that paratactic, comma-laden quality sometimes characteristic of McGahern:

> To lie still in the moment, in the very heart of flesh, the place of beginning and end, to snatch it out of time, to move still in all stillness of flesh, to taste that trembling moment again, to hold it, to know it, *and* to let it go, the small bird that you held, its heart hammering in the cup of the hands, flown into the air. (*P* 57)

The more fully incantatory rhythms of Lawrence's sentences can be heard. Connie's orgasm is syntactically periodic: clauses come in waves and waves: 'it seemed she was like the sea'.[58] Although McGahern's narrator limits the unfurling sex-prose to a few paragraphs, there remains a suggestion of mimetic form.

Sex is described by the pornographer as the moment that 'is always the same and always new' (*P* 57), echoing Lawrence's sense that 'a man and woman are new to each other throughout a lifetime'.[59] More specifically, the representation of sex in the novel as stasis-within-motion – the 'instant of rest', the 'moment of pure rest' (*P* 39) when the man is inside the woman, the perfect equilibrium of lying 'still in all stillness of flesh', of being at rest in the moment and 'out of time' (*P* 57) – is broadly Lawrentian. Connie Chatterley is described as 'swaying to quiescence' as the lovers attain 'a perfect stillness, in which she lay, and he lay upon her', and reference is made to 'the infinite peace of the entry of his body into hers'.[60] In *The Rainbow*, when Will and Anna lie together soon after being married, they are 'beyond the touch of time or change':

> They were at the *very centre* of all the slow wheeling of space and the rapid agitation of life, deep, deep inside them all, at the centre where there is utter radiance, and eternal being, and the silence absorbed in praise: the steady core of all movements, the unawakened sleep of all wakefulness. They found themselves there, and they *lay still*, in each other's arms; for their moment they were *at the heart of eternity*, whilst time roared far off, forever far off, towards the rim. (my italics)[61]

In both writers, the motion of 'kinetic' sex is arrested in a moment of stillness which takes the lovers out of time and brings them to the core, the 'very heart of flesh' (McGahern) or the 'heart of eternity' (Lawrence). It is a 'still-point', like that of T. S. Eliot in 'Burnt Norton', where 'past and future are gathered' and where there is 'Neither movement from nor towards'. Eliot is also conceiving of love – love of God, but also physical love, we must imagine – as beyond the kinetic:

> Love is itself unmoving,
> Only the cause and end of movement,
> Timeless, and undesiring
> Except in the aspect of time
> Caught in the form of limitation
> Between being and un-being.[62]

McGahern not only rewrites low modernist sex, then, but also high modernist love.

The existential framework of *The Pornographer* may alternate between the sex (of the narrator) and death (of the aunt) as if working between opposites. However, this emphasis on the stillness of sex as 'the place of beginning and end' (*P* 57) suggests a less formulaic bringing together of sex and death, such as that imagined by Georges Bataille, in which eroticism opens the way to death. The dissolution of individual identity in sex and death is proof of the 'unknowable and incomprehensible *continuity* of existence' – a continuity that happens without us.[63] For the pornographer, sex brings about an association with his dead parents. As Bataille writes, 'reproduction demands the death of the parents who produced their young only to give fuller rein to the forces of annihilation'. What Bataille terms the 'the crest of the convulsion which gives us shape' is also, for the narrator, the 'shudder that makes us flesh' and 'the shudder that makes us meat' (*P* 30).[64] But the merging moments of death and of creation are described in less zoological terms, too. Josephine's early loss of her own parents underlines both the subjective isolation of both lovers and the strange transcendence of their union:

> We were man and we were woman. We were both the tree and the summer. There was no yearning toward nor falling away. We were one. It was as if we were, then, those four other people, now gone *out of time*, who had snatched the two of us into time. For a moment again we possessed their power and their glory anew, pushing out of mind all graveclothes. We had climbed to *the crown of life*, and this was all, all the world, and even as we surged towards it, it was

> already slipping further and further from one's grasp, and we were stranded again on our own bare lives. (my italics, *P* 42)

The liturgical and biblical allusiveness of the narrator's sex writing is conspicuous because it is in diametric opposition to his pornography. The Lord's Prayer is sounded, but perhaps more surprisingly there is a suggestive echo of the *Book of Revelation*, where the promise is made: 'Be thou faithful unto death, and I will give thee a crown of life' (2:10). Death – not just individual death but a kind of apocalyptic species-death, what St John calls the 'second death', and what is beyond that – is brought within sex, not framed as its opposite. The image of 'the tree and the summer' may be Edenic, but points as much to the 'tree of life' in *Revelation*, protected from the sinning Adam and Eve by a 'flaming sword which turned every way'. The non-virgin lovers may have already fallen but we have come full circle after Genesis: they are again 'new', *un*knowing and out of time. The allusion implicitly associates sex with the apocalyptic 'second death', beyond which the crown of life can be worn eternally. The 'power and glory' of these ill-matched lovers momentarily suggests the kingdom which is to come.[65]

It is significant, then, that Lawrence wrote about the *Book of Revelation* in the same late period that he asserted the life-force of sex in *Lady Chatterley*, a novel with its own apocalyptic sense of the 'tragic age'. A Nietzschean-influenced resistance to Christian ethics marks his analysis of the Gospel, and Lawrence is critical of St John's 'second-rate mind', but he also acknowledges in *Apocalypse* how its language must have permeated his own. For both Lawrence and McGahern, the mystical aspiration to write sex 'high' is manifested in the relation of sex to the universal cycle time of time or, to quote *Revelation*, in 'the Alpha and the Omega'. But the biblical register is liable to be comically debased in *The Pornographer*. Maloney, of course, is delighted to subvert sexual symbolism and to speak in the currency of the market place: he refers to inflamed readers getting 'a rise out of a green tree in Gethsemane' (*P* 51); and, most pertinently here, and in line with all the profane talk of 'blood' in the novel, himself quotes *Revelation*: 'don't imagine you've been washed in the blood of the lamb or any of those cathartic theories' (*P* 243).[66] The narrator's inward-looking, self-sacralizing language is always at risk of being dialogically undercut.

The descriptions of sex in equilibrium should not disguise how love is also presented as an asymmetrical relationship of power and abjection. The narrator of *The Pornographer* has been 'mutilated' by love (*P* 97) in an earlier relationship: love has been 'the loss of my own life in the other' (*P* 104). We take the prior annihilation of the narrator's love to be a supposed cause of his promiscuity, and the tenderness of the descriptions of sex is thus connected to the unsentimental pose he strikes in conversation. The mutilation is reversed in the pornographer's relationship with Josephine: 'The Other would now happily lose her life in me and I would live the nightmare. It would be worse than loss' (*P* 104). The loved will grow to hate the lover, and love will merely increase the measure of disproportion. We may remember the terms in which Ursula first conquers Skrebensky in *The Rainbow*: 'his soul was dissolved with agony and annihilation'; 'She had triumphed: he was not any more'; 'The nothingness was Skrebensky'; 'For he was dead'.[67] McGahern's figuring of love as 'liv[ing] our death' (*P* 97), as a fight which results in the submission of one lover to another, has something of a Lawrentian quality.

However, in Lawrence, the 'unity' of lovers depends on the maintaining of the 'pure duality of polarization', the mutual otherness of man and woman: Birkin refers to stars revolving around a common centre of gravity.[68] The separateness of the sexes is part of an ideal. For example, Lawrence hones in on the singularity of Connie's sexual experience as a woman: 'She was gone, she was not, and she was born: a woman'. This contrasts with the pornographer's sense that 'we were man and we were woman' (*P* 42), suggesting that the mystery is somehow androgynous, even though shared by two such incompatible lovers. The damaging difference between self and other is effaced in an instant of rest, but only fleetingly. In McGahern, the lovers may be briefly united in the sexual sacrament but sex cannot prevent their being 'stranded again on our own bare lives' (*P* 42). More generally, in *Lady Chatterley's Lover*, at least, Lawrence commits himself to presenting sex as a force for moral good. Whatever social conflict there is between Connie and Mellors is worked out through sex. There is an apostasizing moral quality in Lawrence, an assertion that sex can save, which the travestying style of McGahern's novel cannot accommodate.

The representation of solipsism or existentialist alienation in *The Pornographer* sits uncomfortably beside the rare but nevertheless awestruck renderings of sex. We must accept that the pornographer *can* write non-pornographic sex, too. The final upward trajectory, the return to nature and provisional redemption, makes it difficult to place the pornographer's earlier writing of 'high' sex. Psychologically, these passages can be read as the counterfeit or 'pseudo-mystical' justification of devalued sex, and thus as merely symptomatic of the narrator's malaise. However, his assumption of the sacramental language itself creates a tonal problem, an unexplained juxtaposition of cynical-pornographic and mystical-erotic registers.

'The virginity of the soul': Yeats

Mechanical, zoological and spiritual sexual discourses vie with each other in *The Pornographer*. We may finally turn to a last modernist, Yeats, to mediate between 'porterblack' lowness and sacramental highness. Yeats's role in the novel seems initially to emphasize the parodic analogy with unreal pornography, suggesting life-escaping Byzantine artifice, the place away from what teems or what dies. But McGahern's citation of Yeats becomes more complicated. Denis Sampson's sense that Josephine and Maloney can surprisingly be grouped together as similar antagonists to the narrator has a specifically Yeatsian dimension. Maloney claims of Josephine that 'like our friend Yeats she's more of a spiritualist' (*P* 165), and that she too believes in 'the survival of the virginity of the soul in spite of sexual intercourse' and in 'the continuing virginity of the individual' (*P* 165). After his single night of consummation with Maud Gonne, Yeats commented that 'the tragedy of sexual intercourse is the perpetual virginity of the soul'.[69] Maloney thinks the phrase 'shrewd' because it captures how having sex itself does not remove, indeed may even tragically exacerbate, a virginal, unworldly, idealist or spiritualist mentality. According to Maloney, the loss of Josephine's virginity has not led to her becoming a type of Moll Flanders (*P* 165). Maloney may be striking a scathing and worldly tone, but as debased mage, Yeats-surrogate, there is an element of one 'spiritualist's' admiration for another.

In regarding the quotation as 'foolish', the narrator seems to be dissociating himself from the Yeatsian influence. Before sleeping again with the nurse, he remarks that 'our virginity seems well restored in spite of that first night…' (*P* 215), implying the infinite renewability of the sex-instinct which is 'so strong it cancels memory' (*P* 57). The narrator's irritation seems to be with that emphasis, tragic or not, on the 'perpetual virginity of the *soul*'. Despite his entanglements, and the knowingness of his performance with the younger nurse, it is his forgetful, perpetually virginal body which is still restored to its anticipation of the sexual unknown. It is as if the narrator would want to rework Yeats's remark: 'The *comedy* of sexual intercourse is the perpetual virginity of the *body*'.

The novel's ostensible strategic positioning of Yeats as the 'spiritualist' should be adjusted, however. First, the quotation is not from Yeats's poetry: it is not 'art'. In his poetry, Yeats too speaks through the body, and indeed considers its perpetual, promiscuous purity. In the 'Crazy Jane' poems, for example, the decrepit woman emphasizes the undoing of an opposition which may insist on the fairness of body and the foulness of soul. Jane is a type of subversively truth-telling witch, like those in *Macbeth*, whose song of the body is also that of the soul: 'Fair and foul are near of kin, And fair needs foul'. The bishop needs to be reminded that 'Love has pitched his mansion in/ The place of excrement' – a version of Augustine's *inter faeces et urinam nascimur*.[70] The 'foul' is accepted, as in 'The Circus Animals' Desertion': sexual subversion is *incorporated* into romantic love. The experience of Jane's aged, withering body, continually passed over 'like a road', making no moan but singing on, speaks the truth of both grave and bed, one which is 'Learned in bodily lowness'. Jane punningly claims that the soul can only be whole, and death can only be understood, if the (holed) body has experienced love: 'For nothing can be sole or whole/That has not been rent'.[71]

The narrator's relationship with the nurse, which has taken place near his dying aunt, is presented in terms of mortality. The body of the nurse is not sexualized, but is seen rather in the vulnerable 'glory' of its living flesh:

> This body was the shelter of the self. Like all walls and shelters it would age and break and let the enemy in. But holding it now was like holding glory, and having held it once was to hold it – no matter how broken and conquered – in glory still, and with the more terrible tenderness. (*P* 177)

The narrator projects a future when the body will deteriorate, but idealistically insists that it has a kind of permanence, young *and* old, and that age will not disqualify it from 'glory'. In Yeats's 'Girl's Song', the speaker asks, 'Saw I an old man young/ Or young man old?'. Rather than valorize the nurse's youth, the pornographer reaches out to a perception of her as one who, like Yeats's 'withered crone', 'would as bravely show/ Did all the fabric fade'.[72] Sex can be represented as a unifying and vitalizing force, as standing for life, but without discounting that it is situated in the 'broken and conquered' place where we experience death.

The later, more obviously 'embodied' Yeats adds further nuance to high-low modernist intertextuality. In her analysis of the 'Crazy Jane' poems, Elizabeth Butler Cullingford writes that for Yeats, 'excrement is a route to the divine' and 'the low provides access to the high'.[73] Jane can turn the language of the spirit back in on itself: if in the Bishop's words '*All things remain in God*', this must include the 'obscene' body. Cullingford relates the poems to Yeats's role as senator in the post-Treaty Ireland, arguing that they represent a resistance to the sexually conservative mentality of a newly established clerical state. Like a proponent of the Censorship Bill, the Bishop, clutching an old book, *bans* and *banishes* Jack because the lovers lived 'like beast and beast'. As Cullingford reveals, Jane's orality, part of her messy libidinous energy, resists the Bishop's authoritarian textuality. Yeats, like Joyce, has a carnivalesque sense of the body as inverting and upsetting publicly enforced moral hierarchies. The 'heavenly mansion' of the spirit is dialogically inseparable from the 'foul sty' of the body.

In Yeats's 'The Choice', the 'heavenly mansion' is what must be surrendered in achieving 'perfection of the work': the cost, as the title of McGahern's second novel dimly implied, is 'raging in the dark'. Yeats's recycling of the phrase 'heavenly mansion' in 'Crazy Jane Talks with the Bishop' thus takes on added interest. Raging darkness is not only howling existential anguish but darkness as filth, foulness, 'a mound of refuse' (in 'The Circus Animals' Desertion'): what Cullingford calls the 'primacy of pollution over purity'.[74] In the latter poem, the writer is consigned to using the borrowed materials of the 'foul rag-and-bone shop of the heart', including the experience of his flesh. The Jane-like 'raving slut', is a seller. Pornography was originally defined as the selling of writing by 'harlots'. Whether purity is quite relegated like this may be debated, but the lowness of Yeatsian art, like that of Joyce, makes dark or obscene experience inseparable from, a ladder to, the blinding light of love and the artistic image of the 'pure mind'.[75]

In *The Pornographer*, the narrator is careful to note that, when lifted, the aunt's corpse – reduced to bird-like weight, 'a little heap of grey flesh' – leaves 'a brown stain in the centre of the snow-white undersheet' (*P* 238). In holding her racked body, it seems that the nephew is still holding 'glory'. Respect for the ceremony of death will be developed even further in McGahern's last novel, *That They May Face the Rising Sun*, where the wadding up of the rectum is not squeamishly passed over. When the broken human body has become a corpse, it is not then apotheosized in a hackneyed version of the purified, 'snow-white' soul, but is unapologetically shown to leave its material trace. McGahern does not cleanse the stain, and is not willing to sanitize the Yeatsian idea that 'excrement [is] a route to the divine'.

Conclusion

The sense of moral renewal at the end of *The Pornographer* combines with an emphasis on narrative regeneration. The narrator goes back to his beginning in the country, and the narrative goes back to *its* beginning, repeating the scenic 'fragment' of his uncle stepping off the train 'at the beginning of the journey – if beginning it ever had' (*P* 252). The next turn of the wheel, in terms of the narrator's experience in the country, will bring repetition but with a difference: he is without the aunt and presumably with the nurse. Sampson has remarked that for the reader 'the moral challenge [of *The Pornographer*] is a literary challenge', indeed that the subject of the novel is 'the relationship between writing and moral character'.[76] Both the pornographer and Maloney are surrogates of the author (or *poètes manqués*), but Maloney's art is behind while the narrator's lies in the future. In the Proustian terms that Sampson invokes, we reach a point at the end of experience when the 'poet-narrator', will now transform his experience into art with the 'double vision of recollection and symbolic shaping'.[77] Deleuze's view that readers of Proust must decipher the future-directed signs of the artist's apprenticeship, rather than simply immerse themselves in replenished experience of past time, may lead us to focus on the reform of the pornographer's as more of an aesthetically self-reflexive than a moral transformation.[78]

Where does this leave the rereading of the 'low' portions of the novel, and the implied engagement with the history of censored literature, including that of high modernism? The Flaubertian acceptance of the obscene – 'even obscene books are immoral only if they lack truth' – was a precursor to the modernist alliance of impersonal aesthetics and subversive corporeality. The Flaubertian-Joycean concept of an 'indifferent' artist, unworried about including truthful obscenity-within, may justify *The Pornographer*'s 'detaining' of the kinetic language of the market place – the hoarded gift of pornography. The novel is not just about the experience of alienation, suffering and potential recovery, the promise of a redemptive humanist vision, but also about the recurrence of writing. The scattering of literary allusions (to Yeats, Pirandello, Goethe, and de Quincey), and the narrator's copying down and carrying of a quotation as a 'scapular', does more than suggest a marginal dilettantism.[79] We wonder at the extent to which the poet-pornographer's den is really the book-lined study of the artist-in-waiting. Although the narrator's 'voluntary return' to nature may be reconciled with 'a belief in the transformative power of art', in Maher's words, there is an absence of any *direct* articulation of this authorial conversion to a different sort of ritualistic art, such as we would find in the ringing last pages of *Portrait* or *Le Temps Retrouvé*.[80]

A disappointed critic of *The Pornographer* conceded that he was 'not accusing McGahern himself of writing pornography'.[81] That is precisely what McGahern *did* in the novel. After modernism, the post-censorship writer includes the obscene, confuses purity and pollution, and allows the 'rank weeks' of pornography to remain with the symbolic image or mystical diction. Like the Crazy Jane who assimilates the Bishop's words, the dirty writer incorporates a world where '*All remains true*', including dirty words: those too 'are certain good' and not to be excised. It is not so much that the low experience is shaped into transcendent art, more that the low writing must be repeated with a difference. The 'moral reform' of the individual cannot be conclusive: there is still the 'writing ... on the wall', as Sampson observes (*P* 10).[82] If that writing is emptied of metaphysical or moral meaning, in a world in which the Word can no longer be made flesh, then it is still admissible to wonder how to go about distinguishing literature from contingent graffiti – from the Shem-like scrawling of the dirty body. Writing is always contaminated and compromised. Perhaps this is why the very last words of *The Pornographer* are not those of the art-seeking Proustian sign, or of Yeats's so-called masterful images. Rather, the call of the pornographer remains: Maloney's 'Yoo-hoo'. By leaving the silly words in, McGahern allows a colloquial remnant, a not quite joining-up of beginning and end, to persist. High art will always trail its low supplement. The intrinsically dialogic novel cannot abandon its improper and impious serio-comic form.

Notes

1 Douglas quoted in Paul Vanderham, *James Joyce and Censorship: The Trials of 'Ulysses'* (New York: New York University Press, 1998), p. 137.
2 Maher, *The Church and Its Spire*, p. 90.
3 See Adam Parkes, *Modernism and the Theater of Censorship* (Oxford: Oxford University Press, 1996), pp. 3–20.
4 See Sampson, *Young John McGahern*, p. 77.
5 See Valérie Bénéjam, 'The Elliptical Adultery of *Ulysses*: A Flaubertian Recipe for *Succés de Scandale*', in *James Joyce and the Nineteenth-Century French Novel*, ed. Finn Fordham and Rita Sakr (Amsterdam: Rodopi, 2011) p. 78.
6 Oscar Wilde, *The Picture of Dorian Gray* (Harmondsworth: Penguin, 1985), p. 21.
7 H. G. Wells referred to Joyce's 'cloacal obsession' in *Ulysses.*
8 Vanderham, *James Joyce and Censorship*, p. 126.
9 Ibid., p. 144.
10 D. H. Lawrence, *Women in Love*, ed. David Farmer, Lindeth Vasey and John Worthen (Cambridge: Cambridge University Press, 1987), p. 485.
11 D. H. Lawrence, *Pornography and Obscenity*, in *Late Essays and Articles*, ed. James T. Boulton (Cambridge: Cambridge University Press, 2004), pp. 233–53. The essay was published in *Criterion* in November 1929.
12 Lawrence, *Pornography and Obscenity*, p. 246.
13 Alastair Niven, *D.H. Lawrence: The Novels* (Cambridge: Cambridge University Press, 1978), p. 185.

14 Quoted in D. H. Lawrence, *Letters 1928-30*, vol. VII, ed. Keith Sagar and James T. Boulton (Cambridge: Cambridge University Press, 2002), p. 7.
15 McGahern commented as follows to James Whyte: 'In *The Pornographer* the old literary trick is used to trace the sun's shadow in the dust. Pornography is a backcloth to observe the bungling and the human, in its humility and sordidness and glory. The pornography is the mechanical backcloth, the opposite of all that makes up human sexuality' (Whyte, *History, Myth and Ritual in the Fiction of John McGahern*, p. 228). To Eamon Maher, he said: 'Basically, it was a very old theory I was working on: you can trace the progress of the sun better by examining the dust or the shade than by looking directly up into the sky. So the pornography was a kind of backdrop to see if the sexuality, in its vulnerability and its humanness, could be written about. My own feeling is that it probably can't' (Maher, *John McGahern: From the Local to the Universal*, p. 149).
16 Malcolm, *Understanding John McGahern*, p. 90.
17 Michael J. Toolan, 'The Historian and the Pornographer', *Canadian Journal of Irish Studies* 7, no. 2 (1981): 39–55.
18 Sampson, *Outstaring Nature's Eye*, p. 151.
19 McCarthy, *Art of Memory*, p. 190.
20 Ibid., pp. 191–2.
21 Ibid., p. 190.
22 Oscar Wilde, 'The Critic as Artist', in *The Artist as Critic: Critical Writings of Oscar Wilde*, ed. Richard Ellmann (London: Allen, 1970), p. 369.
23 Joris-Karl Huysmans, *Against Nature: A Rebours*, trans. Margaret Mauldon (Oxford: Oxford University Press, 1998), p. 20.
24 Wilde, 'The Decay of Lying', in *The Artist as Critic*, pp. 297, 319.
25 Richard Ellmann, 'The Critic as Artist as Wilde', in *Oscar Wilde: A Collection of Critical Essays*, ed. Jonathan Freedman (Upper Saddle River, NJ: Prentice Hall, 1995), p. 29.
26 See W. B. Yeats, *Autobiography* (New York: Collier Books, 1967), p. 184: '"Art is art because it is not nature," I kept repeating to myself.' Yeats is disturbed to find himself in agreement with a washerwoman and an elderly critic, both of whom dislike Ibsen's *A Doll's House* as much as him. Yeats objects to its lack of 'music and style' – in short, to its naturalism. See Yeats's essay 'At Stratford-on-Avon', *Essays and Introductions* (London: Macmillan, 1960), p. 101. See also Declan Kiberd, 'Oscar Wilde: The Resurgence of Lying', in *The Cambridge Companion to Oscar Wilde*, ed. Peter Raby (Cambridge: Cambridge University Press, 1997), p. 284; and Ellmann, 'The Critic as Artist as Wilde', p. xii.

Yeats's adherence to the art/nature opposition should not be thought of as immutable, however. In response to T. Sturge Moore's objection to the fourth stanza of 'Sailing to Byzantium' 'a goldsmith's bird is as much nature as a man's body' – he was prompted to write 'Byzantium'. See W. B. Yeats and T. Sturge Moore, *Correspondence 1901-37*, ed. Ursula Bridge (London: Routledge & Kegan Paul, 1953), pp. 162–4, 200.

27 Wilde, 'The Critic as Artist', p. 406.

28 Kiberd, 'Oscar Wilde: The Resurgence of Lying', p. 286.

29 Shovlin, 'The Ghost of W.B. Yeats', p. 43.

30 Ibid., p. 44.

31 Fintan O'Toole, 'Island of Saints and Silicon: Literature and Social Change in Contemporary Ireland', in *Cultural Contexts and Literary Idioms in Contemporary Irish Literature*, ed. Michael Kenneally (Gerrards Cross: Colin Smythe, 1988), pp. 33–4.

32 Fintan O'Toole, 'Going West: The Country Versus the City in Irish Writing', in *The Crane Bag* 9, no. 2, *Irish Ideologies* (1985): 114.

33 Whyte, *History, Myth and Ritual in the Fiction of John McGahern*, p. 219.

34 The pornographer goes on to say that there is 'nothing more tiring than so-called beauty' (*P* 161), which tones down the comparison of over-familiar beauty to 'stray vomit' in the early story 'Wheels' (*CE* 10).

35 Sampson, *Outstaring Nature's Eye*, p. 149.

36 Malcolm, *Understanding John McGahern*, pp. 89, 93; McCarthy, *Art of Memory*, pp. 188–93.

37 Joyce, *Ulysses*, pp. 3, 4, 8.

38 See, for example, *Critical Quarterly (Special Issue: 'Low Modernism')*, ed. Rachel Potter and David Trotter 46, no. 4 (Winter, 2004).

39 Joyce, *Portrait*, p. 172.

40 Wilde, Preface to *The Picture of Dorian Gray*; Oscar Wilde, *The Soul of Man and Prison Writings*, ed. Isobel Murray (Oxford: Oxford University Press, 1990), p. 270.

41 See Joyce, *Ulysses*, p. 298: the temperance slogan has been attributed to Robert A. Wilson (pseudonym Barney Maglone, 1820–75).

42 Joyce, *Portrait*, p. 157.

43 Maud Ellmann, 'Disremembering Dedalus: *A Portrait of the Artist as a Young Man*', in *A Portrait of the Artist as a Young Man*, ed. John Paul Riquelme (New York and London: Norton, 2007), p. 393.

44 Maud Ellmann, 'The Name and the Scar: Identity in the *Odyssey* and *A Portrait of the Artist as a Young Man*', in *A Portrait of the Artist as a Young Man: A Casebook*, ed. Mark A. Wollaeger (Oxford: Oxford University Press, 2003), p. 165.

45 Ellmann, 'Disremembering Dedalus', p. 392.

46 James Joyce, *Finnegans Wake*, ed. Seamus Deane (Harmondsworth: Penguin, 1992), pp. 170–87.

47 Joyce, *Finnegans Wake*, p. 179.

48 David Lloyd, 'Writing in the Shit: Beckett, Nationalism and the Colonial Subject', in *Anomalous States: Irish Writing and the Postcolonial Moment* (Dublin: Lilliput Press, 1993), pp. 41–58.
49 Joyce, *Finnegans Wake*, pp. 180, 186.
50 McCarthy, *Art of Memory*, p. 189.
51 Ibid., pp. 192, 190.
52 Joyce, *Portrait*, p. 193; *Ulysses*, p. 74.
53 Rachel Potter, '"Can my Daughter of Eighteen Read this Book"?: *Ulysses* and Obscenity', *Critical Quarterly* (Special Issue: 'Low Modernism') 46, no. 4 (Winter, 2004), ed. Rachel Potter and David Trotter, 22–37: 24.
54 Joyce, *Ulysses*, p. 504.
55 Potter, *Ulysses* and Obscenity, p. 35. There is a continuity here with the delimited language of *Finnegans Wake*, in which the archetypally primal scene of HCE's sexual crime in the park can punningly merge with and contaminate the Crimean War, say, or a Grimm fairy tale. Language has fallen into a post-Babelian 'chaosmos'.
56 McCarthy, *Art of Memory*, p. 186.
57 Ibid., p. 182.
58 D. H. Lawrence, *Lady Chatterley's Lover*, ed. Michael Squires (Harmondsworth: Penguin, 1994), p. 174.
59 Lawrence, 'A Propos of *Lady Chatterley's Lover*', in *Lady Chatterley's Lover*, p. 323.
60 D. H. Lawrence, *The First and Second Chatterley Novels* (Version 2), ed. Dieter Mehl and Christa Jansohn (Cambridge: Cambridge University Press, 1979), pp. 341, 329.
61 D. H. Lawrence, *The Rainbow*, ed. John Worthen (Hardmondsworth: Penguin, 1981), p. 185.
62 T. S. Eliot, 'Burnt Norton', in *Collected Poems 1909-1962* (London: Faber and Faber, 1986), pp. 191, 195.
63 Georges Bataille, *Eroticism*, trans. Mary Dalwood (Harmondsworth: Penguin, 2001), p. 24.
64 Bataille, *Eroticism*, p. 61.
65 The title of the early short story 'Coming into his Kingdom' is another example of McGahern's keenness to exploit the resonance of biblical or liturgical language.
66 See *Revelation* 7:14: 'These are they who have come out of the great tribulation; they have washed their robes and made them white in the blood of the Lamb.'
67 Lawrence, *The Rainbow*, pp. 368–9.
68 Lawrence, *Women in Love*, p. 201.
69 Quoted in Christopher Cahill, 'Second Puberty: The Later Years of W. B. Yeats Brought His Best Poetry, along with Personal Melodrama on an Epic Scale', *The Atlantic Monthly* (December 2003): 116–18.

70 Quoted in Bataille, *Eroticism*, p. 57.
71 Yeats, 'Crazy Jane Talks with the Bishop', in *Collected Poems*, pp. 294–5.
72 Yeats, 'Young Man's Song', in *Collected Poems*, p. 296.
73 Elizabeth Butler Cullingford, *Gender and History in Yeats's Love Poetry* (Cambridge: Cambridge University Press, 1993), p. 242.
74 Yeats, 'The Circus Animals' Desertion', in *Collected Poems*, p. 92; Cullingford, *Gender and History in Yeats's Love Poetry*, p. 286.
75 Yeats, 'The Circus Animals' Desertion', p. 392.
76 Sampson, *Outstaring Nature's Eye*, pp. 140, 141.
77 Ibid., p. 151.
78 Gilles Deleuze, *Proust and Signs*, trans. Richard Howard (London: Penguin, 1973).
79 Thomas Walker has discussed the context of this quotation from Thomas de Quincey: 'Everybody must feel that a man who hates any person hates that person the more for troubling him with expressions of love; or at least, it adds to hatred the sting of disgust' (*P* 137): *A Way of Seeing: Fifty Years of John McGahern in Print*, Conference at Queen's University, Belfast (15–16 March 2013).
80 Maher, *Church and Its Spire*, p. 94.
81 Toolan, 'The Historian and the Pornographer', p. 42.
82 Sampson, *Outstaring Nature's Eye*, pp. 140, 160.

6

Yeats, Nietzsche, Theatricality and Will in *Amongst Women*

Revenant modernism: 'Bogey' and 'boody'

Amongst Women does not indulge the archly self-debasing strategy of the novel that preceded it by over a decade, *The Pornographer*. A strain of formal deflation or disappointment still lingers, however, marked by the revenant presence of both Joycean and Yeatsian modernism. 'As he weakened, Moran became afraid of his daughters' (*AW* 1). Maria DiBattista perceives in the opening sentence of the novel both the male decline and prose rhythm with which 'The Sisters' begins: 'There was no hope for him this time: it was the third stroke'. McGahern may continue to appropriate the early Joycean naturalism of *Dubliners*, but this draws attention to how he refuses to follow that fictional method to its metamorphosis, somewhere within *Ulysses*, into the revolutionary poetics of Joycean high modernism. According to DiBattista, McGahern thus resurrects the 'bogey of realism', a term taken from Joyce's early essay on Ibsen.[1] It is said of the daughters' attempt to reinstate Monaghan Day that it 'revived nothing but a weak fanciful ghost' (*AW* 7). The same goes for the impersonal, austere representational mode of *Amongst Women*: in DiBattista's view, what may be identified as a scrupulously mean, Flaubertian-Joycean mode represents the deliberately archaic performance of a superseded form. Thematically, the novel tarries with 'weakening' and the cooling of revolutionary ardour; formally, it is conscious of its unheroic, belated style. As the ghost of early Joyce reappears, then, a later is implicitly exorcized.

McGahern invites more than one modernist ghost to the feast, however. Mona and Sheila, avidly listening to Rose's stories about living in Glasgow, are described as 'so poised on the edge of their own lives that they listened as if hearing about the living stream they were about to enter' (*AW* 80). Denis Sampson and Declan Kiberd have recognized the quotation from 'Easter 1916':

> Hearts with one purpose alone
> Through summer and winter seem
> Enchanted to a stone
> To trouble the living stream.[2]

The novel ratifies, as it were, the continuing allusive potential of this most canonical of poems. It is not accidental that Moran is described as turning 'stone-silent' whenever the war is mentioned (*AW* 4), or that when hungry for news about Luke, he stands 'like a stone' while reading his daughter's letter (*AW* 65). As Sampson has commented, Moran is like the stone which remains changeless 'in the midst of all'. On the approach of his death, the poem is echoed again: Moran 'had never realized when he was *in the midst* of confident life what an amazing glory he was part of' (*AW* 179, my italics). The language of Joycean realism is thus penetrated by a Yeatsian symbolism which, according to Sampson, intimates that 'the novel is a meditation, following that of Yeats, on the radical disjunction between heroic gestures on the public stage and the private arena of intimate relationships'.[3]

The immovability and immanence of the stone is implicitly contrasted with the minute-by-minute change of the life of Moran's children. As Elizabeth Cullingford has written, the stone of 'Easter 1916' is related to an ironic self-presentation in 'Men Improve with the Years', also written in 1916, in which the ageing or aged speaker is worn out among dreams, 'A weather-worn, marble triton/Among the streams'.[4] McGahern implicitly shows that Moran the Republican guerilla fighter – a soured idealist, a survivor rather than a martyr – has grown triton-like and old 'among the streams'. His growing old is also to be read somewhat ironically in the light of Yeats's reflections on his 'improvement'. The modernist symbol is not so easily reduced. The daughters, who have all moved away, either to Dublin or London, seem disturbingly stone-like in their dream of resurrecting a fallen patriarchal mythology: as Kiberd has argued, their desire to arrest the stream of time itself aspires to stony immutability.[5] The resurrection of Monaghan Day on which they are determined is presented in terms which recall that of the Rising: 'With distance it had become large, heroic, blood mystical, something from which the impossible could be snatched' (*AW* 2). Through their own Yeatsian 'excess of love', the daughters wish to reintroduce the disaffected Moran into his role as a father of the nation, providing those 'handrails to go down into the past' (*AW* 14) and lead him back to glory.[6] That they conveniently forget the fearfulness that the Monaghan ritual had once caused suggests the extent of their diasporic longing for home. The dispersed family is to be recompounded by revisiting a single but recurrent day – by 'snatching at the impossible', like the signatories who dream history into being.

Amongst Women is not reverential but rather self-reflexively conscious of how it inscribes the ideological fissuring and symbolic polyvalence of the canonical text. The novel exploits Yeatsian ambiguity in belatedly representing the future of the past, in the text and in history: the 'time to be' of 'Easter 1916'.[7] Another example of McGahern's undeceived interaction with Yeats in *Amongst Women* that has been noted is the allusion to 'A Prayer for My Daughter', which lies behind the description of the father's storm-threatened house of prayer as a 'frail defence against all that beat around it' (*AW* 90).[8] That Yeats's speaker sings his poem so expansively as 'prayer', as Coleridge does in 'Frost at Midnight', highlights the sometimes fearful instrument of prayer in the Moran household. Certain lines in Yeats's poem may be reread with a wry knowledge of what is to come – not for Yeats's daughter but for Moran's daughters. The suggestion that Great Meadow is akin to Yeats' 'dear perpetual place' prompts intertextual dissonance rather than comfort. Yeats's prayer is for an independent soul who has become 'self-delighting,/ Self-appeasing, self-affrighting', whose 'sweet will is Heaven's will', who can avoid being 'choked with hate'.[9] Moran's hopes manifest a more egoistic paternal will: the desperate dream of arresting individual autonomy so that the selfhood of the child can be subjugated to the locus of the 'larger self of family' (*AW* 12). The poisonous yew tree at the gate is a belated counterpart of the 'spreading laurel tree' in Yeats's poem. In addition, bearing in mind the trepidation with which Moran's sons-in-law are led across the threshold, we may reread with amusement Yeats's hope that his daughter may be brought by her bridegroom 'to a house/Where all's accustomed, ceremonious'.[10] It is worth remembering, however, the ideological tensions in a poem that Terry Eagleton uncompromisingly described as 'artistically admirable, politically revolting'.[11] The political unconscious of the poem has been read by Edward Larrissy as expressing how an 'idealised, desexualised, "feminine" mode' is needed to maintain the continuity of an aristocratic social order.[12] Perhaps, after all, the Yeatsian father – who writes, 'How but in custom and in ceremony/ Are innocence and beauty born?' – is not so far removed from Moran.[13] The unachievable idyll of a family home from which 'all hatred' is 'driven hence' is shared by both Yeats's speaker and Moran. With the mining of the allusion comes an encoded warning: not to regard McGahern's backward glance towards custom, ceremony and canon as uncritical or fetishistically nostalgic.

It is worth continuing to probe the trace of Yeats in the novel in relation to theatricality. Stanley van der Ziel has recently discussed how Moran may be regarded as a Shakespearean, Lear-like figure.[14] Great Meadow is indeed like a kingdom in which the weakening of the patriarch implicates the behaviour of daughters. Although the ascetic Moran may seem to fit a mode of grinding naturalism, he is peculiarly theatrical. When Sheila and Mona are studying, he tries to keep quiet, but instead tiptoes 'in an exaggerated parody of someone trying to enter unheard' (*AW* 77). Earlier he has pulled on gloves comically and groped about the room like a blind man (*AW* 3). He walks through a new house which is 'like an empty stage' (*AW* 151). While being kissed goodnight by Michael, Moran's aspect is 'one of invoking some higher power to help him fulfil his fatherly duty'. We are told that he 'could not have acted in any other way' (*AW* 89). There is a sense, then, in which Moran performs the role of the patriarch in the same way that Sartre's waiter acts as a waiter.[15]

Moran has been an actor in history, an agent of its transformative *agon*. It is no coincidence that we see him as if in a mask: covered with lime, his face has a 'theatrical paleness': he play-acts as 'the boody man' (*AW* 73). At one point, he is said to 'have emptied himself into blankness, aware only that he was still somehow present' (*AW* 91). Moran is, then, both player and ghost – in this sense, a Shakespearean father. But he is more directly a 'Cuchulainoid' figure from national epic, embroiled in oedipal conflict and reshaped into modern tragedy, as Kiberd has remarked.[16] Moran can be aligned in some ways with the Cuchulain of Yeats's *On Baile's Strand*, in which the hero is conceived as an overman whose killing of his own illegitimate son constitutes a Nietzschean act of sacrificial 'self-overcoming'. In the words of Michael Valdez Moses, Cuchulain's fate is 'to have been the instrument by which a peaceful, commercial, and proleptically "modern" and "bourgeois" Ireland come into existence'.[17] It seems Moran is symbolically sacrificed for similar reasons.

The Yeats of 'September 1913' dismisses the grubbiness of post-Parnellite, post-O'Leary Ireland as not having the dimensions for tragedy. The 'time to be' would prove him wrong, as Terence Brown notes: Romantic Ireland was not dead and gone. Nevertheless, that Moran's performance is both tragic and comic does not diminish its Yeatsian resonances. The first to die in the Easter Rising was an actor: the theatrical elements of the political event invite the equipoise of its tragicomic representation in 'Easter 1916'. The poem merges the Rising's vainglory and motley, its 'casual comedy', with the tragedy of its unchangeable and brute deaths.[18] Moran has outlived the romantic nationalism which was the high point of his life, but unlike the player Connolly he continues to tread the boards, his hauteur no longer suited to the modern 'painted scene'. Time renders the grumbling survivor a bogey or ghostly 'boody'. The mock-heroic and occasionally clownish qualities which McGahern confers upon Moran reflect Yeats's own ambivalence about the purity of tragedy and its adulteration.

Moran's theatrical disenchantment derives from a debasing of national mythology which Yeats calls mockery. Moran stands for (diminishing) action and resolution, in opposition to the counter-jumpers. When a retired neighbour watches him ploughing his field, Moran thinks sourly that he would love to see the machinery smash: 'That's all this country seems to be able to do – *gape*' (*AW* 162). At his wedding, he feels that everything 'seemed a kind of mockery. It was as if nothing at all had happened' (*AW* 45). This may be related to Moran's surrendering of his heroic individuality to a new devalued and compromised order. There is something Yeatsian in Moran's scorn. Both Moran and the speaker of the poem 'Nineteen Hundred and Nineteen' are embittered idealists: 'O what fine thought we had because we thought/ That the worst rogues and rascals had died out'. The speaker enjoins the reader ambivalently – 'Come let us mock'; 'Mock mockers after that' – capturing both Moran's unworldly piety and his aloof contemptuousness.[19] Moran continues that Yeatsian indignation for 'the sort now growing up', whose hearts and heads are 'unremembering' ('Under Ben Bulben').[20]

The estranged son Luke is not alone in thinking his father a 'lunatic': the neighbours refer to him as a 'bloody madman' (*AW* 41). In part, this 'madness' can be explained in terms of the tragic waning of his violent power. But for Michael, Moran becomes an increasingly pantomimic king: it is this caricatural deflation which enables him to find a rapprochement with his father, unlike Luke. The book ends among 'chatting and laughter' and 'slow frivolity' which significantly centres on the younger son's skittish behaviour (*AW* 184). Moran is no Major Robert Gregory, who reconciled in youthful death the opposite lives of action and contemplation, but rather a man of former action only, who is examined as he declines into old age.[21] Yeats lingered with the ageing Cuchulain, who in the legend dies young, to inspect the prolonged state of the post-tragic. In another late poem, 'Why Should Not Old Men Be Mad?' Yeats speaks of the impossibility of living with 'an unbroken happy mind', of having a 'finish worthy of the start'.[22] There is quiescent affirmativeness in Yeats's justification of madness. Moran's survival guarantees that his finish, unlike that of the rebels, can never be worthy of the start, and that his happiness too is broken. His final madness is serene, played out in uncharacteristic communion with nature, as Kiberd has pointed out.[23] It is doubtful, however, that the bewildered old man who 'never knew how hard it is to die' (*AW* 179) has 'improved' like Yeats's observant old man, who knows his own madness.

Nietzschean readings: Will

The Nietzschean influence on Yeats has been much discussed. Denis Donoghue, for example, describes a kinship between Nietzsche and Yeats which depends on, among other things, 'Nietzsche's terminology of power, the endorsement of will and conflict, his feeling for the theatrical principle, his sense of tragedy, contempt for the herd'.[24] Nietzsche was, for Yeats, 'that strong enchanter': though 'exaggerated and violent', Nietzsche had nonetheless helped him to build in his mind 'an imagination of the heroic life'.[25] What he perceived as a Nietzschean embrace of heroic violence appealed to Yeats's romantic nationalism in the early 1900s. In later poems which coincided with a rereading of Nietzsche in the mid-1930s, such as 'Lapis Lazuli' – with its 'gay' tragedians, Hamlet and Lear – we again see what is Nietzschean in Yeats: in Valdez Moses's words, the implication that 'the highest duty of the artist is to transform the violence and cruelty of human existence into an object worthy of aesthetic and philosophic contemplation'.[26] The tragic or Cuchulainoid qualities of Moran, such as those we see in *On Baile's Strand*, point to the applicability of Nietzschean epithets. But just as Moran is not purely tragic, and inherits an ambivalent heroic legacy from Yeats, so he is a figure who can be understood through Nietzsche in a similarly paradoxical way: the guerrilla fighter as mock tragedian, the enslaved master; the bourgeois-hating aristocrat whose piety is increasingly liable, as he weakens, to unmask a seething *ressentiment*. More broadly, *Amongst Women* repeatedly names will as a defining force, suggesting that this too can be profitably read through Nietzsche's writing.

The breaking of Moran's friendship with McQuaid is defined early in the novel as a contest of wills: McQuaid's 'growing irritation at Moran's compulsion to dominate, to have everything on his own terms or not at all, had hardened into a sudden decision to overturn the years and quit the house at once' (*AW* 21). McQuaid's feelings of sudden violence are reawakened, reminding us that though he was lieutenant to Moran's commander, he was the original executioner during the War of Independence. The problem of two separate wills coming together and uniting in their memories may be expressed in Nietzschean terms. In *On the Genealogy of Morality*, Nietzsche writes that

> the strong are as naturally inclined to strive to be apart as the weak are to strive to be together: when the former unite, this takes place only with a view to an aggressive collective action and collective satisfaction of their will to power, with much resistance from their individual consciences.[27]

What seems significant is that the threat of violence between competing wills emerges from an apparently consensual set of rehearsed agreements about Moran and McQuaid's former 'aggressive collective action and collective satisfaction'. They have certainly got their story straight through multiple retellings, their storied role in Irish history agreed upon, memorialized and ritualized. It is this which makes the rupture more shockingly irrevocable. Their agreement about the foundational historical moment in Irish history is dangerously monologic, leaving no room to accommodate differences about future national narratives that it brought about.

The Moran-McQuaid scene appears early in the novel, and appears to confirm that will, so defined, is represented in terms of an exclusively masculinist wrangling. Great Meadow is home to a dominant masculine will: that is why the eldest son, Luke, must never return home, and why Michael can only be accommodated to Moran because of his more feminized character. All that the children 'had ever been able to do in the face of violence was to bend to it' (*AW* 54). Although, like *The Dark*, the novel discloses the bullying dominance of the paterfamilias, it also goes beyond the idea of domination and victimhood to explore the enslavement of the will in more abstract ways which are not held in thrall to Moran – or indeed to any personal agency. What emerges in the novel is that McGahern is not restricted to an androcentric conception of will – and that this perhaps surprisingly remains Nietzschean, despite his more notorious comments ('Are you visiting women? Do not forget your whip': words put in the mouth of an old woman).[28] Nietzsche reconsiders the Hegelian dialectical apparatus of master and slave, showing that the will to power is 'always determined at the same time as it determines'.[29] The master is another type of slave, and his slave another type of master: Nietzsche elaborates upon this bondage. Moran's egoism may dominate others in his sphere, but he is equally acted upon by those supposedly 'inferior' others: the reactive force of the daughters, sons and wife is as great as Moran's active force. Nietzschean will to power is not, as is often misrepresented, the desire to gain power, which makes power an object of representation. Will to power is, in Deleuze's words, an '*affectivity*, a sensation, a sensibility'; in Nietzsche's, a '*pathos*'.[30] *Amongst Women* traces the interdependence of weakening and strengthening pathos among the Morans, the pulsions of determined and determinable will, as just such a 'sensibility of force' (*AW* 62), rather than as a hierarchical fixing of objectified power.

Will is seen as a force which defines every scene in the novel. The repetition of the word is no coincidence. 'The will is the important thing', says Moran, referring to the scattered family having the will to stay together (*AW* 137). He is by no means the only possessor of will. Impatient to meet Moran at the post office, Rose is 'able to will her longing into an unexamined haze' (*AW* 25), and much later at the post office the laughter of the women 'seemed to destroy at once an idea that Moran had tried to impose with ferocious will all his life' (*AW* 173). As Moran is dying, the women feel their unified power, 'that they could force their beloved to remain in life if only they could, together, turn his will around … will this life free of death' (*AW* 178). It is Moran's passive acceptance of impending death, a will to nothingness from someone we might expect to rage against the dying of the light, which strengthens the will of his daughters to keep him alive. Moran is eventually disenchanted by the understanding that although he 'had never in all his life bowed in anything to a mere Other', it is only those mere others – his wife and daughters – who can 'will him back to health again' (*AW* 178). As with Elizabeth Reegan and her deathbed priest, the end of life throws up with final insistence the problem of an otherness that cannot be willed away.

We may initially be tempted to interpret female behaviour as continuously abject, and to think of Moran's domineering will as overriding that of his submissive family. But the novel is of course about *male* weakening: how the will of others takes shape as Moran is challenged. During the original courtship, Rose cannot be passive: 'Painfully and in the open she had to make all the running' (*AW* 25). Rose's sister says of her marriage to Moran that 'nothing could stop her … she was determined on it' (*AW* 44). While in early marriage a domineering male will is conventionally imposed, will reacts in its protean way. Rose is 'inordinately careful' (*AW* 49), 'inordinately grateful' (*AW* 56): this immoderacy speaks of an equal and opposite *willingness* – a will-to-passivity. If a direct confrontation is avoided, it may be done so by what might be thought of as wilful strategies. Rose and the girls, although at times 'mastered' by Moran's aggression, are described as 'controlling together what they were mastered by' (*AW* 46). Rose is said to instinctively work 'behind the usual social frameworks … those established forms that can be used like weapons when they are mastered'

(*AW* 24). Armed with such weapons of 'subversive subservience', in Robert F. Garratt's phrase, Rose entraps herself within authority.[31] That is to say, Rose initially imposes her will on Moran, in order to be mastered, but also to control the mastering force. The enfeeblement of the self invites a complementary empowering of the other in a two-way Nietzschean process.

Commentators such as DiBattista and Antoinette Quinn have argued that the decline of the patriarch 'amongst women' allows for a new kind of empathetic 'female realism' in the novel, the culmination of the remarkable imaginative identification which McGahern achieved in his first novel, *The Barracks*.[32] *Amongst Women* appears to be shaped as a sequence of power struggles in which the transferral and assimilation of patriarchal authority from Moran to his daughters is traced – to the extent that they become 'honorary male daughters', in Quinn's words.[33] After his death, it is 'as if each of them in their different ways had become Daddy' (*AW* 183). We may share sympathy with Rose and an admiration for how she extricates herself from her predicament with such passive force. Kiberd credits the wisdom and warm humanity of Rose, who may even stand in as a surrogate for the artist.[34] But she may be viewed less sympathetically. She actively wins Moran but only in order that she can live as a creepily interpellated subject, in Althusserian terms, indistinguishably wilful and submissive. The reader may admire her resourcefulness, fortitude and intelligence, but cannot forget that her 'singleness of attention' (i.e. will) becomes 'so smooth as to be chilling' (*AW* 24). Quinn recognizes Rose's 'warmth and good humour' as 'angel of the house', but also that she uses her shrewdness to collude with and thus perpetuate patriarchy.[35] Rose's powerful, though abject, will supports the social system, abiding by and indeed promulgating its pieties.

The idea that the novel gradually discloses the transference of power from Moran to the women can perhaps be too schematically applied, and should be tempered by the broader philosophical idea – which we see expressed in Nietzsche and his reaction to Schopenhauer – that will is an omnipresent agent-less force which defines us all as humans. The children, no matter how 'frightened of life', how much they used to 'sink into a beseeching drabness, cower as close to being invisible' (*AW* 8), were always already wilful beings. Character, as a conventional realist category, is subordinated to will. The novel largely declines to individuate the separate psychologies of the daughters and sons. The daughters, in particular, become elusively interchangeable in the reader's memory, a group who, having been told by their father that praying together means staying together, also will together. We might argue that the racy Nell Morahan's homecoming, for example, is granted a greater degree of individual empathy than any directed towards the blessed women. This is a clearly deliberate strategy to keep the women at arm's length and to maintain their 'larger self' as a family group.

The archetypal or mythic figure of the patriarch can also be understood as a site of will. Who is Moran but someone who is always expressing volition, willing to power or to nothingness? Likewise, who is Rose but someone who wills to a powerful passivity with the equally remorseless, 'inordinate' force that is called tact? In many realist novels, the self-determination of an individual protagonist may involve contests of will, defeats and victory, in some sort of teleological progress which takes him or her away from home. The Morans are drawn back to Great Meadow, a theatre the reader seldom leaves: the family romance excludes the outside. This dramaturgic type of unity allows McGahern to develop a scenic method in which the behaviour of his characters – the pulsions of their will, willingness, wilfulness – is observed almost as if in an objectively controlled environment.

Rose may be thought of as representing one form of resistance, but a more progressive expression of will is that of Sheila, who despoils the virginity of the house by making love with her husband in it during harvest-time, and who can accurately say of her father that he has 'the manners of a dog' (*AW* 158). Only momentarily perhaps, we see how one of the next generation of women can act in a more dynamic, taboo-breaking way, parading a defiance of Daddy, much to the disapproval even of Michael, and articulating some form of individuation within a newly formed and autonomous family not named Moran. The novel stops short of pursuing such a trajectory. Nevertheless, the realization that domination and dependency are complementary and reversible, and even more that dependency can eventually be triumphant, is consistent with the Nietzschean insight that will (*Wille*) and power (*Macht*) are not coterminous. This may be regarded, up to a point, as potentially progressive and emancipatory. The novel charts how the archetypal patriarchal owner of orthodox will-as-power is dispossessed of it. Will itself may be regarded as a degendered concept which is dramatized and inspected from a distance.

Nietzschean readings: Moran, aristocrat and slave

Recognizing the ranged, reactive forces of nihilism, Nietzsche articulates will as an affirmative, creative force, a will to power as well as to nothingness. Schopenhauerian will is too pessimistic in embracing the inside and projecting an essence of will on to the world as a whole, with the result that will becomes 'less and less bearable, less and less liveable'.[36] This tension lies behind the elaboration, in *On the Genealogy of Morals*, of the morality of master and slave. The disenchantment of Moran – the redirection of his will – seems to suggest a transformation from 'the hyperborean' master to the abject slave which is worth pursuing in greater detail.

A case can be presented for Moran's Zarathustrian spirit. The Morans perceive of themselves as 'unique and separate'; the daughters have inherited an 'unexamined notion of superiority' (*AW* 93); Moran is unwilling 'to deal with the outside' (*AW* 12). He is the head of what is described as an aristocratic family and was a commander to McQuaid's lieutenant. He feels that he and Michael 'could take over everything' (*AW* 108). Moran's isolation and sense of superiority are confirmed by his contempt for the herd of gombeen men and counter-jumpers: 'the crowd of small-minded gangsters' (*AW* 18), the 'bigwigs' in the professions (*AW* 88). This is Yeatsian and Nietzschean. His revolutionary, morality-creating spirit has been contaminated by the ascendancy of those modern slaves, the bean-counting bourgeois.

Moran is also Nietzschean in his resistance to neighbourliness. Zarathustra reverses the wisdom of the Gospels, exhorting the overman to love the most distant rather than the neighbour: 'Your love of your neighbour is your bad love of yourselves'.[37] In *The Gay Science*, again it is distance – though the curious salvation of distance – which is commended: 'I do not love my neighbour near,/ But wish he were high up and far./ How else could he become my star?'[38] It is thus suggestive that the only neighbour to whom Moran is polite (at least initially) is the Protestant Rodden – culturally, 'the most distant' (*AW* 88). Moran is said to 'identify more with this beleaguered class than his Catholic neighbours … he would always contrive to be in permanent opposition' (*AW* 163). Moran's haughtiness is presented in terms of caste. His tendency to refer to his boys as little 'gentlemen' may be sarcastically intended, but he also thinks of himself as taking tea 'like a lord' with his family (*AW* 46). Moran's fields are referred to as bordering a 'demesne' (*AW* 167): Quinn has considered how Great Meadow is a counterpart 'small house' to the tradition of the Big House: though 'not an ancestral seat [Great Meadow] becomes, under his regime, a family seat, more cut off from the life of the surrounding village than any Big House'.[39] Moran comes, then, to admire and share a kind of aristocratic separateness which provocatively shadows the decline of the Ascendancy.

In *Civilization and Its Discontents*, Freud writes of a rift between familial love and civilization which is initially expressed as a conflict between 'the family and the larger community to which the individual belongs'. Civilization, the greater community of society, demands the membership of the individual, but the family will not give that individual up willingly: 'The more closely the members of a family are attached to one another, the more often do they tend to cut themselves off from others, and the more difficult it is for them to enter into a wider circle of life'.[40] The diasporic Morans have not become integrated into this wider circle of society, and their growth as individuals has been stunted. Further to this, the Nietzschean devaluation of friendship, which shares something with that of Proust alluded to in *The Leavetaking*, is another mark of Moran's contempt for the herd. Zarathustra states that 'you should honour even the enemy in your friend. Can you go near to your friend without going over to him? In your friend you should possess your best enemy'.[41] The termination of the honoured friendship with McQuaid speaks of this inimical closeness. To McQuaid, Moran's otherness is his inability to get on in the secular world, his proud retreat into reclusiveness, his piety, his erstwhile seniority in the army – the values whose obverse Moran despises in McQuaid. The withdrawal of ceremonial friendship confirms Moran's sense of his own separateness and defines his 'permanent opposition' in broadly Nietzschean terms: 'in a way he had always despised friendship' (*AW* 22).

Moran may be construed as aristrocratic in these ways, but he is no less slave-like. Nietzsche writes of the man of *ressentiment* who separates the do-er from the deed, would hold birds of prey responsible for their action, and would thereby legitimize his own weakness – Christian passivity, such as turning the other cheek – as an accomplishment of a moral good. Nietzsche argues that, on the other hand, there is no being behind the deed: the doing is everything. The concluding question from Yeats's 'Among School Children', 'How can we know the dancer from the dance?', imagines a kind of union which is beyond the splitting of agency and deed.[42] To Nietzsche, the lightning cannot be separated from the flash, 'strength cannot be separated from the manifestation of strength'; a 'quantum of force is just such a quantum of drive, will, action, in fact it is nothing but this driving, willing and acting'.[43]

The retold history of colonial overthrow in *Amongst Women* can be related to this concept of the agent-less deed. A momentous historical deed is committed – an assassination – and McQuaid and Moran go through the motions of arguing who was more responsible for carrying it off. Both phases of the process, thinking it up, pulling the trigger, were necessary and mutual: there is no wish to atomize responsibility into the individual agency of driving, willing, acting. It is all one: strength in will and action. McQuaid and Moran have in their youth been 'blent', to use that Platonic Yeatsian word. In these terms, the agents of history seem to be Nietzschean, their revolutionary need for unchristian retaliation (against the retaliating Black and Tans) marking them out as appropriately radical, 'strong' in their willed overcoming of abnegation and self-denial. The later rupture between the two men suggests the post-revolutionary narrative fission of the deed, a need to separate and rank agency which is itself a sign of 'weakening' *ressentiment.*

Moran, enchanted to a stone, may have once represented a pure will to power, a serene and noble mastery, but though that idea has a certain appeal, it is not in the end convincing. In Nietzschean terms, Moran's clinging to Christian piety would be termed slave-like. In *The Gay Science*, Nietzsche writes: 'You will never pray again'.[44] Nothing could be further from Moran's almost comical vigilance about the proper conduct of prayer, as the extended family is all too aware. His son-in-law, Sean, ventures to say that some regard the apotheosizing of security as 'the death of life' (*AW* 158), a Nietzschean position which Moran cannot comprehend. He still lives in 'racial fear of the poorhouse or famine' (*AW* 68), drawing ever deeper into the defensive carapace of the 'larger self of family'. Rather than living as if building a city of on the foothills of a volcano (*The Gay Science*), Moran's retreat marks his state of bondage.[45]

Moran's most shockingly anti-Nietzschean, slave-like outburst is his remark to McQuaid that, 'It was better if it [i.e. the War of Independence] never had happened' (*AW* 18). The colonial context complicates the original Nietzschean distinction between master and slave morality. Devout Catholic nationalists like Moran have had to discard those Christian virtues, such as pity, patience and humility, in order to bring into being a 'properly' Christian country, in distinction from a secular, philistine overlord who proclaims that *its* citizens will 'never, never' be slaves. Significantly, Moran's individualistic piety takes its bristling form in spite of his suspicion of priests, and in spite of his contempt for those, like McQuaid, who might complain about those same 'druids' (*AW* 18). Moran cannot divorce himself from the bringing about of theocratic power and corrupt statism. In general, then, a tension is set up between his aristocratic will to power and his Christian *ressentiment.* The completeness of the initiating national deed (the 'snatching of the impossible': the Rising, the assassination of the vaguely symbolized 'colonel or general or whatever he was' (*AW* 16)) is split asunder by its consequences – to the extent that a revolutionary republican would wish himself un-free, again assuming a pious slave morality.

Rather than willing history to recur eternally, he is laden down with the weight of the future that he helped instigate. He has lost the noble man's sense of the aggressive creativity of values, and seeks to blame others and undo history, willing it to nothingness. Nietzsche's overman wills eternal return: '*Einmal ist keinmal*' (once is nothing and by implication everything; misery as well as joy is worth repeating). For Moran, however, once has become too much, more terrible than beautiful: history is excess, an event whose unintended consequence led to a supposed unheroic modernity that outweighed the originary heroic event. There is no sense of accepting history for what it is, of *Amor Fati*, or love of one's fate. Moran is the antithesis of 'the most world-affirming man' in *Beyond Good and Evil*, 'who wants to have it again as it was and is to all eternity, insatiably calling out *da capo* not only to himself but to the whole piece and play'.[46]

In this respect Moran deflates the affirmative Nietzscheanism of Yeats, evident for example in 'A Dialogue of Self and Soul':

I am content to live it all again,
And yet again...
I am content to follow to its source
Every event in action or in thought;
Measure the lot; forgive myself the lot!
When such as I cast out remorse
So great a sweetness flows into the breast
We must laugh and we must sing,
We are blest by everything,
Everything we look upon is blest.[47]

Moran is not content to live it all again. The meeting of friends on Monaghan Day represents the willed return of memorialized history and its wreckage – a return which confirms national self-determination. Such is his dissociation from the state, from his membership of the polity, that for Moran the meeting too must come to an end, not to be lived again. In Nietzschean terms, Moran the revolutionary, the 'aristocrat', was the creator of values, the destructive force for national good, but he has become slave-like in his nihilism, one who thinks that 'here nothing will grow or prosper any longer'.[48] Moran's nihilism leads to his confinement to his bedroom, just like the man of *ressentiment* who 'wants to be loved, fed, watered, caressed and put to sleep'.[49]

Moran's immoderate rages have been matched by his later moderation in other respects: he is careful with money, not greedy, and does not drink heavily. For Nietzsche, this is not praiseworthy, rather fitting the asceticism of slave morality, characterized by 'this fear of happiness and beauty, this longing to get away from appearance, change, becoming, death, wishing, longing itself' and which amounts to 'a will to nothingness, an aversion to life, a rebellion against the most fundamental presuppositions of life'.[50] The daughters fail to 'turn his will around' which suggests, as Nietzsche writes, that Moran's will, a constitutive and reactive force, is directed towards nullity. He has bequeathed this to Luke, who when informed that Moran is dying, says, 'I have nothing' (*AW* 177). Both father and eldest son are trapped in the defeated mentality of the Nietzschean slave who would prefer 'to will nothingness than not will'.[51]

The problem of form

There is a late scene in *Amongst Women*, in which two vying local politicians, having made themselves visible throughout Moran's funeral, fall back from the crowd 'in amiable conspiratorial camaraderie, sometimes turning their heads to look back to the crowd gathered about the grave in undisguised contempt' (*AW* 183). Joe Cleary criticizes this cameo as a 'dismissal of politics as mere gombeenism' which 'betrays [McGahern's] inability to integrate the political dimensions of Irish society' into his fiction: it is a 'comic sketch' which 'substitutes for an articulated political vision'.[52] This scene stands in for Cleary's general view of a novel which does not move beyond 'Daddy's world', to imaginatively project a future beyond Moran for the scattered generation of children who have lived magnetized to Great Meadow. In failing to offer alternatives, suggesting that it is in some sort of imitative thrall to Moran's disappointed version of Irish history (neither endorsed nor repudiated), the novel marks its own limitations.

I would argue that rather than being an evasive erasure of a troublesome past, the hollowing out of dated and event-laden historical time in *Amongst Women* is so emphatic as to be strategic. McGahern's adoption of an 'old-fashioned' aesthetic – what was referred to as the novel's 'bygone cadences' – seems rather too self-knowing to be fully symptomatic of cultural stasis.[53] It is as if McGahern set himself a formal challenge, to write an obviously backward-looking novel about Irish rural society during a finite period – but without writing a densely historical novel at all. The lack of 'official', documented co-ordinates is felt by the reader as a willed resistance to the narrative-providing of authorized historiography, but the emphasis on the metonymic family ensures that the novel is not detached from the processes of mid-century social history, particularly in relation to emigration in the 1950s. The novel may not be future-oriented, but its retrospective strategy still constitutes a form of historical and cultural engagement: a deliberate distancing and objectifying of the national image. The death of a national 'father' is an apt time to punctuate and take stock of a historical period that has now ended.

The presence at the funeral of a little man who, 'old and stiff enough to have fought with Fionn and Oisin' (*AW* 183), and who places the folded tricolour on the coffin, suggests a deliberate acknowledgement of the disjunction between mythical and modern historical time. The novel registers its awareness about its anachronistic representation of a warrior in the midst of politicians, and thus the problem of fictionalizing a man who, in Kiberd's words, 'wants to be in epic but is entrapped in a novelistic world'.[54] The full-blown mock-heroic, mock-mythic method of *Ulysses* is formally remote, to be sure, but the hints that Moran is in some form Cuchulainoid, mythopoeic, gigantic, still belonging to the company of Fionn and Oisin, show that the mock-epic mode relished by Joyce is not entirely ignored by McGahern. In addition, the novel's ideological hesitancy, poised between nostalgia for and condemnation of romantic nationalism and its aftermath, is continuous with the instability of modernist politics: the diverse, self-contradicting Yeatsian selves of, say, 'September 1913', 'Easter 1916', 'Nineteen and Hundred and Nineteen' and 'Politics'. *Amongst Women* may offer the kind of unsatisfactory, alternative-free stasis that Cleary so eloquently outlines, but it does so with an understated knowingness that the texts of Irish modernism can themselves be interpreted as ideologically undecidable, poised between commitment and art, never fully resolved in their aestheticization of action.[55]

The problem of McGahern's form is related to the remainder of modernism: that lacking radical, neo-modernist potentiality, his work comes to stand for an aesthetic symptom of Irish naturalism after modernism: what DiBattista calls, after Joyce, the 'bogey of realism'. In draft form, *Amongst Women* originally ran to over a six hundred pages and was thus significantly condensed. This downscaling of the narrative points to a refusal to write the 'big' Irish novel, to transplant the genre of panoramic social realism, but also to a reluctance to emulate monumentalist forms of mythic modernism. In both cases, a certain formal diminution may be suggested. As DiBattista has argued, a brief reference to Moran's letter-writing suggests one of those covert self-reflexive moments which significantly pepper McGahern's fiction: he has 'a clean, bare style' and writing allows him 'to slip the burden of his personality as he could never do face to face' (*AW* 66). This impersonality of style hints less at realist verisimilitude and more at a modernist flight from expressiveness, be it Joycean scrupulosity or Eliotic abhorrence of the 'face to face'. We wonder about the ethics of that style: 'clean, bare' impersonality is itself a literary personality, a suppression of the drives of a burdensome and dark ego. Again, after Nietzsche, Moran's will to nothingness may initially be related to the undoing of self in language. But there is little affirmative in Moran's epistolary mask: little sense of an ongoing process of Nietzschean 'self-overcoming'. Rather, we register Moran's pathological style-lessness on the page as a purgative and terminal emptying-out. This is far from the Comte de Buffon's idea that style is, confidently, the 'very man', *l'homme même*.[56]

In the end, though, the austere style of the narrator is not neatly analogous to that of the letter-writing protagonist. The pathos of the novel derives from being conducted by a withdrawn narrator who is both sympathetic and ironic, who ceremonially dethrones the Father, but scrupulously avoids *ressentiment*. The reader is not encouraged simply to judge and scapegoat Moran – which would represent slave-like morality – even though Moran is certainly given enough rope to hang himself with. Nevertheless, the invisible narrator presents 'Moran' as a styled self, the object-image of a self, which has now been overcome. The language in which the removing of Moran's mask is narrated is by no means lacking in allusion and bleakly denuded – 'clean, bare' in a pejorative sense – but rich with potential re-enchantment.

Notes

1 Maria DiBattista, 'Joyce's Ghost: The Bogey of Realism in John McGahern's *Amongst Women*', in *Transcultural Joyce*, ed. Karen Lawrence (Cambridge: Cambridge University Press, 1998), p. 22. In the Ibsen essay, Joyce writes: 'It is this doctrine of idealism in art which has in notable instances disfigured manful endeavour, and has also fostered a boyish instinct to dive under the blankets at the *bogey of realism*' (my italics).

2 W. B. Yeats, 'Easter 1916', in *Collected Poems*, p. 204.

3 Sampson, *Outstaring Nature's Eye*, p. 220.

4 Yeats, 'Men Improve with the Years', in *Collected Poems*, p. 152. See Elizabeth Butler Cullingford, *Yeats, Ireland and Fascism* (London and Basingstoke: Macmillan, 1981), p. 103.

5 Declan Kiberd, 'John McGahern's *Amongst Women*', in *Language and Tradition in Ireland: Continuities and Displacements*, ed. Maria Tymoczko and Colin Ireland (Amherst and Boston: University of Massachusetts Press, 2003), p. 204.

6 Yeats, 'Easter 1916', p. 204.

7 Ibid., p. 205.

8 Sampson, *Outstaring Nature's Eye*, p. 235.

9 Yeats, 'A Prayer for My Daughter', in *Collected Poems*, pp. 213–14.

10 Ibid., p. 214.

11 Quoted in Edward Larrissy, *Yeats the Poet: The Measures of Difference* (Hemel Hempstead: Harvester Wheatsheaf, 1994), p. 125.

12 Larrissy, *Yeats the Poet*, p. 126.
13 Yeats, 'A Prayer for My Daughter', p. 214.
14 Stanley van der Ziel, *A Way of Seeing: Fifty Years of John McGahern in Print*, Queen's Belfast Conference, 15–16 March 2013.
15 See Jean-Paul Sartre, *Being and Nothingness*, trans. Hazel E. Barnes (London: Routledge, 1996), p. 59.
16 Kiberd, 'John McGahern's *Amongst Women*', p. 207.
17 Michael Valdez Moses, 'Nietzsche', in *W.B. Yeats in Context*, ed. David Holdeman and Ben Levitas (Cambridge: Cambridge University Press, 2010), p. 267.
18 Brown, *The Literature of Ireland*, pp. 45–60.
19 Yeats, 'Nineteen Hundred and Nineteen', in *Collected Poems*, p. 232–7.
20 Yeats, 'Under Ben Bulben', in *Collected Poems*, p. 400.
21 Kermode, *Romantic Image*, p. 46.
22 Yeats, 'Why Should Not Old Men Be Mad?', in *Collected Poems*, p. 388.
23 Kiberd, 'John McGahern's *Amongst Women*', p. 210.
24 Denis Donoghue, *Yeats* (London: Fontana, 1971), p. 57.
25 Valdez Moses, 'Nietzsche', pp. 266–7.
26 Ibid., p. 274.
27 Friedrich Nietzsche, *On the Genealogy of Morality*, ed. Keith Ansell-Pearson, trans. Carol Diethe (Cambridge: Cambridge University Press, 1994), p. 107.
28 Friedrich Nietzsche, *Thus Spake Zarathustra*, trans. R. J. Hollingdale (Harmondsworth: Penguin, 2003), p. 93.
29 Gilles Deleuze, *Nietzsche and Philosophy*, trans. Hugh Tomlinson (New York: Columbia University Press, 1983), p. 62.
30 Deleuze, *Nietzsche and Philosophy*, p. 62.
31 Robert F. Garratt, 'John McGahern's *Amongst Women*: Representation, Memory and Trauma', *Irish University Review* 35, no. 1 (Spring/Summer 2005): 121–35, 126.
32 Antoinette Quinn, 'A Prayer for My Daughters: Patriarchy in *Amongst Women*', *Canadian Journal of Irish Studies* 17, no. 1 (1991): 79–90.
33 Quinn, 'A Prayer for My Daughters', p. 90.
34 Kiberd, 'John McGahern's *Amongst Women*', pp. 208, 212.
35 Quinn, 'A Prayer for My Daughters', pp. 84–5.
36 Deleuze, *Nietzsche and Philosophy*, p. 84.
37 Friedrich Nietzsche, *Thus Spake Zarathustra*, trans. R. J. Hollingdale (Harmondsworth: Penguin, 2003), p. 86.
38 Friedrich Nietzsche, *The Gay Science*, ed. Walter Kaufmann (New York: Vintage, 1974), p. 53.
39 Quinn, 'A Prayer for My Daughters', p. 83.
40 Sigmund Freud, 'Civilization and Its Discontents', in *Civilization, Religion and Society: Group Psychology, Civilization and Its Discontents and Other Writings* (Harmondsworth: Penguin, 1985), p. 292.

41 Nietzsche, *Zarathustra*, p. 83.

42 Yeats, 'Among School Children', in *Collected Poems*, p. 245. The interdependence of dancer and dance in Yeats's concluding figure is interpreted by Paul de Man as an instance of hermeneutical indeterminacy – of the text's potential difference from itself. See Paul de Man, 'Semiology and Rhetoric', in *Allegories of Reading: Figural Language in Rousseau, Nietzsche, Rilke and Proust* (New Haven: Yale University Press, 1979), pp. 3–19.

43 Nietzsche, *On the Genealogy of Morality*, p. 28.

44 Nietzsche, *The Gay Science*, p. 229.

45 Ibid., p. 228.

46 Friedrich Nietzsche, *Beyond Good and Evil*, trans. R. J. Hollingdale (Harmondsworth: Penguin, 2003), p. 82.

47 Yeats, 'A Dialogue of Self and Soul', in *Collected Poems*, p. 267.

48 Nietzsche quoted in Deleuze, *Nietzsche and Philosophy*, p. 144.

49 Deleuze, *Nietzsche and Philosophy*, p. 118.

50 Nietzsche, *Genealogy of Morality*, p. 128.

51 Ibid.

52 Cleary, *Outrageous Fortune*, p. 177.

53 See Sampson, *Outstaring Nature's Eye*, p. 217.

54 Kiberd, 'John McGahern's *Amongst Women*', p. 206.

55 The complementary critical work of Elizabeth Butler Cullingford (on Yeats) and Dominic Manganiello (on Joyce) reveals that political self-fashioning in modernism is fluid rather than monolithic.

56 Comte de Buffon quoted in Jean-Michel Rabaté, 'Crimes Against Fecundity: Style and Crime from Joyce to Poe and Back', in *Style in Theory*, ed. Ivan Callus, James Corby and Gloria Lauri Lucente (London: Bloomsbury, 2013), pp. 111–12.

7

'Careful Neutrality': Education and Reticence in 'Strandhill, the Sea', 'Hearts of Oak and Bellies of Brass' and 'High Ground'

Introduction

Denis Sampson has argued that McGahern's stories may be interpreted as existential segments in an interrupted sequence. It often seems as is if a single life is being parcelled out through the short-story collections, and that such a life may eventually be recognized, in the words of his first short story 'Wheels', as a 'rich whole'.[1] In this chapter I would like to offer a reading of three short stories by McGahern: two from his first collection, *Nightlines*, 'Strandhill, the Sea' and 'Hearts of Oak and Bellies of Brass', and the title story from the *High Ground* collection of the 1980s. All these stories are first-person narratives in which the isolation of the subject, respectively, a bored boy on holiday, a temporary labourer and a newly qualified teacher, is to some degree informed by the socially divisive consequences of education. Gathering these three segments together, the reader can reconstitute a narrative about education in which the typical tensions of the *Bildungsroman* are recognizable. They speak of that tension Goethe originally distinguished in the developmental *Bildung* between *Vollen* (desire, will, self-fulfilment) and *Sollen* (duty, social obligation).

It follows that some of McGahern's stories can be interpreted in relation to the trajectories of those nineteenth-century novels which Raymond Williams considers in *The Country and the City*. Williams conceives of the internal migrancy of a potentially mobile subject caught between a known community and knowable community.[2] In George Eliot's *Felix Holt*, for example, an emphasis is placed on 'the exposed, separated, potentially mobile individual' who, according to Williams, 'with a divided consciousness of belonging and not belonging, makes his own moral history' (174). We are made aware of the changing subjectivity of characters whose ambivalent sense of both their past and future – loyalty to where they belong, aspiration to where they may belong – is made manifest in a continuous tension, a tearing or rending, in the 'present consciousness' of the protagonist. Thomas Hardy's novels bring to a head this confrontation within the self between education and everyday work. The authorial voice is both that of 'the educated observer and passionate participant' (204). For Williams, being let into Christminster (198), unlike Jude, generates a 'crisis of mobility', a conflict between remaining loyal to a familiar world and aspiring towards the progressive life of the mind, which takes the form of distinct intellectual individualism. Is it possible to hold 'both to education and to social solidarity', to bridge 'the separation from the people who have not made [the] journey' (202–3)? These are the questions which Williams not only asked in *The Country and the City* but also in his own fiction, such as his 'return of the native' novel *Border Country*.

It is just this crisis of mobility, this divided consciousness, which is immediately recognizable in McGahern's numerous narratives of return from the city to the country. But of course these are not realist English novels of problematic education and social advancement in industrialized Britain. Any Irish short-story writer of mid-to-late twentieth century will be subject to scrutiny over his or her formal legacy, in which the tension between the short story's vernacular origins (as an expressive act of telling, the confessional or anecdotal tale of the *seanchaí*) is to be considered alongside the modernist inheritance of impersonality and symbolic density. John Kenny has recently discussed the relationship in Ireland between sociocultural and formalist explanations: that, on the one hand, the short story is the vehicle of those fragmented societies confronting modernity without the confidence of an established national bourgeoisie; and on the other, that its self-conscious aesthetics proceeds from a lyric impulse, a retreat into the private realm of the self. Kenny quotes Adorno: 'The lyric work is always the subjective expression of a social antagonism'.[3] Our admiration for poetic intensity may be tempered with an awareness of what Kenny calls the 'limits of the lyrical', prompting us to wonder whether the alienated voice may represent an immature introversion.[4]

It is worth pondering how McGahern's essay on *Dubliners* may shed light on his own practice of the short-story form. On the one hand, he seems to sponsor O'Connor's social explanation of the short story as flourishing in 'submerged' or marginalized communities. McGahern notes the 'absence of a strong central tradition' in Ireland – that supposed lack of an Irish equivalent to the Anglo-French realist novel recently disputed by Derek Hand – adding that to live in Ireland 'is to come into daily contact with a rampant individualism and localism dominating a vague, fragmented, often purely time-serving, national identity' (*LW* 200). In his introduction to the short stories of the Nova Scotian writer Alistair MacLeod, the same note is again struck, as Kenny recognizes: the short story 'comes into its own like song or prayer or superstition in poorer, more fragmented communities where individualism and tradition and family and localities and chance or luck are dominant'.[5] The theme of a richly microcosmic localism which can be transformed into a universal world-literature, making one place an everywhere – one which may bypass the problematic formulation of a national literary enterprise – is a favourite theme of McGahern's. In this sense, then, we would tend to read the typical narrator's lonely subjectivity as further lyrical expression of an inward-looking privacy produced by antagonistic social forces.

However, in the same essay on *Dubliners*, McGahern goes on to signal the terms by which we may attempt to identify his formal inheritance: that of the Irish, modernist, and of the Irish modernist, short story. What is notable is that he resists co-opting George Moore's *The Untilled Field* and *Dubliners* together into a single unified tradition. Thus, Moore's 'rowdy individualism' – it should be said that McGahern recognizes the freshness, even genius of Moore's writing – is nevertheless 'not applicable to Joyce' (*LW* 200). He writes that 'all of Moore is self-expression: he constantly substitutes candour for truth', whereas in *Dubliners* 'there is no self-expression, its truth is in every phrase' (*LW* 201). The Joycean lineage that McGahern traces is not with Moore or with prior nineteenth-century models in Ireland but rather a development of Flaubertian impersonality.[6] By quoting liberally from the Sand-Flaubert correspondence, McGahern implies the pre-history of Joyce's 'scrupulous meanness' and by extension its appeal to his own fictional practice.[7] It is telling that in referring to how the prose at the end of 'The Dead' draws attention to itself – its chiasmic cadences are indeed lyrical – McGahern writes of its having been 'earned'.[8] From these observations, then, we may expect to find in McGahern's own stories a particularly self-aware negotiation, both in sociocultural and formal terms, of the 'limits of the lyrical' in Ireland both after independence and after Irish modernism. Whatever is spontaneously expressed, post-Romantic, 'poetic', 'lonely', will have to be earned, and it will also have to be placed in the spare symbolical patterning of the short text after modernism.

Mark Schorer neatly contrasts the moral evolution of the novel to the moral revelation of the short story.[9] In the McGahern stories which follow, the process of evolution is arrested and implicitly symbolized, but revelation is withheld. Questions of education, work and affiliation cannot not elaborated, as they might be in the expansive novel, but have to be extricated; feelings occasionally break out, but epiphanies are absent. Those interior moments – of confession, insight, outrage, elation, of reported thought – are tightly controlled. The narrator is subject to the systemic social alienation common to idealized narratives of improvement. His subjectivity is not fetishistically solipsistic, but rather a socially determined structure of feeling, in Williams's terms.

There is a particular quality of silence in these stories: a culturally conditioned reticence which, in 'Hearts of Oak', is called 'careful neutrality'. We understand that the withdrawn or recessed presence of the narrator is a response to being faced with the onrushing need to make his own moral history in a society which will offer independence at a cost. The antagonism of the individual is not expressed but suppressed. The easy conversational fluency of an oral tale 'no longer [rings] with the tone of man's voice speaking', in Frank O'Connor's words.[10] We are invited to supply meaning where we are not spoken to, and this principle of textual occlusion seems to follow the modernist positioning of the *scriptible* reader. Nevertheless, we do not lose a sense of how textual omission – initially comprehensible as the caution of an individual – is produced by a lurking and overarching sociocultural determinism. In this chapter, I would like to approach three stories as interlinked segments in a narrative of conflictual educational development.

'Strandhill, the Sea': Education and 'informations'

'Strandhill, the Sea' illustrates an idiosyncrasy of McGahern's writing: it contains syntactically compressed descriptive paragraphs or sentences lacking main verbs. The effect in the opening paragraph is similar to the impressionistic notational style with which *Bleak House* begins. McGahern's narrator describes a constrictive childhood holiday on the Atlantic coast:

> The street in front of Parkes' Guest House, grains of sand from the street coming on the grey fur of the tennis ball, the hopping under my hand idle as the conversations from the green bench before the flowerbed, red bells of the fuchsia vivid behind them and some roses and gillyflowers, the earth around the roots

> of everything speckled with sea shells, overhead the weathered roughcast of the wall of the house. (*CE* 38)

McGahern is conveying through ellipsis the stultification and claustrophobia of a rainy holiday. Syntactic monotony draws attention to the suppression of the boy's voice, which is not allowed to synthesize and possess the infinitely speckled materiality of the surrounding world, with its walls, benches, voices and overcast weather. Gerundives, noun phrases, and slightly disorientating grammatical elision contribute to masking the agency of the 'I'. Although it is the boy who is bouncing the ball, even that narrative event is depersonalized as 'the hopping under my hand', not to be distinguished from the other phenomena. 'No way to get out from the voices' (*CE* 38) is a declaration made as part of a list, and not afforded preferential narrative status.

The bouncing of the ball is later interpolated into the dialogue as an index of the child's boredom, but in this case the ball's sudden idleness (*CE* 40) suggests a curious attentiveness to the uninspiring adult conversations in the guesthouse. The reader has to supply the idea that the child has reached a point where he must enliven his holiday by stealing magazines. The ball is idle because the boy is bored but also because he notices and listens to the idle words, even as he plots his petty larceny. The emptying out of obvious agency or subjectivity in the first-person 'telling' is part of the strategy of readerly inference which McGahern encourages. The child, as formative subject, must still 'get out from the voices': thus his own voice must not be allowed to predominate retrospectively. The foothold of subjective or retrospective evaluation is withheld in order to convey how the boy is imprisoned within the banality of the world he reports.

Such a strategy blocks the ease of the storytelling voice. It does not completely disappear into the managed polyphony of the impersonal modernist text, but it is 'earned'. The first-person child-narrators of *Dubliners* are not great speakers in the reported dialogue and the same is true in 'Strandhill'. When he is asked by his father why he should read Shakespeare and not comics, as the former could be 'of some use' later, the boy's reply is not recorded. His thought is: 'The old tune. Some use to you later' (*CE* 42). The mocking repetition of the father's words grants the interior life a power that a presumably submissive answer (publicly made, in the company of the holidaymakers in the room) cannot have. In the early Joyce stories, the confessional, epiphanic endings are potent only because the narrative has resisted premature disclosure: 'I saw myself as a creature driven and derided by vanity; and my eyes burned with anguish and anger' ('Araby'); 'And I was penitent, for in my heart I had always despised him a little' ('An

Encounter').[11] In 'Strandhill', the inner voice is similarly deferred: 'it was the world of imagination, among the performing gods, what I ashamedly desired to become' (*CE* 44). The selfhood of the recessed narrator finally emerges out of the sluggish matter of rainy holidays and hackneyed conversations, in a similar Joycean compound of shame and desire – in this case, the fantasy of boys' own heroism.

'Strandhill' sets up an opposition between 'informations' and imagination. Informations are the inert, gravity-laden, empirical facts – racing results, miles to the gallon – which make up the mundane and the material. The odd-looking use of the countable noun signals the deliberate confusion of the boy, hypersensitive to an excess of particulars: 'always informations, informations about everything' (*CE* 38). In a world in which a blood-orange rose can be called '*Climbing Mrs Sam McGredy*', as the retired lecturer says, a kind of nomenclatural glut threatens to overwhelm the imagination: 'A man could spend his whole life learning the names of places and they'd still be as many as the sands of the seashore left' (*CE* 40).

Considerations of good taste, as wrangled over by the retired lecturer Ingolsby and the teacher Ryan, miss the point that both Coriolanus *and* Alf Tupper may fire the imagination. The authoritative voice of the 'educator' (Ingolsby repeats the truism about the 'leading forth' of the pupil) is initially one to which we may be attracted. After all, he defends the value of understanding from an arid triviality: the worth of Wordsworth rather than the ability to name capital cities. He is, though, a disappointed idealist, clinging on to the canonical wreckage, and unable to conceive of a child's rapture with comic books as anything other than a stepping-stone to greater things. He muses on the arbitrary or bizarre naming of the world but needs to 'live through his own voice' (*CE* 43) by expatiating to the less educated: he would no longer be able to see a world in a grain of sand, like Blake, or notice the sand on the tennis ball, like the boy. This is how the writer will really be 'led forth', not by his father's utilitarian implication that Shakespeare will be of 'some use to him later' (*CE* 42). The story complicates the obvious opposition, pitting the transcendent world of the imagination not only against general knowledge (the pub-quiz aggregate of 'informations') but also against the institutionalization of learning.

Adult information fills and staves off 'the dark' (*CE* 39). The narrator, it is implied, will look for light, as 'when a child wiped a clearing on the glass, cabbages showed between the apple trees in the garden, and the green cooking apples were bright and shining in the leaves with rain' (*CE* 44). The world shines with greenness. A dreary guest house may become a place of vivid wonderment where the writer's imagination can be exercised, where even a grey-furred tennis ball can be given meaning. The boy projects himself into the world of the comic-book hero and will eventually become, we intuit in the most general way, the man with a notebook observing and transforming the world in his fiction. A covert self-reflexivity is eventually intimated, as it often is in McGahern. For the child, the performing gods of the imagination are the likes of Wilson the Iron Man, but this is continuous with the emergent artist's new enchanting of the mundane, sluggish or trivial, in the Joycean sense. The boy is, after all, a thief, if not yet a fully fledged Promethean figure. The literature of the imagination is to be an act of transgression, freed from the claims of information or erudition.

'Hearts of Oak and Bellies of Brass': 'Careful neutrality'

'Strandhill' intimates that education is a site of contestation between adults which will bring conflict and expose the individual as an outsider-within. The same is the case in 'Hearts of Oak and Bellies of Brass', in which the isolated subject is now abroad, within and without an expatriate community of labourers on a London building-site, 'not yet completely in [his] situation' (*CE* 30). The story most obviously discloses to the reader the brutalizing and emotionally cauterizing effects of manual labour. In this sense, and bearing in mind how drinking and visits to the local prostitutes are represented as integral to the world of navvying, it is a story about the body. But it is also about the willed denial of the mind. An uneasy and, we guess, temporary equilibrium has been achieved which depends on the intellectual self-abnegation of the narrator: 'I hadn't any wish to live by anything deeper' (*CE* 32). The purported inaction of the mind runs parallel to constant physical action on the site: the title mentions only heart and belly.

The narrative is not told from the point of view of a student 'slumming' during the summer or even by a college-educated dropout. The biographical context – McGahern worked as a labourer for two stints, after graduating from college in 1954 and in the period in the late to mid-1960s after he was sacked from his schoolteacher's job – might lead us to expect this. Rather, the point is carefully repeated that the narrator has spent two years at Secondary School, has passed his exams, but has nevertheless *not* taken the opportunity to 'go on' (*CE* 32). The questions that Raymond Williams raises about the alienation of the educated native are relevant to this story, and we are also aware of how the narrator's consciousness is divided: he has decided not to pursue the life of the mind and declines to tell us why.

The narrator speaks of his ambition being 'in reverse' (*CE* 30) or the 'wrong way round' (*CE* 32). We take this to be an existential exercise of choice to embrace rather than escape drudgery: a rebellion against how human betterment is unquestioningly conceived as social aspiration. The rightness of this bold choice is precarious, however: a co-worker's probing into why the narrator decided against 'going on' prompts, he admits, a 'disturbance' within him (*CE* 32). The narrator attempts to explain his anti-ambition by saying, in an arresting and curious phrase, that he wishes to 'annul all the votes in [himself]' (*CE* 30). The only vow (vote) is to make no vows to others, create no affiliations, express no ardent desires (votes as devotions); choose to make no choices, to cast no votes and to gain no votes (in this sense, perhaps, votes as academic marks, as in the Italian *voti*). Education on a building-site is equated with escape and opportunity and may even admit of the workers' latent admiration: one labourer works so that his children can 'wear white collars' (*CE* 30). However, it is also neighbour to smart-aleckry and thus the occasion of insecure jeering and mistrust. 'Going on' also suggests the breaking of the bonds of social solidarity, and will always involve some sort of betrayal in the novel of development. This is why, for example, Pip's scenes with Joe Gargery are so painful. The narrator of this story refuses this path: he will not 'play Judas' (*CE* 31).

Annulment is aligned with his claim to preserve a 'careful neutrality' (*CE* 32), a phrase which speaks primarily of the tactical evasion of commitment and building-site factionalism but also of willed disempowerment – a type of 'neutering' of the self. We are not convinced by the pose of neutrality, because the fine discriminations of the felt life implied by the narrative voice tell us that he is not and cannot be completely desensitized, and that he, like anybody, does live by something deeper. He is or at least should be, by Frank O'Connor's lights, 'romantic, individualistic, intransigent'.[12] Again, this is fleetingly intimated when the narrator confesses that he has not managed to purge himself of contempt for his work: the 'bitterness of irony' (*CE* 30) in his smile is of a man who has voluntarily rejected the future possibility of better work. Some of the other navvies will assuredly be embittered by their work, but they are not in a position to be ironically knowing about such contempt. The narrator, in Williams's terms, is still the observer as well as the participant, and surely he cannot believe what he claims, that life is 'almost as good behind the mixer as anywhere else' (*CE* 32).

Why is the narrator's self-ironizing account of his 'one and precious *life*' (*CE* 35) – his attempts to persuade the reader he is actually content to be annulled – not quite convincing? Diarmaid Ferriter has written of how the supposed emigrant attitude of 'get up and go' was more or less coerced at state level after the Second World War.[13] But the narrator, the outsider-within, the solitary voice of the short story, implies that he has *willingly* occupied this economic system: rejecting bourgeois aspiration, he has exercised free choice and wishes to make the Marxian transaction nakedly clear to himself: selling hours for money (work) which allows him to sell more hours (the 'leisure' time of the nomadic labourer: boozing and occasional whoring). He is aware of the blandishments of becoming 'a royal incubus' (*CE* 35) – one who buys and profits from the labour of others – and so remains part of the means of production. The narrator's apartness from the others is defined by the analytical justification he articulates. In addition, his avoidance of intellectual or psychological 'depth', a refusal of full confessional disclosure, seems to proceed from a kind of prior and unspoken 'disturbance'. The prostitute can only 'raise desire' through manipulation (*CE* 35) – it is barely desire, then. The desire he has is to live an anaesthetized life, free of desire. The reader must then infer the precondition of a trauma which has produced this willed anti-intellectualism.

The narrator's representation of himself as a cipher creates a mysterious absence in the text. Cause is missing and the structure of feeling purposefully left indeterminate. Our interest in the recessed teller may initially encourage the impression that the story evades an engagement with its wider social context: that these emigrant Irishmen are rebuilding Britain after the war. Ferriter has described the complexity of feelings on both sides of the Irish Sea as to whether it was the emigrant workers or the Irish state who were bringing Ireland into disrepute. For example, in a speech about the harsh working conditions in Birmingham, de Valera attracted criticism for pleading that the labourers should return home, because 'the prestige of our people generally suffers by the suggestion that anything is good enough for the Irish'.[14] Such historical determinants lurk behind the narrator's existential individualism (the emphasis on his 'one and precious *life*'). We are made aware of the labourers' broken relationship with the Irish state: one laughingly wishes for the constant summer rain in Ireland to 'rise higher than for fukken Noah'; another comments that 'they' – the Irish government, it is implied – 'never did much for us except to starve us out to England' (*CE* 31).[15] We speculate on the extent to which such cynicism may be extrapolated to the narrator, who has voluntarily rejected further education rather than being 'starved out'.

The title of the story itself teasingly prompts an ironic postcolonial interpretation. The 'Hearts of Oak' was another name for the Oakboys, an eighteenth-century secret society opposed to the more flagrant exploitation of landowners, particularly relating to road building in Ulster. The implication is that the rebellious spirit of the Oakboys is travestied by the automaton-like desperation of 'shovel or shite, shite or burst' (*CE* 27): a mock-heroic fortitude when building in a foreign land. This becomes clearer when we learn that in the same period as the Oakboys' activities, the actor David Garrick wrote a song, in celebration of British imperial achievements in North America, which included reference to the conquering hearts of oak. What is more, English translations of Book 12 of the *Odyssey* have Circe flatteringly addressing Odysseus' sailors, at the end of their year on the island, and after they have buried Elpenor, as hearts of oak. The prostitute who leans out of the window and flashes her breasts at the navvies can be recast, then, as a low-rent Circe, holding the exhausted men in thrall. The team of men representing modern-day Ireland (metonymically named Tipperary, Galway, Sligo) are, unlike the Oakboys, beaten down, their hearts of oak commandeered to the service of the British imperium, even in its moribund, Suez-era throes. The mock-heroic title encodes a mythic, Ascendancy, and Anglo-Irish context through which we are wryly invited to update the social history of the 1950s. The 'careful neutrality' of the narrator may thus be connected to a deeper political unconscious about the diverse representative Irishmen rebuilding Britain not long after the Emergency. The narrator, as outsider-within, presents his self-annulment in terms of existential alienation, but his apparently willed exile – his refusal to be educated or 'led forth' in his homeland – can be interpreted as an act of neutralizing his affiliation towards the Irish state.

'High Ground': Schism and silence

In these earlier stories from *Nightlines*, the value of education is debated in relation to, respectively, the suppressed enchantment and willed disenchantment of the literary imagination. 'Careful neutrality' is an outgrowth of a social antagonism: the strategic self-censorship of the individual faced with the pressures of affiliation. It is also a principle of form, a literary sensibility, in which repression takes primacy over expression, and the 'limits of the lyrical' in the short story suggest a movement towards modernist impersonality. In the later 'High Ground', first published in the *New Yorker* in 1982, the native has now returned home from an unnamed city bearing the laurels of high academic achievement. Rather than development, though, education has brought even closer to the surface a fracturing in the individual's present consciousness, suggesting that the treacherous necessity of making moral choices silences the storyteller's voice.

The opening of the story hints, I think, at Wordsworthian associations of rural childhood. Moran has gone out on to the lake to savour a night of love and the future promise of a happy union: in a reverie, he lets the boat drift: 'It was only the slow growing distance from the ring of reeds round the shore that told that the boat moved at all on the lake. More slowly still, the light was going from the August evening' (*CE* 190). There is something reminiscent, perhaps, of the episode in *The Prelude* in which a boy also strikes out alone on a still lake at evening, his skiff moving through the water in 'an act of stealth and troubled pleasure', only to be frightened by the unknown forces of Nature: 'the voice/ Of mountain echoes'.[16] In 'High Ground' Reegan's voice comes 'with startling clarity over the water, ... taken up by the fields across the lake, echoed back' (*CE* 191), but the echoing voice in this case represents the irruption of corrupt adulthood, not the pantheistic apprehension of natural sublimity. Williams alludes to the literary tradition that 'an idea of the country is an idea of childhood' – in Wordsworth and John Clare, there is 'the feel of childhood, of delighted absorption in our own world, from which, eventually, in the course of growing up, we are distanced and separated, so that it and the world become things we observe'.[17] Moran refers to the 'harshness of growing up' and to the idea of joyfully entering sexual adulthood – the 'world of love and beauty' (*CE* 190). The potentially enchanted world of adult love is still being conceived with a kind of nostalgia which will be disabused later in the story.

The prominence of 'high ground' as the last words of the story, and as the story and collection title, invites the reader to ponder its potential meanings. Most obviously the lurking cliché alerts us to the narrator's personal code of morality, derived from a country upbringing among the Christian Brothers and now from a university education in the city. Moral decisions are made not in a neutral space but where power seeks to establish itself. The symbolism is also hierarchical and territorial. Reegan is carefully placed in a position of superiority. He sits on the wall above the lake, and is then seen from a distance at the top of the hill, looking back down at the narrator. It is a hill he owns, full of 'his Friesians' (*CE* 192), but one which he has bulldozed and surrounded by electric fencing. Reegan will not work the land – associated with the 'low ground' of ditch-digging – but he both owns it and, as senator, administers it. Although his control of the land is equated with brutalizing modernity, he occupies the military high ground like a feudal overlord who has usurped power. The offer of the headship of the local school which Reegan makes to Moran, at the expense of his former mentor Master Leddy, is a Faustian pact, but there is also something of Satan taking Jesus to the summit and offering him the kingdom of earth below. In addition, the high ground is the contested nation itself. Leddy informs his former pupils that the people with brains stayed in the country and so enjoyed the benefit of water near the source of the Shannon: 'We're very high up here' (*CE* 200). The Shannon Pot rises near Cuilcagh Mountain in Co. Cavan, in the lands between east and west. The country is figured by Leddy as the national fountainhead. Being near the source of the river that divides the country implies a proximity to the origins of the nation: its authentic pre-industrial past, its rootedness in the country, its spirituality. Leddy's 'highness' is precarious: the Master of all the 'toppers' claims the downward slope from the high stool of the bar-room is 'longer and steeper than from the top of Everest' (*CE* 197).

The topography of 'High Ground' sets off this symbolism of verticality against the familiar horizontal journey between east and west. A teasing disjunction is created between conventional signs of technological modernity and country custom: for example, Moran borrows a Ford Prefect but goes to the well for spring water. That sense of Ireland accelerating into modernity while retaining ancient traditions – an emphasis on what one critic has called the 'time-lags' of Irish culture – is a structure of feeling which, although common to much twentieth-century Irish writing, is nevertheless quite characteristic of McGahern's often deliberately anachronous, rather than so-called 'old-fashioned', fiction.[18] The worth of inevitable progress into technological modernity – the world of electric fences – is restlessly questioned. This story, like others, shows how the symbolic values of city and country are enmeshed in such a way that we understand the nation to be 'a contradictory unity', in Terry Eagleton's words, in which modernizers 'want to refurbish an entity part of whose identity is pre-modern', whereas traditionalists 'want to adhere to the organic in a set-up which is inherently a modern idea'.[19] Thus, 'local atavisms and predatory universalism are sides of the same coin'.[20] For the purpose of this story, we read Leddy and Reegan, respectively, as these counterforces. However, just as Williams circles the dialectic of country and city in a greater sense of organic wholeness and interdependence, so McGahern complicates the antipodal opposition. The countryman Leddy is, after all, the educator, whereas the representative of worldly ambition, Reegan, is not a hyper-educated urban sophisticate but one who came to the area poor and worked his way up by means more foul than fair.

The reader must infer the internalization of the forked moral choice that Moran faces. There are no easy nostalgic solutions: the story is neither a homily against the city-bred intellectual pride of which Leddy speaks, nor a reaffirmation of rural honesty and good sense over urban sophistry. Moran's consciousness is divided: he has belonged to rural tradition, to 'his people', but that sense has been undermined by his later education in the city. Moran is a returned native, a Jude who has been let in to Christminster. The unvoiced shame at the end of the story is that of a man for his own kind. As Williams says of Hardy, education confronts the protagonist with a new idea – 'that now we know this world of the mind we can have no respect – and of course no affection – for that other and familiar world' (198). Leddy's unscientific 'reasoning' for the innate brains of the local folk is answered by the narrator's white space. Moran presumably decodes country common sense as superstitious nonsense, convicting the failing alcoholic of an unsustainable ignorance and inanity. We infer his acute feelings of being 'an exposed and separated individual', an 'internal migrant' whose social alienation has 'entered [his] personality' (210). Loyalty (the word is Leddy's) to a fallen, outdated figure would seem to be folly in a bright young man whose future lies invitingly before him. It would render futile – almost, in this sense, betray – the education he has won for himself and which in any case he cannot now unlearn. On the other hand, oedipal betrayal of the 'Master', taking the deal with the corrupt politician, will end his youth and instigate a new life of fallen adulthood. Entrance into a new knowable community requires betrayal of his known community.

Silence is now equated with the end of deferral and delay. The withdrawn narrator is faced with making an irreversible choice and is pushed to the brink, which in the companion story 'Crossing the Line' is symbolized as a picket-line. Crossing the line means losing freedom to one or other grouping, and the young man's healthy instinct is not to plunge into adult life. Although the adult moral subject must nevertheless make some form of commitment, the fragmented text will itself not draw a line, leap across any Rubicon, or 'go on'. In this, 'High Ground' is an incomplete fable, and it conforms to Clare Hanson's view of the modernist short story as a text which 'refuses to seal itself up', leaving us with 'a sense of endless dialectic between two aspects of human experience'.[21]

Lured by competing affiliations, the narrator must now make his own moral history, in Williams's terms. Education may have brought him to this Hobson's choice, but seems not to have improved his chances of taking the right decision. It is important to the sharply penetrative effect of the short-story form that the reader is not told what the moral choice will be. The 'inside' is withheld just when we need it – somewhat in the manner of what Hanson calls the 'false' epiphany.[22] The narrative seems to hinge upon Reegan's offer, but it is important to note the narrator's admission that, on visiting Leddy three days before, he was 'embarrassed, ashamed, confused' (*CE* 196) by a man he was once infatuated with. What Sampson calls the triptych-like structure of the story reveals in its chronology that this shame has not been engendered by the Mephistophelean Reegan but was *already there*.[23] 'It seemed horrible now that I might come to this' (*CE* 197): 'this' is not only his adult disenchantment but the potential for betrayal he felt in Leddy's presence before Reegan's deal was offered. Structurally, this confessional outburst is integrated into the narrative, determining the final silence which follows it.

It is this, I think, which explains Vanina Jobert-Martini's acute description of the silence as having *weight*, and exerting upon the reader an 'estranged, deprived and uncomfortable' feeling. The reader is frustrated by the narrator to the extent of being threatened by his silence.[24] This idea of silence as threat, which in that branch of linguistics called pragmatics is analyzed in the study of dialogue, is particularly important when applied to the end of the text, because it troubles the inevitable dependence upon notions of textual ambiguity or indeterminacy. Or at least it compels the reader to work out the undecidability on moral grounds rather than to indulge in experimental play with the 'idle' or empty sign. We realize that the time for 'careful neutrality' has elapsed, but also that the text has refused either to offer moral revelation or to complete the pattern of the educated individual's moral evolution. Whatever meaning the reader cares to supply will be somehow collusive with the forces of tradition or modernity, dialogically answerable to the voice of the other.

Conclusion

Bertrand Cardin has distinguished between ellipsis and eclipse as differing forms of silence in McGahern's short stories. The latter indicates 'a partial concealment, a sense of semidarkness … a failing message'; aposiopesis may not just be an elliptical gap but a semantic break which 'inserts an objection, a restriction' equivalent to the effect of *abruption* in rhetorics – a syntactic failure to link clause to clause.[25] He also discusses how, in some of McGahern's stories like 'Lavin' and 'A Ballad', the adverb 'now' signals a joining-up, or 'meeting-point' of diegetic and narrative chronologies – so that the 'plot ends with its own writing'.[26] This establishes a temporal blank space within the text, an unwillingness to fill in the intervening time.

Two of McGahern's stories from *High Ground*, 'High Ground' and 'Crossing the Line', expressly avoid that 'now', but rather shift the temporal blank space to what comes *after* the whole narrative. This emphasizes the meaningful failure of short-story endings. The short narrative can exploit the final 'limits of the lyrical', heightening an awareness of the limits of the genre itself: of abruption, of yet-to-be-crossed lines. William James wrote of his brother Henry James's short stories that they gave

> an impression like that we often get of people in life: their orbits come out of space and lay themselves for a short time along ours, and then off they whirl again into the unknown, leaving us with little more than an impression of their reality and a feeling of baffled curiosity as to their mystery of the beginning and end of their being.[27]

Rather than think of the time unaccounted for *within* the story, then, we are presented in these examples from McGahern with a future-directed narrative which whirls off into the unknown, but less with bafflement and mystery, more with a sense of the subject's moral danger, and the reader's complicity with that danger. The next chapter concentrates on another country-and-city story which incorporates that 'bafflement and mystery'. An almost novella-length text like 'The Country Funeral' could not be sustained by the diminished presence of McGahern's compromised first-person narrator. Instead suppression and the threat of silence are largely abandoned, and the longer short story is opened up to loquacity – to the loud, clashing, partial and alcohol-fuelled voices of those who debate their sense of an ending.

Notes

1 Denis Sampson, 'The "Rich Whole": John McGahern's *Collected Stories* as Autobiography', *Journal of the Short Story in English* 34 (Spring 2000): 21–9.
2 Raymond Williams, *The Country and the City* (Nottingham: Spokesman, 2011), p. 210. All subsequent references will be made to this edition.
3 John Kenny, 'Inside Out: A Working Theory of the Irish Short Story', *Frank O' Connor: New Critical Essays*, ed. H. Lennon (Dublin: Four Courts Press, 2007), pp. 99–113.
4 Kenny, 'Inside Out', p. 111.
5 John McGahern, 'Introduction to Alistair MacLeod', in *Island: Collected Stories* (London: Vintage, 2002), pp. xiiii–xiv.

6 Moore scholars have pointed to his own Flaubertian and Russian influences, but whether the former is prominent in *The Untilled Field* is a matter for debate.

7 McGahern, '*Dubliners*', in *The Artist and the Labyrinth*, pp. 66, 68.

8 Ibid., p. 71.

9 Mark Schorer quoted in Dominic Head, *The Modernist Short Story* (Cambridge: Cambridge University Press, 1992), p. 18.

10 Frank O'Connor, *The Lonely Voice* (Hoboken: Melville, 2004), p. 28.

11 Joyce, *Dubliners*, pp. 18, 24.

12 O'Connor, *The Lonely Voice*, p. 20.

13 Diarmaid Ferriter, *The Transformation of Ireland 1900-2000* (London: Profile, 2005), pp. 465–72.

14 Ferriter, *The Transformation of Ireland 1900*-2000, p. 476.

15 See McGahern's essay about localized ambivalence to the Easter Rising in *Love of the World* (*LW* 125) for the biographical source of the first quotation.

16 William Wordsworth, *The Prelude* (London: Norton, 1985), l.90-92, p. 3.

17 Williams, *The Country and the City*, p. 297.

18 David Pierce, *Reading Joyce* (Harlow: Longman, 2008), p. 152.

19 Terry Eagleton, 'Revisionism Revisited', in *Crazy John and the Bishop* (Cork: Cork University Press Field Day, 1998), p. 314.

20 Eagleton, 'Revisionism Revisited', p. 312.

21 Clare Hanson, *Short Stories and Short Fictions 1880-1980* (Basingstoke: Macmillan, 1985), pp. 65–6.

22 Hanson, *Short Stories and Short Fictions 1880-1980*, p. 63.

23 Sampson, *Outstaring Nature's Eye*, p. 203.

24 See Vanina Jobert-Martini, 'Evaluation in "High Ground": From Ethics to Aesthetics', *Journal of the Short Story in English* 53 (Autumn 2009): 249–62. Jobert-Martini usefully borrows the notion of face-threatening from pragmatics, pp. 256–8.

25 Bertrand Cardin, 'Figures of Silence: Ellipses and Eclipses in John McGahern's *Collected Stories*', *Journal of the Short Story in English* 40 (Spring 2003): 56–67, pp. 57, 66.

26 Cardin, 'Figures of Silence', p. 58.

27 Quoted in Ian Reid, *The Short Story* (London: Methuen, 1977), p. 65.

8

The 'Old Pieties': Modernity and 'The Country Funeral'

Introduction

The previous chapter focused on how a crisis of mobility in McGahern's short stories is internalized into the fractured silence of the individual's 'divided consciousness', to quote Raymond Williams's *The Country and the City*. 'The Country Funeral' was originally composed as a pared-down story similarly entitled 'The City and the Country'.[1] The early title indicates the extent to which the story was engendered by the opposition of what have been called Ireland's 'two nations'. The final version of 'The Country Funeral' develops the idea that 'the city and the country' are not to be schematically opposed but rather considered as an interdependent whole. Elsewhere in his fiction, McGahern relishes bringing out the extent to which, in Luke Gibbons's phrase, 'the city in Ireland is simply the country at one remove'.[2] For instance, as Declan Kiberd has observed, a cynical character in 'Parachutes', seeing thistledown floating through Grafton Street, comments of Ireland that 'even its principal city has one foot in the manure heap' (*CE* 164).[3] However, it is in 'The Country Funeral' that the ethically symbolic geography of country and city is explored in particular depth: these antagonistic counterforces are shown to be inescapably bound to each other within the nation in a relationship which is mutually subversive and constitutive.

'The Country Funeral' has been praised for its 'thoroughly objective narration'.[4] The critical epithet *objectivity* may risk being misleading, if it is taken to suggest a certain passivity and ideological detachment. The early draft 'The City and the Country' was much more spare, one might say dramaturgically objective, than the final version. McGahern describes a scene in a city pub. Three brothers enter the pub, talk about a funeral, and then leave the pub; three solitary drinkers and a barman observe this with little comment. This draft story, mainly constituted by dialogue, has an Aristotelian unity: a symmetrically tripartite structure (entrance, conversation, departure) to match the groupings of three. The earlier version is broadly Hemingwayesque: the reader is given only external dialogue and denied interiority. Like the waiters in 'A Clean, Well-Lighted Place', the brothers are not named but simply marked as 'the burly man', 'the thin man', 'the legless man' (or 'the dwarf'), just like the Chorus-like drinkers ('the drinker', 'a second drinker', 'the third'). But in the final version McGahern reverses the conventional paring down (Hemingway's 'iceberg principle' of omission) by expanding his original composition, breaking out from its unities. Interiority is allowed to grow in the journey from city to country and back again, as each of the brothers, now named, are granted a period in which their consciousness is lingered over. Affect is signally readmitted, as is a metaphysically speculative tone which does not belong to the earlier draft.

Conceived like this, the abbreviated objectivity of the earlier draft was not enough for McGahern. The finished story – McGahern's longest, almost a novella – needs more scope, both geographically and formally, in which to develop and work out its dialectics. It is an ethical argument which often takes the more prosaic form of a brooding and protracted argument between brothers. Much of the dialogue consists of sibling bickering: adverbial tags tend to the combative ('heatedly', 'truculently', 'roughly') and there is a lot of 'announcing', 'crowing', 'accusing' and 'deriding'. The expanded story indulges anger, plangency and partiality, but refuses to grant the individual the privilege of revelation, and this is finally shown to be in the scrupulous service of an objectivity which is all too aware of the violent subjectivities it contains.

The final words may give comfort to some readers, but they are purposefully hypothetical: 'as if it was at last a fact' (*CE* 408). The story resists translation into interpretative 'fact'. It is neither a paean to country custom nor a satire of it. One brother's voice, Philly's, sentimentally expresses the values of community, immanence and continuity in the countryside; he defends tradition, continuity and ritual. The other, that of Fonsie, remains furiously resistant to the mortmain of county customs, and is sceptical about mystificatory processes, which often conceal all-too-material, earth-bound hypocrisies. Philly expresses a belated attachment to origin, neighbourliness, fellow man. Fonsie represents independence of mind but also a self-isolating individualism. Philly, too ingenuous, and Fonsie, too caustic, are constantly on edge because 'the strength of their difference betray[ed] the hidden closeness' (*CE* 404), and this marks the formal properties of the text itself, ideologically suspended between affection for and scepticism about 'the old pieties' (*CE* 376). The quietist, 'easy life' position is included in order to be scrutinized: John, the brilliant but taciturn third brother, abstemious and abstentionist, remains *hors de combat* for the most part: a non-participant. We may listen to his rare and moderate interventions carefully, but his voice is also not spared from narrative irony. John's neutral presence – the ethics of opting out, of taking shelter, as if behind a deep hedge (*CE* 388) – is hardly privileged or validated. The story strains to contain the voices of those who speak their moral commitment: we are made aware of how objectivity is hard won.

'The Country Funeral' seems to succeed and update a thoroughly familiar type of tale about the mores of the Irish countryside, traceable back to William Carleton, through George Moore's *The Untilled Field*, and associable with Frank O'Connor's work, among that of many others.[5] But McGahern's scepticism about the notion of a monolithic literary tradition emerges in the formal indeterminacy of 'The Country Funeral', which can be better appreciated if we briefly align it with two other stories about country burial, O'Connor's 'The Long Road to Ummera' and 'The Mass Island'. In both of O'Connor's stories, the dead are shown to exercise unanswerable power over the living. In 'The Long Road to Ummera' an old woman insists to her son that her body is taken back to the mountains where she came from, away from 'the foreigners in the town'.[6] The son is as scornful as McGahern's Fonsie: the country is 'the hunger and misery we came from', the threat of being visited by his mother from beyond the grave, a matter of 'haunts and fairies and spells' (49–50). He is dealt with harshly in the narrative – 'an insignificant little man' with a 'weak melancholy face' (49–50) who enjoys his petit bourgeois trappings in the town – whereas the mother's words echo, albeit in idiomatic vein, those of Kent in *King Lear*: 'I have a journey to go, never you mind where' (53). The contemptuous son is eventually routed by the mother, compelled to speak the exact words the dead woman demanded of her former neighbours in Ummera.

In O'Connor's 'The Mass Island', a priest, Father Fogarty, curiously insists on being buried on a remote lake island, though it is not his native place, much to the disgust of his brother and the bemusement of a fellow priest, Father Jackson. Jackson is a sympathetic character, wry to the sentimentality of Fogarty's wishes – noting that 'romantic men always left their more worldly friends to carry out their romantic intentions' (651). But he is, as it were, 'converted' by the sight of the local people streaming down from the mountains to attend the funeral, lighting up the island with their lanterns 'like a vast piece of theatre' (654). Father Jackson weeps, newly aware of how the parishioners' love speaks of 'something infinitely greater' (653) than mere respect: 'It was like a miracle' (653). Even the aggressive brother is reluctantly won round. In both stories, the reader is left in no doubt that the return to the mountain home or to remote 'sanctified ground' (552) is granted a mystical power to which sceptical others can only accede.

The more reverential accounts of McGahern's writing would tend to suggest that his 'country' fiction replicates similar 'strategies of transcendence', to use James Whyte's phrase. And of course a novel like *That They May Face the Rising Sun* is trying in general to reach out to 'something infinitely greater'. But even if their serio-comic tone cannot be doubted, there is, perhaps, a whiff of didacticism in these O'Connor stories. That is to say, scepticism is in one case conflated with philistine, secular urbanism, or in the other defeated by a romantic spirit of place which is shown not be sentimentalized. The old woman wishes to be *there* with the other souls, much more numerous than those who are here. (The epigraph to 'The Long Road to Ummera' is from a poem by Henry King, 'The Exequy', also quoted by Aldous Huxley in *Antic Hay*: 'Stay for me there. I will not fail/To meet thee in that hollow vale'.) No such victory is allowed in 'The Country Funeral' for *there*, the dead, over *here*, the living. In the analysis which follows, we see that McGahern must indulge the partiality of opposite viewpoints to arrive at a sophisticated, passionately dialectical objectivity which circumscribes the construction of two nations, of 'country' and 'city', of the dead and the living.

Enlightenment and the legacy of modernity

To consider 'The Country Funeral' in the broader context of the Enlightenment is appropriate, particularly if the foundational debates in Irish studies about its legacy are borne in mind. McGahern is inheriting the tradition of assessing tradition: this story is a contemporary evaluation of the clinging on to or rejecting of custom, and of the extent to which modernity's urge to supplant myth is desirable. The odd straying briar 'of the old wildness' (*CE* 378) brushes the windscreen of the gleaming Mercedes as the brothers drive down a road that they expect to be pot-holed but which has been freshly tarred. They are visiting the country of memory. Philly will eventually wish to exchange the empty space of a Saudi desert, where oil is transformed into global capital, for the empty space of the Gloria Bog. Fonsie thinks of the strangeness of his mother, as a girl, seeing the first car in the country, and dismisses the idea that a life before such modern technology could be as 'well off' as one after it (*CE* 391). Such details are part of a carefully laid out symbolic pattern which tests competing ethical positions.

Foucault has written of the need to free ourselves from 'the intellectual blackmail of being for or against the Enlightenment'.[7] Such a comment comes in the wake of Adorno and Horkheimer's *Dialectic of Enlightenment*, the *locus classicus* of the case against. The daring claim that 'Enlightenment is totalitarian' is often quoted: starkly decontextualized, it speaks with increasing specificity of the pessimism of the year it first appeared in print, 1944.[8] Adorno and Horkheimer explode any confidence in the Kantian idea that the Enlightenment was a way out from mystification, superstition and barbarism; that it represented a new ethos or 'attitude of modernity', in which human reason could be put to use, free of authority.[9] In their view, Enlightenment was a systemic 'disenchantment of the world' – a world in which everything could be calculated and structured according to scientific principles, and nothing was incommensurable. 'Abstraction liquidates': every particular lost its identity under the sovereignty of pragmatized thought.[10] History was to reveal that the Apollonian reason of the eighteenth century would be wielded as a destructive instrument of imperial power, enforcing a totalizing absolutism which denied the existence of the anomaly or the outside. Adorno and Horkheimer were concerned to show how Enlightenment does not come into being in a clean opposition to, or progressive movement away, from myth but is rather produced by and wedded to it. Demythologization promises an impossibly utopian state where man can live without fear of the unknown. Enlightenment 'receives all its matter from the myths, in order to destroy them; and even as a judge it comes under the mythic curse'.[11] Enlightenment is a historically conditioned force: it is 'mythic fear turned radical'.[12] Adorno and Horkheimer's reformulation of these dialectics is important to a reading of 'The Country Funeral', connecting to a Raymond Williams-like apprehension of how the city and country are in an ongoing, mutually structuring relationship, not one in which reactionary nostalgia for organicist wholeness predominates.

This animus against the Enlightenment – against the 'curse' of particular-liquidating, radical modernity – has a specific colonial application in Irish history. In his account of Edmund Burke's *Reflections on the Revolution in France* (1790), Seamus Deane shows how Burke equates Enlightenment modernity with the insurrectionary universalism of France. Burke would wish that Ireland might not be treated as 'irredeemably strange' by Britain, but also that it be safeguarded from destructive radicalism by the British polity. Security for Ireland is to be found in the British reality of empirical fact, which is a bulwark against the phantasmic figments visiting the republic of theory across the English Channel. The Burkean counter-revolutionary narrative centres on an 'aesthetic of the actual' to combat 'the despotic encroachments of uniformity'.[13] Universalizing philosophy which allows of no exceptionality, and pays no respect for the obdurately residual particular ('tradition'), can only be barbaric. Deane summarizes Burke's resistance: thought is control, not freedom; universalism a deterritorialized placelessness; theory is the executioner's levelling of difference. Enlightenment reason does not emancipate people from superstition and enslavement but imprisons them in the oppressive units of cosmopolitan sameness. The 'territory of theory' is coterminous for Burke with the 'the territory of modernity'. The demonization of France provides a meta-narrative for Ireland which suppresses the idea that an energetic Hibernian 'fancy' might be directed to theorizing Irish modernity.[14] Whereas the colonialist narrative would emphasize Irish immurement within the oppressive British state, and visualize the utopian project of bringing a strangely self-determining country of its own into being, Burke advocates an adherence to the organic, local and folklorish which should nevertheless be protected from the foreign, the totalizing other, by those same British walls.[15]

Deane's reading of Burke establishes how binarist thinking about tradition and modernity can be deconstructed by attending to ideology. Likewise, McGahern's reading reveals his interest in the ways in which the superficial opposition between superstition and myth, on the one hand, and reason and modernity, on the other, can be dissolved. He was, for example, influenced by E. R. Dodds's *The Greeks and the Irrational*. Dodds, a classicist from Ulster, argued that Greek culture, associated with Athenian rationalism, had been granted immunity from 'primitive' modes of thought, and went about investigating how it, like any other culture, has an immanent religiousness or even religiosity. Dodds took his position against those such as Sir Maurice Bowra who thought of Homer as representing a 'complete anthropomorphic system [which] has of course no relation to real religion or to mortality'.[16] Examples of the 'supernormal' are examined: the 'psychic interventions' and temporary possessions of Homeric characters (a 'shame-culture'); the gradual transformation of the supernatural into an agent of justice, and the human assumption of moral pollution and purification (the 'guilt-culture' which *Oedipus Rex* most clearly illustrates). Dodds was drawn to finding 'the beauty and terror of the old beliefs' in this foundational culture of 'clear-headed' Western civilization, of what we might call Western modernity.[17] McGahern must have been piqued by comments of Dodds such as these: 'I doubt if the early literature of any other European people – even my own superstitious countrymen, the Irish – postulates supernatural interference in human behaviour with such frequency or over so wide a field'.[18] He tells us how reading Dodds's book was like 'finding a clear spring' (*LW* 323).[19]

The Greeks and the Irrational helped McGahern separate out the morality and the culture of his religion, but also to theorize the ways in which the apparent antipodes of myth and modernity may be reformulated. We should approach 'The Country Funeral', then, with this awareness of how 'the city and the country' are symbolic values, and have been set up in a contrapuntal narrative which the reader is required to syncretize and make whole. Our appreciation of the story's objectivity should not imply quietistic detachment, but a much more ideologically dynamic form of undecidability. The brothers' voices are dialogically bound to their own contraries. On the surface, Fonsie's position, in relation to the country and traditional values, could not be more forthright, not to say insulting. 'The whole thing was barbaric, uncivilized, obscene' (*CE* 382); 'the people are savages' (*CE* 386). In both the life that his uncle led on the Gloria Bog and the death that his community are giving him, the rural community is indicted by Fonsie of backwardness, of adhering to 'useless ceremony' (*CE* 399). He seems, then, to represent modernity at its most intemperate. Oddly, though, and despite the prejudice, fury and rudeness, there is a sense that Fonsie is adhering to a coherently resistant code of ethics. Why attend the funeral of a man who did not like you and whom you have not seen for twenty years? The compulsion to attend, Fonsie is unafraid to imply, is based on hypocrisy, false piety, and also on social anxiety and a kind of superstitious cowardice: one had better go – so the guilty inner voice whispers – because not to go would scandalize the neighbours (here and there). The adherents of such traditionalism walk more in fear of a vengeful societal superego than of a vengeful God. Fonsie is merely basing his decision on the evidence of the life that he has experienced. He claims that 'if Peter got a chance he'd have put me in a bag with a stone and thrown me in a bog hole like that black whippet' (*CE* 378), and we are not certain that this hyperbole is entirely baseless. At any rate, it is no surprise that Fonsie should feel little loyalty to the family – seen by Burke as under attack from the French Enlightenment – and we must agree that it seems perverse to be asked to celebrate the life of such a man.

It can be argued, if we are to be charitable to Fonsie, that he is used as a mouthpiece for modernity, whether in the Enlightenment sense of self-reflection and self-responsibility which places independent-mindedness above unthinking tribal loyalty, or even in a more revolutionary Nietzschean, proto-existentialist form. We admire this brave rationalism and faith in his own judgements, this refusal to be cowed by tradition. Fonsie's self-perception is of a modern, urban man: 'The whole lot of you could have come right out of the Dark Ages. … I thought a standard of living had replaced the struggle for survival years ago' (*CE* 405). While Philly and John seem to evade the truth of the situation, Philly is nearest to seeking it out. He unmasks Peter's lack of compassion for what it was, despite Peter's acting out of family duty – 'standing to' (*CE* 373) – when required. Peter was himself trapped by an inherited attachment to 'the old pieties': his loyalty was begrudging, and in bad faith. Nietzsche objected to such Enlightenment truth-seeking as much as to Christianity, but there is something of Nietzsche's contempt for Western slave morality in Fonsie's reflection on the hillside mourners' 'deep love of hardship or enslavement' (*CE* 399). Fonsie sees that sentimental attachment to notions like 'respect' and to death-bound duty can conceal the existing problems of life. According to Fonsie, the dead are easy to respect because they do not have to be lived with any more (*CE* 404); people enjoy getting out of the house to attend funerals: pitiless and bleak observations, to be sure, but acute nevertheless.

McGahern has brought to life a powerful voice of modernity and disaffected rationalism, then. Equally though, Fonsie, is acting *un*reasonably. He jeers and gibes; he could not be less impartial. 'There's no manners round here' (*CE* 386): we are invited to reverse this view, reflecting on the absence of his manners compared to the courtesy of others. He glowers with silent resentment in the company of the Cullens: 'His lips moved from time to time but they were speaking to some darkness seething within' (*CE* 381). This is more a pent-up fury than an enlightened sense of justice or brave individualism. He is also a stay-at-home Irishman to Philly's expatriate in Saudi Arabia: Esau to Jacob, the resentful brother of the Prodigal Son. Adorno and Horkheimer's insight, that Enlightenment emerges from myth, is apt: Fonsie's truculence is not a detached rationalism but rather grows out of an unconscious Old Testament-like need to avenge his dead uncle. He is tainted by the supposedly 'barbaric' superstitions of unenlightened folk like Peter who keep thousands of pounds out of banks (does this seem such a bad idea in the early twenty-first century?), and think it unlucky to make a will. There is little to admire in his disparagement of the mores of Jim Cullen, who seems to embody the Christian injunction to 'love thy neighbour', though an implication is allowed to stand that Cullen has profited from the mismanagement of bad neighbours (*CE* 397) – in other words, that altruism may have its rewards on earth.

Moreover, how critical is Fonsie of tradition itself? It appears that he is not so much critical of Catholic ritual, but more of the perceived lack of decorum with which it is administered. It is not that a corpse is presented, but that it is presented with the cotton still showing. It is not that a coffin should be carried so conspicuously uphill but that it is carried badly by 'a crowd of apes' (*CE* 405). It is not that there is a priest, but only that he arrives late and has to hurry, bent double 'like an enormous black-and-white crab' (*CE* 399). An element of purely social, city-bound snobbery is at work: the Dubliner laughing at his country cousins, who lack class in the way they perform any social ceremony, just as they might at a wedding. Though his voice is sceptical and, on the surface, representative of coldly rational fury, it is not that of, say, Jürgen Habermas, who seeks to salvage something of the Enlightenment 'project' of modernity out of the wreckage of twentieth-century history. Could we really imagine Fonsie committing himself to a revolutionary cleansing of such 'cultic dross' (the phrase is Habermas's) from provincial Ireland?[20]

The answer is that we cannot, and this attaches to another question: why does McGahern choose to make Fonsie disabled? Whyte suggests that there is a parallel between his physical and emotional disability, that he is a 'large child'.[21] Though his behaviour is indeed often childish, he is importantly placed in the narrative as the citified decrier of country tradition and of the sort of archaic ideology which took disabled people to be benighted. Implicitly, then, he would be an advocate of modernity, inclusive of instrumentality, positivism, technology and scientific progress. However, although he may have been a victim of the same 'Dark Ages' (*CE* 405) to which he alludes, he would also have suffered from Nazi 'progress'. 'Enlightenment is totalitarian': this is the terror of the absolute ideal, the modern barbarism, of which Adorno and Horkheimer write. Fonsie's immobility and dependency have an ambiguous metaphoric function in relation to his disabused independent-mindedness. One might even say that his frustration is that of the incomplete, 'disabled' modern Enlightenment figure who has not the power to go with the reason, and is at the mercy of the 'mythic curse' which tradition has imprinted on modernity.

Philly, on the other hand, initially seems to occupy a naïve, mystificatory and old-fashioned position, invoking values such as 'honour', 'respect' and 'mystery' (*CE* 404) in his enthusiasm for the conducting of the funeral. He acknowledges his feelings as those of the 'the rough unfinished man he knew himself to be in the eyes of others' (*CE* 395). There is an echo here, perhaps, of the self in Yeats's 'A Dialogue of Self and Soul' who has endured the 'toil of growing up' and 'ignominy of boyhood', and has become 'the *unfinished man*' brought 'face to face with his own clumsiness' (my italics). Such an embedded allusion may further associate Philly with a world-weary entrenchment in Yeats's 'ditch' and underline how he lacks the 'finish' of the educated intellect.[22] His nostalgia for rural customs is conditioned by his being stranded in the modern world, though financially a beneficiary of it: he is 'alone and companionless' not only in Saudi Arabia but also in his native Dublin, where his homecoming excites him for a few days before he realizes that he 'did not belong' (*CE* 370). The desperation of his largesse continues in the country, where it is a transgression of what 'custom allowed'; the way he highlights that he has been 'roughing it in the oilfields' (*CE* 394) speaks of the outsider's city-bred anxiety. The narrative tells us without qualification that the country has been a place of suffering for the brothers (*CE* 377) but what Fonsie unsparingly acknowledges, Philly represses.

However, McGahern ensures that Philly, perhaps borrowing some of the final affirmativeness of Yeats's 'unfinished' self, is a worthy philosophical opponent of his brother. Philly resists the automatic privileging of 'enlightened' urban ways. An elaborate funeral wake may be considered vulgar but is better than 'having the whole thing swept under the carpet as it is in the city' (*CE* 382): the hygienic disposal of death in urban and secular environments is denaturalized denial, and attacked as representing an arrogant type of humanism. Fonsie blunders by saying 'If I were to go…', to which Philly replies, 'There's no *if* in this business, it's just *when*' (*CE* 407). The atheistic fetishizing of nullity, or the brave existentialist declaration of finitude (the end is the end, not the beginning of the hereafter), masks an unconscious need to internalize and erase the painful knowledge of mortality, just as religion externalizes this basic human need.

'Nothing is ever over'

The meaning of the 'end' or of ending is a common McGahern motif. In 'Sierra Leone', for example, the narrator responds to the non-occurrence of nuclear annihilation, the greatest of endings, by concluding that 'nothing ever seems to end except ourselves' (*CE* 226). In 'The Country Funeral', we hear a similar expression, and it extends the implicit argument about post-Enlightenment metaphysics in a not-fully-secularized country. John observes: 'One of the things that made the last days bearable for me was that everything we were doing was being done for the last time' (*CE* 405). Philly counters: 'It's far from over … As far as I can make out, nothing is ever over' (*CE* 405–6). John's comment suggests that he sees the funeral as 'bearable' – Nietzsche refers to 'the greatest weight' in *The Gay Science* – precisely because it is unrepeatable. But John could not espouse Zarathustra, who faced with life inextricably both great and small, interdependently both joyful and sorrowful, does not wail about the burden of perpetual return: 'Was *that* – life? I will say to death, 'Very well! Once more!'[23] John resists the affirmative idea of recurrence, though, preferring to think of human action as self-identical, singular, exceptional: in Nietzschean terms, he is perhaps too near the late nineteenth-century European nihilist position, fetishizing the idea of nothingness as a terminus. 'The colour of laughter is black. How dark is the end of all life' (*CE* 401): such Bergsonian or Beckettian lines may be attributable to the interpolated comment of a pessimistic omniscient narrator, but I would argue that they suit the focalized consciousness of John, the brilliant scholar, and his life-denying shudder of revulsion which follows. John has carried off the ceremonial duties of the nephew with aplomb, behaving with the 'respect' sentimentalized by Philly. If we attribute the revulsion to John, it casts his good manners, his fence-sitting politeness, in a slightly less admirable light. Fonsie's rude radicalism may appear more authentic.

At face value, Philly appears an orthodox figure. His uncle's death will probably prompt a return from the materialist, non-Christian Saudi Arabia to the Gloria Bog and with it the Catholic Church. Read in these terms, Philly's 'nothing is ever over' represents both a traditional faith and a faith in tradition – the afterlife validated by recurring ceremonies of community. In this, Nietzsche would find him a weak participant in the continuing slave morality which the priests continue to sustain. Comfort is to be had in the ubiquity of death and thus in respectful, meaning-giving rituals of this sort: the funeral is not 'over' because its like will happen over and over again, and when it happens to him he will join the throng of souls, rather like the old lady in O'Connor's story. However, there is another way of regarding Philly's vague, homemade formulation 'nothing is ever over' which need not be slavishly Christian. It may be less the strident propaganda for old-fashioned eschatology, and more like a grasping for a quasi-cosmic sense of immanence, of a remorseless continuation of life. Philly might feel with Nietzsche that the 'eternal hourglass of existence is turned upside down again and again, and [he] with it, speck of dust'.[24] His contention is no more or less fragile than Fonsie's supposedly more enlightened but ill-mannered attitude, or John's resigned faith in non-recurrence. Oddly, it is the brother actuated by nostalgia for a deeply Christian culture who seems closest to Nietzsche's anti-Christian sense of recurrence. Philly's will be an elective rather than unthinkingly inherited affiliation with the country.

Fonsie comments that 'there's nothing more empty than a space you knew once when it was full' (*CE* 383), reminding us of an earlier image of feet passing the open doorway of a Dublin pub: 'When it was empty the concrete gave back its own grey dull light' (*CE* 371). McGahern complicates the simple opposition of presence and absence. Such images suggest deficit, loss, absented space, space emptied out. Eamonn Grennan has interpreted such figures as having 'the sense of possessing what has passed' from Irish culture, but also as representing the 'symbolic stock' which gives McGahern's writing its particular 'sacramental vision'.[25] Bleak material nullity cannot quite account for a sense of the world now emptied of the meanings imposed by ritual. Philly will assume 'his dead uncle's knowledge and presence' (*CE* 383) – one family member will replace another, guaranteeing persistent human presence through time. The end is deferred. *Pace* John, everything is not being done for the last time but rather takes its place in a sequence which establishes culture. This is obviously a way of thinking about mortality, the coexistence of 'the living and the dead', and about death's presence within life.

All three brothers are moved by the country funeral. Philly is moved because the repetition of such customs in the past and in the future guarantees some sense of communality and human identity stretching over time, and this immanence is itself founded on stasis and rootedness-in-place (being in the Bog, being of the Bog, in an almost Heaneyesque way). John endures and is moved by the funeral because it happens only once: it is self-identical, will not recur, and its unique particularity is a contingent comfort in the present only. In a brilliant stroke in the execution of the story, Fonsie, observing the funeral scene from the car, is also moved despite himself, and this *seems* to offer the epiphany, the most rarefied plane of perception which may redirect the direction of the story and potentially transform it. It is a purely private moment which his public persona (the face he shows to his brothers) could not countenance. This draws attention to the object of his observation – a scene which ceremonializes the relationship between the honoured individual (who lived alone, had good neighbours and is now dead) and the community. The deep seriousness and comic banality of the funeral – which simultaneously moves and irritates Fonsie – seem to offer a saving psychological empathy, but the story is too even-handedly 'objective', in this intellectually passionate sense, to linger with Fonsie's subjectivity for too long.

We cannot leave Philly behind. It is a mistake to conflate his naivety and nostalgia with metaphysical recidivism. Philly may resist John's existentialist investment in the non-repeating singularity and presence of life for 'good' Christian reasons, but his vague words perhaps unwittingly raise a philosophical objection to the cult of 'the last time'. The story's own ending is appropriately non-terminal, provisional: '"Anyhow, we buried poor Peter," Philly said, "as if it was at last a fact"' (*CE* 408). Whyte concludes that with this lack of resolution the debate is brought out into the social arena in 'a comedy of manners [which] is a ceremony in itself'. However, the last line suggests more than his assertion that 'the only fact that can be established is the inevitable truth of death'.[26] Doubt still remains about the meaning of burial, and how its symbolic, ritual value can be granted the status of empirical fact. If the completed fact, the ceremony borne or carried through to its conclusion, suggests finitude, then that too is denied. The truth of death is deliberately and aporetically left hanging. They have buried Peter, and that is a fact (in fiction). Do we last after our last moment? We will wait indefinitely for the last 'fact' of our end. The line contains an awareness of its own linguistic collapsibility. What I think must be an implicit or coded allusion to 'the last end' of another story which takes us from the city to the country graveyard, 'The Dead', extends that intratextual irreducibility to the intertextual signifier.

The story will not give us easy satisfaction in its own ending. In the mood of 'The Country Funeral' there is, as Denis Sampson writes, a 'sense of eternal rightness in the accommodation to death', and a 'calm in the face of mortality' that is induced in part by the mystery of nature.[27] In this, the story anticipates *That They May Face the Rising Sun*. But that calmness should not be equated with the end of questioning, an acceptance of death as a mere fact of our existence. 'As if it was at last a fact': the story does not close serenely but hypothetically, interrogatively, dialectically. The formal hesitancy of the text is a manifestation of Adorno and Horkheimer's intrinsic dialectic of the Enlightenment, in which it is argued that, in the empire of modernity, '*the fact* becomes null and void, and might as well not have happened' (my italics). That is, a law of immanence imprisons man in a cycle in which every event loses its self-identity and is explained as repetition. For all its aspiration towards the free action of the subject, Enlightenment's 'arid wisdom' derives from the causal structure of action and reaction in myth.[28] In reason as in myth, an end can never just be an end. What goes for the musing over the 'fact of our ending' in 'The Country Funeral' also goes for these last words of the whole collection of *Creatures of the Earth*, an interconnected series of existential segments in which language detonates meaning under cover of denotative naturalist facts.

Notes

1 See document P71/619 in the John McGahern archive, James Hardiman Library, NUI Galway.

2 Luke Gibbons, *Transformations in Irish Culture* (Cork: Cork University Press, 1996), p. 84.

3 Declan Kiberd, *Inventing Ireland*, p. 485.

4 James Whyte, *History, Myth and Ritual in the Fiction of John McGahern*, p. 122.

5 See, for example, Heather Ingman, *A History of the Irish Short Story* (Cambridge: Cambridge University Press, 2009), pp. 49 and 272. Ingman refers to an article by Peter Denham which discusses the continuities between Carleton and McGahern: Peter Denham, 'William Carleton and Samuel Ferguson: Lives and Contacts', in *William Carleton: The Authentic Voice*, ed. Gordon Brand (Gerrards Cross: Colin Smythe, 2006), pp. 360–77.

6 Frank O'Connor, *Collected Stories* (New York: Knopf, 1981), p. 55. All subsequent references to this edition are made in the text.

7 Michel Foucault, *The Foucault Reader*, ed. Paul Rabinow (London: Penguin, 1984), p. 45.

8 Theodor W. Adorno and Max Horkheimer, *Dialectic of Enlightenment*, trans. John Cumming (London: Verso, 2008), p. 6.

9 Foucault, *The Foucault Reader*, pp. 38–9.

10 Adorno and Horkheimer, *Dialectic of Enlightenment*, p. 12.

11 Ibid., p. 12.

12 Ibid., p. 16.

13 Seamus Deane, *Strange Country: Modernity and Nationhood in Irish Writing Since 1970* (Oxford: Clarendon, 1997), p. 23.

14 Deane, *Strange Country*, pp. 7–8.

15 Ibid., p. 18.

16 E. R. Dodds, *The Greeks and the Irrational* (Berkeley, CA: University of California Press, 1951), p. 2.

17 Dodds, *The Greeks and the Irrational*, pp. 49, 13.

18 Ibid., p. 13.

19 McGahern quotes Dodds in a brief review: 'I need hardly say that religion and morals were not initially interdependent in Greece or elsewhere; they had their separate roots. I suppose that, broadly speaking, religion grows out of man's relationship to his total environment, and morals out of his relation to his fellow-men' (*LW* 323).

20 Jürgen Habermas, *The Philosophical Discourse of Modernity* (Oxford: Blackwell, 1990), p. 115.

21 Whyte, *History, Myth and Ritual in the Fiction of John McGahern*, p. 124.

22 See W. B. Yeats, 'A Dialogue of Self and Soul', in *Collected Poems*, p. 266.

23 See Friedrich Nietzsche, *Thus Spoke Zarathustra*, trans. R. J. Hollingdale (Harmondsworth: Penguin, 2003), p. 326.

24 Friedrich Nietzsche, *The Gay Science*, trans. Walter Kaufmann (New York: Random House, 1974), p. 273.

25 Eamon Grennan, '"Only What Happens": Mulling Over McGahern', *Irish University Review* 35, no. 1 (Spring/Summer 2005), p. 17.
26 Whyte, *History, Myth and Ritual in the Fiction of John McGahern*, pp. 125–6.
27 Sampson, 'The "Rich Whole"', p. 34.
28 Adorno and Horkheimer, *Dialectic of Enlightenment*, p. 12.

9

Habit, Memory and Time: 'A Slip-Up', 'The Wine Breath', 'All Sorts of Impossible Things' and 'Gold Watch'

Introduction

This chapter concentrates on the relationship between habit, memory and time in four stories, all of which appeared in the later American edition of the *Getting Through* collection of 1980. Although the importance to McGahern of a paradigmatically Proustian involuntary memory cannot be doubted, these stories consistently test the restorative power of memory against other modernist legacies of memory and time. In 'A Slip-Up', McGahern explores models of voluntary memory, related to a continued aphasic dependence on mnemonic habit, as much to be understood through Bergson as through Proust. Although 'The Wine Breath' is indeed initiated by an involuntary memory which irrupts into the habitual present, it goes on to question the limits of memory as a replenishing force, and in this it recalls Beckett's early response to Proust.

In the second part of this chapter, the idea is pursued, as it is in the following commentary on *Rising Sun*, that McGahern's fictions do not inevitably lead to the idea that restorative memory is an all-encompassing transcendent signified. McGahern writes complex fictions of time. This continues to involve his Proustian inheritance, as there are examples in his fiction, albeit rare, when the prose texture embodies time, syntactically intermixing actual and hypothetical planes of time, as in 'All Sorts of Impossible Things'. Differentiating between such obviously overlapping concepts as memory and time is worthwhile, as it brings out certain Augustinian and Bergsonian qualities in McGahern's rendering of philosophically aporetic time. McGahern's most self-aware story of time, 'Gold Watch', is notable for relating the tyranny of habit not only to memory but to expectation. This story considers the working of time as both an impersonally 'endless' and personally end-directed process.

Willed memory: 'A Slip-Up'

'A Slip-Up' lingers upon a displaced old man's reliance on an extreme form of voluntary memory – a desperately willed daily habit which takes him out of the present. Having retired in an unnamed, implicitly suburban and probably British environment, Michael has adopted a daily routine for years – walking with his wife to Tesco's and waiting for her outside while she shops. While he walks with his wife, in his mind he walks with his mother along the lake to the farm, 'safe in the shelter of those dead days' (*CE* 85), and while waiting at the supermarket he sets himself the mental tasks of repairing the run-down old farm and reclaiming its fields. Michael's memories are incorporated into the present, rigorously and habitually cultivated, like the fields he used to own. He undertakes what might be thought of as 'virtual' tasks, and so complete is his identification with his brainwork that he takes breaks, leaning on his shovel, as if experiencing physical tiredness.

Though the story is concerned with the relationship between habit and memory, it does not invoke memories which are overlaid by habit and can only be recovered involuntarily. Rather, McGahern explores how the old man habitually preserves memory in the present, and is careful to exploit free indirect discourse in deleting the more obvious signal that a border is being crossed between past and present. Michael's interior life ousts the threadbare and vacant 'real' (waiting outside of Tesco's), and these remembered events take on a disconcerting solidity in the narrative, materially penetrating the present scene, almost as if the shovelling, unblocking and pruning is taking place in the precinct of a superstore car park: 'For all that time he was unaware of the shopping bag, but when all the water had flowed down towards the pool he felt it [the shopping bag] again by his side' (*CE* 86). Michael is 'working' in his memory, and this is connected to the idea that he is voluntarily undertaking the work *of* memory itself, something which Bergson's *Matter and Memory* helps to elucidate.

Bergson distinguishes between two types of memory, the memory-image and the repeated memory. The memory-image is stored in the past and coloured by its specific time and place, of which it bears the unique outlines; it is a personal image, a spontaneous representation of the past which cannot be repeated. This is broadly comparable to Proust's involuntary memory. The repeated memory, on the other hand, is a motor-mechanism which makes use of the past in the present; it is memory as forward-moving action which renders the original image-memory somehow alien to us; it is a repeated habit which helps us live in and cope with the present, rather than represent the past. It is clear from this distinction that Michael, making daily use of his memory as a stable mechanism, and giving solidity to his mental activity in the present, conforms to Bergson's second category. Michael's routine of memorized farm-clearing is accurately described in Bergson's definition of mechanical memory:

> It has retained from the past only the *intelligently co-ordinated movements* which represent the *accumulated efforts of the past*, not in the memory-images which recall them, but in the *definite order and systematic character* with which the actual movements take place. In truth it no longer represents our past to us, *it acts it*; and if it still deserves the name of memory, it is not because it conserves bygone images, but because it *prolongs their useful effect into the present* moment. (my italics)[1]

Bergson's allusion to dementia and aphasia in *Matter and Memory*, consistent with his interest in the mechanical elsewhere (say, on laughter), points to how language works as reflex, so that patients suffering from dementia can 'imitate intelligence' at a complex and subtle level, even if in other respects they are losing their minds. The automatism of Michael's behaviour itself suggests the senility that is the ostensible theme of 'A Slip-Up'. Michael's mnemonic habits are the pelmanist gymnastics of a man staving off dementia. He drains and clears his land, pushing back the barbed wire with the hope of making the whole field into a garden. This is a complex, enclosed mental space, and one which he hopes to extend, as if fighting off the diminishment of his physical life in featureless suburbia. Although the story seems to centre on his wife's forgetfulness – leaving her husband standing in front of the supermarket, and then remembering she has done so – it is perhaps more strongly, though less signally, about Michael's own 'slip-up' or slipping away. For two hours, and despite increasing irritation, he merely stands in the same place, tiring himself out with more manual-mental work on the farm. The habits of his memory, 'bent upon action, seated in the present and looking only to the future', as Bergson puts it, have almost entirely supplanted his consciousness of a physical self in the present.[2]

Reading the story through Bergson does not discount its Proustian elements, particularly the Proust constructed by Beckett. The artist needs to forget in order to remember: Beckett half-jokingly claims that Proust had a bad memory.

The banality of 'good' memory Beckett likens to a clothes-line, on which hang past images of dirty linen: such a memory 'is uniform, a creature of routine, at once a condition and function of … impeccable habit, an instrument of reference instead of an instrument of recovery'.[3] Michael is orientating himself by pacing around the farm, which he has lost in real life but has never been lost to memory: it is just this daily instrument of reference.[4] It may be said that his memories are not dormant because they are not so distant: he sold the farm in later life before becoming a school caretaker. This does not account, however, for his mental reliance on also walking with his mother in a deeper past, which is allied to more recently lost days clearing the overgrown fields and unblocking the drinking pool. The 'shelter of those days' constitutes a temporal refuge from the material habits of the present, such as taking a bottle of Bass at the Royal. Michael's habit 'drapes the formless pain of being', in Proust's words, protecting him from suffering; or in another metaphor which Beckett appreciated, and which speaks of the impoverishment of Michael's daily routine, his habit 'requires the least fostering, and is the first to appear on the seeming desolation of the most barren rock'.[5] Michael's mental behaviour brings out the Beckettian-in-Proust, or vice versa – what lies behind lines such as *Godot*'s 'habit is a great deadener'.[6] Michael is one in whom 'memory is so closely related to habit that its word takes flesh', as Beckett puts it, and may be compared to one of Beckett's routine-reliants, those exhausters of the closed system trying to keep out the void, a failing Cartesian figure clinging on to the mind he is losing.[7]

Bergson emphasizes how the automatism of the habit-forming human subject threatens creativity and autonomy. The implication is that creative art must be free of such motor-mechanism: it is because of this disturbing loss of agency that Michael clearly cannot stand in as one of McGahern's shadowy artist surrogates. Proust, like Bergson, is clear about how art must overcome the inertia which prevents the enrichment of memory through unique lost images: McGahern's aesthetic statement, 'The Image', is just such an apotheosis of the memory-image. This does not, however, stop McGahern from exploring other workings of memory which are traceable to his interest in Proust and Beckett's rendering of Proust. A. E. Pilkington has argued that Proust's references to the analgesic effects of habit (*l'effet analgesique*), or to the barrier of habit (*le cloison d'habitude*), signal an ambivalent view that even for the artist – after all, like Michael, an extreme case – habit is necessary to ward off constant suffering or delight.[8] The hyper-sensitive artist must be blunted by habit, otherwise life would be unliveable, and it is just that blunting which allows something unremembered, untouched by habit and re-emerging from the depths of forgetting, to have such force. Michael is the self-protecting subject pushed to a certain limit, but his restoration of the past is *not* linked to the creative composition of art. The story is a portrait of the old man as a retired caretaker – an astringent to the potentially sentimental view of the artist rejuvenated by memory. The same might be said of another more overtly Proustian story in *Getting Through*, 'The Wine Breath'.

The overdetermined text: 'The Wine Breath'

'The Wine Breath' immediately declares its Proustian structure. Like Marcel tasting the madeleine, treading on the uneven paving-stone, or hearing the clattering of a spoon, a priest's glimpsing of sunlight on the beech chips is a connecting instant or 'simple trigger' (*CE* 112) to the childhood memory of a snowbound funeral which occurred in the bitter winter of early 1947. The priest 'found himself stumbling into these dead days' (*CE* 112): the accidental sense-impression grants access to a more powerful form of memory than that called up volitionally, precisely because the memory has been forgotten. In this story, McGahern seems to elaborate on his statement that 'what we forget is as revealing as what we remember' and that involuntary memories 'are more true because they surprise us, evading will and habit'.[9] In case the initial emphasis in 'The Wine Breath' on the visual may seem out of kilter with Proust, it is also mentioned that the smell of crushed mint had once given the priest back a day, making him feel as if he had 'fallen through time' (*CE* 112). The story begins by clearly emulating this Proustian 'stumbling' upon memory.

However, the title, a quotation from Yeats's 'All Souls' Night', tells us that this is also a Yeatsian story about the presence of ghosts, as Frank Shovlin and Bertrand Cardin have so persuasively demonstrated.[10] The three friends that Yeats calls up, purgatorial spirits abroad after midnight, are implicitly likened to one of the lingering souls whom the priest's mother imagines neglected in purgatory, to the ghost of the dead mother and eventually to the priest himself. The priest enters a liminal zone where the dead walk as 'shadows among the living', as McGahern put it in late essay (*LW* 149), reminding us that though our gross palates may drink from it, yet 'No living man can drink from the whole wine'.[11] The supposedly Proustian recuperation of memory can be reconfigured as a Yeatsian 'dreaming back' from the underworld or a drawing upon Yeats's storehouse of images.[12] What is more, the blanket of snow which is 'general' over Ireland in the winter of 1947 inevitably brings to mind a Joycean sense that 'the world of the dead was as available' to the priest 'as the world of the living' (*CE* 112). The story cannot be regarded as uniformly either 'Proustian' or 'Yeatsian', then, but rather bears the weight of potentially conflicting modernist inscriptions. Modernists throng at the priest's door, as if the ghostliness of the story is itself a manifestation of its overdetermined allusiveness.

'The Wine Breath' moves between rendering 'time present as a flimsy accumulating tissue over all the time that was lost' (*CE* 115), which suggests the transcendent displacement of the present by the past, and recognizing the stubbornness of the material world. The 'actual day' – that is, the present (*actuel*) day of everyday actions – stands 'solidly and impenetrably there' (*CE* 113), despite the effulgence of the past scene. It is implied that the priest's duties in the present, such as making arrangements for an operation on a parishioner's piles, have smothered the essence of things, chaining him to the 'tortuous existence of the everyday' (*CE* 115). In celebrating the power of involuntary memory in recapturing the past 'dead day', the story also insists upon the immovability of the 'actual' day which is irrupted into. The present may be unwilling to yield up memory at the behest of human will, as is exemplified when Marcel, deliberately stumbling again on the same stone, is unable to conjure the Venetian Baptistery into existence.

To Proust, it is the delicate coexistence of time past and present, not the wholesale substitution of one by the other, which reveals what he calls the 'essence of things'. We move beyond the recuperation of lost time towards the timeless:

> But let a noise or a scent, once heard or once smelt, be heard or smelt again in the present and at the same time in the past, *real without being actual, ideal without being abstract*, and immediately the permanent and *habitually concealed essence of things* is liberated and *our true self, which seemed – had perhaps for long years seemed – to be dead but was not altogether dead, is awakened* and reanimated as it received the *celestial nourishment* that is brought to it. A minute freed from the order of time has re-created in us, to feel it, the *man freed from the order of time*. And one can understand that this man should have confidence in his joy, even if the simple taste of a madeleine does not seem to logically contain within it the reasons for this joy, one can understand that the word *'death' should have no meaning for him*; *situated outside time*, why should he fear the future (my italics)?[13]

This eventual entrance into the extra-temporal order finally creates the right conditions for the Proustian artist, ending his apprenticeship to signs so that he can now re-descend into his depths, or range about the distant epochal peaks of his life, this time as an artist as well as remembering subject. The making of the timeless object is the artist's defence against death: Time the destroyer is supplanted by Time the artist.

McGahern's priest is also 'freed from the order of time': the lost day awakens in him a sense that he is 'bathed in the eternal' (*CE* 113), so that it 'was all timeless, and seemed at least a promise of the eternal' (*CE* 118). Memory grants him access to a form of the 'celestial nourishment' Proust describes. He became a priest in order to vanquish death, of which he was afraid. Although involuntary memory initially radiates as a model of the afterlife, conceived of as the timeless 'world of God' (*CE* 113), the priest's belief in the 'promise of the eternal' is put in doubt. It may offer an increasingly chilly comfort – an absence which 'does not cast a shadow' and which is, after Yeats in 'A Cold Heaven', 'riddled with light'.[14] Unlike for Proust, the consolation of art is not available to the priest.

Paul Ricœur has written of Proust that in regaining time he regains death. Marcel recovers his grandmother, after the mismatch between desire and time which is named 'the intermittence of the heart', only when he fully recovers her loss. The priest regains the dead man, Michael Bruen, and also stumbles into the 'dead days' of his own lost mother, similarly demonstrating that the replenishment of memory is co-extensive with the experience of loss. By recovering Bruen's death he also remembers the communal ritual of the funeral, and the apprehension of 'the Mystery in such awesomeness' (*CE* 111). This seems to suggest a transcendent spiritual replenishment which the seemingly confident inception of 'The Wine Breath' has encouraged. It is true that the priest's apprehension of eternal timelessness is distinct from what Beckett conceived of in *Proust* as a Schopenhauerian annihilation or 'obliteration' of time.[15] Nevertheless, a sense of Beckettian impoverishment cannot be entirely banished. For the priest, we might say that there is a growing awareness of his 'unself', a confirmation of that earlier thought that 'he'd miss nothing, being nothing' (*CE* 114). This is not the full Beckettian 'poetics of indigence', but the recuperation of the self in eternity does not radiate with the priest's initial awe.[16]

Yeats's friends drink the fumes of muscatel at high table: they are 'companionable', suggesting that the priest may be comforted by the notion that he can experience death as 'but passing from one room to another', as Yeats put it.[17] However, the priest is finally imprisoned within his 'walls of sense', in a room that is 'empty and dead and dry', a 'room that was an end' (*CE* 120). He is left with only his oaken (rather than high) table and scattered books, the equivalent of what Beckett's Malone calls his 'whole family of objects'.[18] Victor Sage argues that the priest lingers like a Beckettian solitary in a 'purgatorial endgame', eventually deprived of the transfiguring sense of Mystery, and that a kind of post-Enlightenment uncanniness remains in the priest's own ghost.[19] Beckett's configurations of nothingness linger on the threshold in all their denied sublimity: like Nietzsche's nihilism standing at the door, they are 'the uncanniest of all guests'.[20] Yeatsian and Beckettian ghosts are hardly mutually exclusive, though. McGahern commented that he saw 'some of Beckett's works as full of Yeats'.[21] One of Beckett's spectral TV plays, '… but the clouds …', in fact takes its title from Yeats's *The Tower*, as 'The Wine Breath' does. Just as the story is overcrowded by its literary ghosts, overdetermined by allusion, it is finally indeterminate about what the priest feels his accompanying ghost, an 'absence that does not cast a shadow' (*CE* 120), may be beckoning him towards: the timeless afterlife, a state of purgatorial lingering, or 'nothing'.

At the end of the story, the priest displaces his life on to a ghostly other, a young man clutching a wine bottle before meeting a woman: a secular double who feels himself to be 'immersed in time without end', and who will (grossly) taste the wine and live the life the priest did not (*CE* 120). This is the alternative life of what Shovlin calls the 'carnal joy' which the priest might have led – say, with Michael Bruen's pretty daughter.[22] It is suggestive that the priest's end is ghosted, as memory extends into imagination, by an alternative beginning: the young man's embedded future-in-the-past which did not happen but might have happened. That young counterpart should not be seen as occupying a privileged position over the priest, because *his* time would also have an end, and also because, as Yeats's speaker of 'mummy truths' says, 'No living man can drink from the whole wine'. The priest is not suddenly transformed into the Proustian apprentice artist, or into the Yeatsian elegist of 'All Souls' Night', for bringing this young man to life from within the sanctum of his dead room. However, the merest shiver of poetic potentiality is permitted – the inference that the past may be transformed and made present by the imagination. This intimation of artistic autonomy forms part of the conclusion to another story in *Getting Through*, 'All Sorts of Impossible Things'.

The sentence as site of time: 'All Sorts of Impossible Things'

The title of 'The Wine Breath' is designed to 'call up' Yeats's literary ghost: the allusion conforms to a model of intertextuality which is semantic or 'lexicocentric', in David Duff's phrase. However, the clear dependence in the story on a Proustian narrative of recovered memory suggests that intertextual engagement may be regarded not only in semantic terms but also, as Julia Kristeva has conceived, at a syntactic and phonic level.[23] A closer *intertextual* inspection of 'All Sorts of Impossible Things', a story that culminates with a long, unspooling periodic sentence, suggests that temporal complexity is embodied in syntax.

The story is centred conventionally enough on death and the apprehension of mortality. Two friends have enjoyed training a greyhound: Lennon, the agricultural instructor with a weak heart on the wrong side, and Sharkey, who always wears a hat to cover his baldness. Lennon dies before he can be made permanent in his job. Sharkey lost the love of his life because he pushed too quickly for marriage. Premature baldness, a reminder for Sharkey of '*timor mortis*' (*CE* 97), destroyed the illusion that 'time would wait for them forever' and the covering up of his head is a mark of the 'passion to secure his life as he felt it slip away' (*CE* 95). The story plays on the idea of the temporary and the permanent. The instructor's early death preserves his professional temporariness: in an archaic etymological meaning, he is temporary in that he occurs or exists in time, not in eternity. For Sharkey, the permanent placing of the hat is a defence against his own ageing – his same existence in time, or temporariness.

Time is thematized in these ways, but the story is lifted into greater temporal complexity in a single-sentence paragraph which contrasts to the laconically witty dialogue which has preceded it. Sharkey has taken ownership of the greyhound after Lennon's funeral:

> As he petted her down, gripping her neck, bringing his own face down to hers, thinking how he had come by her, he felt the same rush of feeling as he had felt when he watched the locks of hair fall on to the towel round the neck in the room; but instead of prayer he now felt a wild longing to throw his hat away and walk round the world bareheaded, find some girl, not necessarily Cathleen O'Neill, but any young girl, and go to the sea with her as he used to, leave the car at the harbour wall and take the boat for the island, the engine beating like a good heart under the deck boards as the waves rocked it on turning out of the harbour, hold her in one long embrace all night between the hotel sheets; or train the fawn again, feed her the best steak from town, walk her four miles every day from months, stand in the mud and rain again and see her as Coolcarra Queen race through the field in the Rockingham Stakes, see the judge gallop over to the rope on the old fat horse, and this time lift high the red kerchief to give the Silver Cup to the Queen.
>
> And until he calmed, and went into the house, his mind raced with desire for all sorts of such impossible things. (*CE* 103)

The sentence enacts the simultaneity of past and future, what has happened, what might have happened, but what can no longer happen. The desire to find a girl, on the one hand, and to train and race the greyhound, on the other, are mutually exclusive futures held in equipoise by the grammatical pivot of the conjunction and the semicolon. Both futures are remodellings of the past. Shared passion remained open and possible, the teacher's hair luxuriant, until a decision had to be taken whether to marry or to delay: thereafter, this love died and the teacher covered his head. The greyhound was also trained with great passion, until it was realized that it could never be a champion. The sentence is forward-flung, propelled by desire towards two ideal futures. Short stories often end with wild longings for things that, the ironic matter of the main story has shown, can no longer happen. This story amplifies that shiver of potentiality at the end of 'The Wine Breath', encoding an alternative future-in-the-past. The recycling of the text disturbs linearity, back-tracking to a plane of time contained in the teacher's imagination. The impossibility of those imagined futures – he will not find 'some girl' like Eileen, the unexceptional hound cannot become a champion, no matter how many prime cuts he eats – is only asserted in a final short paragraph.

Developing Adorno's idea that the living totality of Proust's text is apprehensible in the 'rank vegetal proliferation' of its particulars, Malcolm Bowie argues that the Proustian sentence, with its birfurcating and ramifying syntax, is itself a site of time.[24] The unruliness of the prose must not be smoothed out to answer to those parts of the novels when the narrator explains the temporal architecture of the whole. Instead, according to Bowie, the heterogeneity of the sentence is imitative of the immediacy of time as we experience it – an intermixed condition of desire, expectation, anticipation and retrospection, prematurity and belatedness, of memories not so much relived as manipulated and remade; a time when the present is haunted both by the past and by a future which may be pre-ordained or may still be open or 'free'. The Proustian sentence frustrates linearity, defers its destination, as if reformulating the goal of its own meaning in its very unfolding; in this it is like 'the rough-and-tumble of lived time', acting directly upon the reader's sense of how 'we live like this, now too early and now too late'.[25] Even as we marvel at the last passages on geological time, as the narrator looks down from his giddy summits as he reaches towards a summation of his temporal credo, we must continue to respect embodied time, *temps incorporé*, and to resist closure.[26]

The economy of the short story leaves the 'syntactic travail' of McGahern's long sentence in stark isolation, emphasizing the miniaturization of Proustian form.[27] There is a self-recapitulating, synecdochic quality to the prose fragment. The simile 'like a good heart' is of course not accidentally chosen but recalls the instructor's own fatally misplaced heart. We might say that the transferring of the physical 'heart' to the vehicle of a literary figure is deliberately conspicuous, an almost clumsy signal that the reader should attend to language itself. The syntactic bifurcation and pulse of the sentence enact the binary structure of the whole story: the white flag or the red flag, the hare escaping or being caught, the heart beating on the right side or failing on the wrong side, the possible or impossible. The story considers the philosophical excluding of the middle: like the greyhound which is neither champion nor dud, it is claimed that the 'in-between' is 'the very worst' (*CE* 91). The hypothetical narrative is the path not taken in life, like that of the priest in 'The Wine Breath'. The language of imagination offers some consolation, but the Aristotelian possibility of poetry is not indulged for too long: the short coda cools the excitement of exfoliating language, insisting on what time, with ruthless determinism, makes impossible.

Tick-tick and tick-tock: 'Gold Watch'

The meeting of the lovers which opens 'Gold Watch' again appears to be circumscribed by Proust. For the narrator, the scent of coffee in Bewley's which blows through the vents out on to Grafton Street is 'for ever mixed with the memory of that morning' (*CE* 134). Although coffee seems to stand in for the madeleine as the memory-releasing sense-impression, the temporality of the sentence interferes with the idea that memory has been instantaneously restored. Retrospect and repetition are built into the narrator's account: *every* time he passes by Bewley's (he is a Dublin resident), he remembers meeting his lover. It is a habitual and associative rather than involuntary memory. There is something immutably benign about the narrator's memory of this first meeting and the 'peace and loveliness that [he] will always link with those high-ceilinged rooms' (*CE* 135). This may be Proustian in the sense that, say, Albertine is always 'linked' to, and inseparable from, the seaside of Balbec. However, Marcel's memory signs are 'always' and 'for ever' subject to reinterpretation. When this involves the perception of the beloved by the lover (be it Odette by Swann, Albertine by Marcel or Morel by Charlus), the instability of the memory is more extremely felt. In Proust, memory can be deception: the truth behind the lie, and the source of jealousy and anguish. This is not the case in 'Gold Watch' but it nevertheless becomes clear that the peace of cherished memory is not going to be a sustaining force in the story, and will be supplanted by an apprehension of time, conceived of as alternately tyrannical and indifferent.

One of the distinctive features of the story is that it connects habit to time, rather than to memory. Habit in this case is not diurnal but annual: the narrator's 'habitual going home' (*CE* 136) will allow him to outwear his father by harnessing Proust's concept of destructive time. By helping stack the hay, he resists the charge of filial betrayal which the father is desperate to impute to him. He is not recovering the lost time of familial childhood like the remembering Marcel, but prolonging its routines into the present. There is no breaking away from habit because this would expose him to the suffering of being (the final rift with the monstrous father), and to the destructiveness of onrushing time. This story particularly brings out Beckett's observation that 'habit is the ballast that chains the dog to its vomit', reminding us of the equally monstrous father in 'Wheels' who dismisses the claims of Romantic pastoralism: 'stare at beauty every day and it'll turn sicker than stray vomit' (*CE* 10).[28] The city-dwelling son in 'Gold Watch' is chained to the 'vomit' of his natural childhood, and is not yet afforded the freedom of the autonomous, implicitly creative subject who experiences loss and forgetting in order to remember.

The narrator is preoccupied by time, whether it be 'the right time' or 'the wrong time', 'just time' (*CE* 143) or indeed unjust time. Time is endless, as the 'endlessly circling' (*CE* 143, 150) watch tells him. Equally, though, it is determined by ends: the 'natural end' of generational change which nature insists upon and must be fatalistically accepted. No privileged meaning should be bestowed upon that which is 'just … the end of something that has gone on for a very long time' (*CE* 146). There is, in contrast, the 'unnatural' end which has been imposed by human agency. 'It had been ended' (*CE* 146): the father attempts to stop or kill time by bringing the family gathering of the hay to a premature or unnatural end, by not passing on the watch, thereby arresting patrilineal succession, and most obviously by trying to smash and corrode the watch. The son, too, wishes to impose his own end – the stamp of his own telic shape and that of his generation – by gathering the hay for the last time, so that he is free to make a new beginning with his pregnant wife. But he also comes to realize that the human need to differentiate time is an anthropomorphizing urge finally contrasted to the indifference of 'time that did not have to run to any conclusion' (*CE* 150).

If time has ends but is endless, it is conceptually abyssal. 'Gold Watch' can be read alongside expositions of aporetic time philosophy, beginning with St Augustine's *Confessions*, a book revered by McGahern, and in which it is declared that 'time exists in the sense that it tends towards non-existence'.[29] Augustine puzzles about how we measure what cannot be measured: 'the times we measure are not those which do not yet exist, nor those which already have no existence, nor those which extend over no interval of time, nor those which *reach no conclusions. …* Yet we measure periods of time' (my italics).[30] As he draws out the corroding watch from the barrel, the narrator tries to articulate the aporia of time: 'only what *was* increased or diminished as it changed, became only what is, becoming again what *was* even faster than the small second hand endlessly circling in the poison' (*CE* 119). Such an obdurate observation draws upon the Augustinian paradox that present time is both threefold thick with past, present and future (*distentio*), and yet also a vanishing point (*intentio*) which occupies no space.[31] The accent is on the word 'only'. 'Only what is' can mean that the present is a fugitive moment instantaneously erased. 'Only what was' is a lengthening time we measure and on which our habitual behaviour may be reliant but which no longer exists.

Bergson calls this Augustinian notion of *distentio* 'extensity', and argues that we 'project time into space', though space does not preserve any trace of the successive moments of the present. Bergson looks at the hands of a clock:

> When I follow with my eyes on the dial of a clock the movement of the hand which corresponds to the oscillations of the pendulum, I do not measure duration, as seems to be thought: I merely count simultaneities, which is very different. Outside of me, in space, there is never more than a single position of the hand and the pendulum, for nothing is left of the past positions. Within myself a process of organization or interpenetration of conscious states is going on, which constitutes true duration.[32]

Like Bergson, the narrator knows that he is counting simultaneities, aware that the position of the second hand vanishes without trace. This does not negate, however, the inner experience of duration – 'what was', between father and son, has built painfully enough to 'what is', and will soon at last become 'what was'. Despite the invisibility or indifference of time, the ego perceives itself as enduring in a set of interpenetrating states of memory, attention and anticipation. It is this which allows the disabused narrator still to wait hopefully in a perfect moonlit night for some 'word or truth', and to be 'amused at the expectation' which poisoned time still renews (*CE* 150).

Whereas Bergson follows the clock with his eyes, the insistence in 'Gold Watch' is more on listening. 'I *heard* the ticking'; 'The ticking of the watch down in the barrel was so completely *muffled* by the spray that *only by imagination* could it be *heard*; the watch was '*silent* or running' (my italics, *CE* 150). While staying with Saint-Loup in Doncières, Marcel considers what he calls 'the problem of sound'.

He hears the ticking of his friend's watch in the barrack-room but cannot initially place where it is coming from; when he locates the ticking, he reflects that rather than hearing the tick 'in a fixed place' he rather 'saw it there, for sounds have no position in space'.[33] Sounds are temporal, warning us of movements and making them appear necessary and natural. A person who has wadded his ears, or who has become deaf, is deprived of 'the perceptible form which the cause of a movement assumed', whereas objects which 'moved soundlessly now seemed to be moved without cause'; they 'seem to be alone' and to 'move, halt, alight of their own accord'.[34] According to Marcel, the deaf man lives in a kind of fairy-tale world without sounds and without consecution – in effect, without teleological time. The narrator of 'Gold Watch' hears *by imagination*: perhaps by imagining the causality of ticking, he is trying to reactivate his faith in the capacity of time to outwear his father.

The 'time that did not have to run to any conclusion' is equivalent to what Frank Kermode, in *The Sense of an Ending*, describes as *chronos*.[35] *Chronos* is 'waiting time', perhaps 'one damned thing after another', or the time that Beckett says 'would have passed anyway'. *Kairos*, on the other hand, represents our very efforts to pass this time: that is, to divide the empty *chronos* and find concord between its demarcations. Apocalypse, epoch, season: *kairos* is 'fated' or 'charged' time: human beings, and more particularly fiction writers, impose ends to create transformative 'moments of significance which harmonize origin and end'.[36] In a well-known example, we are asked by Kermode to consider the man-made narrative of 'tick-tock' (not tick-tick): tock, as the anticipated ending to tick, confers meaning on the plot 'in the middest'. This is the intensely experienced, end-directed *kairos*, whereas the gap between tock and tick is formless chronicity, lying outside of the structure of expectation. The narrator's consideration of 'what was' and 'what is', and his mention of that very expectation caused by the ticking of the gold watch, conform to the innate need for *kairos*, for the tick-to-tock of the natural end. But the second hand of the watch is 'endlessly circling in the poison'. The tick-tick is of time as pure *chronos*, of time passing, increasing or lessening: the time without conclusion which lies outside and beyond concatenated human fictions.

Finally, the eponymous emblematizing of the timepiece is a notably self-conscious strategy, both in McGahern's fiction and elsewhere, as the final chapter on McGahern's last novel takes into account. It thus seems significant that Patrick Kavanagh's minor poem from the early 1930s, 'Gold Watch', which he regarded as part of a turn to an objectivist style, shares the same title as McGahern's short story. The represented everyday object speaks with the sincerity of the poem itself, and the same goes for the compressed and symbolic form of the short story which, in its sophisticated time-writing, demands to be lingered over as a precious textual object. In both the poem and the story, the watches are made by Elgin and have the same features: for McGahern, the 'delicate hands were of blue steel' (*CE* 142); for Kavanagh, 'Slender hands/ Of blue steel'. Kavanagh's watch, twice mended, is seen as careworn and feminine, and in the last stanza is implicitly personified as a queen who has usurped the male counting-house, from where she will dole out the subject's mortality, his 'pennies of time'.[37] This in turn emphasizes the extent to which time is gendered in McGahern's story. The gold watch remains an object of oedipal conflict – the Elgin company used Old Father Time as its company insignia – even after the narrator's lover has it mended. As for Kavanagh, the gold watch in McGahern's story is emblematic of the art-object itself: as Sampson argues, an 'artefact that is both separated from chronological time and yet defined by it'.[38] The aesthetic autonomy of this short story can be defined through its own narration of time, the way its claim to span tick-to-tock is balanced by an existential amusement at the endlessness of tick-tick. The narrator's sense of an ending is a model for how fiction must always mark its segments of undifferentiated time, and there is something irresistibly self-referential in the last word, 'conclusion' (*CE* 150).

Notes

1 Henri Bergson, *Matter and Memory*, trans. N. M. Paul and W. S. Palmer (New York: Zone Books, 1991), p. 82.

2 Bergson, *Matter and Memory*, p. 82.

3 Samuel Beckett, *Proust and Three Dialogues with Georges Duthuit* (London: John Calder, 1999), pp. 29–30.

4 Elsewhere, McGahern associates the quasi-pelmanist practice of memory with 'keeping going' in the present: see essay on Ernie O'Malley 'walking' down the right bank of the Shannon (*LW* 254), and also Rose's walking a lane in her mind while living in Glasgow in *Amongst Women* (*AW* 30).

5 Beckett, *Proust*, p. 28.

6 Samuel Beckett, *Waiting for Godot* (London: Faber and Faber, 2010), p. 87.

7 Beckett, *Proust*, p. 31.

8 A. E. Pilkington, *Bergson and His Influence* (Cambridge: Cambridge University Press, 1976), pp. 163–7.

9 Quoted in Whyte, *History, Myth and Ritual in the Fiction of John McGahern*, p. 231.

10 Frank Shovlin, 'The Ghost of W.B. Yeats', *The John McGahern Yearbook* 2 (2009): 42–51; Bertrand Cardin, '"Absence Does Not Cast a Shadow": Yeats's Shadowy Presence in McGahern's "The Wine Breath"', *Journal of the Short Story in English* 53 (Autumn 2009): 111–26.

11 See Shovlin, 'The Ghost of W.B. Yeats', p. 49; Yeats, *Collected Poems*, p. 259.

12 See Cardin, 'Absence Does Not Cast a Shadow', p. 120, Whyte, *History, Myth and Ritual in the Fiction of John McGahern*, p. 127 and Shovlin, 'The Ghost of W.B. Yeats', p. 45.

13 Marcel Proust, *Time Regained* (London: Chatto & Windus, 1992), pp. 224–5.

14 Yeats, 'A Cold Heaven', in *Collected Poems*, p. 140.

15 Steven Connor has argued that Beckett may pessimistically undervalue the Proustian possibility of 'rediscovering those selves lost to time', and John Pilling of Beckett's admiration for the way in which Proust constructed an auto-symbolic self, irrespective of the claims of the unself. Steven Connor, *Samuel Beckett: Repetition, Theory and Text* (Cambridge: Cambridge University Press, 1988), p. 49.

16 The phrase is John Pilling's.

17 Yeats's *On the Boiler* quoted by Cardin, 'Absence Does not Cast a Shadow', p. 121.

18 Samuel Beckett, *Malone Dies*, in *Trilogy* (London and New York: John Calder, 1994), p. 251.

19 Victor Sage, 'McGahern's Inverted Uncanny', in *Territoires de L'Étrange Dans la Littérature Au XXe Siècle*, ed. Gaid Girard (Rennes: Presses Universitaires de Rennes, 2009), pp. 197, 205.

20 Friedrich Nietzsche, *The Will to Power*, quoted in Shane Weller, *A Taste for the Negative: Beckett and Nihilism* (London: Legenda, 2005), p. 3. Weller provides the original German: *dieser unheimlichste aller Gäste.*

21 McGahern quoted in Maher, *The Church and Its Spire*, p. 192.

22 Shovlin, 'The Ghost of W.B. Yeats', p. 49.

23 Duff, 'Intertexuality versus Genre Theory', pp. 59, 68.

24 Adorno quoted in Malcolm Bowie, *Proust Among the Stars* (London: HarperCollins, 1998), p. 33.

25 Bowie, *Proust Among the Stars*, pp. 34–5.

26 Ibid., p. 67.

27 Ibid., p. 37.

28 Beckett, *Proust*, p. 19.

29 St Augustine, *Confessions*, trans. Henry Chadwick (Oxford: Oxford World's Classics, 1992) p. 231.

30 St Augustine, *Confessions*, p. 241.

31 See Paul Ricœur, *Time and Narrative*, vol. 1, trans. Kathleen McLaughlin and David Pellauer (Chicago and London: University of Chicago Press, 1984), pp. 5–31.

32 Henri Bergson, *Time and Free Will* (London: Allen & Unwin, 1910), p. 108.
33 Marcel Proust, *The Guermantes Way* (London: Chatto & Windus, 1992), pp. 78–9.
34 Proust, *The Guermantes Way*, p. 81.
35 Frank Kermode, *The Sense of an Ending: Studies in the Theory of Fiction* (Oxford: Oxford University Press, 1967), pp. 46–7.
36 Kermode, *The Sense of an Ending*, p. 48.
37 Patrick Kavanagh, *Collected Poems*, ed. Antoinette Quinn (London: Penguin, 2005), p. 8.
38 Sampson, *Outstaring Nature's Eye*, p. 187.

10

'Everything that had Flowered had now Come to Fruit': Modernist Time and *That They May Face the Rising Sun*

Modernist Time: 'Askew with the clocks'

Modernism was perceived as an art of time. By 1927, Wyndham Lewis in *Time and Western Man* had seen enough of the pervasive Bergsonian 'time-cult' which had unduly influenced contemporary writing. Lewis rebutted flux and continuity, instead declaring for space and divisibility: 'As much as [Bergson] enjoys the sight of things "penetrating" and "merging" do we enjoy the opposite picture of them standing apart – the wind blowing between them, and the air circulating freely in and out of them. … To the trance of music, with its obsession of Time, with its emotional urgency and visceral agitation, we prefer what Bergson calls "obsession of space"'.[1] Lewis complained about many of the modernists, aiming at Joyce's new unfolding 'time-book', *Work in Progress*. Joyce inevitably wove this polemic into the parodic play of what became *Finnegans Wake* – in punning allusions to Lewis's book ('*Spice and Westend Woman*'), to Bergson ('the sophology of Bitchson … driven under by a purely dime-dime urge') and Einstein ('the theorics of winestain'), or to the temporal Gracehoper's (grasshopper's, Shem's, Joyce's) taunting of the spatial Ondt (ant, Shaun, Lewis): '*Your genus is worldwide, your spacest sublime! By Holy Saltmartin, why can't you beat time?*'[2]

This of course does not mean that modernism cannot be conceived spatially, as Joseph Frank's theory of 'spatial form' attempts to do. Even Proust's recuperation of time can be made to work spatially: Frank thinks of Marcel conceiving of his extra-temporal signs, now to be immortalized in the artwork, like a mountain range, and this informs the way Beckett and Deleuze write about

Proust, too.[3] Nevertheless, in the reader's experience of the modernist narrative, it is hard to ignore the primacy of that 'implied immensity' of inner time which, as Paul Ricœur says, slows and enriches the narrative, while also suggesting the anticipatory trajectory of its future (for example, Clarissa's party in *Mrs Dalloway*, the sense that Bloom and Stephen will eventually meet in *Ulysses*).[4] This is the immensity which extends from Proust even to Beckett's Molloy, who dashes off the 'vast frescoes' of his memories, albeit 'with loathing'.[5] We might add that immensity is not so much implied as there for all to see in the long interior monologues of Woolf, Joyce and Richardson, but it nevertheless holds true that that part of our appreciation of richness derives from knowing that the narrator could seemingly pass with ease to any other consciousness. Erich Auerbach talks of the 'multipersonal' subjective method of *To the Lighthouse* – the way in which Mrs Ramsay is encircled by the consciousness of others, often directed towards her.[6] Woolf's time can be thought of speleologically as an underground network where the reader may pass between the protagonists' caves of consciousness.[7] These are the abstract subjective potentialities of modernism to which Lukács objected: the sense of all those individual inner lives occurring independently of one another, fragmentary and disunited.

Despite its adjacency to *Memoir* and McGahern's general reputation as a writer of memory, *Rising Sun* is notable in largely not excavating the private time of its characters' minds. There is little prolonged representation of the interior life as an experiential process, and no first person remembering subject who, in Proustian style, bridges the day of the present to the 'dead day', as in *The Leavetaking*. There is a retreat from modernist self-consciousness and an effacement of the Proustian subject as *moi profond*. The novel is costive about its depths, something perhaps teasingly encrypted in the symbolism of the lake itself, a mirror turned to 'the depth of the sky', hinting at 'the teeming energy and life of the depths' (*RS* 177). Memories are largely contained within discretely told stories which implicitly make up a collective history, and it is this rather than the time of the mind which purposefully retards the slow narrative. Ricœur observes that the modern novel produces an enrichment of the notion of action through 'mimesis of consciousness': in Molly's monologue, for example, 'saying is still doing' (156). This applies to the residual oral traditions of Irish writing which *Rising Sun* in some ways recuperates, but it also suggests how the novel writes over modernist narrative form. Though insisting upon the almost constant presence of the Ruttledges, McGahern equally resists exploring their cavernous depths, thereby intensifying the pressure on the paltriness of the novel's plot, on the constitutive role of dialogue, and on Jamesie's demands of the ongoing present – that is, for news. There is a deliberate lack of disclosure, despite the teasing hints about Joe's life as a former seminarian and advertising man, or about Kate's job in London.

The ostensible abandonment of profoundly interior modernist time seems to suggest primacy of space. 'It appears to be a novel of place': Daniel Soar's review of *Rising Sun*, aided by an Ordnance Survey map, emphasizes the extent to which the outsider is thrown into the specific but often unnamed localities of Leitrim.[8] We are told at the beginning of the novel that the people by the lake had 'the entire world to themselves' (*RS* 1). Soar compares the special rootedness and entirety of the characters to the birds that Joe imagines crying '*this is mine* out of their separate territories' (*RS* 20). McGahern too cries out '*this is mine*'. The novel expresses that fidelity to the local explained in a late lecture: 'No one comes out of nowhere; one room or town or locality can be made an everywhere. The universal is the local, but with the walls taken away' (*LW* 11). Here McGahern echoes Donne's 'The Good-Morrow', whose lovers may make 'one little roome an every where'. In mapping the new world, explorers have pluralized the very idea of world ('worlds on worlds have showne'), but this need not detain Donne's lovers, who may 'possesse one world' as 'each hath one, and is one'.[9] The sheer topographical solicitude of *Rising Sun* stands for a similarly loving possession of 'one world' – a reticular 'somewhere' in which immanent universalism is perceived. This spatial conjoining of the local to the universal has appealed to critics, offering a way of establishing McGahern's appeal as a writer both of the Irish west midlands and of the world. This foundational localism is embedded as a literary method in various moments in *Rising Sun*: for example, the rafters form squares of light so that 'the whole sky grows from that *small space*' (my italics, *RS* 68). Theorists and translators such as Michael Cronin have written persuasively about how the endless diversity of the micro-space is a universalizing force against blandly monocultural, homogeneous globalism.[10] By framing and gazing upon such an interconnected 'small space', and tarrying with it in his imagination, McGahern seems to endorse such sentiments.

What implications does this enrichment of the separate territory – more generally this adherence to place – have for the reading of time in *Rising Sun*? It does not suggest that, ousted by the complex diversity of localism, time has been relegated to a subsidiary or functional status in the narrative. Rather, the discipline of *Rising Sun*'s immovability allows time to be conceptualized in fully philosophical ways. McGahern exploits the interdependence of time and space in narrative, exemplifying what Bakhtin thought of as the 'intrinsic connectedness' of the chronotope, described as an axial intersection 'where the knots of narrative are tied and untied'.[11] To Mary's question 'What are *we* doing?', Ruttledge answers, 'Standing put while going past' (*RS* 293), speaking as much for the novel's own chronotopic narrative form as for himself. By 'standing put' for a year *Rising Sun* sharpens our awareness of place as a *site of time*: how time, in Bakhtin's metaphor, takes on flesh, or is visible or palpable in the chronotope.[12] *Topos* does not outweigh *chronos*. *Rising Sun* invites eco-critical interpretation partly because in its chronotopes there is an insistence upon how a place, no matter how entire, cannot be untied from the universal processes of natural time.

It is also important to recognize that *Rising Sun* shares the modernist resistance to the threat of the clock – the mechanization which Lawrence called the 'terrible bondage of this tick-tack of time'.[13] This is the tyrannical punctuality of the Harley Street consulting room in *Mrs Dalloway* where the June day is subjected to 'shredding and slicing, dividing and subdividing', or that of patriarchal Big Ben, which imposes the man-made unit of the hour.[14] In general, this is the time which Bergson objected to as 'false … public, spatial, extensive'.[15] Commentators point to the way in which this resistance to the spatializing of time is manifest in various symbolic ways in modernist fiction. Gatsby knocks over the clock on the mantelpiece; in Joseph Conrad's *The Secret Agent*, there is a thwarted act of terrorism directed against the Greenwich Observatory, where the newly standardized and public 'mean time' was being beaten out; in William Faulkner's *The Sound and the Fury*, though Quentin Compson tries to twist off the hands of his watch, 'the watch ticked on … the blank dial with little wheels clicking and clicking behind it'.[16] This last example accords with the father's futile attempt to destroy time in 'Gold Watch'. McGahern's Augustinian sense of time as immeasurable yet endlessly measured is at the heart of modernist scepticism towards the human willing of temporal order and development in a contingent world. *Rising Sun* is utterly in sympathy with this modernist view of time.

This is illustrated in the way the novel rather curiously appropriates from the earlier fiction temporal figures in which, as in modernist texts, meditations on time were signposted by making clocks, watches or calendars conspicuous. The irregular chiming or 'broken medley' (*D* 75) of the priest's clocks in *The Dark* is returned to in *Rising Sun*. Mary and Jamesie have inherited seven or eight clocks from Jamesie's father, who could set them perfectly. Jamesie, the son, is no connoisseur of regular clock time, however: 'Who cares about time? We know the time well enough' (*RS* 99). Although it is hard to 'know' the largely suppressed historical time of the novel itself, we know that it no longer belongs to the Old Father. Jamesie's apparent indifference to the clocks equally suggests time's indifference to him: that mankind's need for conclusions, or its sense of an ending, are not of concern to cyclical nature. It takes until the end of the book for the watchmaker to be summoned. Adjusting or correcting time is itself an object of procrastination. The removal of the clocks from Jamesie and Mary's house, which leaves the walls looking 'impoverished and plain', leaving its trace in 'distinct and pale' shapes (*RS* 288), repeats a motif in 'High Ground', in which several calendars had faded into the declining Master's wallpaper (*CE* 98). Time acts upon and makes futile what we unreliably measure time with. It is appropriate that the local watchmaker, for all his skill, ultimately cannot get the time quite right: although most of the clocks are successfully synchronized, two still strike late.

Even by the end of the novel there is still something 'askew with the clocks' (*RS* 289), their belated beating still not quite under human control. To Jamesie, the many clocks in the house have looked upon the activity of its inhabitants with a spirit of aloof non-participation:

> Wise. No daws. Never got into trouble. ... All they said was tick-tock. Tick-tock. Pass no heed. Tick-tock. Say no bad. Tick-tock. Turn a blind eye. Tick-tock. Get into no trouble. ... Ask why not but never why. Cleverer than the wisest that ever tried. (*RS* 293)

This is the comic, 'three wise monkeys' equivalent of the 'time that did not have to run to any conclusion' in 'Gold Watch' (*CE* 150): time which, if it is to be given existence by human beings, is personified as being uncaring of the memories and expectations it arouses. It is the human need for teleology (for the charged, end-related *kairos* rather than the 'passing time' of *chronos*) which ascribes the sound 'tick-tock' to a clock which may simply 'say' 'tick-tick'.[17]

In *The Pornographer*, the narrator's psychological pre-history is generally occluded, with the exception of an anomalous memory of his mother's faded calendar, on which every date is crossed out for seven years – except the last ten days of her life:

> I sensed that God, having veiled the earth in darkness and seen all nature to restoring sleep, could hardly have closed down each day with much greater sense of personal control than the march of my mother's Xs across the years seemed to proclaim. Maybe I had been lucky in my mother's death. Before she could get those Xs properly to work on me she'd been taken away. (*P* 201)

The dead mother has erased time and been erased by it. It is implied that the burden of crosses (the pun is surely intended) has been released from the son, releasing him into life, more particularly sex. The same figure is repeated in

Rising Sun. The Ruttledges have taken over a run-down property in which a butcher's calendar was hanging: again, after all the crossed days, the uncrossed day signifies the former owner's death. The inscription on the calendar, '*high-class beef, mutton and lamb*' (*RS* 18) may even be a joke about mortal flesh which comments on *The Pornographer*'s emphasis on carnality – indeed on 'raw meat' (*P* 57). The difference is that the pornographer's claim that the dead mother's march of days has not had an effect on him rings hollow, whereas the end of the butcher's crosses is part of the habitation and vacation of the earth in which the Ruttledges are participating. The recycling of the motif in *Rising Sun* draws our attention to the broader tension between end-directed linearity and recurrence, suggesting that narrative temporality is self-reflective and dynamic.

Moment and duration; subject and object

Although the interior immensity of modernist time is effaced from *Rising Sun*, which stands apart from self-designating works of recuperative memory like *The Leavetaking* and *Memoir*, it is important to recognize that McGahern is still preoccupied by the ways in which time and memory are conflictingly held in the mind. There are passages in *Rising Sun* in which inner life threatens to irrupt into and supplant the external object-world of the present, but such transitional moments are not expanded upon: the impersonal temporality of the narrative, like the surface of the lake, ripples with the teeming depths underneath. When Ruttledge visits his uncle's 'half-wasteland' of a scrap yard on the edge of town, a memory-image momentarily overlays the present scene: the old railway station, 'the hub of the town', now 'stood there so vividly *in his mind*, like an oil painting of great depth, that the substantial square looked deranged' (my italics, *RS* 227). The present is ousted by the past only momentarily, soon supplanted by Ruttledge's concerns for the Shah's retirement. The Ruttledges are constantly occupied with the maintaining of social networks *in the present*, day-to-day. Ruttledge is a catalytic presence, essential to the delicate flows of the interpersonal, and a model of the manners on which, as Declan Kiberd argues, the novel places such a premium.[18] Stanley van der Ziel convincingly characterizes Ruttledge as a 'mind-reading' man of Augustan restraint and solicitude.[19] That concern with present traffic, the interpersonal rather than the personal, is mirrored by the Austen-like novelist himself, one result of which is that Ruttledge's own mind is largely *not* to be read: his flood of subjective time is held at bay, and it is only rare moments like this which remind us of the absence. We note that again this remembered scene – down to the hose which hung down like an elephant's trunk – is largely recycled from *The Pornographer*, emphasizing that the earlier existential brooding of McGahern's narrator has now been excised.

The 'keeping' of moments in memory is vulnerable. One of the Ruttledges' black lambs, which Kate had seen with his mother in a patch of sunlit lawn, is later trampled to death during disinfectation. The couple are brought low by this loss, but are given succour by the moment: 'The black lamb became an instant of beauty, safe by the side of the young ewe on the bank in the sun, and was gone' (*RS* 250–1). The Wordsworthian moment in nature has a sacred beauty which 'goes' easily and can 'only be kept now in the mind' (*RS* 251). However, the recovered image may even be entirely disconnected from original subjective perception. Patrick Ryan 'remembers' a scene from his childhood, in which a young horse, driven wild by a swarm of red bees, cuts itself to death on a mowing machine. He now 'sees' the horse, mower and meadow, even though he did not see the incident. That it remains as 'real as if he had been there' (*RS* 73) suggests the importance of the oral transmission of memory, touching as in *The Leavetaking* on a more flexible notion of memory, such as Hirsch's 'post-memory', or Toni Morrison's concept of 're-memory' in *Beloved*.[20] There is something almost Berkeleyan about Kate's response to Patrick's assumed memory: the 'past and present are all the same in the mind. … They are just pictures' (*RS* 73). Her comment is lightly undercut by her husband: 'Are you sure you haven't been drinking, Kate?' (*RS* 73). It is as if Ruttledge wishes to retreat to the present social realm, to avoid the abyssal philosophical complexities of time.

Rising Sun is both a novel of duration and of moments, but not of epiphanies. It is indeed the negotiation of this relationship between the moment and duration which pushes back against the privileging of either memorial replenishment or of momentary transcendence. McGahern's equivocal response to the bequest of modernist time can be discerned in the way in which *Rising Sun* works through this modernist tension between fragmentation and flux, between rupture and loop, Proustian intermittence and Bergsonian continuity. Proust wondered that 'on ne se réalise que successivement' (translatable as 'We become ourselves only in the course of time'); Woolf too whether 'we are somehow successive and continuous, we human beings'.[21] Modernism rebuts the idea of mechanical succession, of treating time as a divisible spatial form, and is thus associated with *durée*, but this does not mean it rejects the *experience* of temporal succession. Likewise, *Rising Sun* simultaneously announces both a division in time (Ruttledge: 'I think the winter is here'), and a continuous present (Jamesie: 'It's been here for weeks' (*RS* 191)). The compression and distending of time, or the movement between moment and duration, is sometimes shown to be aporetic and potentially inhibiting. Bill Evans 'could no more look forward than he could look back. He existed in a small closed circle of the present. Remembrance of things past and dreams of things to come were instruments of torture' (*RS* 167). Bill may be viewed as in some ways representing a psychopathological extremity of the novel's own straitened temporality. The direct association of torture with Proustian 'remembrance' (in the line from Shakespeare's sonnet 30, used in the earlier translated title of *In Search of Lost Time*) suggests the constraints put upon modernist interiority – an acknowledgement of the 'sweet silent sessions' that are *not* being summoned up. Although, as Eamon Maher comments, Bill's refusal to look back speaks of the trauma of his upbringing as an orphan and brutalized Homeboy, his need for perpetual presentism also alerts the reader to the novel's broader time philosophy.[22] Bill's equilibrium precariously derives from the 'small closed circle of the present', but when he begins to take weekly bus rides into town, a pattern of expectation and memory is imposed which leads to disorientation.

Perceiving duration, forced out of his extra-temporal bunker and to live a new schedule 'in the mind', Bill is confronted by an extending Augustinian present which, threefold-thick with past, present and future, eludes measurement and is never divisible to a point. Present time contains the present of things past (memory), the present of present things (attention) and the present of future things (expectation). For the consciousness trying to grasp time, discordance emerges from the concordance of the moment: the more the mind tries to locate the *intentio* (the one, that which can hold firm, be measured, the point-like intent which the mind engages), the more it experiences *distention* (extension, dispersal to the many, distraction).[23] Augustine writes that 'the past has no existence' and that 'a long past is a long memory of the past', and likewise that the future exists only as 'a long expectation of the future'. These are the long memories and long expectations which torture Bill.[24] Time experienced as extensity is inimical to him and defence must be sought in an enclave of perpetual attention to the present.

Rising Sun never manifests itself as a more complex 'time-book' than when, on the return of her son and daughter-in-law from holiday, Mary wonders

> how so much time had disappeared and emerged again in such strange and substantial forms. Across her face there seemed to pass many feelings and reflections: it was as if she ached to touch and gather in and make whole those

scattered years of change. But how can time be gathered in and kissed? There is only flesh. (*RS* 125)

This is Proustian and Augustinian. The idea of time acting dynamically as an estranging force calls to mind the famous scene in *Le Temps Retrouvé* when Marcel, after many years as a recluse, emerges from the library at the Guermantes ball. He is shocked to see that his old friends appear to be wearing grotesque disguises: he is 'appalled to see that all the while he has been living in Time'.[25] He has missed all the successive images which would allow him to make sense of how time has aged those he knew: like Mary in *Rising Sun*, Marcel now understands how time has disappeared and, after intermittence, re-emerged. The allusion to 'scattered years' and 'gathered' time also brings Augustinian metaphors to mind. Augustine writes of memories being 'dispersed and disordered … hidden, scattered, and neglected'. They can easily slip away into 'remote recesses' and must be effortfully 'brought together (*cogenda*) … gathered (*colligenda*) from their dispersed state'. Augustine relished etymological euphony: the Latin *cogo*, from which *cogito* derives, means both 'collect' and 'compel'; *colligo* also means 'gather together', 'collect'. The cogitating, remembering, learning mind collects in order to recollect.[26]

Dermot McCarthy's memory-oriented reading of *Rising Sun* includes commentary on Mary's meditation on time: 'Only in the mind, in memory, in the imagination that is memory,' McCarthy writes, 'is there a wholeness that time cannot outrun or leave behind'.[27] It does seem significant that these thoughts are conferred upon *Mary*, as McCarthy suggests. The Ruttledges are apparently childless and the mother assumes a fleeting centrality. This psycho-biographical interpretation emphasizes the recuperation of the son's early life with the lost mother. Fiction makes whole and defeats time, something which is finally expressed in the last words of *Memoir* and the final union with the mother. However, *Rising Sun* is not, like *The Leavetaking* or *Memoir*, a self-advertising narrative of memory, and this passage does not quite bear out the idea that memory reconstitutes. We may initially expect from Mary a yearning for unrecoverable familial unity, carried in the cherished storehouse of memory. What is more manifest in this passage, though, is a melancholic acknowledgement, an 'ache', caused by the ungraspable diffuseness of time, which memory is not allowed to displace. Although the metaphor of *colligenda*, of gathering in what has been scattered, is traceable to Augustine's book on memory rather than time, Mary is nevertheless thinking of time as working independently of memory. Time cannot be gathered. 'There is only flesh', as the dead butcher's calendar reminds us – and, as the Book of Isaiah says, 'all flesh is grass'. The centripetality of memory, implicitly authorial 're-collection', is shown to be displaced by the scattering of time. Time is apprehended as it re-emerges in its newness, as in the Guermantes scene. Again, the narrative takes us to the precipice of the character's depths, assimilating free indirect discourse but also reading the expressions on her face. The economy of impersonality is threatened by the onrush of subjectivity, yet the remembering subject is swiftly demagnetized, and what might be taking shape as a character's epiphany – an intuition of ungatherable, estranging time – is quickly swept away by the indifferent time of the narrative.

The memory-image is the author's declared source, but this should not minimize how *Rising Sun* turns memory outwards, resisting confessional disclosure. The way is cleared for the novel to explore the working of time as much on the object as on the subject. In Patrick Ryan's room, Ruttledge sees a reproduction of the Virgin and Christ which has been there for fifty years – 'all faded now with damp spots underneath the glass, the cheapness moving, since it too had been touched and held in depths of time' (*RS* 201). Time redeems cheapness, making the object dear, whatever it might be. Moments are 'held' in and changed by the duration of time. Ruttledge is moved – the object does indeed need him to perceive it – and yet the reader is led away from the subject to the thing itself. In the case of this icon (from the Greek for 'image'), we are made aware that a Christian culture may regain its lost sacredness through the working of time.

Time can be laid out or symbolically spatialized in *Rising Sun*, like the Proustian mountain range conceived by Joseph Frank. A roof is described, a seventh of which is thatched every year, with the result that 'the seven years could be seen side by side in the different shades of the straw in the thatch, from golden brown to what was nearly black with rain' (*RS* 30). Serial or successive time is apprehended as a spatial whole. Is there an understated implication that the text itself (Lat. *texere* – to weave) is like this thatch, woven together and laying out its lingered-over, successive phases in adjacent spaces? The narrative will not allow us to decode its apparently naturalized object other than speculatively, as a most understated symbolic complex of space-time. Nevertheless, reading after modernism, it is tempting to recall the way Joyce assimilates G. E. Lessing's *Laocoön*, which argues that poetry is the art of time and sculpture that of space, into Stephen Dedalus's aesthetics. This will inform that juxtaposition in *Ulysses* of the spatial and synchronic *nebeneinander*, one thing next to another, to the temporal and diachronic *nacheichander*, one thing after another.[28] In *Rising Sun*, the observant eye, looking at the rain-soaked thatch, sees time in space.

'Dying back'

The novel renders seasonal time carefully. The vetches are green, they blacken and then reappear. The wild strawberries cover the banks, to be pecked away by blackbirds; their dark leaves reappear in early summer. We begin and end with the scent of wild woodbine. The rowan berries glow 'for a few brilliant days', 'a shining red-orange in the light from the water' (*RS* 182), but soon their stones lie under the trees like droppings. The sloe gains a blue bloom; the briar rusts. Each stage of growth and decay is recorded; each process supplanting and then itself being supplanted. In *Rising Sun*, neither organicism nor decay is given the upper hand, as they are equally bound to each other.

A formulation such as Jamesie's excited 'Everything will have started to grow' (*RS* 232) may imply his wonder about natural rejuvenation, and the way in which the working lives of those by the lake are tied to that growth. As Eamonn Hughes has argued, the implication of being told that the 'mower, the tedder, the baler were put away for the year' (*RS* 120) is that such equipment will be taken out again: 'The future is constantly imagined … as a matter of time being repeated.'[29] There are broader implications about how we may view *Rising Sun* as a future-oriented narrative. During the Christmas period, the Ruttledges 'did not feel particularly quiet or happy but through them ran the sense, like an underground river, that there would come a time when these days would be looked back on as happiness' (*RS* 206). As Mark Currie has written, the present can be experienced as 'the object of future memory', in anticipation of retrospection.[30] The Christmas days of happiness will be succeeded, it is implied here, by days of sadness which condition the very experience of the present. What the Ruttledges feel is consistent with Heidegger's notion of the unified 'ecstases' of past, present and future, which allow present time to be experienced authentically.[31] Forearmed against the complacency of defining and thus destroying happiness, they do not feel exhilaration in the present, but their sense of the future-within-the-present still allows them to appreciate an as yet unnamed state which will have belonged to this present. Even John Quinn speaks in a temporally complicated way: reflecting on the consummation of his marriage to a woman who immediately leaves him, Quinn compares her to a ripe plum picked when about to fall, with whom sex would be 'like going into and out of a most happy future' (*RS* 175). The mystically extra-temporal, Lawrentian sex described in *The Pornographer* – 'the place of beginning and end' snatched 'out of time' (*P* 57) and not 'caged in any nightmare of the future' (*P* 63) – is replaced by the violent patriarch's unfounded anticipation of continued sexual empowerment, one which highlights what a curiously anachronistic figure he is: one, we hope, without a happy future.

Seamus Deane has observed the musicality of McGahern's sentences, alluding to how their percussive syntax transmits 'the beat of an impersonal process' in the physical object-world.[32] Stanley van der Ziel argues too that incantatory prose rhythms seem to bear out McGahern's comparison of art to prayers.[33] The prose is itself an object of attention, and the reader notices that a complex temporality is built into it:

> The sloes *were already ripening* on the blackthorn. Patches of yellow *were appearing* in the thick wall of green along the shore. *There was* rust on the briar leaves. Certain grasses and *early* vegetables were *dying back*. … The reeds *had lost* their bright greenness and *were leaning* towards the water. Everything that *had flowered had now come* to fruit. (*RS* 177, my italics)

The difficulty of locating the present emerges in the mixtures of tenses. There is an interfusion of completed action in the past (*had lost, had flowered*), completed action in the present (*There was rust*), and continuous action in the past (*were ripening, were dying, were leaning*). Next to this, temporal adverbs act upon their verbs – *already* ripening, had *now* come – to suggest a process of surprise, recognition and confirmation. Vegetables *were* 'early' and grasses not just dying but dying *back*, implicitly in order to grow again. Things have either come or are coming, have gone or are going, but they are unable to extricate themselves from the flux of time. The reader may not be immersed in the 'rank vegetal proliferation' of Proustian syntax, but McGahern surreptitiously merges into his rhythmic writing that heterogeneous temporality held in constant tension between prematurity and belatedness.

Rising Sun is concerned with the representation of a supra-human natural time which subsumes our individual endings. Plenitude may be found in the perhaps idealized interactions between people, the shared sociolect of a particular community, but it is also to be found 'beyond the social', as Denis Sampson has put it.[34] This may tempt the reader to apotheosize nature, and thus to think of the novel as structured in a passively mimetic way, slowed down to a humble, observant purpose. However, the time of the narrative and the time of nature should be distinguished from one another. The very first paragraph is almost exactly repeated much later in the text, with the sole addition of the word 'Easter'. Whereas the opening paragraph might be any morning, any Mass, the repeated words have conferred upon them the liturgical singularity of a Christian day when, a strangely unattributed voice tells us, the 'whole of heaven is dancing in its joy that Christ has risen' (*RS* 238). The text's recycling of itself, pointing up repetition with a slight difference, transforming any Sunday into Easter Day, signals that this is a wrought fiction.

Looking more closely, we see that the novel's progress through the year is not evenly paced or parcelled out equally between the seasons. It is only half-way through the book that we are told that, after the cutting of the meadow, the aftermath has a bluish tinge (*RS* 147), and only well after this (roughly three-fifths through) that a firm temporal marker is laid down for the first time: September and October are noted down as 'lovely months' (181). Exterior, summer time begins by inching along, slowed by the recounted time of the past: the introduction of each new character, often at the Ruttledges' porch, prompts the expository telling of their past stories, and this has an inevitable retarding effect. No month pertaining to present time is named during the high summer, whose mythical, undated slowness calendar time is not allowed to mark with its divisions. On the other hand, May, September, October, November and February are named and fixed. Summer dominates and winter is compressed: so much for the idea of the annual cycle or drama. Beyond the snow-flecked rain and later, the 'precious days of frost' when 'Thin ice glittered along the shore and clinked and chimed when there was any movement of water' (*RS* 212), there is no great evocation of nature in winter. Christmas is marked by its social exchanges and the bustle of the town.

There is a structural *acceleration*, then, through the primroses, blossom and Easter (*RS* 244), May coming in 'wet and windy' (*RS* 249), towards the destination of next summer's 'ripening' (*RS* 296) – not fully ripened – meadows at the end. The reader can be hoodwinked into accepting that an apparent submission to natural rhythms runs through the novel consistently, and thus to underestimate how the gathering, accelerating narrative momentum hurries on through parts of the year. We come to appreciate what Genette, in his study of Proust, termed the 'narrative's capacity for temporal autonomy'.[35] Narrative form is beaten out in its own self-achieved, distended and compressed, time.

The reader's experience of *Rising Sun* – our reading time – is an educative process by which we learn to appreciate this self-fashioned momentum. That momentum is towards death, and in this sense the narrative, for all its circularity, reveals itself to be end-directed. Within the remorseless repetition of time by the lake – an organizing trope of stillness which contrasts to the Heraclitean simile of the 'underground river' (*RS* 206) – comes the knowledge that the future will also comprise, again, what follows ripeness: the mould on the blackberry; 'the traceries of branches stripped of their leaves' (*RS* 183). In nature this is accepted as cyclical, but human mortality is less easily accepted, though it must be. The cycle of *Rising Sun* will contain in its narrative future the death of that endlessly recurring summer figure, the returning emigrant, Johnny. Johnny is trapped in his own alphabetical sequence: when we last see him, he is 'somewhere between Y and Z', as Jamesie puts it (*RS* 270). The vetch and woodbine will keep on appearing, but Johnny will not.

However, that end is temporally 'placed' before the fictional end, as it was with Elizabeth in *The Barracks*. Johnny's corpse is granted its full ceremonial time in the narrative. The slow depiction of the rites of a single culture is accorded a prominence which, while showing the effects of the remorseless temporality of nature, also marks a small resistance to it. That is, the movement towards the supra-human or metaphysical does not exclude a reverence for the human too – 'the innate sacredness of each single life' (*RS* 273) registered in the form of Johnny's superb body. As in 'The Country Funeral', we unapologetically see not only what a human is, but what is done to a human and what humans do *after* death. Johnny's silver digital watch, whose red numerals pulse away on his corpse 'like a mechanical heart' (*RS* 272), draws symbolic attention to the encompassing of temporal contraries: to repeat two of McGahern's short stories, both that 'nothing seems ever to end except ourselves' (*CE* 226) and that 'nothing is ever over' (*CE* 406).

Nature and history

In his preface to the *Phenomenology of Spirit*, Hegel writes of natural time in terms which surprisingly recall McGahern's rendering of recurring moments within the natural cycle:

> The bud disappears in the bursting-forth of the blossom, and one might say that the former is refuted by the latter; similarly, when the fruit appears, the blossom is shown up in its turn as a false manifestation of the plant, and the fruit now emerges as the truth of it instead. These forms are not just distinguished from one another, they also supplant one another as mutually incompatible. Yet at the same time their fluid nature makes them moments of an organic unity in which they not only do not conflict, but in which each is as necessary as the other; and this mutual necessity alone constitutes the life of the whole.
>
> Impatience demands the impossible, to wit, the attainment of the end without the means. But the *length* of this path has to be endured, because, for one thing, each moment is necessary; and further, each moment has to be *lingered* over,

> because each is itself a complete individual shape, and one is only viewed in absolute perspective when its determinateness is regarded as a concrete whole, or the whole is regarded as uniquely qualified by that determination.[36]

Hegel's preface captures the temporality of *Rising Sun*: how successive moments are patiently lingered over as intrinsically true, but also how they relinquish that truth to other moments of truth and thus to a universal natural wholeness. The mutual necessity of each discrete phase allows the life of the whole to be grasped; the truth of the moment, the complete individual shape, will serve the truth of a great organic unity. In *Rising Sun*, the reflection of the rowan berries on the lake is self-bounded, complete, recurrent. It has inspired ancient bards to praise the lips of women. Nevertheless, the rowan stones-as-droppings are equally true in their dull matter: nature is its waste. It may almost be the case, as Hegel says, that one moment almost 'refutes' the other, but the moment's assertion of its independence is chained to its temporal dependence on other such moments. The enduring truthfulness of the moment cannot be purely self-contained, but is connected to its place in time, which tells us that the moment will die and be reborn.

In this natural analogy, Hegel is introducing the problem of philosophical paradigms supplanting one another, how one truth is rendered false by a succeeding truth. A model of mutual exclusivity, of the acceptance or rejection of *epistemes*, misrepresents the interdependence of parts to each other and to the whole, the due ongoing process of philosophical inquiry which makes up a unified 'life of the whole'. Hegel is reaching to nature for metaphors so that he can apprehend the eternal presence of the spirit (*Geist*) of *history* in the stages of human civilization. In the rest of the text, however, he is more inclined to contrast nature and spirit, or biological time and historical time, and sees historical development as a 'hard and obstinate struggle with itself', not a peaceful organic unfolding, as Ricœur has written.[37] There is enough 'cunning of reason' in each of the successive stages of history (*Stufengang*) for the end of history (*Endzweck*) to be deciphered, and so for the eternal present of history to be grasped in its unity. The 'surpassed past' is retained in 'the present of each age'.[38] Hegelian totalization is an expression of mankind's world spirit (*Weltgeist*). Written in the aftermath of the Battle of Jena, it may also be associated with the nascent national spirit of *Volksgeist* during the Napoleonic era – the seed of German unification. Hegel is not eulogizing nature for its own sake but rather writing analogically, and this explains why the language of *Rising Sun*, which on the surface seems to have little obvious affinity with Hegelian philosophy, bears an unexpected resemblance to the preface of the *Phenomenology of Spirit*.

The mixing of natural and historical time-narratives nevertheless alerts us to how the seasonal time of the novel should not be held apart from culturally symbolical time. The eponymous 'rising' is the most hoarily and historically materialist of political tropes. There is an allusion in *Ulysses* to *The Freeman's Journal*'s sunburst headpiece above the motto 'Ireland a Nation': Bloom amusedly notes the 'homerule sun rising up in the north-west'.[39] On Easter Day in *Rising Sun*, Jamesie recounts his boyhood memory of seeing the Black and Tans machine-gunning a group of young republicans who had planned to ambush them. The tale from the War of Independence has been prompted by the republican march taking place, ceremonially marked to coincide with Easter, in Shruhaun. After the gunning-down, Jamesie and his father had come across an injured IRA soldier, who had evaded capture, half-whispering 'Hel-lo … Hel-lo … Hel-lo' from a clump of sallies by the river (*RS* 241). Jamesie turns the 'hel-lo' of the injured republican into 'the high cry of a bird calling out of the depths of the bog' (*RS* 242), reminding us of the suffering which attends upon crying out 'this is mine'. The first spoken words of the novel have been Jamesie's same soft calling of 'Hel-lo. Hel-lo. Hel-lo' (*RS* 1), another marker of the novel's recycling of itself. Such circularity is linked here to the Marxian idea of history becoming farce. Kate bathetically imagines the monument of the stone soldier in Shruhaun as a talking dummy, repeating this same 'Hel-lo' every minute. Heroic sacrificial nationalism is obviously demystified – 'The dead can be turned into anything' (*RS* 244) – but the implications go further. In terms of historical time, we understand that because the traumatic initiatory narrative of the nation is unrepeatably singular and 'stony', in the Yeatsian sense, it will be memorialized recurrently, in stone. What is more, nationalist time is not exempt from the Augustinian splitting open of the present as it becomes past, implied here by the 'terrible gap' between 'Hel' and 'Low' (*RS* 244). Any form of time which announces a teleological beginning is condemned to being out of joint, as premature or belated, as the history of the Rising eloquently demonstrates. To make a beginning is to make a cut in time, and to apprehend its terrible gapped-ness.

This applies to any act of historical agency, and suggests that the reader is being encouraged to read beneath the surface of an episode when the IRA man, Jimmy Joe McKiernan, asks Ruttledge for the time because his time 'is plainly untrustworthy' (*RS* 286). Ruttledge acknowledges that to a man of action he may look like an 'eejit' (*RS* 286). We can reread the passage from Hegel not in relation to nature, but to a radical politics in which the eternal presence of the end – the spirit of the historical project – is always perceptible in the struggle of each stage. In Hegelian terms, Jimmy Joe McKiernan's time may be equated with an attempt to 'totalize' historical time and its ends (*Endzweck*). *Rising Sun* is not only restricted to mortal ends, such as Johnny's, but touches here on the due process of end-directed historical narratives, and on how to evaluate the impatient demand for the attainment of the end without the means, in Hegelian terms. The slowness of the novel seems to endorse the idea that 'the *length* of this path has to be endured, because, for one thing, each moment is necessary', and to resist the demands of remorseless teleology, including the sort of political 'hurry' which requires Hegel's concept of history as struggle. Politically as well as philosophically, the problem is where to begin in time, how to say 'Hel-lo'. The dialogue between Ruttledge and Jimmy Joe, characterized by wariness but not by enmity, concludes with their agreeing on 'making a start' (*RS* 286).

Modernity and recurrence

That the commemoration of national beginning is by now a recurrent echo underlines that Ireland, far from being a laggardly example of a marginalized culture attempting to catch up with a supposedly progressive metropolitan centre, has rather accelerated into modernity during and after decolonization, unimpeded by a prior history of industrialized bourgeois capitalism. As the analysis of 'The Country Funeral' argued, McGahern is aware that the opposing of atavistic ethnic tradition and universal enlightened modernity conceals how mutually constitutive those ideological antipodes are. But in what ways may this modify the obvious temptation to read *Rising Sun* as an elegy for, or at least a nostalgically anthropological record of, a vanishing way of traditional life, and thus as a jeremiad against modernity?

The arrival of technological modernity is finally hinted at the end of the novel by the mention of a 'new telephone pole' (*RS* 296) around the lake. In what is a studiedly complex time-book, this looks like strategic anachrony, especially as the term itself seems to be substituted for the more commonly used 'telegraph pole'. For all their speaking, the characters have not used the telephone much, but that is often the case in fiction. Is it possible that they do not have landlines, or is it rather that the pole is a replacement? We are teasingly asked to entertain the possibility that the coming of the telephone is somehow simultaneous with the era of *Blind Date*, with the post-industrial decline of the Dagenham car plant and with the pre-Good Friday period of the later Troubles (signalled by the mention of the Enniskillen bombing). Most pertinently, perhaps, the book was published during the era of the mobile phone mast, in a period later even than Jameson's late capitalist, postmodernist phase. The modernity of the second Industrial Revolution is at least a century old, its consequences on present time long since felt. The setting of *Rising Sun* implies the bust future of the Celtic Tiger, in which many houses in this Leitrim locality stood empty. So McGahern's new 'telephone pole' should not be retrospectively conflated with, say, the encroaching technology implied by the telegraph poles in Chekhov's *The Cherry Orchard* nor with Conrad's 'sparse row of telegraph poles' in *Nostromo*, which 'strode obliquely clear of the town, bearing a single, almost invisible wire far into the great campo – like a slender, vibrating feeler of that progress waiting outside for a moment of peace to enter and twine itself about the weary heart of the land'.[40] More generally, the rural time of *Rising Sun* cannot be taken as synonymous with Bakhtin's conception of the agricultural chronotope, where human life and nature are perceived in the same categories, so that seasons 'plot the course of an individual life and the life of nature' and time is 'sunk deeply in the earth, implanted in it and ripening in it'.[41] It should not be possible to align the Ruttledges' belated agricultural time with that described by Lawrence in *The Plumed Serpent*: the 'old, uncounted manner of the past … strange, old, uncounted, unregistered, unreckoning days', or with that of Hardy's fabulated Wessex implicitly hedged in by technological advance.[42]

Yet the structure of *Rising Sun* does seem designed to imitate such distant time-narratives. Eamonn Hughes has pointed to McGahern's comments on Tomàs Ó Criomhthain's *An tOileánach* (*The Islandman*, first published in Irish in 1929), an account of life on the Blasket Islands during the late nineteenth century. According to McGahern, that book is characterized by a 'sense of timelessness … of being outside time' which 'comes from the day, a single day breaking continually over the scene and action' (*LW* 265). Hughes convincingly argues that the many anecdotes of past time draw Ó Criomhthain's narrative back as it moves forwards, and that neither the linear motion of *Rising Sun* throughout the year, nor the pattern of circularity suggested by seasonal recurrence, can fully account for the time-scheme. As in the figure of the day 'breaking continually' in *An tOileánach*, time in *Rising Sun* is described as 'wave-like', 'tidal'.[43] McGahern covertly reprises the narrative template of the arrival of modernity, borrowing and replaying the idea that this community, like the Brangwens, will suffer 'ejection from a secure society and a collective historical life', or that, in Ó Criomhthain's words, 'One day there will be none left in the Blasket of all I have mentioned in this book – and none to remember them'.[44] Deeply implied, though, is a consciousness in McGahern that the perennial dialectic of tradition and modernity is indeed being recast in the digital era of post-postmodernity. The slowing-down of *Rising Sun* is dialogically counterposed to the post-Fordian cultural 'speed-up' of which David Harvey writes. Anachronistic jaggedness is made even more pronounced: we now read *Blind Date* as a historical artefact, and wonder why there are still no telephones around the lake. What is produced is not an elegiac, future-less nostalgia but a sense of historical constellation or recurrence – something regarded, when applied to Benjamin or Nietzsche, as sophisticatedly 'modern'.

The impossibility of recuperating the pre-modern is inscribed, even caricatured. Every era has its invading new technology, its 'feelers of progress' waiting to penetrate the heart of the land. To enact that recurrent historical pattern in the literary figure of the telephone poles is less the refuge of retrospective, even reactionary political quietism, but more a self-knowing, even playful resistance to technological advance, and by implication to teleological onrush. *Rising Sun*, itself trapped in its own phase of chronological succession, cannot *be The Islandman*, and thus it creates a kind of simulacrum of its passed time-world: a deliberate, performed anachronicity. Writing after modernism as well as after modernity, McGahern knows that Ó'Criomhthain's being 'outside of time', of having 'a strange sense of timelessness', is also the province of elegiac time-writers like Proust and Woolf. The tidal time of *Rising Sun* may be indebted to *The Islandman*, but we should not forget that Woolf wrote *The Waves*, in which the time-compressing monologues are intercalated with the fragments of a single day under a rising and falling sun. By asking us to consider timelessness as an anthropological and literary category, McGahern implicitly bridges the great divide between so-called metropolitan and provincial cultures. Part of his courteous request is not to pass off the complexity of his own time-narrative as a plangent pastoralism or unconsidered naturalism.

Image and time

McGahern is concerned with the way nature subsumes, gathers in and overlays human culture, be it communal or familial. As the gravediggers stand about the ruin of a great monastery, Ruttledge looks 'at the traces of the streets and huts and the buildings that could be traced through the lines and indentations on the short grass where the cattle lay' (*RS* 280). In the middle of the living room where Mary grew up, 'an ash tree had taken root where they had played cards and said the Rosary', and in the shallows of the lake by the house lie fragments of broken blue delft, an index of the family's former prosperity (*RS* 88). The ruin is the most manifest site of time, and of course particularly associated with Gothic-Romantic writing, but it is not disconnected from modernist chronotopes like the 'Time Passes' section of *To the Lighthouse*, that wartime corridor between two day-long tracts of consciousness. Here Woolf imagines a process of miscegenation in which the butterfly rests on chintz, the thistle pokes through the tile, and projects forward to a future in which picnickers sit outdoors in a 'room' where hemlock grows. 'Did Nature supplement what man advanced?'[45] Woolf's question is implied by the grassed over monastery and the ash tree in the living room in *Rising Sun*. Time is shown to work outside of human perception. Woolf empties the house of human perceivers so that the process of growth – the appearance of carnation and cabbages – remains unobserved: likewise in *Rising Sun*, though the narcissi beautifully fringe the lake near Mary's ruined house, 'there was no one near at hand to notice' (*RS* 88). The dilapidation of human space allows the past to extrude into the present, to assert its simultaneous coexistence with the present, in a way which emphasizes archaeological trace and circumscribes anthropocentrism. The last line of the novel confirms the emptying-out of the human: both 'Jamesie and Mary had long since disappeared from the sky' (*RS* 298).

The human subject, the one who notices, is the viewer of the image, and by extension the artist and the reader. Stanley van der Ziel regards the plotlessness of *Rising Sun* as 'exalting' the pure image, and that this is part of the process of writing which, as McGahern said, 'memorializes, stops time'.[46] Art aspires to the status of the extra-temporal symbolic image. The blue delft in the shallows may be regarded as a representation of 'stopped' human time, emblematic of the vulnerable chinawork of art itself: in modernist terms, like James's golden bowl, or like Eliot's fragments. But we have come to see throughout this monograph how oblique are McGahern's hints about his own aesthetic approach *within the artwork*, and no less so in this novel: as Martin Ryle has written, in *Rising Sun* 'the quasi-authorial protagonist is registered only at the margins' and there is no evidence of 'writerly self-making'.[47] The reader must infer, for example, the self-reflexivity of Kate's art: she keeps going with her drawings, she says, because it brings what she sees closer (*RS* 64).[48] This book began by considering Joe Ruttledge absorbed in a postcard of Giotto's *Flight into Egypt*, and making the claim that his viewing of this image is in some ways analogous to our reading of *Rising Sun*. Ruttledge's memory of the railway station is compared to 'an oil painting of great *depth*' (*RS* 227), an aesthetics of perspective after Giotto which would confer mimetic solidity upon the represented object. But whatever such moments encourage the reader to think about McGahern's own aesthetics remains largely speculative. As Sampson writes, even though *Rising Sun* has a pictorial, framing, 'still-life' quality, in it 'the place of art in human culture is only implicitly suggested'.[49] Writing a novel as an eternal artwork is anachronistic, and aesthetic aspiration is scaled-down or concealed.

Together with an outward-turning appreciation of man's diminished, decentred role, McGahern unobtrusively positions the art of his last novel. The cheapness of the Virgin Mary 'held in depths of time' (*RS* 201), and thus made dear by time, intimates ways in which *Rising Sun* may itself be critically construed as an object of future memory. Patrick Ryan's 'whole cathedral of a shed' (*RS* 297), that *mise-en-abyme* of the novel, is finally left unfinished, open to future time. In this sense, the art-image is chained to the future and thus can never be freed into the eternal. Benjamin writes of the 'arresting' force of the constellated image: 'It isn't that the past casts its light on the present or the present casts its light on the past: rather, an image is that in which the Then [*das Gewesene*] and the Now [*das Jetzt*] come into a constellation like a flash of lightning.' The image as conceived by Benjamin in the *Arcades Project*, itself a kind of artistic ruin, is not timeless but rather a dynamically trans-historical site of time: 'Image is dialectics at a standstill.'[50] The work of culture is caught up in a continuous process of change which includes what Benjamin called its own afterlife (*Nachleben*), and which does not simply follow the work but is constitutive of it. We may thus view the image as static but as dialectical, not extra-temporal, and read McGahern's last novel as aesthetic object *and* anthropological record, knowing that it too will be held in duration, interpretable in its successive historical moments.

Notes

1 Quoted in Stephen Kern, *The Culture of Time and Space 1880-1918* (London: Weidenfeld and Nicolson, 1983), p. 27.

2 James Joyce, *Finnegans Wake*, ed. Seamus Deane (Harmondsworth: Penguin, 2000), pp. 149, 292, 419.

3 Joseph Frank, *The Widening Gyre* (New Brunswick, NJ: Rutgers University Press, 1963).

4 Paul Ricœur, *Time and Narrative*, vol. 2, trans. Kathleen McLaughlin and David Pellauer (Chicago: University of Chicago, 1985), p. 104.

5 Beckett, *Molloy* in *Trilogy*, p. 63.

6 Erich Auerbach, *Mimesis: The Representation of Reality in Western Literature* (Princeton, NJ: Princeton University Press, 1953), p. 536.

7 Ricœur, *Time and Narrative*, p. 112.
8 Daniel Soar, 'Alphabetical', *London Review of Books* 24, no. 4 (21 February 2002): 30–1.
9 'The Good-Morrow', in *The Complete Poems of John Donne*, ed. C. A. Patrides (London: Everyman, 1985), p. 49.
10 Michael Cronin, *Translation and Globalization* (London and New York: Routledge, 2003).
11 M. M. Bakhtin, *The Dialogic Imagination* (Austin, TX: University of Texas Press, 1981), pp. 84, 250.
12 Bakhtin, *The Dialogic Imagination*, p. 250.
13 Quoted in Randall Stevenson, *Modernist Fiction* (Harlow: Pearson, 1998), p. 141.
14 Virginia Woolf, *Mrs Dalloway*, ed. Claire Tomalin (Oxford: Oxford World's Classics, 1998), p. 133.
15 Bergson quoted in Jesse Matz, 'Hulme's Compromise and the New Psychologism', in *T.E. Hulme and the Question of Modernism*, ed. Edward P. Comentale and Andrzej Gasiorek (Abingdon: Ashgate, 2006), p. 115.
16 Stevenson, *Modernist Fiction*, p. 141.
17 Frank Kermode, *The Sense of an Ending: Studies in the Theory of Fiction* (Oxford: Oxford University Press, 1967), pp. 44–7.
18 Declan Kiberd, 'Fallen Nobility: The World of John McGahern', *Irish University Review* 35, no. 1 (Spring/Summer 2005): 164–74.
19 Stanley van der Ziel, 'McGahern, Austen, and the Aesthetics of Good Manners', *Essays in Criticism* 63, no. 2 (2013): 203–22.
20 Toni Morrison, *Beloved* (London: Picador, 1988), p. 36.
21 Quoted in Stevenson, *Modernist Fiction*, p. 138; Proust, 'We realise our own natures only in the course of time', *Sodom and Gomorrah* (London: Chatto & Windus, 1992).
22 Maher, *The Church and Its Spire*, pp. 159–60.
23 Paul Ricœur, *Time and Narrative*, vol. 1, trans. Kathleen McLaughlin and David Pellauer (Chicago: University of Chicago, 1985), pp. 20–1.
24 St Augustine, *Confessions*, p. 243.
25 Marcel Proust, *Time Regained* (London: Chatto & Windus, 1992), p. 298.
26 St Augustine, *Confessions*, p. 189.
27 McCarthy, *Art of Memory*, p. 287.
28 See Joyce, *Portrait*, pp. 177–8; Joyce, *Ulysses*, p. 36.
29 Eamonn Hughes, 'All That Surrounds Our Life: Time, Sex and Death in *That They May Face the Rising Sun*', *Irish University Review* 35, no. 1 (Spring/Summer 2005): 147–63, 158.
30 Mark Currie, *About Time* (Edinburgh: Edinburgh University Press, 2007), p. 5.
31 Currie, *About Time*, p. 53.

32 Seamus Deane, 'A New Dawn', *The Guardian*, 12 January 2002.

33 Stanley van der Ziel, 'The Aesthetics of Redemption: John McGahern's *That They May Face the Rising Sun*', *Studies: An Irish Quarterly Review* 93, no. 372 (Winter, 2004): 473–86, 481.

34 Sampson, 'Open to the World', pp. 136–46.

35 Gérard Genette, *Narrative Discourse Revisited*, trans. Jane E. Lewin (Ithaca and New York: Cornell University Press, 1988), p. 85.

36 G. W. F. Hegel, *The Phenomenology of Spirit*, trans. A. V. Miller (Oxford: Oxford University Press, 1977), pp. 2, 17.

37 See Ricœur, *Time and Narrative*, vol. 3, p. 199.

38 See Ibid., pp. 198–206.

39 Joyce, *Ulysses*, p. 55.

40 Joseph Conrad, *Nostromo*, ed. Martin Seymour-Smith (Harmondsworth: Penguin, 1990), p. 162.

41 Bakhtin, *The Dialogic Imagination*, pp. 207–8.

42 See Stevenson, *Modernist Fiction*, p. 128.

43 Hughes, 'All That Surrounds Our Life', p. 148.

44 Stevenson, *Modernist Fiction*, p. 151.

45 Virginia Woolf, *To the Lighthouse*, ed. Stella McNichol (Harmondsworth: Penguin, 1992), p. 146.

46 Stanley van der Ziel, 'The Aesthetics of Redemption', pp. 473–6.

47 Martin Ryle, 'John McGahern: Memory, Autobiography, Fiction, History', *New Formations* 67 (Summer 2009): 44.

48 See also van der Ziel, 'The Aesthetics of Redemption', p. 475.

49 Sampson, 'Open to the World', p. 144.

50 Benjamin quoted in Ronald Schleifer, *Modernism and Time: The Logic of Abundance in Literature, Science and Culture 1880-1930* (Cambridge: Cambridge University Press, 2000), p. 22. Walter Benjamin, *The Arcades Project*, trans. Howard Eiland and Kevin McLaughlin (Cambridge, MA and London: Belknap Press, 1999), p. 463.

Conclusion

This book began by conceding that it is untenable to claim for McGahern a radical form of belated modernism. It acknowledged the burden of those adjectives Proustian, Joycean, Yeatsian and Beckettian, and staked out the general theoretical problem of continuing or containing modernism after modernism. McGahern declines to imitate modernist form, but even if he did, this would be a sign of his difference from it. The very unlikeliness of constructing McGahern as a formally disruptive late or neo-modernist is a deterrent from reading his works in relation to modernist texts, and that is where this book has hoped to intervene, insisting on the various ways in which McGahern passed through modernism or in which it passed through him.

Lingering with the difference between McGahern and the renegade but increasingly canonized body of modernism has kept a number of questions open. On the matter of the necessary difficulty of the high modernist text, its dislocation into meaning, and of McGahern's apparent diffidence in testing his own mimeticism, the following may be observed. The representation of Elizabeth's dense, encased consciousness in *The Barracks* may be thought Tolstoyan, but there is also a sense of deep and fluid subjectivity not out of keeping with the interior immensity of Woolf and Joyce. At the opposite end of McGahern's career, in a novel of localized surfaces where such immersion into consciousness is largely resisted, *Rising Sun* still reveals itself to be a complex work of time. The reading experience of this chapter-less and not easily consumed novel can be retrospectively misrepresented. It is austerely objective rather than confidently panoramic or expressive, for all its whiskey and vernacular. We cannot ignore the discrepant remains of literature in *The Leavetaking*, a book which follows the channels of the symbolic and the path of the signifier, nor the low supplement of writing in *The Pornographer*. A number of the short stories no longer ring out with the confidence of the speaking voice, rather attaining a symbolic concentration and self-referential emblematic quality similar to that of some modernist short fiction. Shorter narratives may often be unsettling, bringing the narrator and reader to a threatening silence which is structured by internalized conflict. A few earlier stories can be construed, perhaps surprisingly, as palimpsest-like rewritings of earlier modernist texts, or may be ghosted by modernism to the point of overdetermination. McGahern's acute 'sense of an ending' and of abyssal temporality is, in its understated way, consistent with the more strenuously chiliastic aspects of the modernist preoccupation with time. The riotous play of the high modernist signifier is rejected in McGahern's work, and neither is there the remotest hint of postmodernist relish for extrovert ludic narrative, but there is throughout an intentness upon 'the sentence in itself beautiful', as Woolf said – on language 'making' rather than mimetic 'matching'.[1] Language is often more detonative than denotative, as might be suggested by Anne Enright's comparison of a McGahern story to a hand grenade rolled across the kitchen floor.[2]

Frequently this book has touched upon a reluctance in McGahern's work to indulge the idea of a surrogate artist in the text. That displaced self-referentiality is manifest in oblique ways: the crypto-authorial personas of a young boy entering the comic-book realm of the imagination, of a theatre director confusing art and life, of a pornographer creating a fictional artifice, of a weakening father writing a letter. McGahern did not like the idea of the Romantic artist, and did not like this aspect of the Dedalean Joyce.[3] Aesthetic self-inspection is repressed but returns around the edges of the text, as in the multipersonal novel *The Dark*, which is very far from being a modernist *Künstlerroman*, but which cannot eventually resist playing out a downbeat epiphany in which its own clichéd language is mentioned. The poet may be seen as a figure of failure. *The Pornographer*'s Maloney is exemplary: formerly responsible for deadening verses, he expatiates on the aesthetics of pornography, is given enough rope with which to hang himself, but just about clings on to utter the last words of the novel. McGahern's characteristic diffidence may explain why Proust's doubled narrator was so important to him: a withdrawn, muffled but catalytic subject, an unfeasibly absent presence. The architecture of Proustian narrative determined that it would always inherently be about the memorializing process of art, and that its signs of remembered experience *and* aesthetic representation would be 'real without being actual, ideal without being abstract', as Marcel puts it. McGahern's strictures on expression being bad for art point to an orthodox, Flaubertian-Joycean modernist scrupulosity which is easily apprehended in the common evasion of omniscience, except in cases like 'Oldfashioned', when the bird's eye authorial role is being self-consciously resurrected, or *Amongst Women*, when archaic form – the 'bogey of realism' – is anti-heroically performed, occasionally with the used materials of modernism.

'The task of art is to redress, essentially or existentially, the formless universe of contingency. Reality is not a material given, and nor is it a positivistic historical sequence. The act of fictionality thus becomes the crucial act of imagining'.[4] These words would accurately describe some facets of McGahern. They come, however, from one of the most venerable synopses of modernism, by Malcolm Bradbury and James McFarlane. McGahern's backward look to the modernist library may bring out an unresolved tension in two vying models of modernism. On the one hand, the movement in modernism towards the aesthetics of impersonality, to use Maud Ellmann's term; on the other, the self-reflexive reaction against mimetic realism which, relishing the play of the signifier, forces art back upon its own imagining. The former model may suggest a refined objectification which trains upon the static extra-temporal image, and is thus hard to reconcile with the latter sense of a restlessly impatient, processual art of de-creation and iconoclasm (or, the breaking of the image). Like the modernist and unlike postmodernist fiction writers, McGahern does not threaten to remove his fictional world – to suggest its ontological dissolution. But he is uncomfortable with the modernist idea that semiosis or consciousness might be allowed to take control of the fast-receding represented world, so that the materiality of language or the epistemological quest is thrust to the fore.

Most readers of McGahern instinctively know that the writing is rich and carefully self-fashioned, rather than wielded with instrumental mimetic intent. Nevertheless, it is increasingly tempting to submit to thinking of his work, now that it is regarded as a posthumous whole, as primarily valuable for representing an Ireland that is 'dead and gone'. Despite the privacy of his vision, a new kind of historical petrification may set in which above all emphasizes McGahern's representative status and representational mode. His increasing cultural importance in Ireland was well summed up by President MacAleese's eulogy, which alluded to his having 'made an immense contribution to our self-understanding as a nation'.[5] While this is indisputable, it also suggests the way in which a lauded, then banned, then lauded writer may be reabsorbed into a newly disseminated narrative of state, and lionized for a once painful but now symbolically central role as a faithful and elegiac recorder of a vanished era in rural Ireland. While I acknowledge that this book's constant return to intertextual questions is made at the expense of socio-historical investigation into mid- and late-twentieth-century Irish culture, this is justified by the insistence upon evaluating the extent to which literary modernism, at whose heart is Irish modernism, is belatedly assimilated into McGahern's work. This can indeed be reconfigured as a cultural question, but not unless the literary one has also been considered.

McGahern's general unwillingness to tarry with the self-referential, to include too much modernist erudition or express too great an aesthetic ambition, may suggest a kind of old-world courtesy and humility, a privacy to be admired in contrast to the proud egoistic solitude of the exiled modernist. But there is something culturally strategic about appearing to be *hors de combat* or in refusing to dramatize the struggle of art. The feeling persists that there is a shortfall between the almost hieratically Leavisite way in which McGahern sometimes writes of the vocation of his art in his essays or artistic statements, and the partial concealment of this in the artwork itself, which can often be acerbically and wonderfully worldly. If a McGahern author-figure were to speak as he does in one of his essays, he might be cut down to size by one of his characters as being too 'hi-falutin'. Unlike Flann O'Brien, McGahern is not going to put the author in the dock to be judged by his characters. In the end, the evidence of McGahern's commitment to aesthetic autonomy, that 'art is art because it is not nature', is always encoded, encrypted, embedded, joked upon and problematically contained. Such aesthetic reticence may be regarded as a fault if the fiction leaves itself open to being confused with a functional type of realism. Nevertheless, it is still fair to propose that in his quiet, perhaps overly quiet, resistance to the blander norms of realist practice, and in the covert inscribing of modernism, McGahern radicalizes both his diffidence and his difference, to adapt a phrase quoted earlier. Perhaps this is what Declan Kiberd hints at when deliciously referring to McGahern, after Orwell's evaluation of Swift, as a 'real Tory anarchist'.[6] Diffidence may be radicalized into dissidence.

Notes

1 Virginia Woolf, diary quoted in the *Edinburgh Companion to Virginia Woolf and the Arts*, ed. Maggie Humm (Edinburgh: Edinburgh University Press, 2010), p. 9.

2 Anne Enright, Introduction to *The Granta Book of Modern Irish Short Stories* (London: Granta, 2010), p. xii.

3 See Interview with Liliane Louvel in *La Licorne*, p. 26.

4 Malcolm Bradbury and James McFarlane, 'The Name and Nature of Modernism', in *Modernism*, ed. Malcolm Bradbury and James McFarlane (Harmondsworth: Penguin, 1976), p. 50.

5 Mary MacAleese quoted in Ryle, *New Formations*, p. 35.

6 Kiberd, 'John McGahern's *Amongst Women*', p. 212.

Works Cited

Adorno, Theodor W. and Max Horkheimer, *Dialectic of Enlightenment*, trans. John Cumming (London: Verso, 2008).

Alexander, Sarah C., 'The Residuum, Victorian Naturalism and the Entropic Narrative', *Nineteenth-Century Contexts: An Interdisciplinary Journal* 35, no. 2 (2013): 99–120.

Allen, Graham, *Intertextuality* (London and New York: Routledge, 2000).

Arnold, Matthew, 'Dover Beach', in *Poems*, ed. Kenneth Allott and Miriam Allott (London and New York: Longman, 1979), p. 253.

Attridge, Derek, *J. M. Coetzee and the Ethics of Reading: Literature in the Event* (Chicago: Chicago University Press, 2004).

Attridge, Derek, *Joyce Effects: On Language, Theory, and History* (Cambridge: Cambridge University Press, 2000).

Auerbach, Erich, *Mimesis: The Representation of Reality in Western Literature* (Princeton, NJ: Princeton University Press, 1953).

Baguley, David, *Naturalist Fiction: The Entropic Vision* (Cambridge: Cambridge University Press, 1990).

Baguley, David, 'The Nature of Naturalism', in *Naturalism in the European Novel*, ed. Brian Nelson (New York and Oxford: Berg, 1992), pp. 13–26.

Bakhtin, Mikhail, *The Dialogic Imagination*, ed. Michael Holquist (Austin, TX: University of Texas Press, 1981).

Barthes, Roland, *Camera Lucida*, trans. Richard Howard (London: Vintage, 2000).

Barthes, Roland, *The Pleasure of the Text*, trans. Richard Howard (New York: Hill and Wang, 1980).

Barthes, Roland, *Roland Barthes by Roland Barthes*, trans. Richard Howard (New York: Farrar, Straus and Giroux, 1977).

Barthes, Roland, 'Theory of the Text', in *Untying the Text: A Post-Structuralist Reader*, ed. Robert Young (London and Boston: Routledge and Kegan Paul, 1981), pp. 31–47.

Barthes, Roland, *Writing Degree Zero*, trans. Annette Lavers and Colin Smith (London: Jonathan Cape, 1967).

Bataillard, Pascal, 'Love and Solitary Enjoyment in "My Love, My Umbrella": Some of John McGahern's Uses of *Dubliners*', *Journal of the Short Story in English* 53 (Autumn 2009): 79–90.

Bataille, Georges, *Eroticism*, trans. Mary Dalwood (Harmondsworth: Penguin, 2001).

Beckett, Samuel, 'Dante and the Lobster', in *More Pricks than Kicks* (London: Faber and Faber, 2010), pp. 1–14.

Beckett, Samuel, 'Dante ... Bruno. Vico.. Joyce', in *Our Exagmination Round his Factification for Incamination of 'Work in Progress'* (London: Faber, 1972), pp. 3–22.

Beckett, Samuel, *Proust and Three Dialogues with Georges Duthuit* (London: John Calder, 1999).

Beckett, Samuel, *Texts for Nothing* IV (London: John Calder, 1999).

Beckett, Samuel, *Trilogy: Molloy, Malone Dies, The Unnamable* (London: John Calder, 1994).

Beckett, Samuel, *Waiting for Godot* (London: Faber and Faber, 2010).

Beckett, Samuel, *Watt* (London: John Calder, 1976).

Belsey, Catherine, *Critical Practice* (London and New York: Methuen, 1980).

Bénéjam, Valérie, 'The Elliptical Adultery of *Ulysses*: A Flaubertian Recipe for *Succés de Scandale*', in *James Joyce and the Nineteenth Century French Novel*, ed. Finn Fordham and Rita Sakr (Amsterdam: Rodopi, 2011), pp. 76–93.

Benjamin, Walter, *The Arcades Project*, trans. Howard Eiland and Kevin McLaughlin (Cambridge, MA. and London: Belknap Press, 1999).

Benjamin, Walter, 'Theses on the Philosophy of History', in *Illuminations*, trans. Harry Zorn (London: Pimlico, 1999), pp. 245–55.

Bergson, Henri, *Matter and Memory*, trans. N. M. Paul and W. S. Palmer (New York: Zone Books, 1991).

Bergson, Henri, *Time and Free Will* (London: Allen & Unwin, 1910).

Bibby, Peter, 'Taking the Road Out', *Imprint: The Short Story Magazine* 8, no. 3 (1986): 62–7.

Bloom, Harold, *The Anxiety of Influence* (Oxford: Oxford University Press, 1973).

Bowie, Malcolm, *Proust Among the Stars* (London: HarperCollins, 1998).

Bradbury, Malcolm and James McFarlane, *Modernism* (Harmondsworth: Penguin, 1976).

Bradbury, Nicola, 'High Ground', in *Re-reading the Short Story*, ed. Clare Hanson (Basingstoke: Macmillan, 1989), pp. 86–97.

Brontë, Charlotte, *Jane Eyre*, ed. Stevie Davies (Harmondsworth: Penguin, 2006).

Brooks, Peter, 'Freud's Masterplot', in *Psychoanalytic Criticism: A Reader*, ed. Sue Vice (Cambridge: Polity, 1996), pp. 30–40.

Brown, Terence, 'Redeeming the Time: The Novels of John McGahern and John Banville', in *The British and Irish Novel Since 1960*, ed. James Acheson (New York: St Martin's Press, 1991), pp. 159–73.

Brown, Terence, 'John McGahern's *Nightlines*: Tone, Technique and Symbolism', in *The Irish Short Story*, ed. Patrick Rafroidi and Terence Brown (Gerrards Cross: Colin Smythe, 1979), pp. 289–301.

Brown, Terence, *The Literature of Ireland: Culture and Criticism* (Cambridge: Cambridge University Press, 2010).

Cahill, Christopher, 'Second Puberty: The Later Years of W. B. Yeats Brought His Best Poetry, along with Personal Melodrama on an Epic Scale', *The Atlantic Monthly* (December 2003).

Camus, Albert, *The Myth of Sisyphus*, trans. Justin O'Brien (Harmondsworth: Penguin, 1975).

Camus, Albert, *The Plague*, trans. Stuart Gilbert (Harmondsworth: Penguin, 1948).

Capecci, John, 'Performing the Second Person', *Text and Performance Quarterly* 1 (1989): 42–52.

Cardin, Bertrand, '"Absence Does Not Cast a Shadow": Yeats's Shadowy Presence in McGahern's 'The Wine Breath'', *Journal of the Short Story in English* 53 (Autumn 2009): 111–26.

Cardin, Bertrand, 'Figures of Silence: Ellipses and Eclipses in John McGahern's *Collected Stories*', *Journal of the Short Story in English* 40 (Spring 2003): 57–67.

Castle, Gregory, 'Coming of Age in the Age of Empire: Joyce's Modernist *Bildungsroman*', *James Joyce Quarterly* 40, no. 4 (Summer 2003): 665–90.

Chekhov, Anton, *'The Lady with the Little Dog and Other Stories'*, trans. Ronald Wilks (Harmondsworth: Penguin, 2002).

Chekhov, Anton, *Short Stories*, ed. Ralph E. Matlaw (New York and London: Norton, 1979).

Cleary, Joe, *Outrageous Fortune: Capital and Culture in Modern Ireland* (Dublin: Field Day, 2007).

Coad, David, 'Religious References in the Barracks', *Études Irlandaises: Études sur* The Barracks *de John McGahern* (October 1994): 131–8.

Connor, Steven, 'Beckett and Sartre: The Nauseous Character of all Flesh', in *Beckett and Phenomenology*, ed. Ulrike Maude and Matthew Feldman (London: Continuum, 2011), pp. 56–76.

Connor, Steven, *Samuel Beckett: Repetition, Theory and Text* (Cambridge: Cambridge University Press, 1988).

Conrad, Joseph, *Nostromo*, ed. Martin Seymour-Smith (Harmondsworth: Penguin, 1990).

Cooper, David E., *Existentialism: A Reconstruction* (Oxford: Blackwell, 1999).

Corcoran, Neil, *After Yeats and Joyce* (Oxford: Oxford University Press, 1997).

Cronin, John I., 'The Frightful Mill of Love': John McGahern's *The Barracks*', *Études Irlandaises: Études sur* The Barracks *de John McGahern* (October 1994): 107–18.

Cronin, John I., '*The Dark* is not Light Enough: The Fiction of John McGahern', *Studies: An Irish Quarterly Review* 58, no. 232 (Winter 1969): 427–32.

Cronin, Michael, *Translation and Globalization* (London and New York: Routledge, 2003).

Cullingford, Elizabeth Butler, *Gender and History in Yeats's Love Poetry* (Cambridge: Cambridge University Press, 1993).

Cullingford, Elizabeth Butler, *Yeats, Ireland and Fascism* (London and Basingstoke: Macmillan, 1981).

Currie, Mark, *About Time* (Edinburgh: Edinburgh University Press, 2007).

Deane, Seamus, 'Joyce and Nationalism', in *Celtic Revivals: Essays in Modern Irish Lliterature 1880-1980* (Winston-Salem, NC: Wake Forest University Press, 1987), pp. 92–107.

Deane, Seamus, 'A New Dawn', *The Guardian* (12 January 2002).

Deane, Seamus, 'Dead Ends: Joyce's Finest Moments', in *Semicolonial Joyce*, ed. Derek Attridge and Marjorie Howes (Cambridge: Cambridge University Press, 2000), pp. 21–36.

Deane, Seamus, *Strange Country: Modernity and Nationhood in Irish Writing Since 1970* (Oxford: Clarendon, 1997).

Deleuze, Gilles, *Nietzsche and Philosophy*, trans. Hugh Tomlinson (New York: Columbia University Press, 1983).

Deleuze, Gilles, *Proust and Signs*, trans. Richard Howard (London: Penguin, 1973).

Denham, Peter, 'William Carleton and Samuel Ferguson: Lives and Contacts', in *William Carleton: The Authentic Voice*, ed. Gordon Brand (Gerrards Cross: Colin Smythe, 2006), pp. 360–77.

Derrida, Jacques, *Of Grammatology* (Baltimore and London: Johns Hopkins, 1976).

Derrida, Jacques, *Spurs: Nietzsche's Styles/Éperons: Les Styles de Nietzsche* (Chicago and London: University of Chicago Press, 1978).

Devine, Paul, 'Style and Structure in John McGahern's *The Dark*', *Critique* 21, no. 1 (1979): 49–58.

DiBattista, Maria, 'Joyce's Ghost: The Bogey of Realism in John McGahern's *Amongst Women*', in *Transcultural Joyce*, ed. Karen Lawrence (Cambridge: Cambridge University Press, 1998), pp. 21–36.

Dodds, E. R., *The Greeks and the Irrational* (Berkeley, LA: University of California Press, 1951).

Donne, John, *Complete Poems*, ed. C. A. Patrides (London: Everyman, 1985).

Donoghue, Denis, *Yeats* (London: Fontana, 1971).

Duff, David, '"Intertextuality versus Genre Theory": Bakhtin, Kristeva and the Question of Genre', *Paragraph* 25, no. 1 (March 2002): 54–73.

Eagleton, Terry, *Crazy John and the Bishop: And Other Essays on Irish Culture* (Cork: Cork University Press Field Day, 1998).

Eco, Umberto, *Interpretation and Overinterpretation*, ed. Stefan Collini (Cambridge: Cambridge University Press, 1992).

Eliot, George, *Middlemarch* (Harmondsworth: Penguin, 1988).

Eliot, T. S., *Collected Poems 1909-1962* (London: Faber and Faber 1986).

Eliot, T. S., *Selected Prose* (London: Penguin, 1953).

Ellmann, Maud, 'Disremembering Dedalus: *A Portrait of the Artist as a Young Man*', in *A Portrait of the Artist as a Young Man*, ed. John Paul Riquelme (New York and London: Norton, 2007), pp. 389–403.

Ellmann, Maud, 'The Name and the Scar: Identity in the *Odyssey* and *A Portrait of the Artist as a Young Man*', in *A Portrait of the Artist as a Young Man: A Casebook*, ed. Mark A. Wollaeger (Oxford: Oxford University Press, 2003), pp. 143–81.

Ellmann, Richard, 'The Critic as Artist as Wilde', in *Oscar Wilde: A Collection of Critical Essays*, ed. Jonathan Freedman (Upper Saddle River, NJ: Prentice Hall, 1995), pp. 22–35.

Enright, Anne, ed., *The Granta Book of the Irish Short Story* (London: Granta, 2010).

Ferriter, Diarmaid, *The Transformation of Ireland 1900-2000* (London: Profile, 2005).

Flaubert, Gustave, *Madame Bovary* (Genève: Droz, 2011).

Flaubert, Gustave, *Madame Bovary*, trans. Gerard Hopkins (Oxford: Oxford University Press, 1991).

Fludernik, Monika, 'Second-person Narrative as a Test Case for Narratology: The Limits of Realism', *Style* 28, no. 3 (Fall 1994): 445–79.

Foster, John Wilson, *Colonial Consequences: Essays in Irish Literature and Culture* (Dublin: Lilliput, 1991).

Foucault, Michel, *The Foucault Reader*, ed. Paul Rabinow (London: Penguin, 1984).

Frank, Joseph, *The Widening Gyre* (New Brunswick, NJ: Rutgers University Press, 1963).

Freud, Sigmund, 'Civilization and its Discontents', in *Civilization, Religion and Society: Group Psychology, Civilization and its Discontents and Other Writings* (Harmondsworth: Penguin, 1985), pp. 251–340.

Freud, Sigmund, *The Freud Reader*, ed. Peter Gay (London: Vintage, 1995).

Freud, Sigmund, *The Interpretation of Dreams*, trans. James Strachey (Harmondsworth: Penguin, 1985).

Frow, John, 'Intertextuality and Orality', in *Intertextuality: Theories and Practices*, ed. Michael Worton and Judith Still (Manchester: Manchester University Press, 1990), pp. 45–55.

Galsworthy, John, *Selected Essays and Addresses* (London: Heinemann, 1932).

Garfitt, Roger, 'Constants in Contemporary Irish Fiction', in *Two Decades of Irish Writing: A Critical Survey*, ed. Douglas Dunn (Cheadle: Carcanet Press, 1975), pp. 207–43.

Garfitt, Roger, 'Silent Traveller', *The New Review* 1, no. 11 (February 1975): 63–5.

Garratt, Robert F., 'John McGahern's *Amongst Women*: Representation, Memory and Trauma', *Irish University Review* 35, no. 1 (2005): 121–35.

Genette, Gérard, *Narrative Discourse Revisited*, trans. Jane E. Lewin (Ithaca and New York: Cornell University Press, 1988).

Genette, Gérard, *Palimpsests: Literature in the Second Degree*, trans. Channa Newman and Claude Doubinsky (Lincoln: University of Nebraska Press, 1997).

Gibbons, Luke, *Transformations in Irish Culture* (Cork: Cork University Press, 1996).

Graver, Lawrence, *Waiting For Godot: A Student Guide* (Cambridge: Cambridge University Press, 2004).

Grennan, Eamon, '"Only What Happens": Mulling Over McGahern', *Irish University Review* 35, no. 1 (Spring/Summer 2005): 13–27.

Habermas, Jürgen, *The Philosophical Discourse of Modernity* (Oxford: Blackwell, 1990).

Hamon, Philippe, 'The Naturalist Text and the Problem of Reference', in *Naturalism in the European Novel*, ed. Brian Nelson (New York and Oxford: Berg, 1992), pp. 27–46.

Hand, Derek, *A History of the Irish Novel* (Cambridge: Cambridge University Press, 2011).

Hanson, Clare, *Short Stories and Short Fictions 1880-1980* (Basingstoke: Macmillan, 1985).

Head, Dominic, *The Modernist Short Story* (Cambridge: Cambridge University Press, 1992).

Heaney, Seamus, *Opened Ground* (London: Faber, 1998).

Heath, Stephen, 'Realism, Modernism, and "Language-Consciousness"', in *Realism in European Literature: Essays in Honour of J.P. Stern*, ed. Nicholas Boyle and Martin Swales (Cambridge: Cambridge University Press, 1986), pp. 103–22.

Hegel, G. W. F., *The Phenomenology of Spirit*, trans. A. V. Miller (Oxford: Oxford University Press, 1977).
Herman, David, 'Textual "You" and Double Deixis in Edna O'Brien's *A Pagan Place*', *Style* 28, no. 3 (Fall 1994): 378–410.
Hirsch, Marianne, 'The Generation of Postmemory', *Poetics Today* 29, no. 1 (2008): 103–28.
Hughes, Eamonn, 'All That Surrounds Our Life: Time, Sex and Death in *That They May Face the Rising Sun*', *Irish University Review* 35, no. 1 (Spring/Summer 2005): 147–63.
Humm, Maggie, ed., *Edinburgh Companion to Virginia Woolf and the Arts* (Edinburgh: Edinburgh University Press, 2010).
Hunter, Adrian, *The Cambridge Introduction to the Short Story in English* (Cambridge: Cambridge University Press, 2007).
Huysmans, J.-K, *Against Nature: A Rebours*, trans. Margaret Mauldon (Oxford: Oxford University Press, 1998).
Ingman, Heather, *A History of the Irish Short Story* (Cambridge: Cambridge University Press, 2009).
Jackson, Robert Louis, ed., *Reading Chekhov's Text* (Evanston, IL: Northwestern University Press, 1993).
Jacobus, Mary, *Psychoanalysis and the Scene of Reading* (Oxford: Oxford University Press, 1999).
James, David, ed., *The Legacies of Modernism* (Cambridge: Cambridge University Press, 2012).
Jobert-Martini, Vanina, 'Evaluation in "High Ground": From Ethics to Aesthetics', *Journal of the Short Story in English* 53 (Autumn 2009): 249–62.
Johnson, Barbara, 'The Frame of Reference: Poe, Lacan, Derrida', in *Psychoanalytic Criticism: A Reader*, ed. Sue Vice (Cambridge: Polity, 1996), pp. 84–100.
Josipovici, Gabriel, *What Ever Happened to Modernism?* (New Haven and London: Yale University Press, 2011).
Joyce, James, *Dubliners*, ed. Jeri Johnson (Oxford: Oxford University Press, 2008).
Joyce, James, *Finnegans Wake*, ed. Seamus Deane (Harmondsworth: Penguin, 2000).
Joyce, James, *A Portrait of the Artist as a Young Man*, ed. Jeri Johnson (Oxford: Oxford University Press, 2008).
Joyce, James, *Selected Letters*, ed. Richard Ellmann (London: Faber and Faber, 1966).
Joyce, James, *Ulysses*, ed. Jeri Johnson (Oxford: Oxford University Press, 2008).
Kavanagh, Patrick, *Collected Poems*, ed. Antoinette Quinn (Harmondsworth: Penguin, 2005).
Kenny, John, 'Inside Out: A Working Theory of the Irish Short Story', in *Frank O' Connor: New Critical Essays*, ed. H. Lennon (Dublin: Four Courts Press, 2007), pp. 99–113.
Kermode, Frank, *Romantic Image* (London and New York: Routledge, 2002).
Kermode, Frank, *The Sense of an Ending: Studies in the Theory of Fiction* (Oxford: Oxford University Press, 1967).

Kern, Stephen, *The Culture of Time and Space 1880-1918* (London: Weidenfeld and Nicolson, 1983).

Kershner, R. B., *Joyce, Bakhtin, and Popular Literature: Chronicles of Disorder* (Chapel Hill: University of North Carolina Press, 1989).

Kiberd, Declan, *Inventing Ireland* (London: Vintage, 1995).

Kiberd, Declan, 'Fallen Nobility: The World of John McGahern', *Irish University Review* 35, no. 1 (Spring/Summer 2005): 164–74.

Kiberd, Declan, 'John McGahern's *Amongst Women*', in *Language and Tradition in Ireland: Continuities and Displacements*, ed. Maria Tymoczko and Colin Ireland (Amherst and Boston: University of Massachusetts Press, 2003), pp. 195–213.

Kiberd, Declan, 'Oscar Wilde: The Resurgence of Lying', in *The Cambridge Companion to Oscar Wilde*, ed. Peter Raby (Cambridge: Cambridge University Press, 1997), pp. 276–94.

Kristeva, Julia, *Desire in Language* (Oxford: Blackwell, 1980).

Larrissy, Edward, *Yeats the Poet: The Measures of Difference* (Hemel Hempstead: Harvester Wheatsheaf, 1994).

Lawrence, D. H., *The First and Second Chatterley Novels* (Version 2), ed. Dieter Mehl and Christa Jansohn (Cambridge: Cambridge University Press, 1979).

Lawrence, D. H., *Lady Chatterley's Lover*, ed. Michael Squires (Harmondsworth: Penguin, 1994).

Lawrence, D. H., *Letters 1928-30*, Vol. VII, ed. Keith Sagar and James T. Boulton (Cambridge: Cambridge University Press, 2002).

Lawrence, D. H., 'Pornography and Obscenity', in *Late Essays and Articles*, ed. James T. Boulton (Cambridge: Cambridge University Press, 2004).

Lawrence, D. H., *The Rainbow*, ed. John Worthen (Hardmondsworth: Penguin, 1981).

Lawrence, D. H., *Women in Love* (Harmondsworth: Penguin, 1985).

Lloyd, David, 'Writing in the Shit: Beckett, Nationalism and the Colonial Subject', in *Anomalous States: Irish Writing and the Postcolonial Moment* (Dublin: Lilliput Press, 1993).

Louvel, Liliane, 'John McGahern: *The Barracks*: Requiem un Jour Ordinaire', *La Licorne*, 32 (UFR Langues Littératures Poitiers, 1995): 87–105.

MacKay, Marina and Lyndsey Stonebridge, eds, *British Fiction After Modernism* (Basingstoke: Macmillan, 2007).

MacLeod, Alistair, *Island: Collected Stories* (London: Vintage, 2002).

Maher, Eamon, *The Church and Its Spire: John McGahern and the Catholic Question* (Dublin: Columba, 2011).

Maher, Eamon, *John McGahern: From the Local to the Universal* (Dublin: Liffey Press, 2003).

Malcolm, David, *Understanding John McGahern* (Columbia: University of South Carolina Press, 2007).

Malcolm, Janet, *Reading Chekhov* (London: Granta, 2001).

Mann, Thomas, *Tonio Kröger*, trans. H. T. Lowe-Porter (Harmondsworth: Penguin, 1955).

Matz, Jesse, 'Hulme's Compromise and the New Psychologism', in *T.E. Hulme and the Question of Modernism*, ed. Edward P. Comentale and Andrzej Gasiorek (Abingdon: Ashgate, 2006).

Mays, Michael, *Nation States: The Cultures of Irish Nationalism* (Lanham, MD: Lexington, 2007).

McCarthy, Dermot, *John McGahern and the Art of Memory* (London, Berg et al: Peter Lang, 2010).

McGahern, John, *Amongst Women* (London: Faber and Faber, 1991).

McGahern, John, *The Barracks* (London: Faber and Faber, 2009).

McGahern, John, *Creatures of the Earth* (London: Faber and Faber, 2007).

McGahern, John, *The Dark* (London: Faber and Faber, 2002).

McGahern, John, *Getting Through* (London: Faber and Faber, 1988).

McGahern, John, *The Leavetaking*, 2nd edn (London: Faber and Faber, 1989).

McGahern, John, *Nightlines* (St Albans: Panther, 1973).

McGahern, John, *The Pornographer* (London: Faber and Faber, 1990).

McGahern, John, *That They May Face the Rising Sun* (London: Faber and Faber, 2002).

McGahern, John, *Love of the World*, ed. Stanley van der Ziel (London: Faber and Faber, 2009).

Document P71/619 in the John McGahern archive, James Hardiman Library, NUI-Galway.

McGahern, John, 'Entretien de John McGahern avec Liliane Louvel, Gilles Ménégaldo and Claudine Verley', *La Licorne* 32 (UFR Langues Littératures Poitiers, 1995): 19–31.

McGahern, John, 'Entretien de John McGahern avec Nicole Ollier: Step-by-Step through *The Barracks* with John McGahern', *La Licorne* 32 (UFR Langues Littératures Poitiers, 1995): 55–86.

McGahern, John, Introduction to Alistair MacLeod, *Island: Collected Stories* (London: Vintage, 2002).

McGahern, John, *A Private World*, dir. Pat Collins (Harvest Films, 2005).

McHale, Brian, *Constructing Postmodernism* (Abingdon and New York: Routledge, 1992).

McHale, Brian, '"You Used to Know What These Words Mean": Misreading *Gravity's Rainbow*', *Language and Style* 18, no. 1 (Winter 1985): 93–118.

Mikowski, Sylvie, 'L'Expérience Fictive du Temps dans *The Barracks*', in *Études sur* The Barracks *de John McGahern, Études Irlandaises* (October 1994): 27–44.

Mitchell, Juliet, 'Femininity, Narrative and Psychoanalysis', in *Modern Criticism and Theory: A Reader*, ed. David Lodge (Harlow: Longman, 1988), 425–30.

Molloy, F. C., 'The Novels of John McGahern', *Critique* 19, no. 1 (1977): 5–27.

Moretti, Franco, *The Way of the World: The Bildungsroman in European Culture*, 2nd edn (London and New York: Verso, 2000).

Morrison, Toni, *Beloved* (London: Picador, 1988).

Muller, John P. and William J. Richardson, eds, *The Purloined Poe: Lacan, Derrida and Psychoanalytic Reading* (Baltimore: Johns Hopkins, 1988).
Nabokov, Vladimir, *Strong Opinions* (New York: McGraw-Hill, 1973).
Nietzsche, Friedrich, *Beyond Good and Evil*, trans. R. J. Hollingdale (Harmondsworth: Penguin, 2003).
Nietzsche, Friedrich, *The Gay Science*, ed. Walter Kaufmann (New York: Vintage, 1974).
Nietzsche, Friedrich, *On the Genealogy of Morality*, ed. Keith Ansell-Pearson, trans. Carol Diethe (Cambridge: Cambridge University Press, 1994).
Nietzsche, Friedrich, *Thus Spake Zarathustra*, trans. R. J. Hollingdale (Harmondsworth: Penguin, 2003).
Niven, Alastair, *D.H. Lawrence: The Novels* (Cambridge: Cambridge University Press, 1978).
Nolan, Emer, *James Joyce and Nationalism* (London: Routledge, 1995).
Norris, Margot, 'A Walk on the Wild(e) Side: The Doubled Reading of "An Encounter"', in *Quare Joyce*, ed. Joseph Valente (Ann Arbor: University of Michigan Press, 1998).
O'Brien, Edna, *A Pagan Place* (Harmondsworth: Penguin, 1970).
O'Brien, Edna, 'The Art of Fiction', *Paris Review* 82 (Summer 1984), pp. 22–50.
O'Connor, Frank, *Collected Stories* (New York: Knopf, 1981).
O'Connor, Frank, *The Lonely Voice* (Hoboken: Melville, 2004).
O'Toole, Fintan, 'Going West: The Country Versus the City in Irish Writing', *The Crane Bag* 9, no. 2 (1985): 111–16.
O'Toole, Fintan, 'Island of Saints and Silicon: Literature and Social Change in Contemporary Ireland', in *Cultural Contexts and Literary Idioms in Contemporary Irish Literature*, ed. Michael Kenneally (Gerrards Cross: Colin Smythe, 1988), pp. 11–35.
Parkes, Adam, *Modernism and the Theater of Censorship* (Oxford: Oxford University Press, 1996).
Pierce, David, *Reading Joyce* (Harlow: Longman, 2008).
Pilkington, A. E., *Bergson and His Influence* (Cambridge: Cambridge University Press, 1976).
Potter, Rachel, '"Can my Daughter of Eighteen Read this Book"?: *Ulysses* and Obscenity', *Critical Quarterly* (Special Issue: 'Low Modernism'), 46, no. 4 (Winter, 2004), ed. Rachel Potter and David Trotter, 22–37.
Proust, Marcel, *Against Sainte-Beuve and Other Essays*, trans. John Sturrock (Harmondsworth: Penguin, 1988).
Proust, Marcel, *The Guermantes Way*, trans. C. K. Scott Moncrieff, Terence Kilmartin and D. J. Enright (London: Chatto & Windus, 1992).
Proust, Marcel, *Sodom and Gomorrah*, trans. C. K. Scott Moncrieff and Terence Kilmartin (London: Chatto & Windus, 1992).
Proust, Marcel, *Time Regained*, trans. C. K. Scott Moncrieff, Terence Kilmartin and D. J. Enright (London: Chatto & Windus, 1992).
Quinn, Antoinette, 'A Prayer for My Daughters: Patriarchy in *Amongst Women*', *Canadian Journal Of Irish Studies* 17, no. 1 (1991): 79–90.

Quinn, Antoinette, 'Varieties of Disenchantment: Narrative Technique in John McGahern's Short Stories', *Journal of the Short Story in English* 13 (1989): 77–89.

Raban, Jonathan, 'Exiles. New Fiction', *Encounter* XLV, no. 6 (June 1975): 77–79.

Rabaté, Jean-Michel, 'Crimes Against Fecundity: Style and Crime from Joyce to Poe and Back', in *Style in Theory*, ed. Ivan Callus, James Corby, Gloria Lauri Lucente (London: Bloomsbury, 2013), pp. 111–40.

Rajan, Balachandra, *W.B. Yeats: A Critical Introduction* (London: Hutchinson, 1969).

Rayfield, Donald, *Chekhov: The Evolution of his Art* (London: Paul Elek, 1975).

Reid, Ian, *The Short Story* (London: Methuen, 1977).

Ricœur, Paul, *Time and Narrative*, 3 Vols, trans. Kathleen McLaughlin and David Pellauer (Chicago: University of Chicago, 1985).

Riffaterre, Michael, 'Syllepsis', in *Critical Inquiry* 6 (Summer 1980): 625–38.

Riquelme, John Paul, *Teller and Tale in Joyce's Fiction: Oscillating Perspectives* (Baltimore and London: John Hopkins Press, 1983).

Ross, Ciaran, 'Some Painful Thoughts about *The Barracks*', *Études Irlandaises: Études sur* The Barracks *de John McGahern* (October 1994): 119–30.

Ryle, Martin, 'John McGahern: Memory, Autobiography, Fiction, History', *New Formations* 67 (Summer 2009): 35–45.

Sage, Victor, 'McGahern's Inverted Uncanny', in *Territoires de L'Étrange Dans la Littérature Au XXe Siècle*, ed. Gaid Girard (Rennes: Presses Universitaires de Rennes, 2009), 195–206.

Sampson, Denis, *Outstaring Nature's Eye* (Washington: Catholic University of America Press, 1993).

Sampson, Denis, 'The Lost Image: Some Notes on McGahern and Proust', *Canadian Journal of Irish Studies* 17, no. 1 (July, 1991): 57–68.

Sampson, Denis, '"Open to the World": A Reading of John McGahern's *That They May Face the Rising Sun*', *Irish University Review* 35, no. 1 (Spring/Summer 2005): 136–46.

Sampson, Denis, '"The 'Rich Whole": John McGahern's *Collected Stories* as Autobiography', *Journal of the Short Story in English* 34 (Spring 2000): 21–9.

Sampson, Denis, *Young John McGahern: Becoming a Novelist* (Oxford: Oxford University Press, 2012).

Sampson, Denis and John McGahern, 'A Conversation with John McGahern', *Canadian Journal of Irish Studies* 17, no. 1 (1991): 13–18.

Sartre, Jean-Paul, *Being and Nothingness*, trans. Hazel E. Barnes (London: Routledge, 1996).

Sartre, Jean-Paul, *Existentialism and Humanism*, trans. Philip Mairet (London: Methuen, 1973).

Sartre, Jean-Paul, *Nausea*, trans. Robert Baldick (Harmondsworth: Penguin, 1965).

Schleifer, Ronald, *Modernism and Time: The Logic of Abundance in Literature, Science and Culture 1880-1930* (Cambridge: Cambridge University Press, 2000).

Shattuck, Roger, *Proust* (Glasgow: Fontana, 1974).

Shattuck, Roger, *Proust's Way: A Field Guide to* In Search of Lost Time (London and New York: Norton, 2000).

Shovlin, Frank, 'The Ghost of W.B. Yeats', *The John McGahern Yearbook*, ed. John Kenny, Vol.2 (NUI Galway, 2009), 42–51.

Shovlin, Frank, 'Four Ducks', *The John McGahern Yearbook*, ed. John Kenny, Vol.4 (NUI Galway, 2011), 48–53.

Šklovskij, Viktor, 'A.P. Čexov', in *Anton Čexov as a Master of Story-Writing: Essays in Modern Soviet Literary Criticism*, trans. and ed. Leo Hulanicki and David Savignac (The Hague and Paris: Mouton, 1976).

Soar, Daniel, 'Alphabetical', *London Review of Books* 24, no. 4 (21 February 2002): 30–1.

St Augustine, *Confessions*, trans. Henry Chadwick (Oxford: Oxford World's Classics, 1992).

Steiner, George, 'Extraterritorial', in *Extraterritorial: Papers on Literature and the Language Revolution*' (Harmondsworth: Penguin, 1972), 14–21.

Stern, J. P., *On Realism* (London: Routledge & Kegan Paul, 1970).

Stevenson, Randall, *Modernist Fiction* (Harlow: Pearson, 1998).

Taaffe, Carol, 'Irish Modernism', in *The Oxford Handbook of Modernisms*, ed. Peter Brooker, Andrzej Gasiorek, Deborah Longworth and Andrew Thacker (Oxford: Oxford University Press, 2010), 782–96.

Thornton, Weldon, *The Antimodernism of Joyce's* A Portrait of the Artist as a Young Man (Syracuse, NY: Syracuse University Press, 1994).

Toolan, Michael J., 'The Historian and the Pornographer', *Canadian Journal of Irish Studies* 7, no. 2 (December 1981): 39–55.

Valdez Moses, Michael, 'Nietzsche', in *W.B. Yeats in Context*, ed. David Holdeman and Ben Levitas (Cambridge: Cambridge University Press, 2010), pp. 266–75.

van der Ziel, Stanley, 'The Aesthetics of Redemption: John McGahern's *That They May Face the Rising Sun*', *Studies: An Irish Quarterly Review* 93, no. 372 (Winter, 2004): 473–86.

van der Ziel, Stanley, '"All this Talk and Struggle": John McGahern's *The Dark*', *Irish University Review* 35, no. 1 (Spring/Summer 2005): 104–20.

van der Ziel, Stanley, 'McGahern, Austen, and the Aesthetics of Good Manners', *Essays in Criticism* 63, no. 2 (2013): 203–22.

van der Ziel, Stanley, '*Nightlines*', in *The British and Irish Short Story*, ed. David and Cheryl Malcolm (Oxford: Wiley-Blackwell, 2009), 488–97.

Vanderham, Paul, *James Joyce and Censorship: The Trials of* Ulysses (New York: New York University Press, 1998).

Weller, Shane, *A Taste for the Negative: Beckett and Nihilism* (London: Legenda, 2005).

Whyte, James, *History, Myth and Ritual in the Fiction of John McGahern: Strategies of Transcendence* (Lewiston et al.: Edwin Mellen Press, 2002).

Wilde, Oscar, *The Artist as Critic: Critical Writings of Oscar Wilde*, ed. Richard Ellmann (London: Allen, 1970).

Wilde, Oscar, *The Picture of Dorian Gray* (Harmondsworth: Penguin, 1985).

Wilde, Oscar, *The Soul of Man and Prison Writings*, ed. Isobel Murray (Oxford: Oxford University Press, 1990).

Williams, Raymond, *The Country and the City* (Nottingham: Spokesman, 2011).

Wilson, Edmund, *Axel's Castle: A Study in the Imaginative Literature of 1870-1930* (Harmondsworth: Penguin, 1993).

Woolf, Virginia, *To the Lighthouse*, ed. Stella McNichol (Harmondsworth: Penguin, 1992).

Woolf, Virginia, *Mrs Dalloway*, ed. Claire Tomalin (Oxford: Oxford World's Classics, 1998).

Woolf, Virginia, 'Tchehov's Questions'', in *Virginia Woolf: Essays 1912-18*, Vol. II, ed. Andrew McNeillie (London: Hogarth, 1987), pp. 244–8.

Wordsworth, William, *The Prelude 1799, 1805, 1850* (New York and London: Norton, 1979).

Yeats, W. B., *Autobiography* (New York: Collier Books, 1967).

Yeats, W. B., *Collected Poems* (London: Macmillan, 1985).

Yeats, W. B., *Essays and Introductions* (London: Macmillan, 1960).

Yeats, W. B., *Representative Irish Tales* (Gerrards Cross: Colin Smythe, 1979).

Yeats, W. B., and T. Sturge Moore, *Correspondence 1901-37*, ed. Ursula Bridge (London: Routledge & Kegan Paul, 1953).

Index

CPSIA information can be obtained
at www.ICGtesting.com
Printed in the USA
LVOW13s2306290618
582305LV00007B/81/P